S

# The Somme

# The Somme

Robin Prior and

Trevor Wilson

Yale University Press
New Haven and London

For information about this and other Yale University Press publications, please contact:
U.S. Office: sales.press@yale.edu yalebooks.com
Europe Office: sales @yaleup.co.uk www.yaleup.co.uk

Set in Minion by Northern Phototypesetting Co. Ltd, Bolton
Printed in Great Britain by St Edmundsbury Press Ltd, Bury St Edmunds

Library of Congress Cataloging-in-Publication Data

Prior, Robin.
The Somme/Robin Prior and Trevor Wilson.
p. cm.
Includes bibliographical references and index.
ISBN 0–300–10694–7 (cl.: alk. paper)
1. Somme, 1st Battle of the, France, 1916. I. Wilson, Trevor, 1928– II. Title.
D545.S7P75 2004
940.4′272—dc22

2004028497

A catalogue record for this book is available from the British Library.

10 9 8 7 6 5 4 3 2 1

# Contents

# Illustrations



Photographs reproduced by kind permission of the Imperial War Museum, London.

# Maps

# 1 The Context

## I

There is a widely held view about the initiation and prosecution of the Battle of the Somme. It is that the Somme campaign was the brainchild of the British and French military commands alone. That is, the political leaders of Britain (like those of France) played no effective part in this decision-making. Such a proceeding was at odds with British constitutional tradition, whereby high military strategy remained the province of the civilian heads of government.

A large generalisation follows from this. It is that what was true of the Somme battle in 1916 was true of the First World War as a whole. The British military command, who are deemed men of desperately limited strategic horizons and a fixed unwillingness to learn, did the deciding all the way through. Invariably, they opted to strike where the enemy was strongest and best prepared, which meant the Western Front. As a consequence, civilian leaders blessed with more imagination, and dismayed by heavy casualties, went unregarded. The results for the devoted rank and file of the British army were tragic: vast casualties sustained for derisory gains.

The civilian leaders of the nation, according to this scenario, were overall possessed of larger vision and greater strategic insight. They recognised the folly of hammering away on the stalemated Western Front, and perceived hopeful ways of proceeding elsewhere. But ultimately they proved incapable of imposing their views. The contrast with the Second World War is taken to be marked. In that struggle the political rulers of Britain exercised their rightful dominion over the making of strategy, and thereby avoided the terrible bloodbaths of 1914–18.

# II

In this version, the Somme campaign stemmed from a conference held at French military headquarters in Chantilly early in December 1915. It was summoned by the French commander-in-chief, Marshal Joseph Joffre, and attended by representatives of the other Allied armies: British, Russian, and Italian. The principal British figures were Sir John French, commander of the British Expeditionary Force on the Western Front, and Sir Archibald Murray, Chief of the Imperial General Staff.

The decisions taken at Chantilly were as follows.

First, it was agreed that large offensive actions by the four Allies would be undertaken in 1916, and would be launched as near simultaneously as possible. Thereby Germany would be assailed on every front at the same time, and so be prevented from deploying its forces first against one adversary and then against another.

Second, it was decided that Allied endeavours in areas away from the major fronts would either be abandoned altogether, as in the case of Gallipoli, or reduced to a minimum, as with Mesopotamia and Salonika. The British representatives even argued for the total abandonment of the Salonika operation, given that the initial object of sending an Anglo-French expedition there (the rescue of Serbia) had conspicuously failed. The decision however – at French insistence – was for quiescence rather than complete evacuation.

The third decision, and that most germane to this study, concerned the objectives of the Allies' near-simultaneous offensives. The Italians would resume their Isonzo offensive northwards into the territory of Austria-Hungary. The Russians, who had spent most of 1915 being forced into retreat by better equipped and led German forces, would launch a great effort on their more northerly front against the German army, with a lesser holding action in the south against the Austro-Hungarians. The British and French armies would act side by side in a great endeavour on the Western Front, with the French providing the major component but with the British offering a much larger participation than hitherto. Its location would be Picardy, on either side of the River Somme.

These concentric offensives, aimed at closing the ring on the Central Powers, could not be initiated early in 1916. For one thing the Russian army, following its numerous setbacks sustained at the hands of the Germans in 1914 and 1915, needed many months for recuperation and re-equipment. For another, Britain required time to train and, even more, to munition the huge volunteer army it had been accumulating since the outbreak of the war. So it was agreed that the three Allied offensives, including the campaign on the Somme, would go ahead not earlier than the spring of 1916.

As it happened, the presence at this conference of Sir John French and Sir Archibald Murray, Britain's principal military figures for the moment, was pretty much their swan song. There was a generally held opinion in British governing circles, in the upper echelons of the British army, and even at Buckingham Palace, that the nation needed a more independently minded figure than Murray as CIGS, and that Sir John French had proved conspicuously inadequate as chief of the BEF. So in short order French was supplanted by Sir Douglas Haig, and Murray by Sir William Robertson. This was of no strategic significance. Each replacement was utterly convinced of the wisdom of the decisions taken at Chantilly: that the sideshows should be abandoned or placed on the defensive, and that the Western Front should be the focus of Britain's military endeavours. Certainly, Haig had been contemplating, not a joint Anglo-French action on the Somme, but a predominantly British offensive (with French and Belgian assistance) on the northern part of the Western Front directed towards the Belgian coast. But Joffre's proposal for a great wide-front offensive further south, to which the French would be the main contributor but with a significant British participation, was entirely acceptable to him.

Only in one serious respect was this proposal unwelcome to Haig. Joffre intended that, in the months preceding the great offensive, the German reserves would be worn away in a succession of spoiling attacks. Thereby the scene would be set for an Allied breakthrough victory. And given the huge sacrifices already borne by French forces, and the large British army now coming into Haig's hands, Joffre considered that this preliminary task should fall to the British.

Haig did not agree. He had no enthusiasm for seeing his army drained away in unspectacular activities that would lay the foundation for a primarily French triumph. He persuaded Joffre to agree that the proposed preliminary action should be undertaken by both armies, and that it would be confined to just a few weeks immediately preceding the great attack.

In the event, that matter was decided by neither Joffre nor Haig. Late in February the German commander-in-chief, Falkenhayn, launched a vast offensive against the fortress of Verdun in the French sector of the Western Front. This seemed a curious choice, seeing that Falkenhayn had long argued that Germany could only triumph in this war by beating the British, whom he regarded as the major adversary, rather than the French. But (or so he alleged) he concluded that the elimination of Britain could be accomplished by bleeding white the French army, which he called 'Britain's best sword' – as if not noticing that

Britain had now accumulated a considerable army of its own. His assault on Verdun was intended to remove this 'sword'.

So, during the four months preceding the opening of the Somme campaign, the French army was forced to ward off a vast German offensive. This had the effect of whittling away the German reserves, as Joffre had stipulated, but only by imposing the sort of heavy cost on the French army which Joffre had sought to avoid. Thus the scene was set for an Allied offensive which would still occur on the Somme in mid-1916 but would be radically changed in important particulars. As a result of France's grievous losses at Verdun, the French contribution to the Anglo-French assault would be much reduced, the length of front to be attacked would be considerably diminished, the predominant force undertaking the offensive would now be the British army (with the French as a lesser contributor), and the commander chiefly responsible for directing the operation would be not Joffre but Haig. Yet these concessions to necessity did not appear to render the Somme campaign anything but the military operation devised at Chantilly.

## III

This narrative of preliminaries to the Battle of the Somme seems to sustain the established account. It is all about military conferences, military figures, and military decisions.

But it is not a complete account. For one thing, it lacks context. Whatever may have been true of the Somme in 1916, it was plainly not the case that up to that point the great decisions on British strategy had been taken without significant civilian input.

Events at the outbreak of the war illustrate this. Certainly, as evidence had mounted in the years before the war that Germany might be preparing to strike against France by transgressing Belgian territory, the British military command had worked out an appropriate response. They would send an expeditionary force to Europe to stand on the left of the French army. But the political chiefs of Britain were not ignorant of these preparations. It was the choice of the British government that these military preparations should proceed, but on the clear understanding that they were not sanctioning an offensive. As its response to the crisis of July–August 1914 made apparent, the British cabinet reserved to itself the decision whether or not to enter the war at all, and where to direct the forces at its disposal if it did choose to enter. In the event, the British government showed an inclination to abstain from intervention should Germany bow to its demand to withdraw its forces from Belgian territory. And when the German government chose to disregard Britain's ultimatum, the British cabinet opted to send just a part, not all, of its meagre military resources to stand alongside the French. The other part, in defiance of pre-war military arrangements, was kept at home to guard against invasion. A third decision, of vast importance, owed nothing at all to military initiative: the decision that Britain, while preserving its hallowed practice of voluntary service in the armed forces, would straightway abandon its reliance on a small standing army. It would set about raising a huge military force eventually running into millions of men. This striking innovation, without which there could have been no Battle of the Somme, was the spontaneous decision of the British cabinet, and was both thoroughly endorsed by the House of Commons and widely agreed to by the community at large. The role of the military was that of a consenting onlooker.

That the course of events in Britain in the opening days of the war was the outcome of civilian decision-making has been obscured by a personal matter. A large role was soon being played in the conduct of affairs by Horatio Herbert Kitchener, victor over the Dervishes at Omdurman, a major participant in Britain's endeavour in the South African war, and Britain's most famous soldier. That the 'new armies' which Britain set about raising were instantly known as 'Kitchener Armies' has contributed to the conception of a British war effort under military direction. The point needs to be stressed that Kitchener was not acting at this time in a military capacity. On 3 August 1914, having spent three years as ruler of Egypt under the title of British agent and consul-general, Kitchener was prevailed upon by the British Prime Minister to accept the post of Secretary of State for War in the government. That is, Kitchener had become a civilian cabinet minister with special responsibility for military affairs. (His opposite number at the Admiralty was Winston Churchill, who has never been thought of as a member of any sort of 'military hierarchy'.) The fact that Kitchener played an influential role in the decision to send four of Britain's six divisions to France, while retaining the other two in Britain, and that he argued strongly for raising a mass army in what he foresaw as a long war, was no evidence that decision-making on the key matters of strategy and mobilisation had been wrested from civilian grasp.

## IV

It is evident, therefore, that in the momentous events of July–August 1914 the civilian rulers of Britain made the crucial decisions. Likewise, in the following year they exercised appropriate control over the large aspects of strategy. The scheme for launching a naval operation in the Dardanelles was entirely the brainchild of civilians: principally Winston Churchill, but endorsed by the War Council of the cabinet. The only contribution of the chiefs of the navy was a reluctant and half-hearted assent. And when that naval operation came to grief on 18 March 1915, it was again the appropriate government figures, not any military person outside the government, who decided to redeem the setback by launching a military invasion of the Gallipoli peninsula. (For at least one prominent member of the military hierarchy, the whole Gallipoli venture was a 'Brobdingnagian bumstunt'.)

Parallel with its exercise of strategic initiative away from the Western Front, the cabinet and its war committee were agonising actively about the military situation which had developed in Belgium and France. By the end of 1914 it had already become evident that the sweeping movements of great armies on the Western Front, which had been such a feature of the opening weeks of the war, were now a thing of the past. In that region, modern weaponry was bestowing on defence a marked superiority over offence. This appeared to have generated a paradoxical situation. The reason why Britain had entered the war was to rescue Belgium, and ultimately Western Europe, from conquest by the German army. Correspondingly, expelling the German invader from Belgium and France was the fundamental strategic objective of Britain's endeavours. Yet the onset, by the end of 1914, of stalemate in the west, and the ominous power of defensive weaponry (such as machine-guns and shrapnel and barbed wire and trenches) against advancing human flesh, called this Western strategy into question – as Churchill indicated when he inquired whether there was no better use to be made of Britain's new armies than 'chewing barbed wire in Flanders'.

The British War Council (a subcommittee of the cabinet with special responsibility for military affairs) pondered these matters on 13 January 1915. Powerful voices had already been raised against further hammering away on the Western Front. Churchill, for one, wanted to strike against the German coast well to the north of the trench line in Belgium. And David Lloyd George, who railed against any notion that British strategy should be determined by the whims of the French commander-in-chief (he was not at that stage concerned about any whims of the British military commander), urged the institution of an inquiry into the possibility of action in the Balkans. Such action, he argued, might rally the Balkan states to the Allied side, and ultimately bring Germany down 'by knocking the props under her'.[1]

That the War Council as a whole shared this reluctance to launch further bloody actions in Flanders is apparent from some of its proceedings. For one thing, it agreed to Churchill's proposal for 'a naval expedition in February to bombard and take the Gallipoli peninsula, with Constantinople as its objective' – which would prove the first step towards a considerable (if ill-conceived) diversion in strategy away from the Western Front. And it also resolved that, if by the spring of 1915 it had become evident that a stalemate had indeed developed in the west, then British forces would go elsewhere. For this purpose, a subcommittee of the War Council should be appointed to identify 'another theatre and objective'.

All this, however, fell a good deal short of any decision by the civilian leaders to refrain hereafter from assisting the French in their endeavours on the Western Front. No doubt military advice played a part in maintaining a Western orientation. Sir John French argued that the German lines in France and Belgium were not impenetrable, that with the aid of a large supply of high-explosive shells they might be overwhelmed, and that: 'Until the impossibility of breaking through on this side was proved, there could be no question of making an attempt elsewhere.' (This remark, incidentally, was not as obtuse as it may seem. The German trench defences had not, at that time, reached such sophistication that they could ward off assault by a large accumulation of high-explosive shells. The problem, of course, was that such an accumulation of shells happened not to exist. But then, their absence would have been equally an obstacle to British military operations in any other region.)

Whatever weight these arguments by the military may have carried with the War Council, there were other powerful reasons for postponing a precipitate departure from the Western strategy. One is indicated by the War Council's decision to appoint a subcommittee to fossick out 'another theatre and objective'. Such 'theatre and objective' was not immediately obvious. There was simply no more attractive area where the British could make their major effort. Churchill's hankering to strike at the German coast north of the Western Front invited palpable objections. It would require locating irreplaceable units of the British fleet at considerable risk. And as the Germans with their advanced railway system could move promptly to whatever part of their coastline was threatened, the most probable outcome of such a diversion – apart from total failure – would be a further episode of trench deadlock.

As for action against Germany's allies, such proposals ran up against an obvious objection. Notwithstanding Lloyd George's striking imagery, these countries were not 'props' holding up Germany. Germany's great 'prop' in wartime was its powerful army. So, for the Allied cause to prosper, Germany's army had to be engaged and fought to defeat somewhere. And in the dominating circumstances of geography, the only feasible area for mounting operations against the German army, and for keeping those operations supplied and reinforced, was the Western Front. The Balkans, despite Lloyd George's ill-developed inclinations to proceed there, held few promises and many problems: for example the uncertain loyalties and profound animosities towards each other present among the Balkan states, the crushing difficulties of transportation awaiting an army so far from its home base and operating in such poorly developed territory, and the comparative ease with which Germany could move its own forces south to meet any attack directed against Austria-Hungary.

There was a yet larger matter rendering perilous for Britain any diversion to a non-Western strategy. Lloyd George might rail against the attempts of the French commander to influence British decision-making. But he was choosing to forget that, were it not for this French commander (and his army), Britain would no longer be in a position to do any deciding. If the Kaiser's army had managed to sweep across Western Europe, as promised by the Schlieffen Plan, the game would have been up for Britain. Its prospects of liberating a Europe lying under German conquest hardly merited contemplation. And Germany, following such a triumph in the West, would have been in a position to enlarge its economic base substantially by employing conquered industrial areas in Belgium and France. Thereby it might greatly expand its fleet and so challenge Britain's final frontier: the North Sea.

Even with the Schlieffen Plan thwarted, the French army was in 1915 the only bastion standing in the way of a German victory in Western Europe. What, in military terms, Britain had to offer, whether in holding back the invader or driving him out, was (for the moment) decidedly limited. In such circumstances, to send a signal to the French authorities that Britain had decided to fight a different war against other enemies would – simply in terms of Britain's most vital interest – have been folly of a high order.

## V

The War Council of 13 January 1915, if with the utmost misgivings, opted not to commit this folly. The proposed subcommittee which was intended to discover 'another theatre and objective' met once and came to no conclusion. And when Sir John French's force did attack at Aubers Ridge in May and failed conspicuously, the conclusion was not drawn in political circles that this proved a Western strategy to be invalid. The setback was attributed, not to faulty strategy, but to a lack of the necessary weaponry (what the newspapers trumpeted as the 'shell scandal'). The solution, correspondingly, did not lie in seeking out fresh fields of endeavour, but in undertaking a huge mobilisation of industry for war purposes under a newly created Ministry of Munitions. This would generate the quantities of guns and ammunition needed to batter down German defences in the west and so terminate the deadlock there. It is notable that the political figure who agreed to take on the headship of this new ministry was David Lloyd George. His appointment served to show that even those who – periodically if not too persistently – presented themselves as advocates of an alternative strategy were not always steadfast in that assessment.

Nothing that happened during the remainder of 1915 created the impression that the direction of British strategy was passing under military control. It was certainly no initiative on Sir John French's part which caused him to embark on another dismal operation on the Western Front, this time at Loos. (Nevertheless, his failure there finally meant that he no longer had any credibility as a commander of the BEF.) Nor was it the military chiefs who took the decisions both to send British forces to Salonika in a doomed attempt to save Serbia, and to close down the Gallipoli campaign. Sometimes, certainly, Britain's decision-making was powerfully influenced by pressure from its allies. But it was still the appropriate constitutional bodies within Britain which responded to these pressures.

This was true in other areas. For example, the conversion of operations in Mesopotamia, originally undertaken (quite sensibly) to safeguard Britain's oil supplies, into a hazardous and uncalled-for expedition to Baghdad was the handiwork of the British War Council and the government of India. Far more significantly, the mounting pressure to alter the basis of army recruitment within Britain from voluntary service to enforced conscription was not set in train by the military command (even though most army figures probably favoured it). The campaign to curtail civil liberties in this fundamental matter was generated by conservative forces in Parliament and the electorate, supported by some prominent figures in the Liberal Party.

More generally, it is evident that what produced the context from which emerged the Battle of the Somme was not any seizure of decision-making by military elements. It was the whole course of the war in 1914 and 1915.

The vital developments were these. First, any notion that Britain, as one member of an alliance, might confine its contribution to just the exercise of command of the sea and the employment of its financial power and productive capacity, with no more than a token military contribution, steadily lost all validity. In short, Britain's allies were going to lose the war on land unless Britain agreed to contribute mightily in that sphere also. This was not because the endeavours of France and Russia were anything but large, devoted, and sacrificial. It was because their endeavours were fearfully costly, and did not prosper.

In the early weeks of the war, and twice in 1915, French forces had launched massive offensives against the German army. These had proved ill-rewarded and had sustained staggering losses. As for the Russians, their early offensives into East Prussia in 1914 had been shattered at Tannenburg and thrown back at the Masurian Lakes, and during 1915 their armies had been driven out of Russian Poland with huge casualties. If the war was ever to be won by the Entente powers, Britain by the start of 1916 had no choice but to engage in a large and mounting contribution to the war on land.

Anyway, from the start of the war the British cabinet, the House of Commons, and a considerable section of the general public had made it clear that they expected Britain to embark on a major military commitment. Moreover, before many months had passed it had become evident that this commitment was incompatible with the economic practice of 'business as usual'. There must be extensive mobilisation of the economy by the government for military purposes. As a consequence, Britain by the end of 1915 possessed a mass army undergoing extensive military training, and an industrial and financial base in the process of being converted to the generation of unprecedented (if not necessarily sufficient) volumes of weaponry and ammunition.

Something else, to all appearances, was patently obvious by the close of 1915: the matter of where Britain must direct its great military effort. At the start of the war, this issue had not seemed in doubt. In so far as Britain had an army to send abroad, it must be directed against the German hordes pouring over the territory of Belgium and into France. A German conquest of Western Europe would be for Britain an irreversible calamity.

In the aftermath of the onset of stalemate on the Western Front, certainly, noteworthy political figures did contemplate employing Britain's military resources in areas far from Flanders and France. But by the end of 1915 these inclinations had run into the ground. Campaigns against the Turks, supposedly attractive as directed against a soft target, were now discredited. For one thing, as they were not directed against the German army, they seemed quite beside the point. For another, they had proved anything but painless. The Gallipoli operation had failed conspicuously and was in the process of being abandoned. And the expedition to Baghdad, having been driven into retreat, was entering a quite ominous phase.

As for speculations that Britain might strike at Germany's other principal ally, Austria-Hungary, through the Balkans and at the head of a Balkan coalition, these entirely vanished during 1915. They had never been based on anything of substance. No Balkan state was eager to invoke the wrath of the mighty German army, just then hammering to pieces the forces of the Tsar. And at least some Balkan states were confident that they had more to gain by striking a deal with the Kaiser than by ganging up against him. From the moment in September 1915 that the German commander, Falkenhayn, decided to call off his campaign against the Russians and set about disposing of Serbia, the matter of which major contestant could actually wage a successful campaign in the Balkans passed beyond doubt.

So events in 1915 put paid to a widely held notion: that Britain, thanks to its command of the sea, might choose from a variety of strategic options. In a war against Germany, Britain's dominance at sea in fact provided no choices of strategy for the simple reasons that Britain needed to keep its fleet on its doorstep, to watch over the Kaiser's battleships; and no amount of journeying far afield would bring British forces into meaningful contact with the Kaiser's armies.

It seemed to follow that Britain in 1916 had just one sensible destination for its great military endeavour – the same destination that it had chosen in August 1914. And as it happened, the need for such an endeavour had become imperative. Back in 1914, France would almost certainly have survived even had the BEF stayed at home. After a year and a half of slaughter, France was unlikely to survive much longer without substantial military aid from Britain. And, evidently, the only locale for that aid was – if only *faute de mieux* – the Western Front.

This takes us back to our starting-point. The notion that the Somme campaign must have been the handiwork of bone-headed militarists, acting in disregard of the wisdom of responsible civilians, springs from the evident futility of the Anglo-French offensives which had already been delivered on the Western Front in 1914 and 1915. And the view that the attempted breakthrough on the Somme in 1916 was, therefore, a ridiculous undertaking for which the political leadership could not have been responsible has since been powerfully endorsed: by the widely read memoirs of Winston Churchill and Lloyd George.

But this deduction begs a large question. We have observed the fundamental nature of civilian input into military decision-making in 1914 and 1915. So when did the supposed transference of power from politicians to the military, with the Somme campaign of 1916 as its consequence, take place? To elucidate this matter, it is appropriate to observe in detail the role of political decision-making in the run-up to the Somme campaign.

# 2 'Absolutely Astonishing': The War Committee and the Military

A somewhat bizarre episode of May 1916, of no great moment in itself, will help to set the scene.

On 18 May 1916, the War Committee[1] turned its attention to a rather specific issue. This was the great numbers of horses being maintained on the Western Front by Haig's army. These, it was noted, particularly on account of the huge quantity of fodder they consumed, were tying up a lot of shipping space.

The spokesmen for the military sought to justify this outlay. The Quartermaster-General discoursed on the role of horses as beasts of burden: hauling supplies and weaponry to and from the battlefield. And Kitchener argued that 'if they reduced the number of horses, they could not keep men efficient as cavalry officers'.[2] That is, the horse retained a large role on the battlefield, both in providing transportation and in prosecuting conflict.

The War Committee was not convinced. It conceded that horses were required for moving about artillery, although even here Lloyd George wondered whether so many were necessary 'in view of the employment of so much traction'. But the pressure on shipping made it necessary to dispense 'with everything not essential', and cavalry had apparently ceased to possess a place in military engagements dominated by the products of industry. Lord Crewe bluntly inquired 'why Cavalry should be kept up, when it was never used at all'. The War Committee decided that – following consultation with the CIGS and Haig – 'an independent investigation should be made into this question'.

This decision was profoundly unwelcome both to Haig and to the Army Council. In their view the War Committee might have responsibility for deciding about grand strategy: where campaigns were to be waged, with what overall resources, and for what duration. That did not give it a role in the actual conduct of battle or the employment of specific instruments of warmaking. Haig's response, as Lloyd George interpreted it, was in effect to tell the War Committee (the words are Lloyd George's) 'to mind their own business' and not interfere with his. And the Army Council came back with what Lord Curzon considered 'a very stiff letter'.

Faced with this double riposte, the War Committee might have concluded that it had trespassed beyond its province. That, however, was not its response. Faced with this display of military obduracy, the committee exploded in wrath. The issue promply turned from a mundane matter concerning horses into a constitutional challenge to civilian primacy over the military.

The charge was led by Curzon. (In an earlier incarnation, as Viceroy of India, he had suffered much at military hands – ironically those of Lord Kitchener.) 'The Army Council,' Curzon proclaimed, 'had written a reply of the most surprising nature.' As for Haig's missive, 'according to his feelings [it] was absolutely astonishing'. The War Committee, Curzon insisted, had been carrying out its duty of seeking to alleviate the undue pressure on shipping resources; 'if this was to be the attitude of the Army Council towards them, he could only characterize it as most extraordinary'. Lloyd George agreed. He considered it 'most surprising to receive such a letter which amounted to the Army Council setting itself up against the Government', and deemed Haig's letter 'perfectly insolent'. In words which addressed directly the issue of where, under the British constitution, authority lay in military matters, Lloyd George said of Haig:

> The latter talked about his responsibility – to whom was he responsible? He was responsible to them, to the Government, and through the Government to Parliament, and through Parliament to the people .... He thought that the documents of the Army Council and of Sir D. Haig were most improper ... they could not say 'hands off' to the War Committee, who were the real responsible body.

The Prime Minister joined the chorus of disapproval. Countering a suggestion by the CIGS that only a military expert 'could say what was the number of horses required', he responded that that was not at all the issue.

The point was that the War Committee was faced with a big question – not the minor question of how many horses they should have, but the large question of the best way of prosecuting the war.

Significantly, Asquith went on to make a decidedly pungent judgement on a strictly military matter which he clearly saw as his concern:

> the horses out in France were of no use now. They were only there for prospective use when we had broken through. We were maintaining in France an enormous number of horses which were temporarily useless.

As for the statement by the Army Council, it 'should never have been written nor presented'.

A few voices were raised in defence of the military, but only in a decidedly half-hearted way: either the army chiefs had not got the hang of what was being said, or they had not intended their views to reach the War Committee. So Balfour suggested that the whole thing arose from a misconception:

> The War Committee were thought to be mixing themselves up with questions of detail, whereas they were [actually] concerned with the great part of two big questions. The men who had written the memo had no idea of the real issue.

As for Haig, Balfour felt that had he known 'what was at the bottom of the proposed investigation, he would not have written as he did'.

Robertson took a slightly different, but no more combative, line in defending the military. Haig's letter, he said, had been addressed to himself, not to the War Committee, and he regretted having shown it to the latter body. Countering a proposal that he should draw Haig's attention to 'the impropriety of his having written as he had', Robertson requested that this should not be pressed, 'as it was a private letter'.

What eventuated from this lively exchange? As it happened nothing of consequence. After exerting themselves in committee, Britain's civilian leadership, perhaps exhausted by their own audacity, sank into torpor. They dispatched no instructions to Haig ordering a reduction in the number of horses or to disband the cavalry. The supposedly urgent need to save shipping space by reducing fodder supplies was never raised again. While constitutional supremacy had been vigorously asserted, in practice it was the military who emerged victorious from this encounter. This pattern – of assertion and inaction – of acerbic criticism and an inability to direct – would dog the War Committee's dealings with the high command from the first day of the Battle of the Somme until the last.

# 3 Decision-making, January–February

## I

On 28 December 1915, the War Committee gathered to consider the resolutions of the Chantilly conference. So began the process of passing judgement on the proposed Anglo-French offensive in the spring of 1916.[1]

Britain's political chiefs, a month earlier, had taken two decisions which bore directly on this subject. On 23 November, the War Committee had felt bound to recommend 'the evacuation of the Gallipoli Peninsula, on military grounds, notwithstanding the grave political disadvantages which may result'.[2] And on 1 and 15 November, it had ruled out further devotion of British resources to the campaign at Salonika – first resolving on the evacuation of British forces, then amending this to read that any increase in men or guns must be provided by the French.[3]

Thereby, the War Committee had set aside two areas of strategy potentially alternative to the Western Front. That is, even before receiving the proposals from Chantilly, it had begun moving to a situation where the only field of action open to British forces in 1916 – assuming it intended a serious offensive anywhere – lay in France or Belgium.

The War Committee meeting of 28 December took five decisions.[4] The first two were crucial. They deemed that France and Flanders were to be 'the main theatres of operations', and that every effort was to be made to prepare for an offensive there 'next spring'. It would take place 'in the greatest possible strength' and in close co-operation with Britain's allies. Three subsidiary conclusions followed. Operations in East Africa would continue 'with the force already determined'; a body of troops should be kept in Egypt sufficient 'for its defence'; and operations in Mesopotamia (in the aftermath of the abortive thrust to Baghdad) would be 'of a defensive nature' employing 'the existing garrison of India'.

All of this seemed to point to a smooth endorsement by the War Committee of the Chantilly proposals. That, soon however, ceased to be the case. On 29 December, one of its members, A. J. Balfour, wrote a memorandum which was quite at odds with the conclusions reached just the day before.[5] A former Conservative Prime Minister and now First Lord of the Admiralty, Balfour had been a regular member of the Committee of Imperial Defence even when his party was out of office. Already in recent weeks he had made clear his opposition to the decision to evacuate Gallipoli. And while accepting that he had been overruled on that matter, he continued to deplore the high command's view that the Western Front constituted the only region for fruitful operations. He agreed that the purpose for which the expedition to Salonika had been undertaken – namely the salvation of Serbia – had been 'wholly illusory'. And he accepted that 'erroneous information' had caused British forces in Mesopotamia to be placed in a difficult position. But he would not conclude that this made exclusive concentration on the Western Front the only appropriate direction for British endeavours.

The origins of the war, Balfour argued, lay in the east, where Germany's main ambitions were centred. Certainly, British and French concerns were concentrated in the west, and the total defeat of Germany there might bring down its allies, 'whether Christian or Mahometan': 'But we have no right to regard the crushing defeat of the Central Powers at some new Waterloo...as the only possible issue of the present struggle.'[6] If anything short of a decisive victory in the war turned out to be all that the Allies could achieve, Balfour argued, then 'every loss of prestige by Britain and France in the East...must raise against us new enemies that will make victory in the war more difficult'.

As it stands, Balfour's argument is downright obtuse. He appeared to be saying that a conclusion to the war that fell short of a definite victory over Germany would 'make victory in the war more difficult'. Nevertheless, his conclusion on military matters was clear enough. In a war whose outcome was indecisive, Britain would be advantaged by having maintained a strong military presence in the east. Consequently, as regards Salonika, 'it may be foolish to abandon an adventure which it was foolish to undertake', because, as long as Britain was not turned out from there, Germany's 'triumph in the Near East is incomplete'.

What also emerged from this was Balfour's lack of conviction that a great Western Front offensive, even though employing all Anglo-French resources, would be an incontrovertible success. Certainly, the Entente powers were seeking to achieve over Germany a great superiority in men and weapons. 'But.... the Germans are straining every nerve to make their line absolutely impregnable'. Further, 'we have found no sufficient reply to the obstacles provided by successive lines of trenches, the unlimited use of barbed wire, and the machine gun'. He asked whether the Western powers could afford to fight on terms 'which may involve a far heavier loss of men for them than for their opponents'. And he offered the judgement that 'if at the end of these spring operations' the strategic position remained unchanged 'while the attackers have lost far more men than the attacked', then 'the position would...be one of extreme peril for the Entente'.

At the very least, Balfour argued, Britain should not engage in a Western offensive as early as the spring of 1916. For this there were two reasons. First, by then British armaments would still be inadequate. The required level of firepower could not be reached before mid-year. Second, the absence of a British offensive in the west in the spring would force the Germans to act there. Germany's 'theories of war' and 'internal necessities' would compel it to assume the offensive in the west. When Germany had attacked there and had failed; when Germany had sacrificed three men for every two of the Allies; and when Germany's reserves had been seriously drained and its people discouraged by months of 'unrewarded hardship', then the time would have come for an Allied Western offensive.

## II

Balfour's memorandum (despite its sustained incoherence) carried sufficient weight to elicit a powerful rejoinder from the Secretary of State for War, Lord Kitchener.[7] He rejected Balfour's apparent view that Germany's objectives were limited to Eastern and south-eastern Europe. 'Germany's primary object was', he asserted, '... to establish a predominant position in Europe, first by crushing France completely, and then by compelling her other adversaries to accept the terms she chooses to dictate'. Kitchener strongly endorsed actions to render Egypt secure, but deplored locking up forces in Salonika, 'where they can exert no effect on operations in the main theatre, where they may not detain a single German or Austrian soldier, and where, from a military point of view, they are wholly wasted'. In addition, an active policy in the Near East, even if intended only as a prelude to later operations on the Western Front, would deny British troops the necessary training in trench warfare and would place a strain on Britain's inadequate shipping resources.

Kitchener went on to challenge Balfour's advocacy of delaying the opening of the Allied offensive in the west beyond the spring. He rejected as 'wholly illusory' Balfour's claim that this would force the Germans – to their cost – to launch their own offensive in that region:

> They are in occupation of the whole of Belgium and all the north-eastern provinces of France, comprising the most valuable mining and manufacturing districts in that country. They may well conclude that, providing they can continue to hold their gains, they will be in a favourable position to impose their own peace terms, and that the Allies will tire of the struggle before they themselves do so.

Delaying the attack until June (when the Allies had reached their maximum strength) would leave insufficient campaigning time to accomplish a victory on the required scale. What was being contemplated, Kitchener insisted, was not a single battle on the lines of Waterloo, but a succession of battles prolonged over several months. Any postponement in the commencement of this process would result in an extended campaign, 'protracted too late into the year'. The opportunity to end the war before the onset of winter would be lost, with unhappy consequences:

> it must be apparent to all my colleagues that it will be extremely difficult for this country to sustain the strain imposed upon us by keeping our forces in the field during the winter [of 1916-17] for a spring campaign in 1917, and that France will be also in a similar condition.... we shall be running a great risk of losing the war through the exhaustion of our resources.

Finally, Kitchener turned his attention to an assertion by Balfour about 'our "relative deficiency in guns"':

> In November of last year [1915] the number of guns on the Allied front from the Somme to the sea was – Field guns, 2,950; heavy guns, 1,269. The Germans on this front had – Field guns, 1,746; heavy guns, 604. Since November the number of our guns has been steadily increased.

## III

Balfour was not alone in resisting the proposals emanating from Chantilly. At a meeting of the War Committee on 13 January 1916, further dissenting voices were raised.[8]

The Prime Minister was at pains to point out that the resolution agreed upon on 28 December was not a firm endorsement of an Anglo-French offensive in the spring. All that had been concluded was that 'every effort is to be made to prepare' for such an offensive. That, Asquith argued, 'left the matter open for final decision'.

In response, a number of members spoke in ways at least suggesting that the 'final decision' might go another way. Austen Chamberlain, the Secretary of State for India, indicated that 'possibly our plans on the Western front might be upset by the Germans acting against the Eastern front', and inquired: 'In this case should we then settle down to the defensive?' And when Kitchener affirmed, yet again, that 'the only chance of finishing the war this year was by a great offensive in the West', he was challenged by Reginald McKenna, the Chancellor of the Exchequer. McKenna stated that unless Kitchener could say 'with positive conviction' that such an undertaking would certainly succeed, 'he could not accept it'. 'Such an effort would be contemplating the exhaustion of our resources.' Responding to a question by Kitchener, McKenna was even firmer: 'if we were exhausted we were done'. Lloyd George (not personally an ally of McKenna) chimed in with what appeared to be support. He claimed that in such circumstances 'we should have nothing to bargain with'.

Lloyd George's interventions at the meeting of 13 January are of particular note, if only because in his war memoirs (written in the 1930s) he usually – although not invariably – presented himself as a devoted opponent of a Western strategy. Lloyd George on 13 January interpreted Balfour's memorandum as requiring the War Committee to decide whether or not the Somme offensive should proceed. He pointed out that Britain had (in 1915) already participated in two Western offensives, 'both of which had come to nothing'. And he insisted:

> We could not have another of the same sort. That would amount to a defeat. Therefore we ought to delay until we were really strong enough.

Equally as important as British concerns, Lloyd George went on, was the matter of French preparations. 'On every occasion hitherto the French had understated the amount of ammunition they required' – with (by implication) disastrous results. Now, however, they were adopting a more considered approach, as revealed in a document emanating from the French Xth Army 'which showed that they would not be ready by June'. Lloyd George pressed this point:

> On the figures which he had, by every computation we should not be ready by March–April.... We must postpone in order to make for ourselves a fair chance of success.... By June we should have a large number of heavy trench weapons, and the French would have complete artillery with a sufficient supply of munitions.

Lloyd George's contributions on this occasion are notable for their ambiguity. Up to this point, he seemed to be arguing (as Balfour too may have been) against a premature Western Front offensive rather than against such an offensive in any circumstances. His prime concern appeared to be a sufficiency of guns and ammunition. But at other points in the discussion, Lloyd George appeared to be inclining against any Western offensive.

For example, in a discussion stemming from a suggestion that the Turks might, in about May, embark on a big offensive into Egypt, Lloyd George aired what looked like a proposal for action far from the Somme: a campaign against this ally of Germany, 'forc[ing] the Germans to do what we had to do in Servia'. Lloyd George argued:

> In the main, it was our business to sit tight on the Western frontier, and then take the offensive in Egypt, Mesopotamia, or Salonika. If we attacked in either [*sic*] of these places, the Turk must be there, and the German must come to his assistance. We could not do both things. It meant the selection of an alternative.

Warming to his subject, Lloyd George revealed that he had even more to offer than just a British offensive against Germans or Turks. There was, he argued,

> a third alternative, namely to send equipment to France and Russia. Russia had a long front, and it might be easier to break through on it. It was worth considering the question of sending heavy guns and equipment direct to the Eastern Front.... Supposing France and ourselves sent 1,000 heavy guns to Russia, they might be able to break down the defence.

Plainly, for some highly placed members of the British government, the issue of strategy was wide open.

## IV

Yet if the meeting of 13 January showed the War Committee prepared to look askance at the Chantilly proposals, in what direction were the dissenting voices pointing?

Clearly, some contributors seemed opposed to any British offensive on the Western Front. McKenna – without suggesting an alternative – was alarmed at the probable effect on British resources of a Western offensive that was not totally successful. He was also concerned that conscription, to which he was implacably opposed, would inevitably follow from a large campaign in the west. Lloyd George spoke approvingly of offensive action against Turkey rather than Germany, or of offensive action against Germany conducted only by the Russians (employing weaponry supplied by the British and French). And Balfour urged the maintenance of the operation at Salonika – an operation which Lloyd George (puzzlingly) seemed to think was directed against the Turks, not the Bulgarians.

But all of these were kites flown, not developed schemes. Lloyd George grounded his support for action against the Turks on the palpably insubstantial premise that the Germans would be forced to come to their aid (as, supposedly, the British had been obliged to do in the case of Serbia). He ignored the plain fact that the Germans had done precious little to aid the Turks during the British campaigns in Gallipoli and Mesopotamia. (For that matter the British, apart from their belated and wholly ineffective action at Salonika, had noticeably failed to come to the aid of Serbia.)

As for Lloyd George's suggestion that one possible strategy would be to send large quantities of armaments to the Eastern Front and await a Russian breakthrough, that ran counter to discussions already made in the War Committee on 13 January. In a discussion about 'Material for Russia', great stress had been laid on the incompetence of the Russian authorities in arranging for the distribution of supplies from Britain. Balfour 'thought it a scandal that such a state of affairs should exist'. No one offered a different opinion, Kitchener expressing doubts about whether, even if a British officer were sent to oversee distribution, 'even then delivery will be assured'. (Subsequently, Lloyd George made it plain on a number of occasions that he would support sending to the Russians only such weaponry as was surplus to British requirements for offensive action on the Western Front.)

What is evident is that, although some critics of the Chantilly proposals seemed to favour either an offensive elsewhere or no British offensive at all, this was not where their main emphasis lay. What Balfour and Lloyd George were principally arguing against was a premature offensive in the west. Kitchener might claim, and with some sense, that the protracted campaign being envisaged must commence in the spring so as to ensure sufficient campaigning weather. Balfour and Lloyd George were, on the contrary, convinced of the merits of delay beyond the spring. This, Balfour claimed, would oblige the Germans to attack first, and so wear out their reserves. (He was expressing the common belief that attack cost more than defence – a view to which he would continue to cling even as the progress of Germany's Verdun offensive called it into question.) And Lloyd George insisted that the Western offensive must wait upon the production of an overwhelming sufficiency of guns and ammunition

– something that would not occur before the middle of the year. The dissenters did not argue in vain. The meeting of 13 January amended its earlier decision in order to show, as Balfour had stipulated, 'that the War Council was not definitely committed to the plan of an offensive in the West'. The resolution still read that every effort should be made to prepare for a great offensive in the spring 'in the main theatre of war'. But to it was added the rider: 'although it must not be assumed that such offensive operations are finally decided on'.

A further decision was taken, at Lloyd George's prompting. A conference of British and French military and munitions authorities was to be convened, in order to compute the numbers and calibres of guns and ammunition 'necessary to assure the success of the next great offensive operation on the Western Front'. 'This information was considered essential to any final decision regarding both the desirability of undertaking an offensive in the West and the best time for commencing such an operation.'

Two things had emerged pretty clearly. First, in response to the Chantilly proposals, the nation's political leaders were not prepared to relinquish their constitutional right to make the big decisions about strategy. The military command might propose, but the civilian chiefs would still dispose.

But, secondly, although the War Committee reviewed differing ways of proceeding, their discussion hardly revealed that they saw themselves as having an attractive range of alternative operations. Some members might speak of action in regions far from the Western Front, or of Britain's forces adopting a posture of immobility. But neither idea enjoyed sustained advocacy, even from the people who raised them. What seemed the matter for serious dispute was the timing of action on the Western Front: not whether, but when.

## V

On 22 February, the matter of strategy for 1916 again came before the War Committee.[9] The question was raised by Lloyd George, who 'thought the time had arrived to discuss the projected summer campaign'. His choice of words was noteworthy; that is, his unqualified, and thereafter unchallenged, reference to a 'summer campaign'. No further reference would be made to an offensive in the spring, despite Kitchener's earlier claim that only this would provide sufficient good weather for the campaign to be carried to fulfilment. Lloyd George, in the course of the discussion, quoted Haig as believing that the British army would not be ready to attack on a 25 kilometre front until May or June. And that was that.

The matter which Lloyd George believed remained open for discussion was that 'before the offensive could be contemplated the relative forces in men and material should be carefully weighed'. Sir William Robertson, the government's main adviser on military matters, looked to a conference of Allied commanders-in-chief on 1 March to clarify the situation regarding men, guns, and munitions. However, whether accurate figures concerning German resources could also be supplied was a matter of dispute.

Lloyd George offered the tentative opinion that the Allies were slightly superior to the Central Powers in men but inferior in weaponry. Asked by Bonar Law whether 'we should be ready, as concerned munitions, in May and June', Lloyd George replied 'Yes, we should'. But he then added that 'the awkward point was that the Germans were now accumulating huge stores' and that the British would 'have to catch up. France was the only country of the Allies which had already reached a great output.' And he threw in the observation that 'If we had no facts to go upon, he did not understand how we could decide on offensive action.' Given these negative observations, his affirmative reply to Bonar Law's question about whether the British would possess a sufficiency of munitions by May or June becomes decidedly puzzling. So is the issue of whether he did, or did not, regard the issue of the offensive as having been settled.

One thing, nevertheless, was clear. As Minister of Munitions, Lloyd George was spearheading a great endeavour to accumulate munitions whose only proposed purpose was a (summer) offensive on the Western Front. The man most stubbornly resisting that campaign remained McKenna. He insisted that 'it was essential to know the real strength of the combatants in guns'. And he plainly did not believe that it was enough to be assured that the Allies possessed a large superiority in numbers. The lesson of the war, he argued, was that such superiority might not be enough:

> He thought that at Ypres in October 1914, the German preponderance in troops and guns was overwhelming, and our troops had no trenches, and yet the Germans did not succeed in getting through.

Again, in the huge French offensive in the Champagne in the autumn of 1915: 'the French had fired away 7,000,000 rounds of gun ammunition and had been two or three times as strong in numbers, and yet they had not got through.'

McKenna wanted 'an analysis of all the attempts of the offensive'.

> It seemed to him in the contemplation of the offensive we were relying too much on hopes. We should have more definite knowledge, considering the number of times that the efforts at the offensive had already failed.

These negative observations did not go unchallenged. Kitchener and Robertson both spoke in defence of their actions. Yet McKenna's misgivings carried weight. The Prime Minister concluded that the matter must remain undecided 'until the possession of the facts, or at least the conjectured facts'. Without these 'facts', evidently, the British government would continue to withhold authorisation of the offensive.

Yet, equally evidently, the War Committee was failing to follow through on any alternative ways of proceeding. No voice was raised in favour of redirecting British attention towards the Balkans. Balfour offered the judgement 'that from a Naval point of view such operations would be very bad'. And Lloyd George, asked by McKenna how long it would take to produce the 688 mountain guns required for an operation there, 'said it could not be done'. It seemed to follow that when the weaponry and trained manpower for a major operation started coming to hand, the place of their employment was not really in doubt.

# 4 Decision-making, March–June

## I

In March 1916, the apparent confidence among members of the War Committee that they possessed control over British strategy, and so over the Allied prosecution of the war, began to falter. Doubts surfaced concerning the way events might be about to unfold, and under whose direction.

It would be easy to attribute these misgivings to a major development on the German side. Late in February, the German high command seized the strategic initiative by unleashing a huge offensive against the French fortress system of Verdun. During March, the War Committee found itself uncertain both about the extent of German aspirations in this undertaking, and about how threatening the operation was actually proving.

So on 10 March, the Prime Minister inquired of Robertson what was the German objective. 'Was it Verdun?' Robertson replied unhelpfully that he 'supposed it was, although he did not know why'. And he then added: 'The Germans were out for crippling the French, and then to turn on us or Russia.' His puzzlement seems obtuse. Regarding the degree of menace presented by the German assault, Robertson offered Joffre's assessment that 'the French losses were 30,000 and that the Germans had lost twice as many', but then interposed his own opinion that 'Probably the French had lost as many as the Germans.'[1] The War Committee was entitled to be a bit bewildered.

Yet the developing unease in the War Committee was not primarily a response to German action at Verdun. It was much more about the course of French strategy, and even more about what the Russians – without reference to their allies – might be planning. On 21 March Lloyd George expressed strong fears that the Entente powers were in danger of reverting to an earlier situation, where haphazard offensives had been launched without reference to the War Committee.

> The point bore on the constitution and function of the Committee, who ought to know all facts and proposals.[2]

He 'feared that the same thing would happen as last year – i.e. that one Ally would go off before it was ready [he was apparently referring to Russia], and that would entail other allies being brought in to relieve the pressure'. Balfour chimed in: 'The Committee had not got to the bottom of the Russian plan'. And Asquith insisted that, 'When they went to Paris...they ought to have some information both from France and Russia'. It was, he concluded, 'all very slippery and sloppy'.[3]

In the ensuing weeks, notwithstanding Germany's startling action at Verdun, what continued to trouble the War Committee was this matter of the exercise of strategic initiative among the Allies. For the Prime Minister, as for Balfour and Robertson, what mattered above all was that the Entente powers should deliver their offensives simultaneously and in combination. The War Committee even passed a resolution stressing the 'utmost importance' of this.[4] What particularly worried them was that the Russian command might, without consultation, be about to launch a great operation which would in time oblige the British and French to come to their rescue.[5]

Another matter, equally unconnected with events at Verdun, worried the War Committee. While the British were making plans to diminish their contingent at Salonika, leaving the French and Serbs to preside over what should remain a quiet sector, the French kept generating plans for a great endeavour there – plans that would involve an increased, not reduced, British contribution. What muddied the situation was the fact that, while overall the War Committee opted for inaction in this region, some members spasmodically threw out remarks apparently sympathetic to operations at Salonika. So Balfour opined, if only in passing, that the presence of a substantial British contingent in Salonika would compel Bulgaria to maintain a watching force there.[6] Others expressed the belief that the same contingent might nudge Romania towards entering the war on the Allied side. And Lloyd George could not forget that once – at least theoretically – he had strongly preferred British action in the Balkans to operations on the Western Front. So he punctuated the War Committee's deliberations with inquiries about how the Russians would react to a British withdrawal from Salonika, and spoke of a plan for 'smashing the Turks'. ('That would be very unpleasant for Germany.')[7]

None of this – when action was actually called for – was going to affect the War Committee's prevailing view on strategy. It would proceed with its decision to withdraw at least one division from Salonika (in Robertson's view 'It was useless there and wasted').[8] And it would resist firmly any offensive there, Lloyd George going so far as to assert that any such offensive, even if intended to aid the Russians, 'would be fatuous'.[9]

While moving, via these assorted ambiguities and speculations, to a firm stance against extraneous operations, the War Committee was girding itself to take the one decision that mattered. They might continue to contemplate providing weapons for their struggling Italian allies and even for the still neutral but ever-wavering Romanians. They might agonise about what action to take concerning the grandiose ambitions and palpable fragility of the Russians. But their firm conclusion would be that any aid in weaponry to the Italians or Romanians must be from what was surplus to the requirements of a great British offensive in the west. And their conclusion about the circumstances of their Eastern ally would be that the only effective way of advancing or redeeming Russia's situation was to launch a large Anglo-French operation on the Somme.

Lloyd George made this clear late in March. He had been arguing that the British should, for reasons of morale, send a limited quantity of machine-guns to both Italians and Romanians. Robertson responded that Haig, at that moment, possessed only 1.5 machine-guns per battalion whereas, for a major offensive, he required eight. Lloyd George replied that by June Haig's requirements would be fully met. The War Committee resolved that only after full provision had been made for Haig's forces (along with home defence and the air force) would any surplus – assuming one existed – be directed to the Italians and Romanians.[10]

In more respects than this, the nation's leaders were concerned to ensure that the coming offensive in the west would be well considered and soundly mounted. The military spokesmen were at pains to stress that this would not be a grandiose or reckless endeavour. Kitchener, disregarding warnings he had already received from the Fourth Army Commander, General Sir Henry Rawlinson, assured his colleagues that Haig was not going to do anything foolish.[11] Above all, he would not be lured by the French into taking on all the fighting unaided. If the French tried to convert this into a purely British endeavour, Haig would close it down.[12]

Lloyd George, significantly, spoke in the same vein. He had, he said, received firm assurance from the Minister of Munitions in Paris, Albert Thomas, that the French intended to engage in the offensive on a big scale, and they meant to fight. As long as the offensive did not begin until June, the French would have sufficient ammunition 'to go on forever' (unlike the Germans, who – in the French view – were at the end of their resources).

Warming to his task, Lloyd George offered a forecast of the shape of events to come. He stressed that the offensive must not begin prematurely. First it was necessary to accumulate a superiority in men and materiel. Britain's output of ammunition had recently been checked by blizzards and air raids, but as long as 'the contemplated fighting did not take place until May, we should be able to keep it up right through the summer'. He went on to outline the stages of the operation. The attack should be carried out for a fortnight, then there should be a month of 'joining up forces', then another fortnight of attacking, then another month of reorganisation, and so on. 'It would take from May to August.'[13] When Balfour interposed that the particular manner of carrying out the offensive 'must be left to the General on the spot', Lloyd George concurred.[14]

The War Committee meeting at which these views were expressed, on 7 April, was – for all its low-key nature – an event of great significance. For it placed beyond doubt the essential nature of Britain's involvement in the land war of 1916. Lloyd George provided assurance that – in circumstances where weaponry rather than manpower was becoming recognised as the key to success – the British army would, by mid-year, be fully provided with the wherewithal for a large, and lengthy, offensive on the Western Front. And he did not dissent from the view that the actual conduct of operations would rest in the hands of Haig as 'General on the spot'.

Most of all, at this meeting the qualification which the War Committee had hitherto placed on the launching of the campaign was withdrawn. Since February, while preparations for the Somme campaign were being allowed to proceed, the nation's leaders had withheld authorisation that it would actually be embarked on. That now ceased to be the case. As Asquith summed up the deliberations of that day, Haig was to be informed: 'You have the authority for which you ask.'[15]

## II

Plainly, this decision was not forced upon the controllers of British strategy by the circumstances of the French at Verdun. Lloyd George actually expressed uncertainty about whether the Germans would be making their major endeavour for the year on the Western or Eastern Front, as if unaware that they had been showing their hand for the last month and a half.

This obtuseness continued for another month. The ally whom the War Committee anticipated might soon be needing assistance was Russia, not France, and proposals for helping it out ran the familiar gamut: sending ammunition, or taking action in the Balkans, or launching a great Anglo-

French offensive in the west ('attacking [the Germans] with all the forces with which we are capable').[16]

Only in May did Britain's leaders seem to wake up to the fact that the Germans had for the last three months been making their strategic orientation clear, and that their action was beginning to imperil France's continued participation in the war. Robertson informed the War Committee that the French authorities estimated their casualties at Verdun at 115,000 but that actually they were 'somewhat heavier', and that German casualties, although greater than those of their opponents, were not as large as the French were claiming.[17] And a week later Kitchener warned his colleagues that the Germans were not only bent on wearing out the French forces at Verdun but were succeeding in doing so. After that, he suggested, they would 'wear through and go on to Paris'.[18] It was a great danger to France.

It is evidence of the reluctance of Britain's political masters to take on board the significance of the Verdun operation that, even now, A. J. Balfour could not understand what all the fuss was about. He clung to his view that those conducting an offensive always paid more dearly than those resisting it, and he concluded that therefore the Germans at Verdun seemed to be doing just what the Allies wanted. 'He did not understand why General Joffre did not rejoice.'[19]

Kitchener, along with Sir Frederick Maurice (the Director of Military Operations), struggled to explain why Joffre was not rejoicing. As Maurice put it, thanks to German nibbling 'in the end [Joffre] would have no troops left'. Prior to the attack on Verdun, Joffre had been intending to employ 40 divisions in the Somme offensive. He was now down to 25, and could not look as far ahead as 1 July (the projected date for starting the offensive). And Kitchener warned the committee that Joffre's divisions were getting so knocked about that he would soon have no reserves left.[20]

So, late in the day, Britain's leaders were obliged to come to terms with the fact that the French, after all, would not be the major contributor to Allied strategy in the west in the summer of 1916. The offensive on the Somme would go ahead as planned. But it would be on a reduced length of front owing to the diminished contribution of which the French were now capable. The burden of undertaking the offensive would have to rest primarily on the British.

Lloyd George, for one, firmly accepted the implications of all this. He was still prepared to promise large quantities of rifles to the Russians, but only on a time scale of six months to a year. And he was ready to offer surplus guns and ammunition to the Italians, who were at that moment being roughly handled by the Austro-Hungarians. But on the matter of the substantial employment of British resources he was definite on two matters.

First, he was now firmly opposed to action at Salonika, which might be thought an exhausted alternative but remained one which the French – incomprehensibly, given their circumstances – persisted in taking seriously. (As the Foreign Minister, Sir Edward Grey explained to the War Committee, France's Premier Briand had made it clear to him that French public opinion was 'set on this offensive', and the British government's disdainful response had caused the French Ministry 'great emotion'.)[21] Lloyd George, unmoved, urged that the War Committee should 'take the line of the [British] General Staff that this was an impossible operation'. The French, he said, were proposing to transfer 100 big guns to Salonika for an offensive there, and were 'prepared to cripple the Western Front to do this'. The War Committee ought to refuse to embark on an operation which their military advisers told them would lead to disaster.[22] (Following a remark by Lloyd George that this was 'a mad proposition', Balfour chimed in that not only were Joffre and Briand mad 'but the whole French people were mad'.)[23]

Second, and yet more significantly, Lloyd George was convinced of the necessity for powerful British action on the Western Front. Despite a section of French opinion which favoured action at Salonika, Lloyd George reported that there were stronger currents. On the strength of discussions with Albert Thomas, he told the War Committee that the French were becoming 'rattled'.[24] They had borne the brunt of the fighting for two years and were growing exhausted. The British must come to their aid, otherwise their army would be knocked out. Further, France was developing a jaundiced attitude towards its Entente partners. The idea was developing in France, Lloyd George reported, that the British were accumulating military resources for some future project entirely to their own benefit, and were disregarding France's immediate needs.[25]

These statements decidedly alarmed Lloyd George's colleagues. Robertson was quick to insist that French misgivings about their ally's intentions were unwarranted. At Chantilly in December 1915 the British representatives had agreed to a joint offensive in 1916. Only now had Joffre raised the matter of the date on which it should commence, and Haig had been entirely agreeable to his proposal. Admittedly Petain, the commander in the Verdun region, was saying that his sector could not hold out beyond 20 June, but Joffre was saying it could last until early July. Robertson reiterated that the British had never refused the French assistance.[26]

Grey chimed in, urging Lloyd George to assure Albert Thomas that the forces of Britain were at France's disposal. Lloyd George responded that he had indeed told Thomas that this was the case, but nevertheless the impression obtained in France that the British were doing nothing.[27]

This discussion left Britain's leaders in no doubt that the situation of France in this war was now becoming precarious. Asquith commented that the whole position of that country had deteriorated. Lloyd George expressed the feeling that the French were 'not quite holding their own' at Verdun.[28]

The next day the War Committee, who were also showing signs of being 'rattled', reassembled. Haig was now present and confirmed their worst fears. He told them that the French President was evidently alarmed at the situation, even saying 'Verdun sera pris.' The French were aware, Haig argued, that having started the war as the strongest of the Allies, 'they were now going down and down'. Consequently he had told Joffre that he was prepared to launch his attack on 20 June, as against his preferred option of 15 August when all the artillery he required would be at hand. Joffre had assured him that 1 July would be soon enough.[29]

# III

Two matters here require emphasis. Both diverge from generally held views. First, it is not the case, as often claimed, that the British offensive on the Somme was launched only on account of the French army's parlous circumstances at Verdun. On the contrary, the offensive had been proposed by the military, and at least partially endorsed by Britain's War Committee, weeks before the Germans had even launched the Verdun operation. And such qualifications as the War Committee had placed on its commitment to this offensive were withdrawn before its members woke up to the fact that the French were in serious trouble on account of Verdun. Indeed, some were still imagining that Germany's offensive at Verdun was serving the purpose of the French and British.

In short, the only effect that France's travails at Verdun had on Britain's strategy in 1916 concerned the timing of the offensive on the Somme and the relative contributions of the main participants. The offensive might have commenced in August had the French not been pleading for it to start by 1 July. (As against this, as long as it was recognised that this must be a lengthy operation, it could not be delayed too late into the campaigning season.) Again, French losses at Verdun reduced the size of force that they could contribute to the joint venture. This did not cause the British to increase the extent of their participation. It simply meant that the size of the operation overall was reduced and the British involvement became, relatively, greater than that of the French.

The second aspect requiring emphasis is the way in which the course of events thrust Lloyd George to the forefront of those causing this offensive to happen.

It is a widespread view, which in time Lloyd George would seek to propagate, that his role in the inception of this operation was largely that of querulous onlooker. An examination of the course of events tells a different story.

Simply by his occupancy of the key post of Minister of Munitions, Lloyd George – far more than Kitchener or Robertson or Haig – became the man capable of providing the wherewithal and assurances necessary to this offensive. The grisly experiences of Russians and French and British in 1914 and 1915 had placed the nature of the war beyond doubt. Formidable accumulations of men – even men of sound national character – would not accomplish victory. As the Germans were proclaiming by their *modus operandi* at Verdun, the recognition was now general that only a terrifying accumulation of killing devices could bestow success upon any offensive operation. Only Lloyd George, in his capacity as Minister of Munitions, could provide the necessary assurance that such a volume of weaponry would be available to Haig's army by the due date.

So, at a series of meetings between 21 and 30 June, Lloyd George presented the War Committee with an apparently satisfying array of facts and figures. On 21 June he produced statistics revealing an 'enormous improvement' in the British army's firepower, particularly in heavy gun ammunition. (The Prime Minister deemed it 'a remarkable contrast' with what had gone before.) Further, Lloyd George told his colleagues that Britain was now doing 'extraordinarily well' in the production of heavy guns, turning out 140–150 every month in contrast with France's 20–30. And Haig's army was now in a position to expend shells at a rate of nearly 300,000 a week. Aerial photographs were presented of the bombardment of the German lines at Ypres and St-Eloi. These revealed, according to Grey, that 'the trenches were obliterated'. Grey inquired whether the same could be done to all German trenches. Lloyd George replied 'Certainly'.[30]

There was, the Minister of Munitions admitted, a problem with fuses. Earlier, shells had sometimes exploded prematurely, so damaging the guns supposed to dispatch them. The introduction of delayed-action fuses had solved this problem but produced another: the shells did not explode until they had buried themselves in the ground. The Ministry had therefore reverted to a modified version of the earlier fuse, and the artillerists were delighted. Lloyd George asked if the War Committee was prepared to accept this compromise, still with some risk of prematures but improving the prospect of shells bursting on impact. A committee of experts was appointed.[31]

To complete this generally hopeful picture, Lloyd George provided information on the output of machine-guns (which the Prime Minister deemed extraordinary), and told the War Committee that the output of small arms ammunition was also 'very satisfactory'.[32]

By way of summation, Robertson, responding to an inquiry from Balfour, said he regarded the situation 'with serenity', and Asquith characterised as 'marvellous' 'the improvement in the output of munitions'. A formal conclusion was adopted, recording that 'the War Committee were impressed with the great progress which has been made' regarding the output of munitions 'and the highly satisfactory position which had been reached'. Lloyd George pointed out that prominent men who had set aside their own business concerns to further the output of munitions had been subjected to grossly unfair attacks in the newspapers. So the War Committee agreed that the Prime Minister should make a statement in Parliament embodying its favourable judgement.[33]

## IV

The War Committee engaged in this panegyric to Britain's preparedness for battle on 21 June, just ten days before the commencement of the campaign. In the following days it received less comforting information, not about its own forthcoming offensive but about its allies. Information was received that French casualties at Verdun had risen to a quarter of a million (although the speculation was offered that German losses might be double this), and that so far the Germans had not diminished their exertions at Verdun in response to British preparations for an offensive on the Somme.

Again, messages from the Russian front were, at best, decidedly mixed. On the southern sector, General Brusilov's subsidiary offensive against the Austro-Hungarians was making striking gains. But the main Russian contribution to the concentric Allied operations, on Russia's northern front against Germany, was hanging fire. Further, Hindenburg was reported to be mounting operations against the Russians on a front of 172 miles, and Russia's supply of weaponry was well below requirements.[34] (Lloyd George subsequently commented that whereas British industry was producing 120,000 shells a week, the Russians were bringing forth only 40,000.)[35]

These ominous matters, raised at the War Committee's meeting on 22 June, did not cancel out the hopeful prognosis already established. On 30 June, in a last survey of the Somme battlefield before the infantry went over the top, Robertson exhibited a photographic panorama of the British and German fronts, along with maps showing the lines of attack and the British objectives. The British front ran for 15 miles and the French for 7 miles. The immediate objectives were at a depth of 1.5 miles. The artillery preparation had been proceeding satisfactorily. The British were employing 26 divisions and the French

14 (with more to follow). Robertson laid before the committee figures of the imposing number of guns being used and the miles of railway lines and water pipes constructed in support of the attack. He could not offer figures of the numbers of German guns, as the enemy artillery were not responding to the Allied bombardment, but estimated that the enemy had only six divisions facing the British (although probably with more at call). He took the view that 'we could get on all right'.[36]

One other point emerged during these last days before the battle. On 22 June Robertson surveyed for the War Committee the British situation on the Western Front as a whole. The British, he said, had 51 divisions, which would become 54 divisions by 1 July. The Germans had 36 or 37 divisions facing the British sector 'but a German division was smaller than ours'.[37]

Then, seemingly out of the blue, he remarked: 'We had a superiority in men but he thought the Germans were superior in guns.' A.J. Balfour, in a response of potentially great moment, remarked: 'on the whole our superiority was great except in the one thing that really mattered'.[38] This exchange seemed to cry out for further exploration. But nothing followed. With the British army poised for its greatest endeavour so far in this war, the apparent discrepancy between the rival forces in so crucial an area as munitions excited no further comment. Only by this potent act of omission were the political masters of Britain able, with whatever qualifications, to approach the start of the Somme battle with high hopes and full endorsement.

# 5 'Grasping at the Shadow': Planning for the Somme, February–June

## I

In accordance with the decision taken at Chantilly and confirmed with qualifications by the War Committee the British command began planning for the offensive. The location chosen by Haig and Joffre was the area to the north and south of the River Somme in Picardy. Here the Somme is sluggish and meandering, with wide, marshy banks which preclude military operations in its near vicinity. For this reason the river itself plays little role in the battle which bears its name.

In January 1916 the front to the north of the river (from Rancourt to Curlu) was occupied by the British Third Army commanded by General Allenby. Immediately to the south of the river stood the French Sixth Army commanded by General Foch. In the early phase of the planning the French command proposed that the British should carry out preliminary operations in order to attract and wear down the German reserves. But, as already mentioned, Haig refused to accept such a secondary role and in mid-February the plan was dropped.[1] Allenby was accordingly informed that he was to prepare for an attack north of the Somme in conjunction with an offensive by the much larger French forces to the south. The front of attack laid down by Haig ran from Gommecourt in the north to Maricourt in the south. The French would thus take over some ground to the north of the river which would enable one national army to co-ordinate operations on both of its banks. Overall command of the British section of this battle would reside with Allenby, including the newly established Fourth Army headquarters under General Rawlinson.[2]

This plan soon ran into trouble. The problem was that Rawlinson was senior to Allenby. Haig's solution was to promote Allenby temporarily but this was resisted by the War Office on the grounds that it would be difficult to reverse when the battle had concluded. Tortuous negotiations followed, and King's

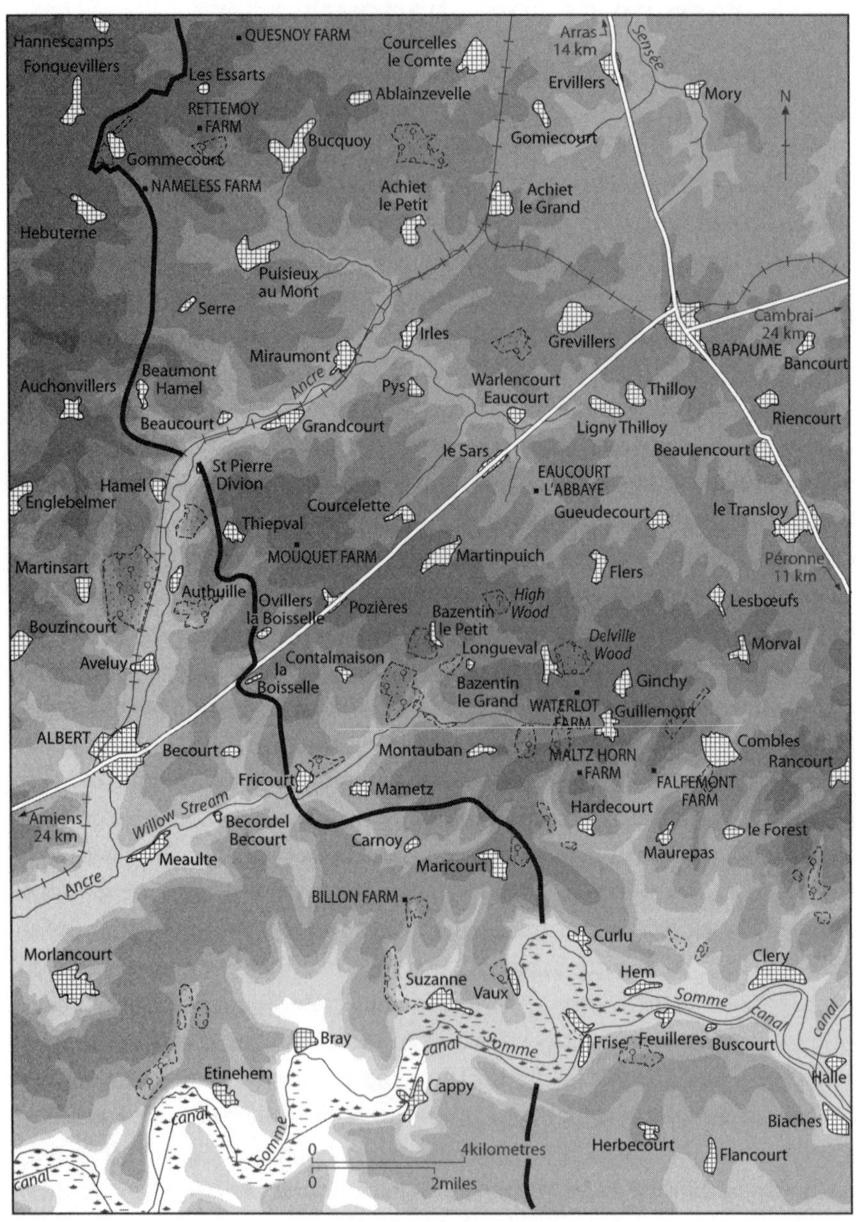


The Topography of the Battlefield

Regulations were quoted by both sides. Robertson eventually pointed out – with some exasperation – that Section 219, which was overlooked by 'most people', allowed junior generals to be placed temporarily in command of their seniors. The thoroughness with which these trivialities were canvassed puts to shame much of the later planning of the battle and in the end the issue was not even decided by Haig or the War Office. As noted earlier, it was decided by the Germans. On 21 February they launched their offensive against Verdun. This brought about an immediate request from Joffre that the French X Army, which was sandwiched between the British First and Third Armies to the north of the proposed area of battle, be relieved. Haig promptly ordered Allenby to take over the French-held section and Rawlinson to take command of the Somme operation.[3] So it was that on 25 February Rawlinson moved into his headquarters at Querrieu. Inauspiciously, the move took place in a blizzard.[4]

Rawlinson's first action as Army Commander was to undertake a series of reconnaissances of the front. His purpose was to select an area of attack and to familiarise himself with the German defences. He found himself in a region of gently undulating hills with green fields and woods still in evidence behind the British and German trench lines. There were no precipitate rises, the highest point being just 300 feet above sea level. However, the British lines were to some extent dominated by the Thiepval–Ginchy Ridge, which from some points provided the Germans with extensive vistas to the west and south. South-west from this high ground lay a gentle slope to the valley of the River Ancre. The reedy marshes of the Ancre bisected the British battlefield between Thiepval and Beaumont Hamel.

Notwithstanding its later evil reputation, the Somme area seemed reasonable campaigning country. Its undulating nature kept the soil well drained and the only swampy areas were around the river banks. It had no industrial wildernesses such as the British had encountered at Loos. Nor had it yet suffered the effects of continuous fighting. Indeed, the area had seen little conflict since 1914. In late August of that year part of Kluck's Second Army passed through it on the way to Amiens and (as they imagined) Paris. After the Marne the same army fell back to the Somme, followed cautiously by the French. Gradually trench lines became established which remained virtually unchanged until the summer of 1916. Throughout 1915 there was the occasional trench raid and intermittent shelling, but this sector escaped all of the major battles of 1915 and remained one of the quietest sections of the Western Front.

During this period of 21 months the Germans had not been idle. At the end of 1914 their defences had consisted of a single trench. By the opening of the Somme campaign this one trench line had been converted into a front system consisting of three lines of trenches 150 to 200 yards apart. Moreover, the defensive power of the system had been greatly enhanced. In front of the trenches the Germans had placed two belts of barbed-wire entanglements, each from 15 to 30 feet wide, all tied to iron stakes to prevent their easy removal. Deep under the trenches the Germans had constructed a series of dug-outs in the chalky soil. (It is this chalk that gives the Somme trenches their distinctive white ribbon effect). These dug-outs were 20 to 30 feet below the level of the trenches, deep enough to give protection to their garrisons (usually of 25 men) from all but a direct hit by the heaviest calibre of shell. The dug-outs were often interconnected to guard against a single exit being blocked.

To strengthen the front system further, the Germans had incorporated into it a number of defended villages. Beaumont Hamel, Thiepval, Ovillers, La Boisselle, and Fricourt consisted of solid stone houses with cellars which could also shelter small garrisons of troops and machine-gunners. To enhance their natural strength the German command provided them with all-round trench defences protected by barbed-wire entanglements

Not content with the considerable strength of this front system, the Germans had both set about building a second line some 2,000 to 4,000 yards behind the first and had placed a series of strongpoints between the lines. The strongpoints (of which Nordwerk and the Schwaben Redoubt were the best known) consisted of a maze of trenches with the capability of all-round defence, incorporating dug-outs and concreted machine-gun posts. These were sited to take heavy toll of troops advancing from the first trench system.[5]

Certainly the second line was not as strong in construction as the first. Its dug-outs were not as extensive and only the occasional village (such as Longueval) had been incorporated into it. Nor was its protecting wire as formidable. Nevertheless, it had its own strengths. Much of it could not be observed from the British front line and was out of range of British field artillery. And a section of it had been placed on the highest ground on the ridge around Mouquet Farm and Pozières.

To complete their defensive system the Germans had begun construction of a third line approximately 3,000 yards behind the second. But this was still in a rudimentary state when the battle commenced.

The garrisoning of these defences was variable. But it was usual to dispose two battalions of a regiment of 3,000 in or near the front system, with the remaining battalion in the intermediate strongpoints or in the second line.[6]

Despite their formidable nature (Churchill called the German defences at the Somme 'undoubtedly the strongest and most perfectly defended positions in the world'),[7] there were some weaknesses in the German defensive arrangements. The front system had been largely constructed in 1914 and 1915 when the overriding concern was for a long, uninterrupted field of fire with good observation for the forward artillery observers. What this meant was that the Germans had placed most of their front system on a forward slope which made it directly observable from the British front line. Consequently, in daytime both relief of troops and repair of wire and trenches were almost impossible for the Germans, and the British could direct artillery fire on to the enemy front system with some ease.

It was the weaknesses of the German position which impressed themselves on Rawlinson after his first tours of inspection. He wrote to Kitchener in surprisingly optimistic terms:

> In this new area which I have taken over there are great possibilities – The artillery observation is excellent; there are an unlimited number of artillery positions well covered from view – within 2000 yds of our present line & the facilities for assembling the assaulting infantry columns behind the trench line are the best I have seen anywhere.[8]

He acknowledged to Kitchener that the wire protecting the German line was good but thought the distant wire 'weak' and that the possibilities for enfilade artillery fire were 'great'.[9]

This mood of optimism did not last. Shortly after writing to Kitchener, Rawlinson contracted the flu and betook himself to Nice for two weeks' rest.[10] On his journey back to the Somme he stopped in Paris where the War Minister was planning strategy with the French. Rawlinson took the opportunity to discuss the coming offensive with him. He found Kitchener in a gloomy mood. He was despondent about the refusal of the French to wind down the Salonika operation and was convinced that they wanted to shift the main burden on the Western Front to Britain.[11] He warned Rawlinson about the demands likely to be made on British manpower and told him that an attack *au fond* in the summer might cause 50,000–60,000 casualties 'which could not be replaced'.[12] Rawlinson, perhaps taking his cue from Kitchener's despondency, immediately pronounced himself in favour of a strictly limited offensive. He warned Kitchener, however, that this was not Haig's view and that he (Rawlinson) 'would have to talk strongly to D.H. who has set his mind on a large offensive here north of the Somme'.[13]

When he returned to the front two other factors confirmed Rawlinson's new-found caution. The first was a talk with his corps commanders, all of whom pronounced in favour of an attack with limited objectives. Indeed, Hunter-Weston, the commander of VIII Corps and not generally known for his reluctance to attack *au fond*, emphasised to Rawlinson that he was 'strongly opposed to a wild

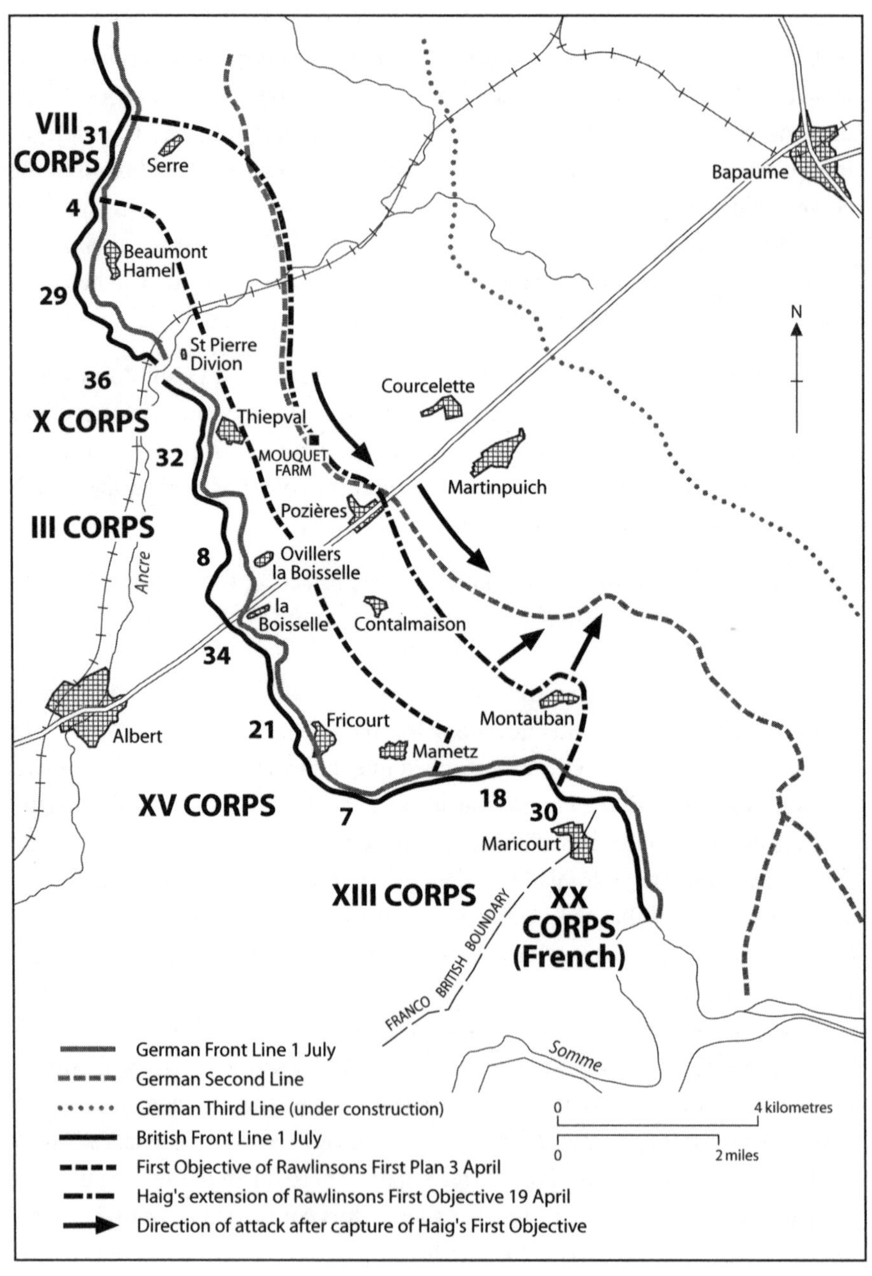

VIII CORPS
31
4
29
36
X CORPS
32
III CORPS
8
34
21
XV CORPS
7
18
30
XIII CORPS
XX CORPS (French)
Serre
Beaumont Hamel
St Pierre Divion
Thiepval
MOUQUET FARM
Pozières
Ovillers la Boisselle
la Boisselle
Contalmaison
Courcelette
Martinpuich
Bapaume
Albert
Fricourt
Mametz
Montauban
Maricourt
Ancre
Somme
FRANCO BRITISH BOUNDARY
N
0
4 kilometres
0
2 miles
German Front Line 1 July
German Second Line
German Third Line (under construction)
British Front Line 1 July
First Objective of Rawlinsons First Plan 3 April
Haig's extension of Rawlinsons First Objective 19 April
Direction of attack after capture of Haig's First Objective

The Haig/Rawlinson Plans, April–May

rush … for an objective 4,000 yards away'. He reminded the Fourth Army commander that 'to lose the substance by grasping at the shadow is a mistake that has been made too often in this war'.[14]

A second factor encouraged this mood of caution. In his absence his Chief of Staff, Archibald Montgomery, had drafted a plan which was also for a strictly limited offensive. Supported by this convergence of opinion, the originally optimistic Rawlinson decided to submit to Haig the Montgomery plan with only minor amendments. Yet he was not unaware of the reception it might receive from the Commander-in-Chief:

> I daresay I shall have a tussle with him over the limited objective for I hear he is inclined to favour the unlimited with the chance of breaking the German line.[15]

# II

Rawlinson sent the Montgomery plan to Haig on 3 April. Essentially it envisaged a two-step 'bite and hold' operation by 10 divisions with seven in reserve. Its aim, Rawlinson stated, was not to gain ground 'but to kill as many Germans as possible with the least loss to ourselves' – a concise definition of a true attritional battle which implied no great penetration of German-held territory.[16] The front of attack was to be 20,000 yards long, ranging from Serre in the north to a point just east of Mametz in the south. This secured the attack on two defensible flanks and required each assaulting division to attack a length of front of 2,000 yards. In addition 20,000 yards constituted the maximum length of front Rawlinson considered could be dealt with by the 200 heavy howitzers (defined by him as 6 inches and above) he had been assigned.

Rawlinson then turned to the proposed depth of advance. Here he saw two alternatives:

> An attack to rush the whole of the enemy's defences in one rush as was attempted at Loos: An advance in two stages, the first to include the enemy's front line system of defences and certain important tactical points [beyond] which are essential to the success of a further advance [to the second German line]. The second to be undertaken as soon as preparations can be made.[17]

He went on to indicate the considerable advantages of this first alternative; namely that experience had shown most ground gained in an attack was secured by the initial rush and that it was important to take advantage of enemy disorganisation and panic, which were also at their maximum in the early moments of an attack. Moreover, he claimed, the 200 howitzers possessed by the Fourth Army were sufficient to deal with the enemy defences to the depth of their second line.

Nevertheless, this first alternative proved not to be where his preference lay. He went on to give six reasons why the second, more cautious, option was to be preferred. Three of these concerned the infantry. First, the New Army troops at his disposal could not be expected to maintain cohesion over the long distance between the British front line and the German second line. Second, once they became disorganised it would prove difficult to put them into a state to meet a counter-attack. Third, if the troops holding the German second line were well prepared, as there was every reason to expect, such a counter-attack might result in a rout.

Other reasons to prefer the second option concerned the artillery. He noted that much of the German second line was hidden from direct observation, and argued that this would make it difficult to establish whether the wire in front of it was actually being cut. Second, the deeper the penetration aimed for, the greater the number of targets the artillery would need to subdue. Third, because of the observation problem, it would be difficult for the gunners to protect from counter-attack troops advancing on the second enemy line.

There is an anomaly here. Rawlinson had argued early on that his artillery could deal with the Germans' trench defences to the depth of their second line. He was now saying that it could not. In particular it could not with certainty cut the distant wire or protect troops advancing on it. Moreover, on the vital matter of destroying trenches and fortified villages and strongpoints, he had implied (although, considering its importance, in a rather oblique manner) that these might constitute more targets than his guns could manage.

The upshot of all this was the conclusion by Rawlinson that he should divide his advance into a succession of small steps. These would set realistic objectives that could be achieved by his green troops, and would make good observation of the German second line possible for his artillery. It may also be noted that, having stated that his purpose was to kill Germans rather than gain territory, his proposed deliberate approach would provide a more certain way of accomplishing the required slaughter.

The next issue dealt with in his plan concerned the length of the artillery bombardment preceding the attack. Rawlinson acknowledged that a short, intense bombardment would aid surprise, might cause a rapid lowering of enemy morale, and would deny the Germans time to bring forward guns and reserves. However, he felt that he had no choice but to opt for a lengthy preliminary bombardment, of 50 to 60 hours. His main reason was that the extensive German wire could not be cut in any less time with the guns available.

Finally, Rawlinson discussed the use of gas. Remembering his experience at Loos where gas had drifted back on the British troops, he considered that the likelihood of a suitable wind to propel the gas towards the enemy line exactly at zero was so small as to constitute an unacceptable risk. So he ruled out gas except to isolate strongpoints such as fortified villages that were not to be assaulted directly. But, also remembering Loos, Rawlinson proposed to employ smoke 'to the fullest extent possible all along both defensive fronts and the fronts to be attacked' as a means of concealing the advance of his troops across no man's land.

Haig received Rawlinson's plan on 4 April. During the next ten days he commented on it in his diary, scribbled notes on his copy of it, discussed it at a meeting with Rawlinson, communicated with Joffre, and finally responded formally in writing to the Fourth Army commander.[18]

The gist of his comments did not vary. Rawlinson's plan made no attempt to achieve surprise; it was too cautious; it paid no attention to the need to assist the French; and there was no role for the cavalry.

Haig deprecated Rawlinson's insistence on a long bombardment, which would obviously remove any chance of launching an unexpected attack. He also considered that Rawlinson was overlooking the effect that a short intensive bombardment would have on enemy morale. He instructed him to reconsider this matter.[19]

Turning to the objectives to be achieved in the first instance, Haig stated that the Fourth Army 'could do better' than Rawlinson anticipated. In particular he suggested that north of Pozières Rawlinson should aim to capture the entire German second line in a single advance. The new 'tanks' would be of great assistance in keeping this northern flank secure. Further south he also considered that the Fourth Army plan was too cautious. Here, the objectives should be extended to the high ground around Montauban and the Briqueterie.

Haig had noted Rawlinson's objections to this course of action: namely the difficulty of providing distant troops with artillery support and the risk in any case of their becoming disorganised after advancing such distances. But he believed these difficulties could be overcome.

> The risks to be incurred can be foreseen and to a great extent guarded against by previous arrangements for providing artillery support, for throwing in reinforcements as required to fill gaps in the line and to cover flanks that become exposed ... and generally, for providing the means of holding what may be gained.[20]

The dialogue between Rawlinson and Haig on this last point is extraordinary. Rawlinson claimed that the artillery could not support distant troops. Haig stated that it could. Rawlinson argued that his troops would become disorganised. Haig said that this could be overcome. Nowhere did Haig engage with the actual problem of how the gunners were to support troops they could not see, or how reinforcements were to be fed to exactly the correct points on a moving and chaotic battlefield, where accurate information was bound to be difficult to obtain.

But there is another, even more extraordinary, feature about this exchange. It is the fact that neither Haig nor Rawlinson was confronting the central issue concerning the capture of the German second line. By setting a more distant objective, Haig was decreasing by a large factor the intensity of the bombardment which could be brought to bear on the defences under attack. The point was that Haig had just about doubled the number of yards of trench to be bombarded by the heavy howitzers. Yet he was not proposing to increase the volume of guns or shells employed. Thereby, he was creating the danger of so diluting the bombardment everywhere that it would be inadequate to quell even the first German positions, in which case his forces would be denied any success at all. This might be thought a matter of the first importance, yet in the Haig–Rawlinson dialogue on the plan it went unremarked.

Haig also raised other concerns. He noted that Rawlinson had paid no attention to the fact that his operations were part of a larger scheme to assist the French. As it happened, there is no evidence that Rawlinson had ever been informed by Haig of the details of the French plan. That is, no attention was being paid to the fact that, at this stage of planning, the Somme operation was still largely a French affair. Joffre was to attack with 39 French divisions, with the aim of crossing the river in the vicinity of Péronne. Haig's attack would be made with just 14 divisions, with the purpose of assisting the French in their larger undertaking. Haig explained to Rawlinson that this could best be done by seizing the Thiepval–Ginchy Ridge from where the Germans would otherwise overlook French operations on the north bank of the Somme. After the first objectives had been captured Rawlinson should swing his main effort south-eastwards down the ridge with the aim of rolling up the German second line south of Pozières. This process would be aided by a simultaneous attack from around Montauban which would catch the Germans between two fires.[21]

As for further operations, Haig was not prepared to speculate. He had already told Joffre (perhaps unnecessarily) that his further actions would be 'directed against the enemy's forces'.[22] More to the point, he assured Rawlinson (if not quite felicitously) that he was not attempting 'to rush the whole of the enemy's defences in one rush', against which the Fourth Army commander had strongly warned. He noted on his copy of Rawlinson's plan that 'I think such a plan wd be impracticable agst. this position.'[23] And he told Rawlinson that he expected operations to be conducted in distinct phases after artillery preparation had been carried out, even though he believed that cavalry might find opportunities to capture advanced positions at any time.[24]

So was Haig opting for an unlimited offensive? Certainly in its detail Haig's amendments to Rawlinson's plan did not amount to converting a 'bite and hold' plan into an attack *au fond*. Haig is plainly proposing a manoeuvre battle, but not yet a breakthrough battle by British forces. His objectives, that is, are more distant than Rawlinson's but not unlimited. His overriding aim was to assist the French. However, there are two references in Haig's plan which perhaps indicate that he was aiming for bigger things. Thus although the operation would be a phased one it is clear that he expected Rawlinson to pass from one phase to the other with minimum delay.[25] And more directly, while agreeing with Rawlinson's object of 'killing Germans', he thought that this could be best accomplished 'if we can get the enemy out of his trenches',[26] so implying that he expected to overrun in fairly short order the entire German defensive system. Perhaps Rawlinson's view that Haig was hankering after a breakthrough was not very wide of the mark.

## III

Rawlinson replied to Haig's memorandum on 19 April. This document is a curious mixture of resistance and capitulation. On some matters there was no dispute. Now he had been made aware of the French plan, Rawlinson would reorient his operations subsequent to the initial attack, directing them southeast towards the French.[27]

On other matters he was not so compliant. He agreed with Haig that the prospect of capturing the German line north of Pozières at a single blow was 'alluring' but he then restated his reasons for resisting this course. He argued that wire-cutting at great distances would be difficult, that his own troops would become disorganised, that the enemy garrisoning the second line might turn this disorganisation into a rout, and that even if the infantry did manage to gain a footing in the second line the artillery would have 'serious difficulty' in supporting them.

Rawlinson also deprecated the extension of the southern flank, noting that it would require an additional division in the initial operation which would have to be supported with his existing artillery resources.[28] He also noted that he did not have sufficient force to extend the northern front as far as the Gommecourt salient.[29]

Thus far Rawlinson had stood his ground and rejected Haig's facile assurances that the risks to be run in capturing the German second line could be foreseen and guarded against. But he then went on to say:

> I, however, fully realise that it may be necessary to incur these risks in view of the importance of the object to be attained. This will, no doubt, be decided by the commander-in-chief, and definite instructions sent to me in due course.[30]

In other words, he would in the last analysis carry out Haig's instructions even if he thought them to be impracticable.

On some other matters, however, Rawlinson would not budge. In his original plan he had tried to make it clear to Haig that there really was no choice about the duration of the bombardment – the wire could not be cut in anything less than 50–60 hours. Haig had failed to grasp this point. So Rawlinson reiterated the need for a lengthy shelling of enemy positions. But in so doing he drifted away from his main argument by emphasising the greater effect on enemy morale of a prolonged bombardment. Haig refused to accept that a long bombardment was superior as a morale-breaker to a short one. For the time being, the matter remained unresolved.[31]

On one final matter, the use of cavalry, Rawlinson took Haig's remarks to mean that a major role should be given to the horsed soldiers. He therefore proposed to push them through *en masse* south of Grandcourt to assist in the protection of the northern flank 'if we succeed in inflicting on the enemy a serious state of demoralisation'.[32] This was a major proviso but in any case Haig had nothing so grandiose in mind. He wrote on his copy of Rawlinson's letter: 'This seems to indicate that you are intending to use the cavalry as one unit. This is not my view…. Certain Corps Cmdrs should have some Cav at their disposal on the flank near Serre.'[33] In the light of future developments this remark is worth noting.

In the following weeks the points at issue between Haig and Rawlinson were settled. Rawlinson raised no more objections about the extension of the objective in the north and this aspect of the plan was made explicit by Haig in a memorandum on 16 May.[34] And Haig recognised that Rawlinson did not have the means to attack at Gommecourt. This operation became a 'diversion plan' and was transferred to the Third Army.[35] Meanwhile Rawlinson agreed to extend the southern flank to Montauban if he could have five additional siege batteries, and this was accepted by Haig.[36] As for the bombardment, Haig finally bowed to the inevitable – it would be a methodical one, spread out over five days. The use of cavalry continued to be a matter of dispute, but in the upshot it made no difference to the basic plan and will be dealt with later.

The Rawlinson–Haig exchange on the nature of the Somme plan raises an interesting question. Why did Rawlinson so readily capitulate to Haig on those aspects of the plan where he plainly thought the commander-in-chief misguided? The simple answer is that he was merely bowing to the authority structure of the British army. But his readiness to yield on matters of importance perhaps has deeper roots. In 1915 Rawlinson had made injudicious remarks about the inadequacies of a divisional general. Haig had backed Rawlinson's criticisms and suggested to Sir John French that the general be sent home. An investigation revealed however that any inadequacies in command in fact lay with Rawlinson. Haig was furious with his subordinate but resisted French, who wanted Rawlinson removed. Haig had no hesitation in telling Rawlinson to whom he was indebted for retaining his post. From that point Rawlinson was Haig's man and although there would be numerous times when Rawlinson resisted the commander-in-chief, it is notable that resistance was only ever taken so far by the Fourth Army Commander

The outline plan for the British aspect of the Somme campaign as it stood in May can now be briefly summarised. It called for an attack by 11 divisions on a 24,000 yard front with defensive flanks around Serre in the north and at the junction with the French around Montauban in the south. In the first instance the German second line would be overrun from Serre to the Pozières–Albert road. To the south of that point the initial penetration would stop well short of the German second line, but it would include the villages of Contalmaison and Montauban. The depth of advance would range from 3,000 to 4,000 yards in the north to 2,000 to 3,000 yards in the south. The attack would be preceded by a five-day bombardment which would include 220 heavy howitzers. Gas would be used to neutralise villages which were not to be directly attacked and the infantry advance would be screened by smoke. When the first objectives had been seized, the troops in the north would endeavour to roll up the remainder of the German second line, which would also be attacked from the south along a line Contalmaison–Montauban. Tanks (if available) and cavalry would be used to protect the flanks and, in the case of the horsed soldiers, to assist the infantry in capturing their objectives.

Further advances would depend on developments.

When all this had been accomplished, operations would be reoriented south-east to secure the left flank of the French.

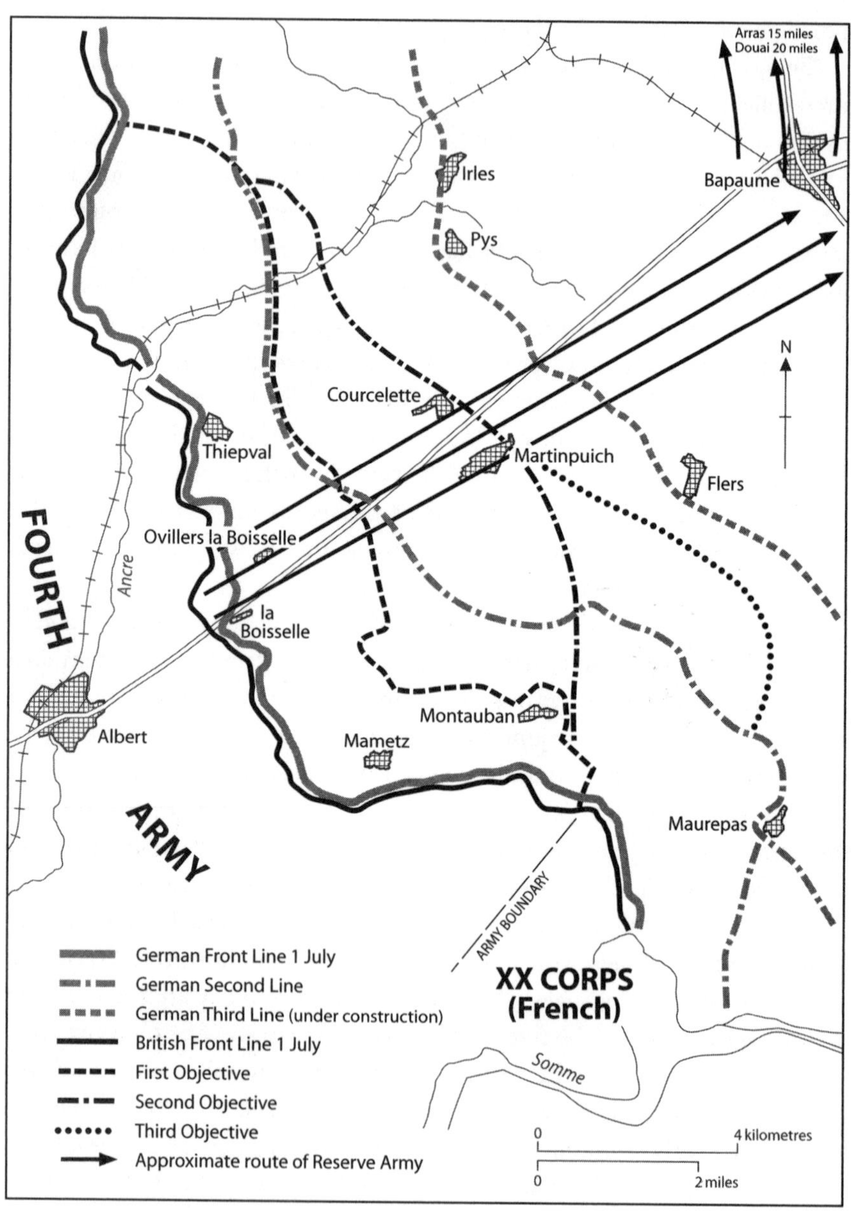


The Change of Plan, June

# IV

With the final decisions made on objectives, artillery, and the type of bombardment, it might be thought that the planning process was at an end. All that remained was the drafting of detailed orders to give effect to the overall plan. This was not the case. By the time that Rawlinson and Haig had ironed out their major differences, the French position at Verdun had undergone a precipitate decline. The Germans had attacked that fortress on 21 February with indecisive results. But three months of heavy fighting had taken its toll on the French army. On 21 April Joffre informed Haig that the 39 French divisions which were to have made the major attack at the Somme would be reduced to 30. The remainder would have to be diverted to Verdun. Then on 20 May the number was reduced to 26. By the end of the month that figure had become 20 and by early June Joffre had stopped specifying the number of divisions he could now spare for the Somme.[37] It was left to Haig to deduce that Joffre's Sixth Army was now the only French unit still designated for northern operations, and that its 12 divisions were all the support he could expect.[38]

How did the shrinking number of French troops assigned to the Somme operation affect the British plan? Seemingly there was no immediate change. Late in April, one week after the first French reduction, Haig created a Reserve Corps, a combined infantry–cavalry force under General Gough to exploit targets of opportunity.[39] The first proposals for the use of the force were put to Haig by Gough in May. After discussions with Rawlinson, Gough had concluded that two brigades of cavalry should be used, one on the northern sector of the front and one in the south, to help the infantry get forward in the event of an enemy collapse. In addition, he suggested that an entire cavalry division should be concentrated in the north to sweep forward to the enemy's second line and assist in rolling it up.[40] However, Haig's response to these proposals indicated that his basic thinking had not changed. He commented that the scheme was too ambitious. 'One Cav Div in all is the utmost that can be allotted or that could be used. In such ground masses of Cav cannot be employed.'[41] Gough was told to reduce the cavalry scheme to the use of one brigade in the area of the Ancre Valley and another in the Montauban area. They were to be used only if clear opportunities presented themselves.[42]

Even by the end of May little had changed. By this time the French contribution to the battle had halved – from 39 divisions to 20. Yet shortly after this, Rawlinson published a set of operations orders which indicated that the plan decided on in April still held the field. The British would confine themselves to the capture of the German second line north of Pozières and then attack along it to the south-east in order to assist the main French operation.[43]

A week later all was changing. The French contribution now consisted of a mere 12 divisions. This might have led to the conclusion that the whole campaign should be scaled down because there was no prospect that the British army could be expanded to the extent necessary to compensate for the lost French divisions. Yet nothing of the sort occurred. Instead, the British, without any major accession of power, took upon themselves a campaign no less ambitious than when the French were to be the major contributors.

So on 14 June Rawlinson issued a new set of operations orders. The first objective remained as before, that is the German second line to the north of Pozières and south of that point an advance of between 2,000 and 3,000 yards towards the German second line. The second objective, however, was now stated to be a line due *east* of the first, namely Grandcourt–Martinpuich–Montauban. And there was now to be a third objective: the capture of the ridge from Martinpuich through High Wood to Ginchy. In short, operations were now to be directed due east instead of south-east towards the French.[44] The aim of the operation had also changed. It was no longer to assist a French crossing of the Somme in the vicinity of Péronne but 'to break the enemy's defensive system and [to] exploit to the full all opportunities opened up for defeating his forces within reach'.[45] With this in mind three divisions of cavalry would be massed with the idea of turning the defeat of the enemy into a rout – their objective, Bapaume.[46]

So Rawlinson's fears, expressed back in March to Kitchener, had been realised. A limited (if quite over-optimistic) attack had been transformed into an unlimited one. But the cause of this transformation was not that the British army had enjoyed a large accession of fighting forces, or that its capability to launch a mass offensive had suddenly become a realistic operation of war. It was simply that the French army was now so diminished that it was incapable of doing the job.

The extension of objectives did not stop here. It transpired that, in Haig's estimation, the army which he had delegated to confine itself to strictly limited objectives but then had deemed equipped to capture Bapaume could do even more. Just two days after Rawlinson issued his revised operations orders, Haig announced that if enemy resistance collapsed a combined force of cavalry and infantry, to be commanded by Gough in what was ominously renamed the Reserve *Army*, was to turn north from Bapaume with the purpose of rolling up the German position from that place to Monchy (a German-held village to the east of Arras) in 'flank and reverse'.[47] So the ultimate objective of the Fourth Army, instead of being a move forward of about 3,000 yards and then a swing south to assist the French, had become a massed advance to positions 40 miles away. And this without any major accretion in British strength.

Nor was Haig satisfied with even this much. Some days after settling on Monchy as the Fourth Army's destination, he received an Intelligence report which suggested that the enemy had 'only' 32 battalions on the main front of the British attack and 'only' a further 65 with which to reinforce this front within the first six days of battle.[48] The use of the word 'only' in this report is puzzling. The course of battle over two years had made it plain that, given the advantage of defence over attack, in the current state of weaponry a small force dug in and equipped with machine-guns and artillery could stop a very much larger force attacking across the open. Further, the Intelligence report indicated that any superiority held by the Fourth Army would entirely vanish after just five days, hardly the scenario for a decisive advance or any sort of breakthrough. Indeed, it foreshadowed, at the very most, a gradual and costly pushing forward of no great significance.

Yet Haig appears to have embraced this information as justifying a further move in the direction of optimism. Soon after reading this document he extended the Fourth Army's objective to Douai, some 70 miles away. Such an objective would only be obtainable if the entire German army holding the line in the north collapsed, so enabling Haig's cavalry to range into territory that the Germans had become incapable of defending. Haig was indeed thinking in Napoleonic terms. As noted, he intended to use his cavalry, he told Robertson, 'on the lines of 1806' – that is, as Napoleon had done at Jena when an infantry break in had been converted into a breakthrough and rout of Prussian forces by the cavalry.[49] Thus machine-guns, quick-firing artillery, barbed wire, and trenches, none of which had been present at Jena, were wished away by the commander-in-chief as he sought to return to simpler times and decisive victories.

Rawlinson, it must be said, was not being swept along by Haig's flights of fancy. On 22 June he addressed his corps commanders on the new plan. He informed them (presumably they already knew) that the British attack had become the main operation and that although the first objective remained the same, subsequent ones had been added by the commander-in-chief. Distant towns such as Bapaume, Monchy, and Douai were to be captured seriatim by the cavalry. Rawlinson then went on to say:

> An opportunity may occur to push the cavalry through, in order to confirm success, and in this connection I will read you the orders which I have received on the subject from the Commander-in-Chief this morning. But before I read them I had better make it quite clear that it may not be possible to break the

> enemy's line and put the cavalry through at the first rush. In the event of our not being able to capture the [first] line until the afternoon, it would not be possible to send the Cavalry through on the first day at all. A situation may supervene later when the attack on the [second] line takes place for pushing the cavalry through; but until we can see what is the [state] of the battle, it is impossible to predict at what moment we shall be able to undertake this, and the decision will rest in my hand to say when it can be carried out.[50]

A more lukewarm endorsement of a plan would be hard to find.

## V

We have looked so far at the infantry and cavalry plans and have seen them transformed. Beginning as an operation designed to capture certain enemy trench lines to assist the French, it had become a grandiose plan for the defeat of the entire German army in the northern area of the Western Front. The artillery aspects of the plan have only been mentioned in passing. But it should be noted, whether or not the military command recognised it, that the artillery was the primary weapon whereby the German trench defenders were to be neutralised or killed. And unless this was to occur along a sufficient portion of the line, there was little to be gained from discussing distant cavalry objectives.

Rawlinson's initial thoughts on the artillery aspect of the plan were made in the light of his recent experience on the Western Front and in particular his experience at the Battle of Loos in September 1915. At the conclusion of that battle, Rawlinson's artillery adviser General Budworth, who was to serve in the same capacity at the Somme, calculated that one heavy howitzer (which he defined as 8 inches and above) was required for every 100 yards of front attacked.[51] We have seen that Rawlinson employed this formula at the Somme to calculate that with approximately 200 heavy howitzers at his disposal he could attack around 20,000 yards of front.

It is quite clear that Rawlinson regarded this situation as most satisfactory. In May he told his corps commanders:

> As regards the bombardment, looking at the operations as a whole, we shall have twice as many guns for the bombardment as we had at Loos, and we shall have an unlimited supply of ammunition.[52]

Yet the situation was hardly as promising as this statement implies. In the first place, Rawlinson himself, on the occasion of presenting his figures to the corps commanders, observed that the attack would be delivered on a front 'rather more than twice as wide as we attacked on at Loos'.[53] So at least in terms of the availability of guns per yard of front, his army would not be better placed than in the previous operation. This is of particular importance given that Rawlinson himself had recognised that the British artillery at Loos was insufficient to destroy the German defences and for that very reason had employed poison gas in a futile attempt to rectify the insufficiency.

Rawlinson's calculation concerning guns had been made purely in terms of the length of front. This had some validity at Loos where the German defences consisted of little more than the front line. It had no validity at the Somme where, as noted, enemy trenches consisted of a front system of three lines, including a strong second line some 2,000 to 4,000 yards beyond the first, and a maze of communication trenches between. Rawlinson, in his first proposal to Haig, intended to penetrate these defences to an average depth of 2,500 yards, in other words to subdue trenches greatly in excess of the actual length of front attacked. This was cause enough to raise doubts about Rawlinson's optimistic view of the artillery situation. Even more alarming, it will be recalled that Haig had extended Rawlinson's original objectives so that the trenches to be reduced were doubled, making any comparison with Loos even less relevant. In fact, if any calculations had been made at this point it would have been discovered that the 24,000 yards of front actually to be attacked had no less than 150,000 yards of trench behind it. The Loos calculation, accordingly, was out by a factor of eight.

It might be thought that these figures reveal that Rawlinson, by some strange mischance was unaware of the complexity of the German trench system at the Somme. This was certainly not the case. When Haig extended the objectives to be captured in the south, he added a further 1,780 yards to Rawlinson's front of attack. Rawlinson immediately pointed out to the commander-in-chief that he was now faced with an additional 16,000 yards of trench to bombard.[54] In this instance he appeared to recognise that it was the whole complexity of the trench system that needed bombardment, not just the length of front. Yet he seems to have drawn no overall lesson from this flash of insight. The Loos calculation, based simply on length of front, remained the basis of the Fourth Army's allocation of heavy howitzers until the day of battle.

But even this is not the extent of Rawlinson's miscalculation. In strength, the defences at the Somme bore no comparison to those at Loos. The trenches were deeper, there were more dug-outs to shelter the defending garrisons, there were more concreted machine-gun posts, and there were a number of all-round fortified positions such as the Schwaben Redoubt. In addition the

Germans at the Somme had incorporated a succession of fortified villages into their front defences.

Even the Loos figure of guns per yard of front could only be reached for the Somme by redefining what constituted a heavy howitzer. Budworth, in his paper, had insisted that only 8 inches and above be defined as 'heavy'. At the Somme Rawlinson arrived at his figure only by including 6-inch howitzers in the heavy category. By Budworth's definition he had only 133 – far fewer than was required even by an attack on a single trench line.[55]

It is possible that Rawlinson derived some comfort from the fact that, unlike at Loos, he would have what he referred to as 'an unlimited supply of ammunition' to fire from his inadequate number of guns. On 20 June it was made apparent that this was not remotely the case. On that day he received a communication from General Kiggell, expressed in the double-speak that was becoming a GHQ trademark.

Rawlinson was instructed that, in relation to the preliminary bombardment, while no one desired to 'fetter' his discretion and bearing in mind that 'it is essential that his artillery preparation should be thorough', he should pay due regard to the limitations of the ammunition supply and the effect that prolonged shooting would have on the guns. If these factors were neglected, 'the continuance of offensive operations during the summer may be seriously prejudiced'. Therefore he must ensure that the desired results were attained 'without expending more ammunition than is required to effect that purpose'.[56] Now Rawlinson had earlier informed GHQ that he intended in the course of the preliminary bombardment to include six periods of intense firing, amounting in total to 8.25 hours. GHQ suggested that this period be reduced, arguing that their 'value against lightly manned trenches ... when not followed by assault is open to doubt'.[57]

Rawlinson entered a quite vigorous protest to this missive. He made it clear that he thought his discretion was being 'fettered', and that if the bombardment had to be reduced, it quite obviously would cease to be 'thorough'. He also informed Haig that the periods of intense firing were not directed against 'lightly manned trenches' but against the strongest fortified locations in the enemy defensive system.[58] But once more, having made a show of resistance, Rawlinson capitulated. Without further argument, he agreed to cancel no fewer than three of his six periods of intense bombardment.[59]

It hardly needs to be stressed that this was a matter of the gravest import. No less than four hours of firing (three periods each of 1 hour 20 minutes) by the heaviest guns against the strongest enemy positions were to be forgone. Yet Rawlinson still seemed to think the bombardment adequate – no 'further' reductions, he said, could be made with safety.[60] As a consequence he failed to entertain the idea that in response to the limitations which had now appeared in the availability of ammunition, the objectives to be attempted should be rethought along the lines of his original plan.

One other artillery matter, that of counter-battery, was given little prominence in any of Rawlinson's or Haig's plans for the Somme. Yet it was Rawlinson who had stated after the Battle of Loos that the 'success of an operation depends largely upon keeping down the fire of the hostile artillery'. Perhaps the commanders once more thought that the Fourth Army was so lavishly supplied with counter-batteries that the question need not be discussed. However, on any objective assessment of Rawlinson's artillery resources, it is difficult to see how such a conclusion could have been reached. For the bombardment Rawlinson had 1,010 guns devoted to wire-cutting and light trench bombardment and 233 heavy howitzers for major trench destruction.[61] This left just 180 guns for counter-battery purposes, of which 32 were the obsolescent and notoriously inaccurate 4.7-inch guns. The remainder consisted of 128 × 60-pounder and 20 × 6-inch guns. So, overall just 12.5 per cent of Rawlinson's artillery was devoted to counter-battery, with 18 per cent of the guns used for this purpose practically useless. Given that the Germans had 476 artillery pieces ranged against the British, and that as preparations for battle became more obvious they reinforced this number by 17 field howitzer batteries and 36 smaller guns, the number of guns devoted to subduing them was quite evidently inadequate.[62]

In the event, not even this pitiful number could devote all their attention to the German batteries. When Haig extended the objectives in the north, Rawlinson discovered that the 18-pounder wire-cutters could not reach the distant wire. His solution was to switch some of the counter-batteries to this task. What effect this decision had overall is difficult to assess. But its effect may be guessed from the fact that, in the case of VIII Corps, 24 of their 32 × 60-pounders and all of their 8 × 4.7-inch guns were required to divide their activities between wire-cutting and counter-battery.[63] So the counter-battery programme was reduced to little more than half its original dimension.

There were other instances which show the neglect of counter-battery. In the case of XV Corps, Rawlinson considered that it had a smaller bombardment task than other corps so he had reduced its howitzer component accordingly.[64] However, during the bombardment the corps found this allocation so unsatisfactory that it switched its counter-battery guns to general bombardment purposes.[65] This action evinced no response from Fourth Army headquarters.

Nor was there a more evident reaction to the extraordinary comment offered by X Corps. In a report on the preliminary bombardment it was stated:

> Our superiority in artillery was not used to destroy the enemy's heavy artillery with heavy howitzers and there was not much counter battery work.[66]

That is, counter-battery activity, which Rawlinson in the light of the battle of Loos had characterised as a prerequisite for victory, was allowed to degenerate under Fourth Army neglect into a matter wholly at the whim of the individual corps commanders. Not one of them had hitherto commanded heavy artillery in battle.

# 6 'Favourable Results Are Not Anticipated': Preparations for Battle, June

## I

While the plans for the battle were being finalised, the officers and men of Fourth Army were set to work to train for the impending battle. Training is a problematical question in the First World War. In the static nature of the warfare between 1915 and 1917 when advances were small and failures many, it is tempting to overlook it altogether. Moreover, the body of a trained soldier is no more able to withstand massed machine-gun and artillery fire than that of an untrained one. However, training could still be important in some situations and, as we shall see, it provides insights into the minds of the command.

It would be a truism to say that many of the New Army formations which were to fight the Battle of the Somme arrived in France with inadequate training. This was not because of lack of intent. Early in the war a six-month programme for training had been laid down by the War Office which included drill, musketry, marching, and fighting in units ranging from platoon, through company and battalion to brigade and division.[1] In practice only some elements of the programme were carried out. Instructors were in short supply, equipment (even including rifles) was scarce, and large unit exercises were difficult to co-ordinate. The result was that the level of training was very variable, and owed much to chance or the enthusiasm or otherwise of individual officers.[2] The unreality of the exercises often made them impossible to take seriously. As one recruit noted:

> Those were the happy days when you could capture a village by merely marching into it; when you could hold up a Battalion by pointing a dummy machine-gun at it, and refusing to budge; when you usually had lunch with the enemy, each side claiming the victory, over cheese sandwiches, chocolate, apples and water.[3]

More seriously, and for reasons which are not at all to the credit of the army command, the artillery received considerably less training in Britain than the infantry. This shows that the command was still thinking in terms of an infantry war. The artillery programmes gave the impression of haste and it seems impossible that the technical detail for even rudimentary gunnery could have been absorbed in the short time available. Lack of sufficient guns and ammunition for training was even more chronic in this branch than in the infantry. In 34 Division (which was to meet with disaster on 1 July) there was time for only three days' practice before embarkation.[4]

In France, GHQ and the army commands tried to rectify some of the most glaring deficiencies. GHQ began to distribute pamphlets on aspects of training to commanding officers but distribution had only just commenced by the time of the Somme. One of the more widely distributed pamphlets was *Training of Divisions for Offensive Action* issued by General Kiggell, Haig's Chief of Staff, in May 1916.[5] It was at least an attempt to impose some uniformity of method on the BEF, but the principles laid down were often so general as to amount to little more than platitudes (for example each unit must have a clearly defined objective, an attack must be driven home until the endurance of the enemy is broken down, and – more ominously – 'all must be prepared for heavy casualties').[6]

Rawlinson, from Fourth Army, issued his 'Tactical Notes', which reproduced much of Kiggell's pamphlet but attempted to go further in giving guidance on how some of the new weapons such as Lewis guns and Stokes mortars, were to be used. These notes also dealt with matters such as air–infantry and artillery–infantry co-operation and drew attention to some of the more specialised GHQ pamphlets on the use of these new methods.[7] A series of 'schools' was also established at the army level where officers and men could be instructed in topics such as co-operation with other arms, the tactical use of ground, map-reading, the latest French infantry doctrine, and the general interchange of ideas.[8] Other schools addressed the burgeoning need for specialists in the handling of Lewis guns, trench mortars, rifle grenades, gas, smoke, and machine-guns.[9]

Nevertheless, despite their best efforts the BEF was beset by difficulties in organising a coherent training programme. The main difficulty was the shortage of labour. Preparations for a battle on the scale of the Somme required an immense amount of physical toil. Yet Haig had only 5,000 men to offer Rawlinson for these tasks.[10] This was so inadequate that the Fourth Army commander had no option but to supplement the force with his infantry. What this meant for the troops is detailed in a report by 32 Division. In the course of two months this division (among other things) constructed new assembly trenches for the attack, dug communication trenches, dug over 50 emplacements for trench mortar batteries, completed a water supply system through to the front trenches, dug 19.6 miles of trench in which to bury the communications cables, laid 160 miles of this cable, erected 28 bridges for the artillery, constructed 72 emplacements for gas cylinders, and carried up 671 of these cylinders to the front.[11] All divisions had similar tasks and the consequences were sourly summed up by General Maxse of 18 Division: 'No rest and training for the infantry, except during the one week.'[12]

Nevertheless, some training was carried out by the corps or divisional commanders. This usually took two forms. The first was to rehearse the attack to be made over models of the enemy trench system they would face:

> In each of these [training] areas a complete system of trenches reproduced exactly from air photographs was constructed representing the whole of the objectives to be attacked by each brigade. Each brigade in the Corps was thus enabled to be practised over trenches exactly representing those it was finally to attack.[13]

The second form concerned the training of men to fight within trench systems, but this seems only to have been undertaken by a few divisions.

Maxse of 18 Division rehearsed his men in the use of Lewis guns and trench mortars to overcome pockets of resistance by working to a flank, attacking the enemy from several directions, and generally manoeuvring in trench systems so that a portion at least of the attacking troops would fight their way forward.[14]

In his summary of the battle Maxse made much of his methods, characterising the battle fighting as a 'picture of hard slogging by determined Company Commanders who used their heads and sent detachments with bombers round the flanks of the enemy'.[15]

But in commenting thus, Maxse (and some observers since) confused primary and secondary sources of success. Maxse's 'determined Company Commanders' could only operate as they did in the south if the artillery had already eliminated a high proportion of the defenders and their weaponry. As many in the VIII, X, and III Corps could have testified, determination in the face of an intact defence would have availed nothing. Training, in short, was valuable only in an environment which gave trained troops a decent chance of exercising their skills.

## II

The next matter that Rawlinson was required to consider was how his troops, well trained or ill, were to traverse the killing zone of no man's land. Two methods of protecting the infantry in this perilous journey had been canvassed earlier – gas and smoke. Both were eventually discarded by the Fourth Army commander because of the inability to predict the wind direction and speed at zero. At Loos the erratic wind had played havoc with gas operations, and in the absence of shells which could deliver gas with some exactitude Rawlinson was not prepared to risk using it again. He argued that the same risk applied to smoke, which would now be confined to forming a screen for troops attacking villages such as La Boisselle and Fricourt. Rawlinson was making a legitimate point here. But his earlier insistence that his troops required the concealment provided by smoke remained valid.

Rawlinson suggested a different type of infantry protection at a meeting with his corps commanders on 16 April, stating that

> The lifts of the artillery time table must conform to the advance of the infantry. The infantry must be given plenty of time. The guns must 'arrose' [spray as if from a hose] each objective just before the infantry assault it.[16]

Rawlinson later made this idea more explicit in his 'Tactical Notes':

> The ideal is for the artillery to keep their fire immediately in front of the infantry as the latter advances, battering down all opposition with a hurricane of projectiles.[17]

These remarks by Rawlinson are some of the first expositions of what would later be called the 'creeping barrage', one of the most important methods of infantry protection devised during the First World War. A creeping barrage consisted of a screen of shells which advanced (or crept) over the ground at a regular, predetermined pace, behind which proceeded the infantry. It had two great advantages. It swept over all enemy defences and was therefore likely to catch machine-gunners or riflemen whether they lurked in front trenches, communication trenches, or shell holes. Moreover, it would force dug-out dwellers to remain concealed while the attackers were traversing no man's land, or risk manning their weapons under a hail of shells. Thus if the infantry followed close behind the barrage they might overpower these defenders before they could emerge and bring their weapons into action.

What is not clear is whether Rawlinson grasped all these advantages in April and May 1916. Certainly after his conference he made no attempt to impose the creeping barrage on his corps or divisional commanders. The decision about whether to adopt it therefore remained in their hands. Unfortunately for the troops, few would use that option on 1 July.

The other matters about the deployment of troops in no man's land to be decided by Rawlinson were the speed and formation they should adopt. The matter of speed was dealt with in the 'Tactical Notes', which stated, *inter alia*:

> Celerity of movement and the necessity of taking immediate and full advantage of the stunning effects [of the bombardment] on the enemy's moral[e] and physical powers are essentially the governing factors. The leading lines, therefore, should carry right through to the furthest limits of the objective. The assaulting troops must push forward at a steady pace in successive lines, each adding fresh impetus to the preceding line. Although a steady pace for the assaulting troops is recommended, occasions may arise where the rapid advance of some lightly-equipped men on some particular part of the enemy's defences may turn the scale.[18]

What seems noteworthy about this document is that, so far from laying down a specific method of proceeding, it canvasses almost every possible speed. Thus 'celerity of movement' may be contrasted with pushing foward at a 'steady pace' or a 'rapid advance' only in particular (but unspecified) circumstances. It seems extremely unlikely that busy corps or divisional commanders could divine from this document any distinct message regarding the speed with which their troops should cross no man's land. They should act as they thought fit.

If Rawlinson did not specify the speed with which his troops should cross no man's land, nor did he dictate the formations they should adopt for their journey. Certainly the Fourth Army 'Tactical Notes' give four illustrations of 'the best formations' in which to advance, and each takes the form of a 'wave'. Yet these formations were not insisted upon. Indeed, Rawlinson stated that 'there can be no definite rules as regards the best formations for attack'. The most suitable, he suggests, would depend on the nature of the ground over which the attack was to be made. As an example he suggested that if full use of folds in the ground were to be made then 'small columns' might be appropriate.[19] Given these generalities, it was entirely appropriate that lower order commanders should develop those formations which they deemed suitable for their circumstances. As we shall see, the solutions they adopted varied enormously.

## III

On 24 June the preliminary bombardment for the great battle commenced with the field artillery concentrating on the German wire. For the next two days the weather continued fine, wire-cutting progressed, the heavier guns were registered on their targets, and counter-battery fire commenced.[20] But on the 26th just as the full bombardment started, the weather deteriorated, with low cloud and showers hampering aerial observation.[21] This was a serious matter because only RFC spotter planes could record if the heavy guns were hitting their targets – the enemy batteries, trenches, and wire. On the 28th the conditions were so bad that Rawlinson was forced to postpone the attack for 48 hours in the hope of better weather.[22] Even then the weather did not fully oblige. Both the 29th and 30th saw periods of low cloud and rain but the ammunition supply would allow for no further delays. The attack would go in at 7.30 a.m. on 1 July.

What effect the weather had on the effectiveness of the bombardment is difficult to estimate. Certainly, given the state of artillery accuracy prevailing at this time, any periods of unobserved fire were in the nature of a lottery. But during the course of the bombardment an unanticipated factor revealed itself which acted to reduce its effectiveness even further. This consisted of the various flaws in the guns and shells employed in the attack. These were the result of the haste with which Britain had been forced to improvise a large munitions industry. Under Lloyd George the Ministry of Munitions discarded quality control to meet production quotas. In addition orders placed externally (mainly for shells from the United States) were given to establishments with little or no experience in munitions production.

Consequences can be illustrated by looking at the experience of X Corps. Regarding their heavy artillery on the first day of the bombardment,one of their 2 × 9.2-inch howitzers had to be condemned when the rifling in the barrel twisted.[23] On the following day *both* of these howitzers were put out of action as a result of the premature explosion of a shell in No. 2 gun. They remained unserviceable throughout most of the bombardment. That same day two lighter howitzers from other batteries had to be withdrawn because of faulty equipment or premature explosions.[24] The next day (the 28th) passed without incident but on the 29th three guns from one battery succumbed to equipment failure and on the 30th a 6-inch howitzer collapsed with a faulty barrel.[25]

Nor were things much better with the field artillery. A single division (32) from the corps reported that during the bombardment

> about 20 × 18Pr and 6 × 4.5″Pr [howitzers] were out of action at one time or another with spring or buffer problems or prematures in the case of 4 × 4.5″[26]

The equipment and ammunition problems were not confined to X Corps. Almost all corps reported problems with their 18-pounder guns.[27] XV Corps also had two of their 9.2-inch guns explode. Many of the shells for this calibre of gun, by contrast, did not explode at all owing to fuse problems.[28] Similar problems were reported with 8-inch howitzer shells, 60-pounder ammunition, and 18-pounder ammunition (an entire consignment from America contained faulty fuses).[29]

Other problems concerned gun design. For example all of the 66 × 8-inch howitzers were makeshift weapons – old 6-inch coastal defence guns with the barrels rebored. All shells fired from them tended to fall short. They also had improvised recoil mechanisms which meant that it was difficult to return the guns to exactly the same position after each firing.[30]

What these defects meant in one instance is described by a German defender, Lt F.L. Cassel, located just north of Thiepval:

> One afternoon while I was lying on my wire bedstead heard the...boom of a heavy gun, the awesome whiz and swish of a rising heavy missile, then the earth was quaking, and while dust was falling through the boards I saw the beams above me bend and slowly descend by about 10 cm. My heart seemed to stop; now comes the end. But the catastrophe did not come. After the momentary paralysis was gone I left my bed and went into the trench ... [I] found a crater with a diameter of several metres made by a 21cm [9.2-inch shell], a dud! Had it exploded whoever was in the dugout would have seen daylight not before the day of resurrection.[31]

How well, despite these many defects and limitations, did the British artillerymen perform? It will be convenient to divide this discussion into the three objectives of the bombardment – cutting the wire in front of the German trenches, destroying the German trench system and its inhabitants, and overwhelming the German batteries in the area of the attack.

Wire-cutting was seemingly the most likely of the three tasks to be accomplished. First, the overwhelming proportion of British guns (1,000 out of 1,500) and shells (1 million out of 1.6 million) were devoted to this task.

Moreover, the wire protecting the enemy's front line was the closest target to the British guns and therefore the most easily observed by the Forward Observation Officers. In addition the success achieved in this task could be checked (and re-checked) by raiding parties sent out at night to inspect the results.

Nevertheless there were some difficulties. Regarding observation, extensive areas of the front were shielded from direct view by sudden folds in the ground. This seemed a particular problem for X Corps, which constantly reported that the exact effect of the guns on the wire could not be seen.[32] Bad light could also hamper observation and this was recorded as a problem by several of the corps during the preliminary bombardment.[33] Finally, such a mundane factor as long grass could raise doubts about the effect of the shelling or even if the wire was being hit.[34]

Then there were problems with the types of shell used. Most wire-cutting guns fired 18-pounder shrapnel or high-explosive shells. If shrapnel was used the degree of accuracy had to be very high. On bursting, a shrapnel shell propels steel balls forward and downwards. So to penetrate the wire at the high velocity needed to cut it, the shell had to explode first a few yards short of and above the target. It is a reasonable supposition that at least a proportion of the British gunners at the Somme had not the experience to achieve consistent accuracy of this sort. High-explosive 18-pounder shells required less accuracy but the problem here was that many shells travelled through the wire and only exploded on impact with the ground. This tended to throw the wire into the air and down again without cutting it.

The distant wire presented a particular difficulty. Here the results could not be checked by patrols, and aerial photographs, which in the case of wire were notoriously difficult to interpret, had to be relied upon. Most gunners considered wire-cutting at 5,000 to 7,000 yards a matter of luck. In III Corps the artillerymen warned that, while they were willing to try to cut a few lanes, 'favourable results are not anticipated'.[35]

Finally the overall task was, despite the number of guns employed, too great for some corps. III Corps calculated that to cut all the wire within 3,500 yards of the front line would require quantities of ammunition which were simply not available. Their only solution was to suggest that the infantry provide a priority list of wire whose removal was essential.[36]

As noted, the only sure way to check on the state of the wire was to send raiding parties or patrols across no man's land at night. Even then the reports presented problems of interpretation. Each patrol could cover only a short length of front in the limited time they could remain in this hazardous area. On a good night parties might assess 100 yards of front; if they encountered hostile troops they might not get close enough to the wire to file a report at all. And difficulty arose in knowing whether these reports were typical of the entire divisional front.

In all, the records of 50 patrols exist for the period of the preliminary bombardment. At best these would have covered just 5,000 of the 24,000 yards of enemy front facing the Fourth Army. The picture they conveyed was decidedly ambiguous. Of the 50 patrols, 24 reported that the wire in their section was not cut, 20 reported that it was cut, and six that it was cut in some places but not others. Nor did the overall picture become any clearer as the preliminary bombardment progressed. Patrols for each night from the 26th–27th to the

29th–30th recorded almost exactly the same proportion of negative, positive, and indeterminate results.[37]

The picture does, however, become clearer if the figures are split into individual corps. In the south, XIII Corps consistently recorded far more positive than negative reports; and XV Corps (for which few reports survive) were confident from a major raid on the night of the 26th–27th that the wire facing them was almost totally destroyed. In the north the picture was also reasonably clear. VIII Corps consistently produced far more negative than positive reports. And on the night before the attack the position was made yet clearer by the 10 raids conducted. The wire was intact on the front of 31 Division, was reasonably well cut on the front of 4 Division, and varied from non-existent to strong on 29 Division's front. The two centre corps (X and III), are the most difficult to analyse. Here the reports showed no consistency and were almost evenly split between positive and negative results.

The patrol reports were collected at Fourth Army HQ, and Rawlinson should have been aware, at least in general terms, of the variable effect of the wire-cutting. Nevertheless, the overall picture eluded him. He directed all his attention to the situation on the front of VIII Corps, even going so far as to discuss it with Haig.[38] Certainly the situation in the area as revealed by the raid reports was not encouraging. But neither was the situation on the III and X Corps front and this elicited no response from Rawlinson. On the eve of battle he pronounced himself entirely satisfied with wire-cutting, 'except in VIII Corps front which is somewhat behind-hand'.[39]

The next aspect of the bombardment was trench destruction. From 25 June to zero hour on 1 July Rawlinson's heavy guns threw 188,500 shells weighing 34.5 million pounds at the German defences.[40] Two points mentioned earlier about the evolution of the Somme plan deserve repetition here. First, this was the heaviest Allied bombardment of the war so far and bound to cause much destruction. Second, for the area it had to cover and the type of defences it had to destroy, it was woefully inadequate.

No methods for assessing the effectiveness of the bombardment on the German trenches were available to Rawlinson. From the air it was difficult to assess the state of an enemy trench and even aerial photographs were difficult to interpret. As for trench raids, these were decidedly hazardous. The raiding parties actually had to enter the German trenches and, if possible, the dug-outs underneath them (where it was known that Germans might shelter during a bombardment).

In the north and centre (VIII, X, and III Corps) information was scarce. As noted, in some areas the wire had not been sufficiently cut to allow raiding parties through. In other areas patrols found the German defences manned in strength and were driven off by rifle and machine-gun fire.[41] One patrol (that of the Royal Dublin Fusiliers from 29 Division) managed to fight its way through the wire. The men were close enough to observe that the German front trench was totally destroyed. But they were unable to proceed further because 'fire from a line or lines in rear very effectively sweeps the ground in front of the first line'.[42] Only in one instance was a patrol from any of these corps able to inspect a dug-out. By chance it had collapsed.[43]

None of this provided warrant for confidence. If trenches were being manned in strength, either the majority of dug-outs were providing sufficient shelter or the bombardment was missing the trenches holding most troops. And as the Dublins found, it was insufficient merely to render the front line uninhabitable. Any trench from which machine-gun fire could be brought to bear on no man's land had to be dealt with, otherwise the attacking troops stood no decent chance of success.

In the south (XV and XIII Corps) there was some reason for optimism. Raiding parties from both corps were frequently able to enter the enemy trenches. They reported that many dug-outs had been destroyed. Even in this area, however, on the night before the attack many patrols were driven back by heavy fire, indicating that a reasonable number of enemy soldiers had survived the bombardment.[44]

What of prisoners' reports? For one reason or another the raiding parties found prisoners hard to capture during the preliminary bombardment. In the north this was because the raiders hardly managed to penetrate the enemy wire, let alone enter the hostile trenches. But even in the south capturing prisoners was no easy matter. In this area the Germans at night evacuated their front line, and even on occasions their second and third lines, so placing their forces beyond the range of the fiercest bombardment and the raiding parties.

So in all just twelve prisoners were interrogated by Fourth Army Intelligence between 25 and 30 June.[45] And they were not just few in number but unrepresentative of the front as a whole. Nine of the twelve were captured by XV Corps; of the remainder one came from the X Corps area, one from III Corps, and one from XIII Corps. Their stories, which anyway should have been treated with caution because of a well-known tendency for prisoners to say what they expect their captors to want to hear, were extremely variable. Of the XV Corps group, three claimed that the dug-outs were being badly damaged, two claimed they were little damaged, and four made no comment on dug-outs. Thus we can contrast prisoner Gregor's statement:

> The dug-outs are still good. The men appear to remain in these dug-outs all the time and are completely sheltered[46]

with that of an unnamed prisoner who commented that his company

> has suffered heavily, most of the casualties being due to the destruction of the dug-outs by our heavy artillery, the occupants being buried.[47]

One of the more interesting comments came from a soldier who had recently been transferred from the Ovillers sector (III Corps) to the XV Corps sector. He too noted that the dug-outs in his new area were being destroyed but stated that these were of much less robust construction than those around Ovillers.[48] Whether this qualification was picked up by Fourth Army or passed on to III Corps is not known.

The evidence from prisoners in the other areas was either unilluminating (XIII Corps) or contradictory. Prisoners in X Corps area, for example, reported that the entrances to the dug-outs were being caved in but that casualties were slight.[49] Prisoner Hornung (III Corps area) noted that new dug-outs were being constructed in the support lines but did not say whether that was because the front line was being destroyed or whether the garrisons were being pulled back to a slightly safer area.[50]

A cautious interpretation of these statements might have concluded that anyway in the south some but by no means all dug-outs were succumbing to the bombardment, whereas in the north the position was too obscure to warrant any firm conclusion. This was not the conclusion reached by Fourth Army Intelligence. On the eve of battle they confidently stated that

> From the examination of prisoners it is apparent that our artillery fire has been most effective. Most of the dug-outs in the [enemy] front line have been blown in or blocked up. Even the deep dug-outs of a Battalion H.Q. were not proof against our big shells.[51]

As an extrapolation from the evidence of twelve prisoners this sweeping statement borders on the irresponsible.

The third element in the bombardment programme was counter-battery fire. In 1916 the problem of firing at distant and precise targets with any accuracy had yet to be resolved.[52] In the event a number of factors told against the effectiveness of Haig's counter-battery programme. The major deficiency was simply a lack of guns. This has been touched on already but it is worth emphasising.

Rawlinson had just 180 counter-battery guns and some of these were old and inaccurate. Some corps were forced by the extension of the objectives to divert guns from counter-battery to cutting distant wire and bombarding trenches. XV Corps suffered an additional disadvantage. Their staff allocated to counter-battery the lowest of priorities. On some days just four batteries (16 guns) were attacking the enemy artillery.[53]

There was one exception to this picture and it reveals how much might have been accomplished had Rawlinson paid more attention to counter-battery. XIII Corps gave counter-battery a high priority and not only allocated their 60-pounders and 4.7-inch guns to the duty but added some heavy howitzers as well. Outstanding results were achieved. Most German batteries in the valleys north of Mametz and Montauban were destroyed. By the eve of battle the Germans could bring only a handful of guns to bear against the southern corps, so cancelling out the failings of XV Corps and ensuring that the troops of XIII Corps had a reasonable chance in their attack.[54]

A further factor was the state of the weather during the preliminary bombardment. This negated a recent improvement in artillery technique. By the time of the Somme the importance of aerial spotting for the artillery had been well recognised. For the preliminary bombardment 20 planes were allocated to this task, a number well in excess of those available in 1915. In addition nine planes were utilised to take photographs of likely enemy battery concentrations. Other photographs could be used to check on results. Unfortunately for the British, most of this went by the board when the weather closed in on the 26th.[55] Of the projected five days of the bombardment only one was fine. The others were plagued by low cloud and rain. Even the two-day extension (the 29th and 30th) had periods when visibility was poor.[56] Deprived of their 'eyes in the air', the counter-batteries had to resort to shooting at previously identified battery positions from map references. Later it was discovered that the maps used were so inaccurate as to render these endeavours useless. Anyway the Germans were quite adept at moving their batteries to new locations to thwart the British gunners.

To what extent was the command aware that in most sections its counter-battery programme was deficient? There was much information for Fourth Army staff to draw on. Each corps and division kept a daily record of enemy artillery retaliation on their front and these were sent to Fourth Army headquarters for collating and analysing.

Overall they should have made sobering reading. Of the fifteen reports received from VIII, X, and III Corps, only two described enemy artillery retaliation as light or fairly light. And even these last were hardly comforting. They occurred during the first two days of the preliminary bombardment on the front of 32 Division (X Corps) and were soon superseded by others for the remainder of the bombardment period which described enemy shelling as heavy or fairly heavy.[57]

Their situation may be contrasted with the reports of the two southern corps (XV and XIII). They sent in twelve reports. Nine described German artillery fire as light or fairly light. Even so, reports on the eve of battle noted that hostile shelling had increased to levels described by XIII Corps as 'active' and XV Corps as 'considerable'.[58]

Given these reports, Rawlinson can have been under little illusion as to the ineffectual nature of his counter-battery programme. Yet his diary shows little sign of this. Only in the area of VIII Corps did he note that the counter-battery programme had not worked well. When battle was joined on 1 July he would find that the problem was much more widespread than that, as the 598 field guns and 246 howitzers of the enemy that had survived the British counter-batteries brought down a curtain of fire on the advancing troops.

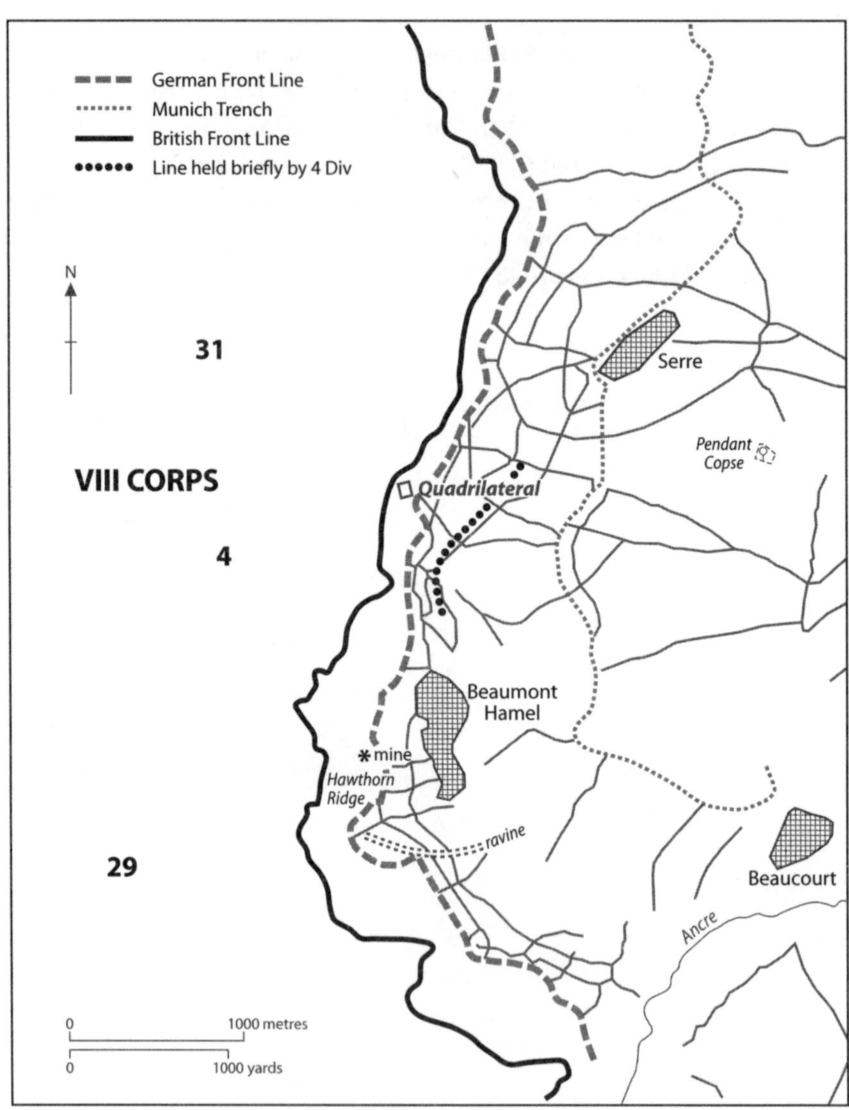
German Front Line
Munich Trench
British Front Line
Line held briefly by 4 Div
N
31
VIII CORPS
4
29
Serre
Pendant
Copse
Quadrilateral
Beaumont
Hamel
mine
Hawthorn
Ridge
ravine
Beaucourt
Ancre
0
1000 metres
0
1000 yards

VIII Corps, 1 July

# 7 'A Short Life': VII and VIII Corps on 1 July

## I

Two miles north of the main operation, the diversionary attack on the Gommecourt salient was to be undertaken by two divisions of the Third Army's VII Corps. It may be dealt with quickly. As the two divisions (56 and 46) replaced the battalion that held the line at Gommecourt, the Germans responded by moving up an extra division.[1] To that extent the diversion worked. To a greater extent it did not. What was to stand in the way of the Fourth Army's attack to the south was not so much enemy troops as enemy artillery. And the German defences in the Gommecourt salient were so formidable that the enemy command did not deem it necessary to relocate even one gun to support their troops. Their confidence was borne out by events. A total of 6,800 men from VII Corps fell in the attack for precisely no gains.[2] A feint attack was probably all that was required at Gommecourt, but that was not Haig's way.

## II

Further south in the area of the main attack, VIII Corps planned to capture the first and second German trench systems. They were then to establish a strong defensive flank in order to secure the advance of the cavalry further south from counter-attack. The German position was formidable. First they had good observation from their front line over the whole of the VIII Corps sector and from further back more extensive vistas were possible as the ground rose amphitheatre-like beyond Serre and Beaucourt.[3] And should the attackers capture the enemy front system they would be faced some 500 yards further on with the fortress-villages of Serre and Beaumont Hamel. Serre was situated on the crest of a ridge and the machine-gunners who manned its encircling defences could direct their fire on most sections of no man's land.[4] Beaumont Hamel lay in a valley shielded by the front defences situated on a ridge. Should these fall to an attack, the many machine-gun posts hidden in rear of the village were sited to take a heavy toll on troops advancing down the bare slope.[5]

A major natural feature along this section of front was Y Ravine, which bisected the area to be attacked by 29 Division. Its steep sides provided shelter for an entire battalion of enemy troops.

The other feature that presented attackers with a difficulty was Hawthorn Ridge, which dominated the ground to its north and south. At its tip the Germans had placed a concentration of machine-gun posts called Hawthorn Redoubt.[6] General Hunter-Weston's (the Commander of VIII Corps) solution to this problem was to place 40,000 pounds of explosive under the ridge and detonate it four hours before zero, thereby seizing it well before the main attack. His rationale for this time gap being that the delay would reduce German fears of an impending assault.[7]

General Headquarters objected and insisted that all mines be exploded at zero hour.[8] For reasons that are not clear (and appear to make no sense) VIII Corps decided to fire the Hawthorn mine at 7.20 a.m., ten minutes before zero.[9] At that point two companies of troops would rush across no man's land so that the tip of the crater would be in British hands when the main attack commenced.[10]

Arguably, the decision to detonate the mine at 7.20 a.m. had a disastrous consequence. So that the troops advancing to occupy the crater might not be hit by their own artillery, the gunners were ordered to lift their fire to the German rear positions the moment the mine was detonated.[11] This decision made sense if applied just to those batteries firing on the Hawthorn Redoubt. But in the event the entire corps artillery was ordered to lift from the front to rearward defences. Apparently this was done to keep the corps troops in step as they attacked the main rearward German defences in this sector. Whatever the wisdom of this, lifting the heavy artillery barrage along the entire front of VIII Corps at ten minutes before zero allowed the German defenders in those areas ample time to man their parapets and bring up their machine-guns from their dug-outs.

As it happened, the crater stratagem proved ineffective. Prompt on the explosion German forces in rear lines moved forward to occupy the lip of the crater nearest to them, just as British forces were advancing across no man's land to occupy the other crater lip. As the German positions were closer to the crater, they arrived at their lip first and directed withering machine-gun fire on to the advancing British troops. The crater remained in German hands.[12]

Then at 7.30 a.m. the main attack by VIII Corps commenced. Their initial advance by no means conformed to the stereotypical view of soldiers leaving their trenches in one body and proceeding across no man's land, shoulder to shoulder at a slow walk. In the far north the battalions of 31 Division had left the trenches ten minutes earlier: they then advanced to within close proximity of the German wire and lay down ready to rush the German front line at zero. The follow-up battalions moved forward in similar fashion.[13]

In the centre, the battalions of 4 Division adopted various stratagems. Some moved into no man's land before zero hour and 'pushed' forward at a good pace.[14] Others such as the King's Own Regiment adopted very complicated formations involving leading groups of specially trained skirmishers and snipers followed by Lewis gun teams. In turn they were followed by the main body of the battalion in highly complex, irregular formations.[15]

The 29 Division also adopted various attack formations. Some units, such as the Royal Inniskilling Fusiliers on the right of the attack, 'marched' up to the enemy front line and – where they were not held up by intact belts of wire – advanced on the support line. Others such as the Lancashire Fusiliers rushed forward in columns from advanced positions in no man's land.[16]

The main comment that can be made about VIII Corps' attack procedures is that most divisions or brigades or battalions chose those tactics which seemed most appropriate to the conditions confronting them. Certainly there was no slavish adherence to the Fourth Army 'Tactical Notes', except to that section of them which gave commanders *carte blanche.*

## III

In the event the variety of tactics adopted by the units of VIII Corps availed them nothing.

The situation was most poignant on the very left of the attack. Here was situated the 31 Division. It was a Kitchener Army unit formed in the main from North Country 'pals' battalions, that is groups from the same local area who had volunteered for service in the first days of the war.[17] They entered battle with high hopes. One of their brigadiers (Brigadier-General H.C. Rees) told them:

> You are about to attack the enemy with far greater numbers than he can oppose to you, supported by a huge number of guns . . . .
>
> You are about to fight in one of the greatest battles in the world, and the most just cause.

> Remember that the British Empire will anxiously watch your every move, and that the honour of the North Country rests in your hands.
>
> Keep your heads, do your duty, and you will utterly defeat the enemy.[18]

As we saw, the lead battalions of 31 Division moved into no man's land before zero and lay down close to the German wire. They then discovered to their horror that the British bombardment had (according to corps instructions) moved beyond the front German trenches, and that the German machine-gunners and riflemen were lining the parapet. Almost immediately heavy machine-gun fire ripped through the prostrate forms in no man's land. In essence the attack had collapsed before zero hour. By then hundreds were dead and hundreds more wounded. One battalion had no functioning officers by 7.28 a.m., two minutes *before* the intended commencement of the attack. A few men from the leftward brigade did reach the German front line and pressed towards Serre. They were never seen again.[19]

Such was the chaos that even troops in close proximity to the front were unsure of what was happening. Morris Bickersteth was a company commander with the 15 West Yorkshire. He was to go over with the eighth wave. His brother, who assembled this story from survivors' accounts, takes up the narrative:

> 'Come on lads', he [Morris] cried, 'Here's to a short life and a good one'.... After going ten yards, they found the remainder of 7 and 6 platoons only a few of whom were left alive lying just behind the rising ground .... Morris apparently gave the order to lie down for a moment to try and disentangle the living from the dead, although there were very few of the former .... Morris ...[then] looked around to see if there was any support from the trenches behind and at that moment a shrapnel bullet struck him in the back of the head; a second later another bullet passed right through his head, coming out through his forehead .... He just rolled over without a word ... quite dead.[20]

In all, the 15 West Yorkshire, or the Leeds Pals as they were better known, suffered 539 casualties out of 750 attacking. Of these, 230 were killed.[21]

The melancholy fact was acknowledged by the brigadier who had so encouraged his unit with visions of success. As he left his men to take up another command he issued another special order of the day which said in part, 'I bid goodbye to the remnants of as fine a Brigade as has ever gone into action'.[22] They had tried to do their duty. But so far from defeating the enemy, they had gained not one yard of ground.

Nor did the follow-up battalions of this division fare any better. By 7.25 a.m. the Germans, in addition to the constant heavy machine-gun fire, had dropped a heavy barrage on the British front line and on the assembly trenches to the rear. Some were wiped out before they reached their own front line.[23] Of those who attempted to deploy in no man's land the experience of the 12 York & Lancasters (Sheffield Pals) was typical. As they left their trenches they found that

> they had to pass through a terrible curtain of shell fire, and German machine guns were rattling death from two sides. But the lines growing even thinner, went on unwavering. Here and there a shell would burst right among the attackers .... Whole sections were destroyed; one section of 14 platoon was killed by concussion, all the men falling to the ground without a murmur. The left half of 'C' Company was wiped out before getting near the German wire .... The third and fourth waves suffered so heavily that by the time they reached No-Man's-Land they had lost at least half their strength .... The few survivors took shelter in shell-holes in front of the German line and remained there until they could get back under cover of darkness. What torture the troops endured in the shell holes they alone knew.[24]

Even worse was the experience of the 16 West Yorkshire. Their battalion was so badly hit that reconstruction of their ordeal was not possible in their war diary. However, survivors were interviewed and the account of one of them (Sergeant Major Cussins) is so graphic that it deserves to be quoted at length:

> Five minutes before 7:25 the enemy Machine Gun, Rifle Fire, and Shrapnel were directed against the parapet of our Assembly trench the Southern half of Bradford trench causing us to suffer considerably. A lot of men never got off the ladder, but fell back; and many fell back from the parapet, in getting over.
>
> On getting out of the trenches to take up our position in front, we lost heavily through the line of shrapnel, machine gun, and rapid rifle fire; by the time we attained our position in front of Bradford trench, most of the Officers, N.C.O's, and many men, were knocked out.
>
> At zero we advanced, and continued to advance until the Company Headquarters, with which I was, found ourselves in front of the Battalion all in front having been hit. We found ourselves then half way between 'Leeds' [trench] and the front line. At this point I continued the advance Capt Smith having been knocked out and carried on until we got to the front line.
>
> In our advance, we passed the majority of 'A' Co. halfway between 'Leeds' trench and the [British] front line, lying on the ground, killed or wounded. I found in the front line, a good many of the 15th W.Yorks, what was left of the D.L.I. Co. attached to us, also a few of the K.O.Y.L.I. I found no officers or

N.C.O's. of any of the above regiments, or of my own regiment. The order came to 'ease off to the left' I proceeded to do this, and found Lt. Jowett, of my Regiment, who ordered me to try to collect and organise the few men who were left, with a view to advancing again. At this moment, the enemy started shelling our front line, very heavily, with Shrapnel and High Explosive this would be nearly one hour after zero, but, of course, I cannot give correct time.

Within a very short time, all the men we had collected were knocked out including Mr Jowett, who gave me instructions to make my way back to Brigade Headquarters and report that there were no men left. He told me that he had already sent back to Battalion Headquarters 3 or 4 times, but without success … I made my way to what I took to be Brigade Headquarters, as I saw a notice board to that effect, but it turned out to be the 94th Brigade who telephoned my information to the Division, and also gave me orders to proceed to the 93rd Brigade Headquarters. This took some time … [as along the way I was] ordered, with others, to line … [a] trench, with a view to quelling a German counter attack which had just started. As soon as the necessity for this was over, I reported myself to the 93rd Brigade Headquarters, who told me that what was left of the 16th West Yorks were being collected in [a trench called] Sackville Street, and I was to return there and look after them.

In the day somewhere between 3 and 4 in the afternoon I was ordered to form up the remainder of the Battalion in Legend Street, near Brigade Headquarters. After two hours I was ordered to take the 16th down to 'Dunmow' trench, which I did.

During the wait at Brigade Headquarters, I took the names and numbers of the men of the regiment, that I had with me about 50 in all. Just as I was going down to Dunmow trench, first re-enforcement's, in the form of Officers and N.C.O's. arrived. Until the arrival of these re-enforcement's, I had no N.C.O. above the rank of Lance/Corporal.[25]

It should be emphasised that the entire scene described by Sergeant Major Cussins took place *behind the British front line.* Almost all the casualties suffered by the 16 West Yorkshires were incurred without them seeing an enemy soldier or getting one of their men into no man's land.

All attempts to try and press home the attack failed. Troops to the rear could hardly struggle forward through trenches filled with dead and wounded. Those who left the trenches and attempted to proceed above ground such as the 13 York & Lancaster Battalion suffered 400 casualties before reaching their own front line.[26] To persist in these conditions was useless. By noon orders had at last got through to halt any further attacks and to improve the original front line for defence against a German counter-offensive. Even this proved costly. The 18 Durham Light Infantry were given this task. Just holding the line and the support trenches between 1 and 5 July cost them 482 casualties, or almost half their infantry strength.[27] In all, nine battalions from the two forward brigades had attacked (about 6,750 men). Of these, 4,300 became casualties.[28] As attacking formations, the 93 and 94 Brigades had ceased to exist.

On the southern section of the VIII Corps stood the 29 Division. The Gallipoli veterans had been much reinforced since 1915 and on 1 July contained the only troops from outside Britain to attack that day, the 790 officers and men from the Newfoundland Regiment. Essentially, the story here was the same as in the northern section of the front. In the main the wire had not been cut, the enemy machine-gunners not subdued, the German artillery not destroyed or neutralised.[29] Even imaginative tactics availed little in these circumstances. On the left the Lancashire Fusiliers had connected a sunken road which extended halfway across no man's land to the British front line via a tunnel. Then two leading companies of the battalion moved via this tunnel to the sunken road on the early morning of the 1st. At zero they dashed forward in extended order. They were wiped out within a few yards by massed German machine-gunners who had emerged unscathed by the bombardment which of course had lifted from the enemy front trenches ten minutes previously to accommodate the explosion of the mine. The follow-up companies hardly fared any better. Not one of the Fusiliers reached the wire, let alone the German front line.[30] From a shell hole near the German wire one of the most advanced troops, Corporal Ashurst, surveyed the scene.

> in my shell-hole … I could look back over no man's land towards our own trenches. Hundreds of dead lay about and wounded men were trying to crawl back to safety …. As I lay there watching their painful efforts to get back to our line I watched these poor fellows suddenly try to rise on their feet and then fall in a heap and lie very still …. Shells whistled over my head and dropped amongst the poor fellows, blowing dead men into the air and putting others out of their agony.[31]

Affairs were hardly different on other parts of the 29 Division front. On the right some troops found a gap in the enemy wire, crossed the front trench and advanced on the support line. However, so heavy was the enemy barrage that follow-up troops were unable even to leave their own trenches until half an hour later. When they finally ventured forth most were shot down. Only a handful reached the advanced troops, who soon had to withdraw to shell holes in no man's land.[32]

The advance of these few men on the right was to have unfortunate consequences. Back at 29 Divisional Headquarters a view prevailed that the entire rightward brigade was across the German front line. At the same time reports arrived that troops to the right and left of the division were making substantial progress. Therefore at 8.37 a.m. General de Lisle ordered the leading battalions of his reserve brigade (the Essex and the Newfoundlanders) to reinforce the supposed success.[33] So blocked with dead and wounded were the trenches in front of the Essex that initially they failed to deploy. Somehow the Newfoundlanders got through. At 9.15 a.m. they advanced from where their Caribou monument now stands down a bare slope towards Y Ravine. What happened next is best described in the War Diary:

> Machine gun fire from our right front was at once opened on us and then artillery fire also. The distance to our objective varied from 650 to 900 yards. The enemy's fire was effective from the outset but the heaviest casualties occurred on passing through the gaps in our front wire where the men were mown down in heaps .... In spite of losses the survivors steadily advanced until close to the enemies wire by which time very few remained. A few men are believed to have actually succeeded in throwing bombs into the enemy's trench.[34]

In other words not one Newfoundlander got so far as the German front line. The cost to the battalion was 272 killed and 438 wounded out of 790 who deployed; a casualty rate of 90 per cent.[35] Attempts made by the British command to halt the Essex were only partially successful. Two companies responded but the remaining two attacked at 9.30 a.m. The result was 229 casualties and no success.[36]

Further attacks were planned but the British trenches were now so full of killed and wounded that the reserve troops could not get close enough to the front to deploy. The attack was postponed, once, twice and then at 1.50p.m. cancelled altogether.[37]

The 29 Division had suffered nearly 5,000 casualties, gained not a yard, and for many months was finished as a fighting formation.

Only in the centre did troops in any number enter the German front defences and then only briefly. Here 4 Division attacked on a one-brigade front with two brigades in reserve. All along their line the results were patchy. Despite encountering heavy machine-gun and artillery fire some units managed to cross no man's land and, finding the wire destroyed, entered the German trenches.[38] One such battalion was the 1/8 Warwicks, on loan to 4 Division from a reserve unit. Here, the men advancing in skirmishing lines with minimal equipment had occupied the German trenches by 7.50 a.m. However, their numbers were insufficient to maintain a coherent defence and it was only a matter of time before they were driven out by counter-attack. When they mustered after the battle only 27 of the 600 men who had advanced were not dead or wounded. Of the 30 officers 13 were dead and 17 wounded, a casualty rate of 100 per cent.[39]

Others, such as the 11 Hampshires, suffered 500 casualties without being able to cross no man's land;[40] yet others (1 East Lancashire) crossed no man's land but were unable to penetrate the German wire.[41] The follow-up brigades had similar experiences. The Royal Dublin Fusiliers were destroyed as a formation before they reached their own front line. The King's Own and the 2 Essex suffered heavily but managed to push some troops into the German positions in support of the original attackers.[42]

The result was that by 9 a.m. some sections of the German line opposite 4 Division were in British hands, most of a formidable strongpoint known as the Quadrilateral had been captured, and a few men had pushed forward towards Pendant Copse in the German second line.

A very different assessment was conveyed by the telephone messages received at divisional headquarters. At 7.42 a.m. it was reported that the entire German front line had been captured. At 10.07 a.m. the leading brigade was thought to be moving on its final objective, Munich Trench some 4,000 yards behind the German front. At noon parties of the 2 Essex were said to be in Munich Trench. Only after 1.14 p.m. did the true situation start to become clear. At that moment the Essex reported, not from Munich Trench but from the Quadrilateral, 'for goodness sake send reinforcements'. Then at 1.40 p.m. two battalions reported that they were back in their own front line. By 2.15 p.m. it was obvious that only in the Quadrilateral were British forces occupying any of the German defences at all.

What is evident from the telephone log is that at no time did divisional headquarters have a clear idea of the state of the battle on their section of the front. In these circumstances, their attempts to reinforce what was thought to be a success only added to the casualty list. Attempts to redirect the artillery (for example in support of the supposed position of the Essex in Munich Trench) were simply inappropriate and by the time the true position was realised most of the division's 5,000 casualties had already occurred. By then the only course of action was to try to supply the men with enough reinforcements and ammunition to hang on until nightfall and then withdraw them. In the end this was done quite efficiently. But it meant that as 2 July dawned, not a man from VIII Corps was occupying even a yard of the enemy defences.[43]

For this result VIII Corps had suffered about 14,000 casualties or about 50 per cent of its strength. But even this horrific figure understates the carnage among the battalions that actually attacked, for there were eight battalions from the corps reserve which did not attack at all and two that were only briefly engaged. So of the 29 battalions that attacked, the average number of casualties was 490 and the casualty rate approximately 66 per cent. And in the case of some unfortunate battalions the rate was even higher: we noted earlier that the Newfoundlanders suffered 90 per cent casualties, but the 11 East Lancashire (31 Division), the 1/8 Royal Warwick, 11 Hampshire (4 Division) and 1 Borders (29 Division) each had about 80 per cent casualties.

Why had the attack of the VIII Corps ended in slaughter? In essence the answer was simple. The British bombardment had failed comprehensively to subdue any element of the German defence: wire entanglements, dug-outs and their garrisons, machine-gunners and artillery. Essentially the story was the same right across the VIII Corps front. As soon as troops began deploying in no man's land, whether that was before zero hour or not, they were met immediately with heavy machine-gun fire. On the front of 31 Division, a German map reveals the position of the 10 machine guns which wiped out the advanced battalions of that formation. Between them, these guns could deliver 6,000 rounds per minute. Troops in no man's land, whether prone or moving, had no chance against this concentration of fire. No doubt the situation was somewhat the same on the front of the 29 and 4 Divisions. And those who did survive devastation by machine-gun fire and endeavoured to get forwards found their efforts frustrated by uncut wire.

So in VIII Corps' area the bombardment had failed in two of its essential tasks: destruction of a fair percentage of the defending garrison, whether located in dug-outs or machine-gun strongpoints, and removal of the wire.

It had also failed in its third task: the destruction or neutralisation of the enemy artillery. All the war diaries record an intense German artillery barrage falling in no man's land and on the British front and assembly trenches. In the north it is recorded as starting as early as 7 a.m. (30 minutes before zero hour). Elsewhere German shells certainly started falling in numbers shortly after the explosion of the Hawthorn mine at 7.20 a.m. No assessment was made of how many German batteries survived the hostile bombardment in this area, but in all probability at least 240 guns opened fire on VIII Corps between 7.00 a.m. and 7.30 a.m. Counter-battery fire, which had been given such a low priority by Fourth Army and which was diluted even further on account of Haig's extended objectives, was evidently wholly ineffective. Furthermore, in the north, German observation over the British positions was almost total. Nothing could be concealed from it. So the bare plateau of the Redan Ridge in front of Serre, which confronted 4 Division and the downward-sloping ground in front of Y Ravine in the 29 Division area made advancing troops perfect targets.

On the very north of this sector it was obvious to the Germans that 31 Division formed the flank of the attack. Assembly trenches dug for the attacking troops stopped abruptly like a straight line drawn on the ground. With this in mind German batteries to the north of the attack could fire on the 'Pals' battalions in the sure knowledge that no attack would eventuate directly to their front. In the area of 29 Division, failure by X Corps to their right exposed them to heavy enfilade fire from around Thiepval.

In certain instances the British command added to their difficulties. The leading troops of 4 Division were reinforced in the mistaken belief that they had been successful. In 29 Division the follow-up attack, which led to the elimination of the Newfoundland Regiment, was based on information that was either false or misleading. Yet not too much emphasis should be placed on these command failures. Divisional commanders acted on the best information they could get. They had been told that opportunities to exploit success might be fleeting and to seize the moment. They did not wilfully sacrifice their men, and all halted their attacks when the true situation became known. The overall fact is plain. VIII Corps was doomed from the start by the failure of the artillery plan. Local decisions may have compounded failure but they did not cause it. The fault for that lay elsewhere.

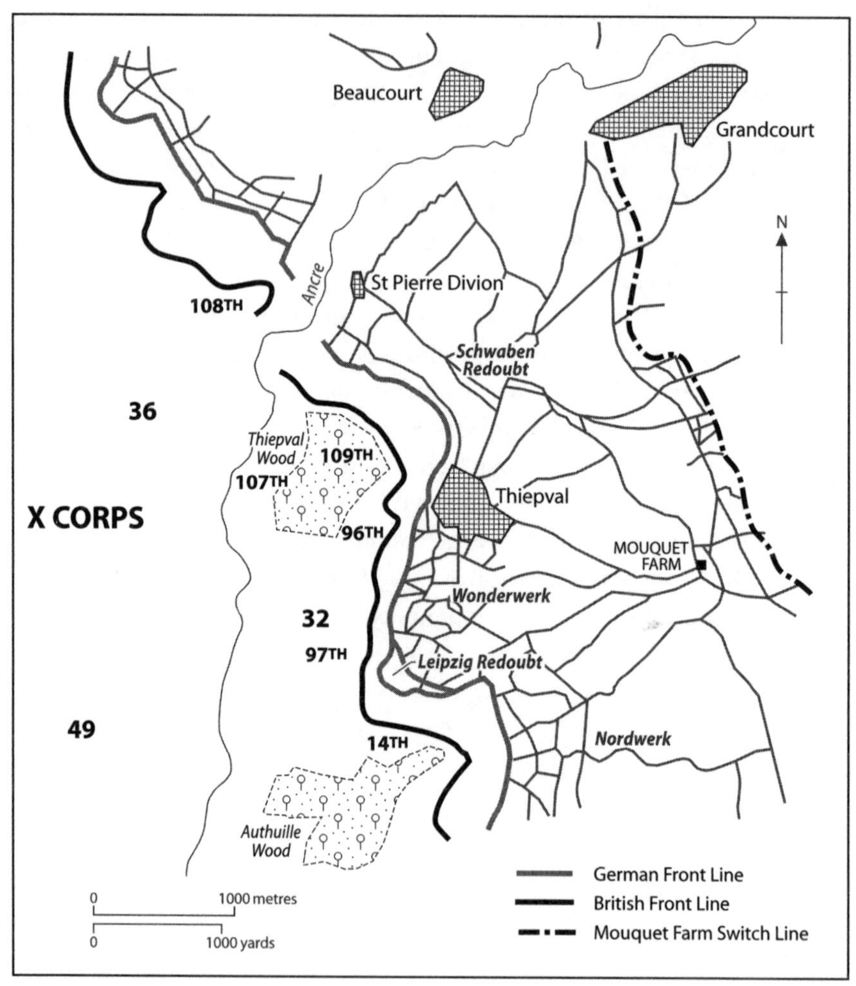
Beaucourt
Grandcourt
N
Ancre
St Pierre Divion
108TH
Schwaben Redoubt
36
Thiepval Wood
109TH
107TH
Thiepval
X CORPS
96TH
MOUQUET FARM
Wonderwerk
32
97TH
Leipzig Redoubt
49
14TH
Nordwerk
Authuille Wood
0
1000 metres
0
1000 yards
German Front Line
British Front Line
Mouquet Farm Switch Line

X Corps, 1 July

# 8 'The Enemy's Fire Was So Intense': X Corps on 1 July

## I

To the south of VIII Corps, the British X Corps under General Morland had been given one of the most difficult tasks of the day. Its two divisions (36 and 32) were to capture the area between Thiepval and Mouquet Farm. This presented a formidable problem for any attacking force. The ridge in this area was 140 to 160 metres high, while the British positions ran through the low-lying marshes of the Ancre Valley on the lower slopes of the ridge. From wherever they attacked, Morland's troops would therefore face a steep uphill advance across bare slopes. In the X Corps sector only Authuille Wood, with its tree canopy intact, offered protection from German observation.

Facing the British was the German 26 Reserve Division. In the 20 months during which they occupied this sector of the front, the Germans had gone to considerable lengths to fortify it. First, the villages of St-Pierre Divion and Thiepval were converted into fortresses with dug-outs for machine-gun crews and infantry. These only the heaviest British guns could penetrate. Then, on some high ground between the villages, they constructed the Schwaben Redoubt, a complex of tunnels and dug-outs which was extensive enough to contain hospital facilities and a telephone exchange. Beyond Schwaben attackers faced further formidable obstacles. To the north of the River Ancre, Bécourt Redoubt housed a nest of machine-guns ideally placed to enfilade troops advancing towards the German second line near Grandcourt. To the south of Schwaben, the Mouquet Farm Switch Line contained a series of equally strong redoubts.

South of Thiepval on the very right of X Corps sector, in a salient in the German front line, the enemy had constructed the Leipzig Redoubt, a maze of interlocking trenches capable of all-round defence and containing many machine-guns. Should this position fall, the advancing troops would be subjected to flanking machine-gun fire from two additional redoubts, the Wonderwerk to the north-east and Nordwerk to the south. Both of these positions were situated on a reverse slope, out of sight of direct British artillery fire.[1]

As ever, the crucial question would be whether the British artillery had managed to eliminate or neutralise those elements of the German defence most deadly to the attacking troops – the distant enemy guns and the more proximate machine-guns.

In the event the results of the preliminary bombardment in this sector proved extremely variable. It was noted earlier that X Corps could not observe with any certainty whether the enemy wire had been cut. The events of the day would reveal (too late) that the wire had been reasonably well cut between the River Ancre and Thiepval but hardly at all elsewhere. Further, as already noted, three of X Corps' super-heavy howitzers were out of action for 'most of the [preliminary] bombardment'. Yet only these guns had the weight of shell which could penetrate into the deep dug-outs inhabited by the Thiepval machine-gunners. In consequence Thiepval was only subjected to sporadic shelling by the less heavy guns. This was sufficient to destroy the buildings in Thiepval but not the dug-outs beneath them. No one in the artillery commented on this matter.[2]

## II

Here, as on other sectors of the front, the troops moved into position in the early hours of the morning. The diarist of the 14 Royal Irish Rifles, which was bivouacking in Thiepval Wood, was moved to lyricism:

> At this time [1.10 a.m.] a lull seemed to settle over all the earth, as if it were a mutual tightening up for the great struggle shortly to commence. A water hen called to its mate midst the reedy swamp, and a courageous nightingale made so bold as to treat us with a song.[3]

Shortly after this dawn chorus came the first indications that all was not well. At 3 a.m. the Germans heavily shelled the remains of Thiepval Wood. Then at 6.15 a.m. sectors to the south of this wood were deluged with shells in response to the commencement of the intense British bombardment.

On the left of X Corps front was the 36 (Ulster) Division, raised by Sir Edward Carson to fight the British government over Home Rule. In 1914 they volunteered almost to a man to fight the Germans instead. Much was made (at least by the leadership of that division) of the fact that the battle would commence on the anniversary of the Battle of the Boyne in 1690, a symbol of the triumph of Protestantism in the province.[4]

The operation of the Ulster Division was divided in two by the River Ancre and its valley. As the subsidiary operation occurred to the north of the river, it will be convenient to deal with it first.

The attack was, in fact, a fiasco. The leading troops found the wire well cut but the trenches strongly held by enemy riflemen and machine-gunners. Those few troops who penetrated to the German front system were cut down by defenders in Bécourt Redoubt, which had entirely escaped the attentions of the British artillery. The experience of the 12 Royal Irish Rifles on the left of the attack was typical. At 7.30 a.m. about 750 men from this unit moved off under the cover of a trench mortar smoke barrage. They were immediately hit by concentrated machine-gun fire and pinned down in no man's land. When at 10.20 a.m. a new attack was attempted only 100 men could be mustered. This too resulted in heavy casualties. At 11 a.m. a third attack was ordered for 12.30 p.m. in conjunction with 29 Division to the north. Just 46 men made ready to advance. Luckily for them, when zero hour arrived the 29 Division was nowhere to be seen. The operation was called off.[5]

The failure of this attack had grave consequences for the main assault south of the river. The German machine-guns at Bécourt Redoubt, which had dealt such a rapid blow to the northern attack, could from about 10 a.m. turn their attention to the troops attempting to advance south of the Ancre. And as events would prove, the further these troops penetrated into the defences, the more effective the fire from this redoubt would become.

In the area of the main attack (from south of the Ancre to Thiepval), the wire had been well cut. And in addition, as the Ulstermen deployed in no man's land, they were hidden from German view by an effective smoke-screen.[6] The operation can be dealt with in two parts – the flanks and the centre.

The flanking forces fared no better than their compatriots to the north of the Ancre. On the left the troops were cut down by machine-gun fire from St-Pierre Divion and the Beaucourt Redoubt, both of which had been left unbombarded by the British artillery.[7] On the right, the Thiepval machine-gunners stopped the attack in the German front system of trenches.[8]

In the centre, a most startling event occurred – the Ulstermen captured the Schwaben Redoubt. As it happened, around Schwaben, the artillery had wreaked havoc with the German defences. In the words of one German account:

> The position had suffered quite exceptionally under the long bombardment; the trenches had been practically wiped out, wire swept aside, and dug-outs mostly battered in. The 9th Company of the 99th west of Schwaben Redoubt,

> suffered particularly severe losses. The enemy assault therefore found favourable conditions.[9]

Facing only sporadic fire from this shaken defence the Ulstermen swept forward into the redoubt. Small parties even managed to advance beyond it and enter the Mouquet Farm Switch Line. The farm itself lay just 500 yards to the south; the German second line a similar distance to the east.

The 36 Division appeared to be on the brink of a major success. But in truth the break-in had been made by too few men on too narrow a front to amount to anything substantial. Just 1,000 soldiers were holding a salient 1,000 yards deep and 200 yards wide. German flanking fire was becoming increasingly severe. Moreover, German artillery had put down a curtain of fire on no man's land. Nothing could penetrate this barrier and so no ammunition, water, or other supplies reached the forward troops. So unpromising did the situation appear to the divisional command that they issued orders for the troops to fall back on Schwaben and consolidate. Orders were also sent to the reserve brigade to remain in place.[10]

Unfortunately for the reserves the orders were never received, so these formations had been set in motion at 8 a.m. according to their original orders. As they attempted to cross no man's land they were hit by the German barrage, the Thiepval machine-gunners, and then by machine-guns in Beaucourt and St-Pierre Divion.[11] Incredibly, a small number survived this ordeal and advanced towards Grandcourt past the troops in the Mouquet Switch.[12] They were never seen again.

By this time the German rear formations were beginning to respond to the attack. A regiment (probably from Grandcourt) overran the most advanced Irish troops. They then swept on and arrived within 600 yards of the Schwaben Redoubt before British fire halted them. Then, as the afternoon wore on, further German counter attacks developed. Soon almost all troops in advance of the redoubt had been killed or captured and the enemy was closing on the redoubt itself from all sides.[13]

On the British side confusion reigned. The position of the advanced troops was not known with any accuracy. Possibly because of some optimistic reports about the situation around the redoubt it was decided to commit the corps reserve division (49) to the fray.[14] This was unfortunate, to say the least. The reserve brigade had already been consumed because the halt order had never arrived. Since then the situation at the front had greatly deteriorated. Now the remainder of the division was to be committed. In the end they were saved by the chaos prevailing near the front. Communication trenches were by this time choked with dead, dying, and wounded. All the attempts by 36 Division staff to arrange an attack (their persistence in this was incredible: they were still trying to commit 49 Division as late as 1 p. m. on 2 July) failed. At the end of the day the two remaining brigades of the division were still intact behind the British front line.[15]

From early afternoon the position of the 36 Division was probably irredeemable. They were starved of ammunition and supplies of all kinds. Reinforcement through the German barrage was impossible. Small remnants managed to hold on to some of the German defences, including the Schwaben Redoubt, until the morning of 3 July. Eventually these men too had to be withdrawn. Despite the promising beginning, permanent gains in the area were zero.

## III

On the right of X Corps' attack was the 32 Division. In detailing its actions on 1 July it is immediately obvious why the Ulstermen, as they advanced on Thiepval, had no support on their right flank. In this area two battalions from 32 Division had been given the task of attacking Thiepval frontally. They were wiped out. No fewer than 21 machine-guns in the village had survived the bombardment and during the course of the British attack they fired 210,000 rounds.[16] In these circumstances the observation of the British Official History that 'only bullet-proof soldiers could have taken Thiepval on this day' is hardly an exaggeration.[17]

The remainder of 32 Division's attack to the right of the village fared little better. In the words of the War Diary of one of the units involved:

> When the barrage lifted [the Fusiliers] ... were instantly fired upon by the Enemy's M.G.s & snipers. The Enemy stood upon their parapet and picked them off with rifle fire. The Enemy's fire was so intense that the advance was checked & the waves, or what was left of them, were forced to lie down.[18]

There they remained until after nightfall, when just 280 survivors of the 800 who had attacked were withdrawn.[19]

Nevertheless, despite this carnage, a few men from one battalion did enter the German line and were seen by British observers to the east of Thiepval.[20] They were soon captured or killed but their supposed presence was to have a 'baleful' effect on the battle.[21] First, the support battalions were ordered forward to reinforce the supposed occupiers of Thiepval. They suffered 200 casualties and gained no ground towards the village.[22] Second, the alleged presence of

British forces in Thiepval prevented X Corps artillery from re-bombarding the village, the only expedient which had a chance of redeeming the position.

Meanwhile, the extreme rightward troops of 32 Division had made some progress. As a result of closely following the barrage some troops had entered the Leipzig Redoubt. However, all attempts by them to advance further were halted by fire from the Wonderwerk and Nordwerk, which had escaped bombardment by the artillery.[23]

So on the front of 32 Division all the troops that delivered the initial attack had failed. Yet that did not put an end to the slaughter. As in many other areas, the almost mechanical forward movement of the reserves proved impossible to halt. The commanders of these units were unaware of the carnage in front of them and devoted all their efforts to fulfilling their task – to provide reinforcement to their comrades. The result was invariably disaster. In the case of 32 Division, first the reserve battalion of the assault brigade was shot down before it reached its own front line, then the division's reserve brigade was mown down in similar fashion as it attempted to debouch from Authuille Wood.[24] Of the two leading battalions (about 1,500 men) barely 100 survived the journey to the German front line.[25] Let the account of the 1 Dorsets serve for the experience of the entire brigade:

> Immediately the leading platoon left Authuille Wood very heavy and extremely accurate machine-gun fire was opened by the enemy from some point on our right not definitely ascertained [it was almost certainly Nordwerk]. As this fire concentrated mainly on the point at the edge of the wood ... past which the whole Battalion had to go – we endeavoured to find some other exit from the wood but could not do so, barbed wire and other obstacles preventing. The whole Battalion, therefore, advanced from this point by sections, and it was during the dash across country from Authuille Wood to our own front trench about 100 yards ahead that at least half our total casualties were sustained. By the time the Battalion had left the wood, the end of ... [the] track and the ground up to our front line trench was covered with our killed and wounded.[26]

The slaughter of the brigade of which this battalion was a part introduced a grim aspect into the fighting. The 2 Manchesters had advanced over ground littered with the bodies of the attacking battalions. They had also suffered heavily from machine-gun fire and, as they neared the front line, snipers. When they finally reached the portion of Leipzig Redoubt still held by British troops, they were given charge of some German prisoners. What happened next is recorded with unusual frankness by the War Diary of the Manchesters:

> Considerable enjoyment was given to our troops by Lieut Robertson who made the prisoners run across the open through their own Artillery barrage, upon reaching our line these men were kept out of our dugouts by the sharp end of a bayonet.[27]

Needless to say, those reinforcements which did reach Leipzig Redoubt had no capacity to alleviate the situation. The survivors were evacuated to the original British line on the following day.

So, the attack of 32 Division was almost a complete failure. The attack on the left had been stopped by the unsubdued machine-guns in Thiepval. On the right the rapid seizure of the Leipzig Redoubt could not be reinforced in strength.

At the end of the day, therefore, X Corps had suffered 10,000 casualties (36 Division 5,100, 32 Division over 4,000 and 49 Division 600). There was no permanent gain of ground. Essentially, the reason for failure was the same as that in the north. The artillery had not managed to subdue substantial German strongpoints (St-Pierre Divion, Bécourt Redoubt, Thiepval, Nordwerk, Wonderwerk) or eliminate much of the German artillery. Only at two points, the Schwaben Redoubt and Leipzig Redoubt, had the guns actually suppressed the defence for long enough to allow occupation. And in these instances occupation was futile unless the troops could be reinforced or other parts of the line from which enfilade fire could be brought to bear were captured. That is, without reinforcement or success on a wider front the noteworthy achievements of the Ulstermen were bound to be transitory.

It is worth noting once again that the zone of the destruction of British forces was not confined to no man's land. Unsubdued machine-guns and artillery proved capable of destroying many British formations before they reached their own front line. This was especially the case in the area of 32 Division where enemy domination of the debouches from Authuille Wood proved devastating to the follow-up formations. As in the north, the killing zone extended some thousands of yards behind the British front. For many soldiers the 'race to the parapet' was actually a race to their own parapet, and it was a race that they lost.

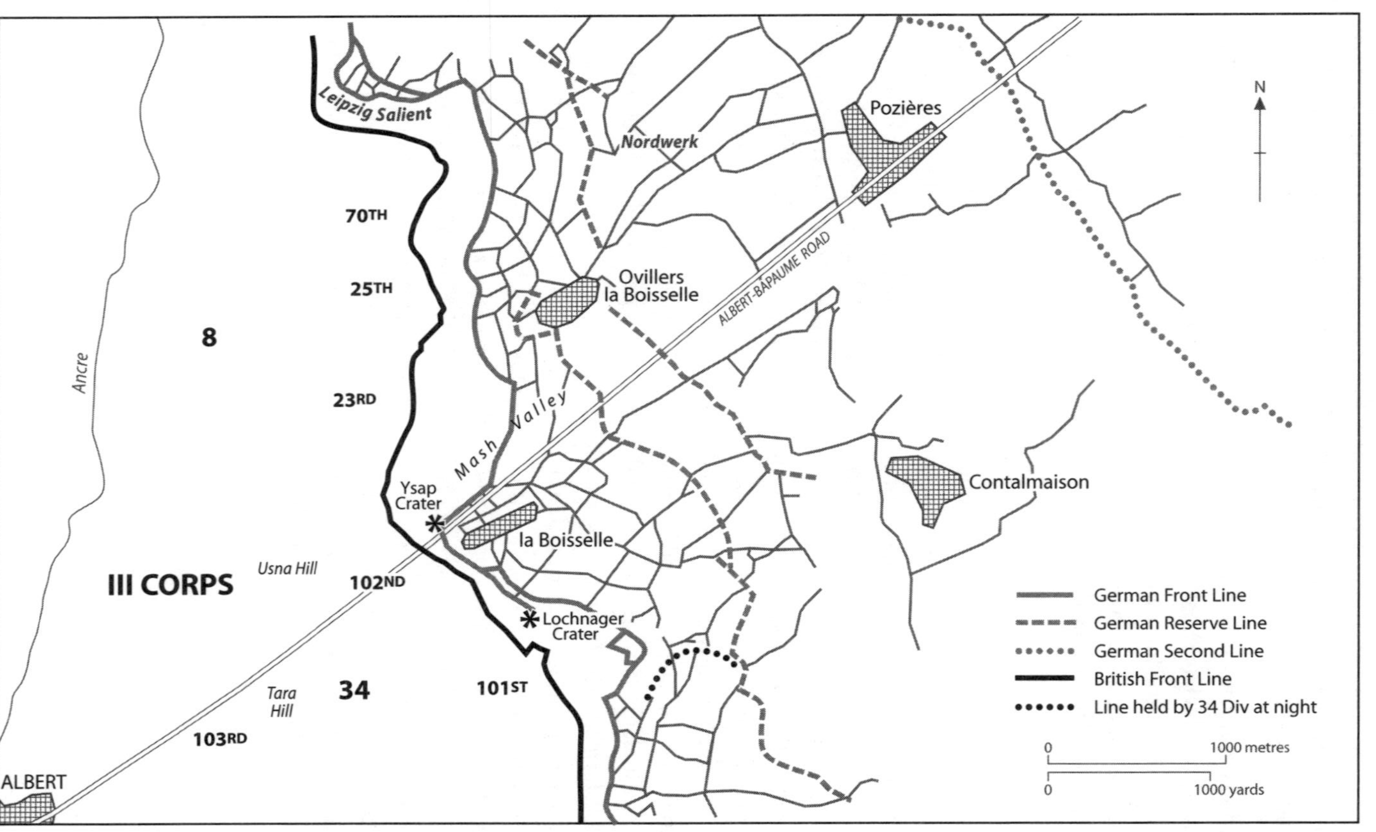


III Corps, 1 July

# 9 'Wave after Wave Were Mown Down': III Corps on 1 July

## I

The centre of the British attack was also central to Haig's great purpose. It was in this area – just south of Pozières – that the breakthrough was to come; that the cavalry, protected from flanking fire by the advance of forces to its right and left, would sweep through to Bapaume followed immediately by Gough's Reserve Army of infantry. However, for Haig's horsemen ever to achieve this sort of advance, it was essential that III Corps first overwhelm the entire enemy trench system confronting them.

Yet there was every indication that III Corps would not succeed in clearing the way for the cavalry. Their gunners had stated during the period of the preliminary bombardment both that no success should be expected from their attempts to cut the distant wire and that they would be hampered even in cutting the more proximate wire by lack of ammunition.

These were surely matters of the utmost import, for if the wire was not cleared, the cavalry could not operate. There is no evidence however that anyone from III Corps headquarters conveyed the doubts of the artillerymen to Fourth Army Headquarters or to GHQ. One possible explanation for this lack of communication is that no one at III Corps or Fourth Army Headquarters was taking the cavalry operations seriously. Certainly clearing the way for the horsemen was given no prominence in III Corps' orders. In this the III Corps was being no more than realistic – the chance of a German collapse and a cavalry sweep was a remote possibility. But underneath all this lay an issue of substance which General Pulteney, the Commander of III Corps and his staff were failing to notice. At the same time that the prospects of a cavalry breakthrough were being discounted, the artillery plan was being extended to encompass the more distant objectives demanded in the plans for that very same breakthrough. But no one at III Corps headquarters made representations to

Fourth Army Artillery to modify their plan along more realistic lines and to concentrate the fire of the guns on the formidable German front defences. No doubt it was considered that any such suggestion would be overruled by Haig. But the failure even to raise the matter left Rawlinson and Pulteney proceeding according to one set of assumptions, yet employing an artillery plan based on a completely different set. A more inappropriate way to initiate a great campaign would be difficult to imagine.

Given the geography of the central section of the front, III Corps could not have been confident of achieving even a fraction of what was expected of it. Behind the British front line there was no cover of any kind, not even the shattered ruins of former woods. The whole rear area consisted of bare, gentle slopes which culminated in the Tara-Usna hills astride the Albert–Bapaume road. This entire area was overlooked by the Germans so that even moving forward small numbers of troops to the front could bring down on them a hail of artillery shells and machine-gun bullets.

In marked contrast, the German positions on the forward slopes of the eastern sector of Thiepval Ridge were of great strength. The key to the German defences were the two villages which lay directly in the path of the British line of advance. To the north of the Albert–Bapaume road on a small ridge which dominated the surrounding countryside stood Ovillers. To the south of the road on lower but still dominating ground was La Boisselle. These villages were small, but before the war had consisted of several score houses with substantial cellars, ideal for the protection of small garrisons and machine-gun nests. In addition, the two villages had small garrisons and were surrounded by trench defences.[1]

Between Ovillers and La Boisselle ran a long, narrow declivity (called, by the British, Mash Valley) which could be dominated by enfilade crossfire from the villages. Finally, the whole northern section of the III Corps front was also overlooked by two strong defensive positions in the attack zone of X Corps: Nordwerk and the Leipzig salient. It was essential then, if the left of III Corps was to get forward, that these positions be eliminated by X Corps artillery.

As well as the inherent strength of the German defences, another problem confronted some sections of British troops. This was the width of no man's land. In the north, this varied from a fairly standard 200 yards to a terrifying 800 yards in the area between the villages around Mash Valley. Further south, the width varied from just 50 yards directly in front of La Boisselle to 600 yards to the north of the village, to 700 yards in the area of 101 Brigade's attack (see map). There is no indication that any special attention was devoted to the matter of how troops were even going to traverse the widest distances.

The two British assault divisions were (in the north) the 8, consisting mainly of Regulars, and (in the south) the 34, consisting entirely of Kitchener volunteers from around Newcastle.

For the attackers to possess any chance of success, it was essential in the first instance to neutralise the enemy machine gunners in the villages. Yet as the bombardment proceeded, there was every indication that this was precisely what was not happening. We have already noted the statement from a prisoner emphasising the strength of the Ovillers dug-outs.[2] During the course of the bombardment, its relative ineffectiveness against this type of defensive position was recorded by Captain Reginald Leetham, a Regular soldier in 8 Division.

> It was always a wonderful sight to see our shells bursting in every direction .... One ... saw the houses of Ovillers destroyed and several nights one saw the flames or fires in these and other towns lighting up the sky. But after [a] raid which found the Bosche line so strongly occupied it made one doubt whether all this bombardment was doing us much good. It was all a very fine exhibition of what our Artillery could do, but what was the use of bombing Bosches 30 feet below the level of the ground.[3]

Given the overall situation – an ineffectual bombardment, strong interlocking defences, and a total lack of cover – any plan made by III Corps was bound to be fraught with danger. The plan they actually made did not address any of these difficulties. At zero hour all six infantry brigades in the corps would be committed to battle. In the 8 Division all three brigades would attack from their front line.[4] In 34 Division two brigades would launch the initial assault but simultaneously the reserve brigade on the Tara-Usna hills would also be propelled forward.[5] Under this plan, once battle commenced, there would be no reserves on which to call, no time for redeployment, no time to rethink a failing strategy, no way to extricate troops from disaster. Moreover, all the senior officers, of both divisions from brigadier to general, would be located well behind the front and in no position to ascertain, even vaguely, how the battle was progressing. So in the area of III Corps there would be no one in the position and with the authority of Brigadier-General Rees of VIII Corps, who stopped the potentially disastrous deployment of the reserve brigade from 31 Division.

There was some attempt in the plans of the two divisions to take into account the defensive strength of the two villages. At two points held to be particularly dangerous, mines were placed under the German trenches. To the north of La Boisselle 40,000 pounds of ammonal were located under a German trench called Y Sap which jutted out into no man's land. To the south of the same village 60,000 pounds of ammonal were placed under a feature of considerable strength called Schwaben Hohe. In this case it was believed that the lip formed by the mine crater might to some extent protect the advancing troops from the La Boisselle machine gunners.[6]

The care taken to place these mines is in stark contrast to the rather sloppy planning of III Corps. The work was carried out by two tunnelling companies who started in early 1916. One of the officers in charge of the tunnellers describes how it was done:

> The gallery to this crater [was] known as the Lochnager tunnel. The enemy had certainly become aware of these operations for he had put down a defensive mining system deeper than the British tunnel [so] the work was done in silence. A large number of bayonets were fitted with handles. The operator inserted the point in a 'crack' in the 'face', or alongside a flint, of which there were any number in the chalk, gave it a twist which wrenched loose a piece of stone of varying size which he caught with his other hand and laid on the floor. If, for any reason, he had to use greater force, another man behind would catch the stone as it fell. The men worked bare-footed, the floor of the gallery was carpeted with sandbags, and an officer was always present to preserve silence. As sand bags were filled with chalk they were passed out along a line of men seated on the floor, and stacked against the wall ready for later use as tamping. Air was forced in from a bellows through armoured hose and 'exhausted' out thro' the gallery. The dimensions of this latter length of tunnel were about 4′6″ × 2′6″. The work was extremely laborious, and if we advanced 18″ in 24 hours we thought we did well. We could hear the Germans quite plainly in their mining system below us, and in their dug-outs. All such dug-outs and the men sheltering in them were destroyed when the mine was blown.[7]

In addition to these measures, the two villages were to be blanketed by smoke at zero hour. Ovillers was to be bombarded by smoke bombs and La Boisselle obscured by clouds of candle smoke which, it was hoped, would drift towards the village from the British front line.[8]

To the very end of the bombardment period the III Corps artillery plan served the troops ill. At 7 a.m., 30 minutes before zero, the heavy artillery lifted from the German front line to the rearward support line. The heavy shells then proceeded on their way to Pozières in 250 yard lifts and played no further role in the battle.[9] This left just the field guns (18-pounder and 4.5-inch howitzer) to suppress enemy fire for the crucial 30 minutes before the attack. As these light shells had no destructive power against solidly constructed trenches, it should have come as no surprise when they failed.

So, in the event, even the stratagem employed by the left brigade (70) of 8 Division, of leaving their trenches before zero in order to close on the German line while it was still being subjected to bombardment, proved futile.[10] Most of the leading troops were shot down by German machine-gunners and riflemen who had emerged from their dug-outs as soon as the heavy artillery lifted. One of the foremost battalions of 70 Brigade had been reduced to just 30 per cent of its strength *before* zero hour and the other probably suffered in equal measure.[11] However, the survivors of these battalions were presented with a brief moment of opportunity. In this sector most of the wire had been cut and many defenders stunned by the bombardment. Further, the enemy were momentarily distracted to the north by the 32 Division assault on the Leipzig salient and to the south by 25 Brigade's (8 Division) advance on Ovillers.[12] This distraction briefly enabled the survivors of 70 Brigade to penetrate the German front system. But as they then progressed on to the German intermediate system they were shot down in such numbers that the attack lost all coherence and the survivors were forced to retreat. A few, however, managed to hang on in the German front line.[13]

Meanwhile the follow-up formations had been trying to reinforce their assault troops. This proved impossible. Just after 9 a.m. the German machine-gunners in the Leipzig salient, having beaten off their assailants from 32 Division, turned their attention to the area of 70 Brigade. One of the unlucky British units described the result:

> It was impossible to stand at all in No Mans Land and the Battalion crawled forward on hands and knees to the help of the Battalions in front.[14]

A second attempt by these units failed; a third made by just 50 men met the same fate. In all, out of a strength of 27 officers and 710 men one unit suffered 529 casualties without reaching their comrades holding out in the German front line.[15] The other reinforcing battalion lost 50 per cent casualties and had ceased to exist as a fighting formation even before it had reached its own front line.[16]

From 10 a.m. in the 70 Brigade area all communication across no man's land had ceased because of enemy shelling and machine-gun fire. All messages instructing the artillery to bring back the barrage were never delivered. Eventually, even the British who had penetrated the German front line were driven out or killed. By the end of the day not a square inch of German territory was held by the brigade.[17] Of the 2,720 men who had moved to the attack, less than 600 could be mustered the next day.[18]

The story of the remaining two brigades of 8 Division, which contained some of the last units of the British Regular Army, can be quickly told. Almost complete disaster overtook them. On only two sections of the front were lodgements made in the German positions, and these were temporary. In every case the battalions were hit by a hail of machine-gun and rifle fire as they attempted to cross no man's land. Even the expedient of forming into small groups and rushing the German line availed them little.[19]

So the 25 Brigade were shot down by fire from Ovillers, the 23 by cross-fire from the two villages. The two small lodgements in the German front in Mash Valley and just north of Ovillers were quickly dealt with by enemy counter-attack.[20] Except in one case the support battalions were not spared. Indeed, some of them suffered the heaviest casualties of the day as the German guns found the range and added a deluge of shells to the hail of machine-gun fire scything down the British.[21] The percentage casualties suffered by the assault battalions of 23 and 25 Brigades tell a bleak tale.[22]

| Battalion | Percentage casualties |
|---|---|
| 2 Royal Berkshire | 53 |
| 2 Lincolnshire | 62 |
| 1 Royal Irish Rifles | 64 |
| 2 Middlesex | 92.5 |
| 2 West Yorkshire | 70 |
| 2 Devonshire | 50–60 |

In all, just over 3,000 men became casualties in this attack for precisely no gains. If these figures are added to the toll taken on 70 Brigade, they amount to the destruction of 8 Division as a fighting unit. Indeed, it was not until October that this division returned to the Somme.

The disaster which overtook 8 Division did not go unremarked at the time. Brigadier-General Tuson, commanding the 25 Brigade, included the percentage casualties for all his battalions to 'explain why … the Brigade failed to reach its allotted objective'.[23] He then went on to make some acute observations. He noted that throughout the attack, his brigade had been 'deprived of artillery support' and that it was futile bombarding distant objectives 'if we are ourselves unable to maintain our hold on the enemy's front line'. His solution was to make the artillery timetable absolutely dependent on the advance of the infantry, thus to some extent anticipating the creeping barrage of artillery shells which would be the main method of infantry protection for the last two years of the war. In concluding his remarks he contrasted his proposed deliberate method with the impractical artillery timetable implemented by III Corps which saw the distant Pozières being bombarded at the very moment that 8 Division was being wiped out in no man's land.

> I have seen the 'hooroosh' [artillery] time-table programme tried upon several occasions in this war, and I have never seen it successful beyond the first two or three trenches. And never expect to.[24]

Whether anyone higher up the chain of command managed to digest this wisdom is another matter.

## II

The slaughter of 8 Division was not to be redeemed by any actions of 34 Division on its right. There were a number of curious aspects of the plan made by Pulteney and his staff for this unit, which have already been mentioned but deserve repetition here. The first was that as all units would advance at zero: there would be no reserves. The second was that, as with 8 Division, the heavy guns would lift from the German front line at zero, leaving just the inadequately equipped field artillery to fire on the German trench systems and the fortified villages.

This meant that the men of 34 Division would have to encounter all the difficulties faced by the 8, but with one additional factor. The village of La Boisselle, as we have noted, occupied a small ridge directly in the line of the British advance. No infantry attack was to be made on this place, the troops relying on smoke candles to screen them from it. So at zero the La Boisselle machine-gunners would be assailed not with a heavy bombardment or an infantry attack but with candle smoke.[25]

These problems might have been offset by one advantage: the mine explosion was intended to coincide with the infantry advance. But the 34 Divisional staff had difficulty in integrating the two events. The mine under the German front line (south of La Boisselle) was only some 100 yards from the British. It was timed to explode at two minutes before zero which, given the narrowness of no man's land at this point, might have provided the attackers with some chance of occupying the crater lip ahead of the Germans. However, the command had instructed the infantry to delay their advance until five minutes after zero so as to allow the debris to settle. Thereby all chance of taking advantage of the shock of the mine discharge was lost.[26]

At 7.30 a.m. the 34 Division attack commenced. The smoke screen on La Boisselle was nowhere to be seen, the wind having failed to oblige by blowing in the right direction. What this meant to the north of La Boisselle was catastrophic. The two assault battalions were forced to cross a no man's land of 800 yards in full view of the German defenders in the village and surrounding trenches. Worse, the enemy knew the exact timing of the attack because one of their listening posts had picked up a message between 34 Division headquarters and one of the forward battalions to the effect that an attack was imminent.[27] Yet more lamentably for the British, the Y Sap mine had been discovered by the Germans and its garrison evacuated.[28] Consequently, the 20 and 23 Northumberland Fusiliers, as they commenced their slow walk over 800 yards of cratered ground, were confronting an alert enemy, spared the shock of the mine explosion and lining their parapets with riflemen and machine-gunners. Both battalions were wiped out within a few minutes. The 20 suffered 661 casualties out of the 800 men deployed. As for the 23, only 120 men from their original 820 were assembled the following day.[29]

To the south of La Boisselle, the stunning effect of the larger Lochnager mine explosion allowed some troops on the left to advance past the village. They were soon counter-attacked but a few clung on in the German second trench for the remainder of the day.[30] Further south still, the battalions attacking the crater five minutes after the initial attack had commenced were predictably annihilated. As the 11 Suffolk reported, 'wave after wave were mown down by machine gun fire ... very few reached the German line'.[31] Within a few minutes the battalion had been destroyed. Of the 800 who had attacked 691 became casualties.[32] The gap caused by the destruction of these units and heavy flanking fire from the village forced the most southward battalions to veer away from La Boisselle. Casualties in these battalions were horrific – 9 in 10 who attacked were either killed or wounded. But at least for the survivors there was some succour. As they drifted south they found fresh troops from the flanking XV Corps dug in and in numbers. With these men they found at least a semblance of safety.[33]

At the exact moment that the lead brigades of 34 Division were being destroyed, calamity was also befalling the reserve brigade. There was however a certain difference. This brigade ceased to exist as a formation even before it reached its own front line. It perished, that is, without a chance even to do any fighting.

The 103 Brigade (the Tyneside Irish) left its position on the exposed slopes of the Tara-Usna Hills at 7.40 a.m. and advanced with its four battalions abreast towards the front. Because of a fold in the ground, none of them could see even their own front line and as all communication with the front had ceased, no one from the brigade was aware of the débâcle ahead. The attacking force had gone only far enough to shake out into regular waves when it ran into a heavy and accurate German artillery barrage.[34] This was soon accompanied by scything machine-gun fire. Even so, in the words of one account, 'the forward movement was maintained until only a few scattered soldiers were left standing'.[35] 'Glorious' is a word often mentioned in accounts describing the martyrdom of the Tyneside Irish.[36] It is hardly appropriate. This episode scarcely amounted even to battle. By the time some units of this brigade had arrived at *their own front line* they had suffered 70 per cent casualties.[37] Two years in the making, the Tyneside Irish lasted just 80 minutes as a fighting formation.

Amazingly, a few of them managed to reach not only their own front line but that of the enemy. And a handful did penetrate some distance further, reaching the edge of Contalmaison near the German second line. They were never seen again.[38] Accurate casualty figures for the brigade are hard to establish but at the very least 2,200 out of the 3,000 attacking were either killed or wounded.[39]

These losses were some of the most visible of the whole war. An official photographer captured line upon line of their dead and wounded. Traditionally, they are represented as having fallen in no man's land. That is a misconception. They lay on the bare slopes of the Tara-Usna Hills well behind their own front line. It needs to be recognised, that at the time of the Somme no photographer ever trespassed into no man's land and none would have survived had he done so.

The attack of 34 Division cost over 6,000 casualties for a derisory amount of ground gained. Indeed, so desperate was the position that elements of the corps' reserve division (19) were rushed forward lest the Germans attempt to take advantage of the carnage to advance on the unprotected ruins of Albert.

The attack of III Corps was meant, at least in the minds of the command, to clear the way for the cavalry by capturing the German defences as far back as Pozières. Instead 12,000 from the corps were dead or wounded and 99 per cent of the German front line was securely in enemy hands. The plans made by III Corps command certainly reflected little imagination or subtlety. But in the light of the comprehensive failure of the artillery bombardment even the most cunning of plans was doomed to failure. It is sometimes said that Haig's cavalry plans mattered little because they had no chance of ever succeeding. In the case of III Corps this was far from the truth. They mattered because they spread the artillery fire of the corps over such a wide distance and against such a multitude of targets that the German front line defenders were not adequately dealt with. And these defenders proved quite capable unaided of stopping the British attack in its tracks.

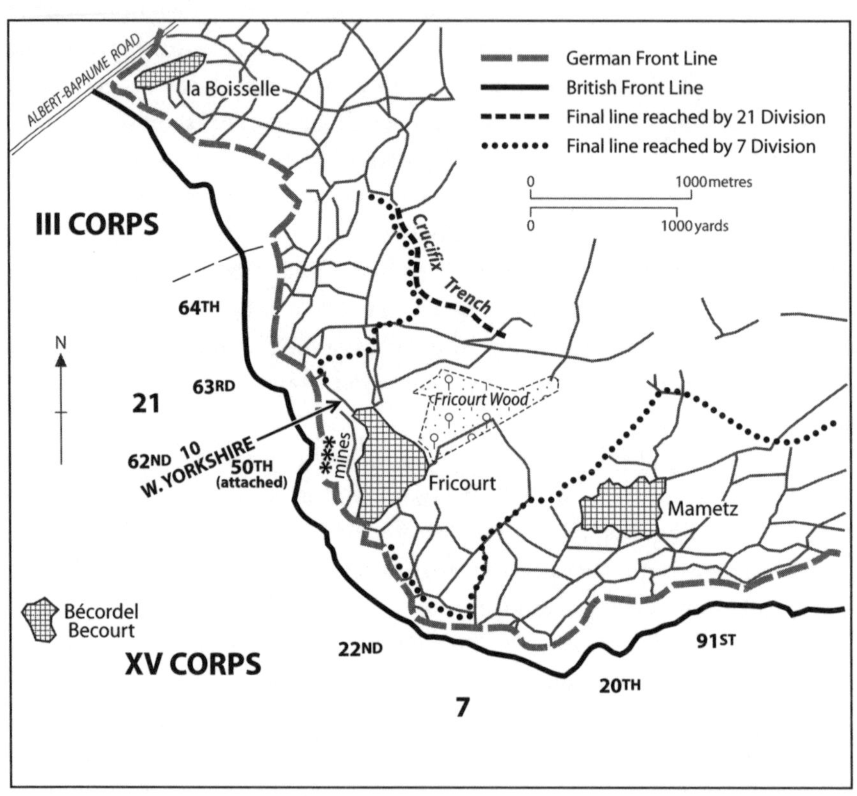
ALBERT-BAPAUME ROAD
la Boisselle
German Front Line
British Front Line
Final line reached by 21 Division
Final line reached by 7 Division
0
1000metres
0
1000yards
III CORPS
Crucifix
Trench
64TH
N
21
63RD
Fricourt Wood
62ND 10
W. YORKSHIRE
50TH
(attached)
mines
Fricourt
Mametz
Bécordel
Becourt
XV CORPS
22ND
91ST
20TH
7

XV Corps, 1 July

# 10 'Cowering Men in Field Grey': XV and XIII Corps on 1 July

## I

To the south of La Boisselle the front line turned sharply to the east around Fricourt, thus presenting the British with a difficult right angle to attack. In addition some of the factors which had proved ruinous to attacks further north also applied here. In particular two villages, reduced to rubble but amply provided with cellars to shelter machine-gunners, stood athwart the line of advance. At the apex of the right angle stood the considerable village of Fricourt. Enfilade fire from its ruins could sweep to the north and east of the British line. Of all the villages incorporated by the Germans into the Somme defensive system, Fricourt was the largest and for the attackers the most awkwardly placed. Then, after the front had turned due east the smaller village of Mametz lay directly in the path of any attacking force.

In other ways however the situation which faced the XV Corps was more favourable than that which applied in the north. First the geography of this area favoured the British. This section of the line was on the lower, forward slopes of the ridge and immediately behind the British front the ground sloped upwards to form the Morlancourt–Maricourt Ridge. This meant that from many areas of British-held territory there were excellent views of the German positions as far back as Mametz Wood. Moreover, because of the right angle, Allied artillery to the south of Fricourt could enfilade the German line to the north and allied artillery around Bécordel could enfilade it to the east.

These factors of improved observation and opportunities for enfilade fire meant that the bombardment of the enemy front line was far more effective than had been the case in the north. Hence the German machine-gun and rifle fire facing the British forces attempting to cross no man's land was considerably reduced.

There was a further factor which contributed to this situation: the employment, if only in embryo, of firing a creeping barrage in front of the advancing troops. In time this procedure became a very sophisticated form of infantry protection by the artillery. The barrage would by then be of sufficient depth to fall both in the area of no man's land just ahead of the advancing troops and on the enemy front line, forcing the German defenders either to remain in their dug-outs or to risk death and injury in the attempt to man the parapets.

As applied on 1 July, the bombardment only fell on the German front line at the outset and moved beyond it at too fast a rate (100 yards in two minutes) for the troops to keep pace. Further, it did not contain the density of shells which would later be a feature of the creeping barrage. The consequence was that enemy defences were sufficiently subdued to allow some of the attackers to make progress but it was by no means sufficient to knock out or keep down all the enemy machine-gunners and riflemen. Nevertheless, by keeping the heavy artillery bombardment on the German front line until zero hour and instructing their troops to move into no man's land before zero and then cling as close to the creeping barrage as safety would allow, the XV Corps staff undoubtedly helped to minimise the casualties inherent in this perilous crossing.[1]

In another matter concerning artillery XV Corps were more lucky than skilful. It has been shown that, in the planning phase, no other corps devoted fewer resources to counter-battery than XV Corps. This had one positive aspect – more of XV Corps' heavy artillery was available to fire on German dug-outs and machine-gun posts in the front trench systems. However, it also might have had a considerable negative aspect. As the situation in the north revealed, unhindered German batteries could wreak havoc on an attack and fatally impede any attempts to reinforce an initially successful advance. Two factors prevented this situation from applying to XV Corps. The corps adjoining it, Congreve's XIII Corps, gave a particularly high priority to counter-battery. And the French, more lavishly supplied with heavy guns than the British, also stressed the importance of counter-battery and directed many of their heavy guns into the general Mametz–Montauban area because they feared that German batteries here might hinder their efforts to advance in the Maricourt salient on the right of XIII Corps.[2] The combination of counter-battery fire from both the XIII Corps and the French wiped out the German guns in the area facing XV Corps during the preliminary bombardment. And on 1 July fire described as 'devastating' kept down the response from those German batteries which survived.[3] On the day, therefore, the men of 21 and 7 Divisions would face far less artillery fire than confronted VIII, X, and III Corps in the north and centre, even though XV Corps had failed them in the matter of counter-battery.

The final factor assisting XV Corps concerned German defensive arrangements. In this area, most of the deep dug-outs had been constructed under the first trench system. There were very few further back. These dug-outs were not as robustly constructed as those in the north but contained a greater proportion of the German garrisons than elsewhere. So the defence in this area lacked depth and the troops were more vulnerable to British shell fire.

The great defensive strength of Fricourt loomed large in the XV Corps' plans. It was not to be attacked directly. The 21 Division would attack to its north, the 7 Division to its east. They would link up only when the village had been bypassed. If the flanking attacks were progressing satisfactorily a direct attack might then be launched on the village to hasten its evacuation. Three small mines were to be blown up at zero in front of Fricourt in order to distract the defence and form crater lips which would shield the troops moving immediately to the north of the village. In addition Fricourt would be deluged with smoke to screen the flanking troops.[4]

In contrast with the British operations which have been described so far XV Corps' operations were a partial success. The overall pattern was that the further the units were from Fricourt, the greater the chance of their achieving their objectives.

Even in areas of success, however, advances did not come cheaply. In the extreme north of the XV Corps area the British bombardment had not proved consistently accurate so as the attack battalions left their trenches at 7.25 a.m. to position themselves close to the barrage they were met with heavy rifle and machine-gun fire before they had gone 25 yards. In one unit, 19 of the 24 officers became casualties in no man's land. Then as the barrage lifted from the German front line, enemy soldiers occupied the parapet and opened fire.[5] Nevertheless, a sufficient force made it across to take the first German system. There they were soon joined by the two follow-up battalions and, in the words of the brigade report, 'all four battalions passed on and the leading lines (now much bunched) appeared to have reached their first objective – Crucifix Trench – Round Wood – <u>close behind the artillery barrage</u>'.[6] So in the space of 45 minutes the combination of the creeping barrage and the relative paucity of German troops behind the front line had enabled 64 Brigade to advance well to the north of Fricourt .

Support on the flanks for 64 Brigade was not to materialise. The destruction of the 34 Division of III Corps to their north has already been described. To their south, the other assaulting brigade from 21 Division (63) had also failed. Neither the bombardment nor the smoke-screen directed against Fricourt had succeeded in neutralising it, with the result that as the men of 63 Brigade left their trenches they were cut down by machine-gun fire from the village. Of the lead battalions probably only two or three hundred men reached the German front line.[7] The follow-up units managed some small advances but fire from Fricourt and Fricourt Wood was too intense to allow significant progress. The survivors dug in just behind the German second trench and waited for night.[8]

While these events were unfolding, just to the north of Fricourt the 10 West Yorkshires from 50 Brigade[9] launched the most disastrous attack of the first day of the Somme. Here the explosion of three small mines was supposed to distract the Germans in Fricourt as the Yorkshiremen skirted the north of the village to provide flank protection for the 21 Division on their left. As far as the first two companies were concerned the expedient worked and they captured the German front line and pushed on to the support trenches virtually unscathed. The rearward companies however were wiped out by the rapidly recovering German garrison within the village. Consequently no reinforcements arrived to assist the forward companies. What happened to these men is not known in any detail.[10] They were certainly split up into small groups which mostly fell victim to German bombing parties in the course of the day.[11] At nightfall just 21 men from the battalion returned to their front line. In all it had lost 23 of its 24 officers and 717 of the 750 men who attacked.[12]

So, in sum, as night fell, the 64 Brigade was in a strong position north-east of Fricourt, the 63 Brigade had captured the German front line but not much more, and the 50 Brigade had failed utterly. Whether this partial success could be turned into anything more substantial rested with 7 Division attacking on the other side of the Fricourt salient.

## II

In the event, 7 Division was almost entirely successful in its attacks. It is clear from the accounts that the crossing of no man's land was greatly assisted by the creeping barrage. Most battalions were just 50–60 yards from the German line at zero and many were occupying the German trenches within one minute of the barrage lifting.[13] Others speak of crossing no man's land close behind the barrage without suffering a single casualty.[14] Of course not all proceeded smoothly. One battalion ran into the only intense artillery bombardment fired by the Germans on this part of the front and lost all cohesion.[15] Another battalion ran into uncut wire and suffered heavy losses finding a path around it.[16] Then as the advance continued and the pace of troops slackened, they lost the protection of the creeping barrage and ran into heavy machine-gun fire from

Mametz and on the left from Fricourt. Nevertheless, nowhere was this fire sufficient to bring the attack to a halt. By 1.30 p.m. the southern outskirts of Mametz had been entered, while on the right follow-up battalions had bypassed the ruined village and captured trenches to its north and east. Finally around 4 p. m. the last vestiges of Mametz were captured and 600 enemy troops surrendered.

The situation on the left nearer Fricourt was not so favourable. Yet even here 7 Division had established a strong defensive flank facing the village.[17] All this meant that XV Corps was threatening the village from the salients to the north and the east and that any German forces holding out were in danger of being cut off by subsequent operations.

The XV Corps headquarters however were not content to wait on subsequent operations. Wildly optimistic reports which seemed to indicate that 21 and 7 Divisions had taken all their objectives and that the German artillery was retreating towards Pozières led them to order a frontal attack on Fricourt at 2.30 p.m.[18] At least one of the battalions involved warned that the situation was not so favourable as was thought.[19] It was overruled and informed by the command that the attack would go in. The result was much slaughter. The defenders of Fricourt had by no means been overcome by 2.30 p. m. Indeed, they were continuing to pour fire into the flanks of the British advance. As they were doing so, from across no man's land (which at this point of attack was some 500 yards wide), came two battalions of British troops, unaccompanied by a creeping barrage, straight for the centre of the village. Within three minutes one battalion had lost 350 casualties.[20] Further south the other battalion managed to capture the German front line and advance to the support trench. By then they had suffered so heavily and so intense was the fire that they could go no further.[21] All told, 600 to 700 men had been lost to no effect.

## III

On the right of the British attack was the XIII Corps commanded by General Congreve and consisting of two New Army divisions, 18 (Maxse) and 30 (Shay). Its direction of attack was due north. There were two main obstacles to the British advance in this area. One was the village of Montauban which with 274 houses was one of the largest in the Somme area.[22] The second was Pommiers Redoubt, a circular trench fortress, 1,000 yards from the front line, lavishly equipped with machine-guns and dug-outs, and protected by belts of barbed wire.[23]

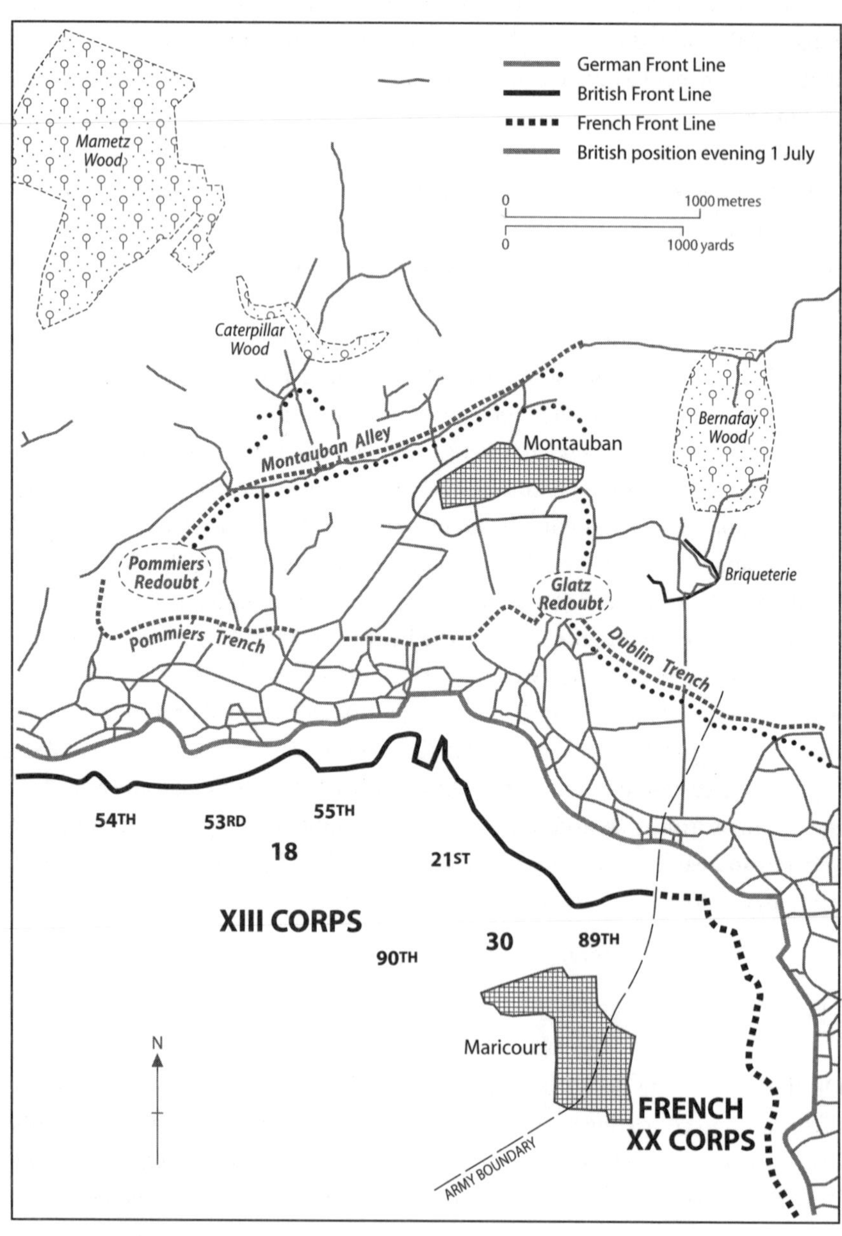


XIII Corps, 1 July

As with XV Corps, the British troops in the southern section of the front had some advantages. The first was artillery observation. The high ground behind the British front gave excellent panoramas over the entire German front line system as far back as Montauban.[24] Further, XIII Corps had optimised this advantageous position by giving counter-battery operations the highest priority of any British corps during the preliminary bombardment. Then there was the advantage of being alongside the French. To the north of the Somme the French XX Corps was also lavishly supplied with heavy guns and could enfilade from the south many German positions facing the British.

This concentration of well-placed Allied artillery proved devastating to the Germans. The batteries of the 12 and 28 Reserve German divisions had been badly knocked around during the preliminary bombardment and by midday on 1 July almost entirely destroyed.[25] The trenches and their defenders opposite XIII Corps had also suffered greatly. Almost all the wire in the area to be attacked had been swept away and many machine-guns in forward areas opposite 30 Division had been destroyed. Moreover, the majority of trenches in both divisional areas had been caved in or, in some instances, obliterated.[26]

In addition, given the accuracy of the XIII Corps and French artillery, German defensive arrangements in the area, like those in front of XV Corps, favoured the British. For reasons that are not at all obvious, the Germans had constructed far fewer deep dug-outs in the south, and those they had constructed were largely under the front line. As a consequence a high proportion of the German garrisons were crowded forward in these dug-outs. Accurate artillery fire and a rapid advance of troops would therefore neutralise large numbers of German defenders in the early minutes of the battle.[27]

It is possible that XIII Corps also aided their infantry by firing a creeping barrage. Certainly the corps orders seem quite clear:

> The field artillery barrage will creep back by short lifts....The infantry will follow close behind the barrage as safety admits.[28]

Anstey, however, in his unpublished history of the British Artillery in the First World War, claims that while 18 Division did fire a classic creeping barrage, 30 Division abandoned it and provided four lifts from trench to trench at zero plus 6, 16, 56, and 146 minutes.[29] In truth a close reading of after-battle reports from the units of both divisions supports the proposition that both fired modified creeping barrages – ones that crept between trench lines and then halted until the designated time for the next lift. In some parts of the front, as will be seen, these pauses may well have delayed the progress of the troops, but at least the troops could be certain that if they could advance in time with the pre-arranged timetable then they would have artillery protection while they traversed the open ground between the trench lines.

So, to sum up: in XIII Corps area, the troops had the advantages of good artillery observation, overwhelming superiority in guns, the high priority given by the corps to counter-battery fire, the French contribution, the faulty German defensive arrangements, and the protection of the creeping barrage.

## IV

The 18 Division attack, on the left of XIII Corps, started well. A series of mines (the largest 5,000 pounds, several others around 500 pounds) were blown under the German front line at 7.27 a.m. – three minutes before zero. In all, nine dug-outs were destroyed along with many of their garrisons.[30] In addition eight 'Russian' saps (shallow trenches dug across no man's land) containing machine-guns and flame-projectors were employed to enfilade the German line or incinerate those trench-dwellers who survived the bombardment.[31]

Nevertheless, all did not go well. In the area of 53 Brigade, some German guns had survived the counter-battery onslaught and managed to inflict heavy casualties on British troops as they huddled in their assembly trenches. The results were particularly grisly, as one observer later noted:

> Our men were lying dead in [the assembly trench], killed by the enemy's shells. In one place a man was kneeling, as if in prayer, his hands covering his face. Lying in the trench behind him was another man, face downwards, half buried in the earth thrown into the trench by the shells. A short distance away another man was sitting on the fire-step, buried to the knees, and looking as if he had suddenly turned to stone. A little further along the trench I stepped on something, and looking down I saw a piece of a man's backbone, and pieces of flesh strewn about the trench. Hanging down from the parapet, in the corner of the traverse, was a mass of entrails, already swarming with flies. And so on, here and there along the trench, wherever the enemy's shells had dropped in.[32]

It is perhaps worth noting that the 53 Brigade report described the enemy's barrage in this area as 'not heavy'.[33]

On the right of the attack facing 55 Brigade, German machine-gunners in a cratered section of no man's land survived the British bombardment, machine-guns, and flame-throwers. They inflicted heavy casualties on the leading waves of the brigade and effectively brought the attack in this section of the front to a halt.[34]

Luckily for 18 Division, the experience of the 54 Brigade, and of the large section of 53 Brigade which had escaped the early attentions of the German artillery, was quite different. These brigades, aided by the confusion caused by the mines, had captured the German front line shortly after 7.30 a.m. Following the creeping barrage, and with only scattered opposition, they progressed rapidly through the support line and rearward trenches of the German front system. So rapid was their progress that most of the strong Pommiers Trench was in their hands by 8.15 a.m. By 8.30 they had advanced 1,000 yards in total and were closing on Pommiers Redoubt.[35] There they encountered their first setback. The wire in front of the redoubt had not been adequately cut and the attack halted. It took them half an hour to cut their way through ('a nightmare for years to come,' according to one participant).[36] Even when the wire was cut the enemy garrison in the redoubt fought on, prepared, as the Bedfords noted, 'to defend this last vital point in their line . . . to the last'.[37] It was at this point that the meticulous training given to the troops by Maxse, and their familiarity with the German trench layout from the realistic models constructed during training, paid dividends. Parties of troops simultaneously swung to the left and right flanks of the redoubt. From the left, it was found, a machine-gun could enfilade the front face of the German position. Some other troops, in contrast, tried to assault from the rear only to be fired on by German troops in a trench behind the redoubt. However, they turned about, charged that trench, subdued the defenders, turned about again, and captured the rear face of Pommiers. By then other troops were entering the trench fortress from all sides. By 9.30 a.m. the formidable Pommiers Redoubt was in British hands.[38]

All this action, and the final subduing of the German garrison in the cratered area at 9.30 a.m., relieved the pressure on 55 Brigade, which, as related earlier, had been brought to a halt.[39] The survivors of the leading battalions of this brigade, reinforced by their support battalions, were now able to advance on their final objective (Montauban Alley just to the north-west of the village). All went smoothly until they reached a trench halfway towards their objective. There some German riflemen and machine-gunners put up a considerable resistance which failed only when they were outflanked by a party led by the intrepid Lt. Tortoise of the Queen's Battalion, who had already performed other startling deeds of bravery that day.[40] At this point German resistance in front of 55 Brigade finally crumbled and the brigade was able to link hands with the 53 Brigade on its left and the troops of 30 Division on its right.[41]

All objectives on the front of 18 Division had fallen. On the left elements of the 54 Brigade were holding positions some 500 yards behind Pommiers Redoubt and in the centre patrols had even been sent forward to Caterpillar

Wood which lay beyond the final objectives. The wood was found to be empty but as evening was now falling and German shelling growing heavier it was prudently decided to consolidate Montauban Alley and await the new day.

## V

On the very right of the British attack the 30 Division achieved the greatest advance, at the least cost, of any British division that day. This applied especially to 89 Brigade, which attacked alongside the French. At zero the men from this unit dashed across no man's land to find the wire well cut. Within a minute the German front line had fallen. Most of its defenders were killed or wounded. The remainder were too stunned by the bombardment to offer much resistance. Many of them were soon streaming back to the British lines as prisoners.[42] Then, after waiting for the creeping barrage to lift from its respective halts, the men followed it until their final objective (Dublin Trench, south of Montauban) was reached. All this was accomplished by 8.30 a.m. At 12.30 p.m. a company had even secured the Briqueterie, a cluster of buildings on the flank of the Allied advance from which, it had been feared, German machine-gunners might have been in a position to enfilade the troops attempting to capture Montauban.[43] So by midday the 89 Brigade had come to a halt, awaiting the arrival of 90 Brigade which was to leapfrog through them and capture Montauban. All this had been accomplished at a cost of just 24 killed.[44] One battalion (17 King's) had escaped even a single death on 1 July.[45]

On the left of 89 Brigade, the 21 Brigade had also made progress, but with much higher losses. The attack started well. The troops crossed no man's land with light casualties, found the wire well cut, and occupied the front trench before the Bavarian defenders could reach the surface from their dug-outs.[46] But then machine-guns in rear and in enfilade, from where the 18 Division to their left were being held up, took a heavy toll. In the case of one company, just 31 of 200 reached the German line.[47] Of the 500 casualties suffered by another battalion most were inflicted in this phase.[48]

Nevertheless, the attack retained sufficient weight to maintain progress against an increasingly disorganised enemy. (A French shell had wiped out almost all the regimental officers of a Bavarian regiment just after zero.)[49] Soon Glatz Redoubt had fallen and contact was made with 89 Brigade on the right.[50] Consolidation commenced as the troops awaited the capture of Montauban by 90 Brigade.

At first glance the Montauban operation bore an alarming similarity to some of 1 July's most unprofitable endeavours. The 90 Brigade had to advance from well behind their own front line, up a slope, to capture the ruins of a large village. In short, it had to accomplish what 32 Division failed to manage at Thiepval, 8 Division at Ovillers and 34 Division at La Boisselle. In all these cases, the result had been much slaughter and little progress. But with 90 Brigade affairs went quite differently. Their operation was covered by a dense smoke-screen put down by the two advanced brigades. It opened at 8.30 a.m., and by 9.30 the leading units had joined up with the troops of the 21 and 89 Brigades just south of the village.[51] Just after 10.30 a.m. the barrage moved on to Montauban, followed by troops from three battalions of 90 Brigade.[52] Ten minutes later the village (which in the event was deserted 'except for a fox')[53] fell into British hands with hardly a casualty.

What had happened was remarkable. Montauban had been all but obliterated by the combined might of the British and French artillery – 'there remained no recognizable ruins although there had been 274 houses there before the war'.[54] Moreover, the substantial cellars that in other areas had protected machine-gun detachments, were here either caved in or their inhabitants had been rendered incapable of resistance. An officer from the 17 Manchester, one of the units which captured the village, described the scene:

> Inside Montauban all was wreck and ruin, a monstrous heap of rubble stinking of death, brick-dust and high-explosive. Down in deep dug-outs, a few of which had survived our heavy shells, cowering men in field grey were taken prisoner. In one, which was equipped with electric light, a Brigadier or Colonel with a staff of six officers was captured. Large parties of Bosch laughing and dancing like demented creatures went streaming back to Maricourt unguarded, holding their arms up and calling, 'Mercy, Kamarad'. They had thrown away their arms and equipment and were utterly demoralised; their uniforms filthy and stinking. In the village the horrors of war were visible on every side; dead and dying Germans, some with terrible wounds lay amidst the brick-dust and rubble.[55]

Briefly the ruins of Montauban came under ferocious enemy artillery fire. The response of the British who had captured the village was to push forward and take Montauban Alley to the north.[56] From this position, the most advanced captured by the British that day, 30 Division troops could see the Germans flooding back towards their second line.[57]

# 11 Reflections on 1 July

The account of the first day of the Somme given here is in agreement with all other accounts on the two most vital matters: the great number of casualties suffered by the British army (57,000) and the small amount of ground gained (three square miles).

In most other ways our account is so at variance with the conventional story that it is necessary to indicate why this is the case before providing a summary of our own findings.

The conventional account of 1 July 1916 is as follows. At 7.30 a.m. the British infantry, reduced to a walking pace by their 66-pound packs, were ordered by a doltish command to walk shoulder to shoulder across no man's land. Obeying this order to the letter, they were slaughtered like sheep by the German machine-gunners who emerged from their dug-outs in sufficient time to man their weapons. This is the story of the so-called 'race for the parapet', a race which the British army lost, according to one arresting phrase, by three minutes. The implication of all this is that, had these three minutes been erased, the result of the day would have been victory, not defeat.

Apart from newspaper accounts, which contain only the sketchiest detail of the events of the first day, John Buchan's book *The Battle of the Somme*, published in 1917, seems to have set this scene. In describing the attack Buchan wrote:

> The British moved forward in line after line, dressed as if on parade; not a man wavered or broke rank, but minute by minute the ordered lines melted away under the deluge of high explosive, shrapnel, rifle and machine-gun fire.[1]

Buchan, as might be expected in a book written in wartime, emphasises the courage and steadiness of the soldiers rather than the inappropriateness of the infantry tactics employed. Later writers, however, especially those from the late

1920s onwards, made essentially the same point as Buchan, but laid great stress on the deficiencies of the high command. In the forefront of these authors was Liddell Hart. In 1930 he wrote:

> Battalions attacked in four or eight waves, not more than 100 yards apart, the men in each almost shoulder to shoulder, in a symmetrical well-dressed alignment and taught to advance steadily upright at a slow walk.[2]

He also added:

> each man carried [a pack of] about 66 lbs, over half his own body weight, which made it difficult to get out of a trench, impossible to move quicker than a slow walk or to rise and lie down quickly...even an army mule, the proverbial natural beast of burden, is only expected to carry a third of his own weight.[3]

Ever since Liddell Hart, this grim depiction of British infantrymen reduced by their own commanders to worse than pack animals has held sway.

It might be thought that the publication in 1932 of the relevant volume of the British official history of the battle would modify this account. After all, its author, Brigadier-General Sir James Edmonds was the first to see the combat records of the campaign. Surprisingly, Edmonds did little more than confirm the by now well-established view:

> the assault on the 1st July was...carried out at a 'steady pace', and with the direction that each line of assaulting troops must leave its trenches simultaneously and make the assault as one man.[4]

These early accounts set the pattern up to the present day. For example, C.M.F. Cruttwell in 1934 wrote of the infantry:

> straightened out into long lines advancing shoulder to shoulder...laden like beasts of burden.[5]

Even defenders of the high command such as John Terraine accept the dominant paradigm. In his biography of Haig written in 1963 Terraine uses the alleged eyewitness account of Sir Edward Spears to describe the opening moments of battle:

> the British rigid and slow, advancing as on Aldershot parade in lines that were torn and ripped by the German guns.[6]

It might be thought that the opening of the official military records in 1965 would have brought forth a reappraisal of the first day. But with one partial exception this has not come to pass. Martin Middlebrook in 1971, Corelli Barnett in 1979, Paul Kennedy in 1988, and a recent BBC documentary of the Great War have all accepted the conventional view.[7]

The partial exception is Anthony Farrar-Hockley. In 1970 he wrote a small book on the Battle of the Somme. It is clear from a close reading that he by no means accepted that all the attacking infantry walked to their doom shoulder to shoulder at a steady pace. He produced examples which demonstrate units formed up in no man's land and not at the edge of their trench; that others advanced at the double and yet others adopted various complicated infantry formations designed to reduce the effect of the German machine-gunners.[8] Yet the impact of these revelations on future accounts was nil, partly because of the tenacious hold of the established view and partly because Farrar-Hockley himself drew no conclusions from what he had written. Later in the same year he wrote a chapter on the Somme in a history of the British army. In it he reverted to the usual view of rigid waves slowly walking into German machine-gun fire.[9]

It will be apparent that the account of the first day of the Somme given in the four preceding chapters challenges the conventional story. Certainly around 20,000 men were killed and about 40,000 wounded on the first day. But the vast majority did not meet their fate by advancing shoulder to shoulder at a slow walk. Nor did the high command order them to do so.

In the first instance, Rawlinson in his 'Tactical Notes' laid down no particular doctrine about the best method of advancing. Indeed his statements were notable for their ambiguity: at one point he states the need for 'celerity of movement'; at another that troops proceed at a 'steady pace' (except in certain unspecified circumstances which required a 'rapid advance of some lightly equipped men'). Most infantry commanders presumably concluded that they had *carte blanche.* Nor did Rawlinson lay down the formations in which the advance should be made. Instead he noted that 'there can be no general rule as regards the best formations for attack'.

It should come as no surprise, therefore, that, as our account reveals, the battalion commanders, who seem to have been the key decision-makers in these matters, did the choosing. They adopted whatever attack formations they deemed appropriate and they decided on the speed with which these formations should advance.

It needs to be reiterated that their decisions on the best method to cross no man's land and come to grips with the enemy were many and various. So in the north the attack brigade of 31 Division moved into no man's land before zero and lay down ready to rush the German line when the barrage lifted. Further south some units of 4 Division such as the King's Own Regiment started from their own parapets but adopted complex formations led by skirmishers and snipers. In the 29 Division on their flank, some battalions 'marched' up to the enemy wire, others such as the Lancashire Fusiliers rushed forward from advanced positions already dug into no man's land.

All along the front these large variations are apparent. In X Corps the Ulstermen formed up close to the German wire and rushed forward at zero. So did some of the battalions from 32 Division and 8 Division in the centre. It is possible that the other division of the centre Corps (III) walked in stereotypical manner, as did many battalions from the successful XV and XIII Corps in the south.

In summary, for the 80 battalions that went over the top in the first attack on 1 July, 53 crept out into no man's land close to the German wire before zero and then rushed the German line, while ten others rushed the line from their own parapet. This leaves just 17 battalions, 12 of which advanced at a steady pace and five for which no evidence exists.

There is a further complicating factor here. At least some of the battalions who walked across no man's land at a steady pace did so because they were following a creeping barrage. These were some of the most successful units of all on the first day.

Yet despite the variety of tactics employed, the pattern of death in prohibitive numbers applied to most of the front. The reason is plain. As long as most German machine-gunners and artillerymen survived the British bombardment, the slaughter of the attacking infantry would occur *whatever* infantry tactics were adopted. To rush German machine-guns might slightly increase the rate of survival over those who walked towards them, but the difference was not significant. A hail of bullets (on some occasions, as noted, to the scale of 6,000 *per minute*) would wreak havoc on human bodies *no matter what expedient was adopted or how sophisticated the tactics.* In the south, significantly, where the 30 Division seemed to adopt no particularly innovative tactics, success was ensured because the British artillery had dealt such severe blows to the German gunners and trench-dwellers. In other words, if the artillery had done their job it mattered little if the infantry walked or ran or executed the Highland fling across no man's land.

Another point should be made. Unsubdued machine-guns and artillery could decimate formations well behind the British line. Thus the follow-up formations of 93 Brigade, so graphically described by our eyewitness (see pp. 75–6), were wiped out before they reached their own parapet. The same applies to units of 4 Division, 29 Division, the Tyneside Irish of 34 Division and, even if to a lesser extent, to the relatively successful brigades of 18 and 30 Divisions.

Although the exact number of casualties suffered by the British *behind their own front line* cannot be calculated, it was probably around 30 per cent of all British casualties suffered on 1 July. For those men the opening engagement was anything but a race for the parapet. The only parapet towards which they were 'racing' was their own; and in many cases, they lost. The killing zone then did not just encompass the width of no man's land, it continued back some thousands of yards into British positions. Death in battle is terrible whatever form it takes and in whatever location it occurs. But there does seem something especially melancholy about death inflicted in a so-called friendly zone, long before the enemy front line comes into view.

What all this confirms is that the determinant of victory in industrial war is the prevalence and effectiveness of killing-machines – in this case predominantly machine-guns and artillery. It is not the specific tactics or attack formations adopted by the infantry. In essence this should not be all that surprising. The infantryman with his rifle and bayonet had long since ceased to be able to compete with the distant and high-intensity fire of weapons such as machine-guns and quick firing artillery. What must be deemed surprising, rather, is the fact that for over 80 years historians have turned this story on its head. They have argued as if the skill, or lack of it, evident in the tactics supposedly imposed from above on the infantry really did, on the first day, make the difference between winning and losing.

All of this raises two historiographical questions concerning the first day of the Somme. Why has the image of the infantry plodding shoulder to shoulder to their doom exercised such an iron grip on our vision of the battle? And exactly why do historians think that, above all else, it was the behaviour and experience of the infantry that determined the outcome of this day's endeavours?

The first question suggests several answers. Of all the observers watching the deployment of the infantry on 1 July, probably only one group actually had a view of the advance not obscured by smoke and dust. This group was in Albert, and what they were observing was the Tyneside Irish marching towards their own front line in close order formation and then being cut down in large numbers. In other words they were not witnessing an attack in rigid formation across no man's land, as at least some of them probably thought. They were watching the deployment of a unit well behind the British front line. As for Edward Spears and other so-called eyewitness observers, they were too distant to observe anything with precision and no doubt lapsed into conventional language and imagery to describe a failed attack.

As for the second question, it is fairly clear that the established portrait of the battle was derived from Buchan and other early writers on the Somme. The portrait seemed to them particularly appropriate because it resonated with their view of the virtues possessed by the British infantry – steadiness under fire and unflinching bravery in the face of disaster. The first day on the Somme, in short, was the foot soldiers' equivalent of the charge of the Light Brigade.

This picture also resonated with that later group of historians characterised by Liddell Hart. For them, however, the conventional image was not associated with the bravery of the infantry. It centred on the stupidity of the high command and on the needless slaughter of an innocent rank and file by those whose duty it was to safeguard them.

So for all these groups, the patriots and the perplexed, the Haig haters and the Haig admirers, for the 'westerners' and for those for whom the Western Front was a synonym for a bloody shambles, the first day of the Somme became the necessary image of the war. By the time later writers made their appearance the conventional image was so strongly embedded that it possessed the status of an established fact, beyond criticism or investigation. When, rarely, an historian did gain an inkling of the real story (as with Farrar-Hockley) he seemed reluctant to believe what he had found, and re-embraced the received wisdom as swiftly as possible.

The mystery of all this is the devotion of military historians to the notion that the outcome of even the largest conflicts is determined by the skill and heroism of the rank and file infantry. Whatever truth this notion may have had in earlier wars, it was clearly inappropriate for the large episodes of industrial war of 1914–18. Plainly, it was the mass-produced, long-range killing-machines that now dominated the battlefield. As Omar Bartov noted:

> The Great War with its depersonalised, industrial killing, should have spelled the end of the heroic image of the warrior yet nothing of the kind happened. The image of heroic individuals on whose supreme qualities [the outcome of battle depends] remained intact.[10]

There is an obvious explanation for this focus on the infantry. Notwithstanding the war-changing impact of industrialisation in battle, it is still the infantry who put their lives on the line. It is the foot soldiers who are required to go over the top and enter the killing zone. So we may understand why historians feel obliged to look upon the terrible experiences of the rank and file with compassion and awe. It is not a large step (even though it may be largely specious) from this position to ascribe to the ordeal of these common men primacy in the outcome of battle.

Furthermore, if 'colour' or 'human interest' is to be added to accounts of war, then again, in the main these elements can only be provided by the infantry.

What seizes the imagination are heroic deeds accomplished, tales of machine-guns overcome, and mates who make the 'supreme sacrifice'.

Bartov adds another, more disturbing factor. He argues that we have an in-built need for the heroic image in war and that as war becomes ever more depersonalised this need has actually grown. The historian's approach to 1 July 1916 demonstrates this. A best-selling book on the subject is Martin Middlebrook's *First Day on the Somme*. Its focus is on the heroism of individuals, while it gives little sense of why such heroism proved largely in vain. If the warrior is to be reinstated as war-winner, then it is necessary that what he does is paramount. And when his endeavours prove futile, as they did on 1 July, again the matter must be reduced to the personal. The explanation has to lie, not clearly where it belongs, in the insufficiency of killing weapons to facilitate such an attack, but in the faulty tactics imposed on the infantry by their commanders. Let it be stressed that there were command errors aplenty on the first day of the Somme. But the most profound misjudgements lay elsewhere. Only an abundance of guns and shells on the Western Front could create the conditions whereby rank and file infantry might operate on the battlefield with any chance of success. When the guns proved insufficient and were employed inappropriately (as happened in the north) the infantry also failed, with great slaughter. When the guns were employed with sufficient numbers and skill (as in the south) foot soldiers were placed in an environment where they could display their skills and gain a modicum of success. None of this may seem glamorous or heroic, but it more nearly represents the reality of 1 July 1916 than any obsessive focus on infantry tactics.

# 12 'Ill-Considered Attacks on a Small Front', 2–13 July

## I

If the first day of the Somme was the most disastrous day of battle in British history, no sense of doom or despair appears to have penetrated the minds of the high command. During the day Haig remarked that 'on a sixteen-mile front of attack varying fortune must be expected'.[1] Even on the 2nd, when the casualty lists were coming in, he maintained his equanimity, commenting merely that over 40,000 casualties 'cannot be considered severe in view of numbers engaged'.[2] Rawlinson showed similar sang-froid. He noted without comment at 7.30 p.m. on the 1st that the casualty total was 16,000.[3] On the 2nd the figure had risen to over 30,000, a total he was prepared to admit was 'heavy', but he remained unconcerned as there were 'plenty of fresh divisions behind'.[4]

One matter was not discussed by the high command. No mention at all was made of how far short of expectations the achievements of the day had fallen. Rawlinson quietly dispersed the cavalry during the night.[5] No mention at all was made of Bapaume or points east.

So, with an insouciance that was perhaps a necessary façade in the face of the lamentable results achieved, Haig and Rawlinson set about planning the next stage of the campaign.

Several choices seemed to confront them. Would they attack all along the original front, as Rawlinson proposed, to bring the British line to within striking distance of the second German position? Would they, as Haig favoured, confine themselves to further advances in the south, the only area in which gains had been made? Or would they make a second attempt to obtain the commanding heights of the Thiepval Ridge?[6]

A meeting was held to discuss these issues on the 3rd. Tempers flared. Joffre 'ordered' Haig to give priority to capture of the Thiepval Ridge. Haig demurred. Rawlinson remained silent.[7]

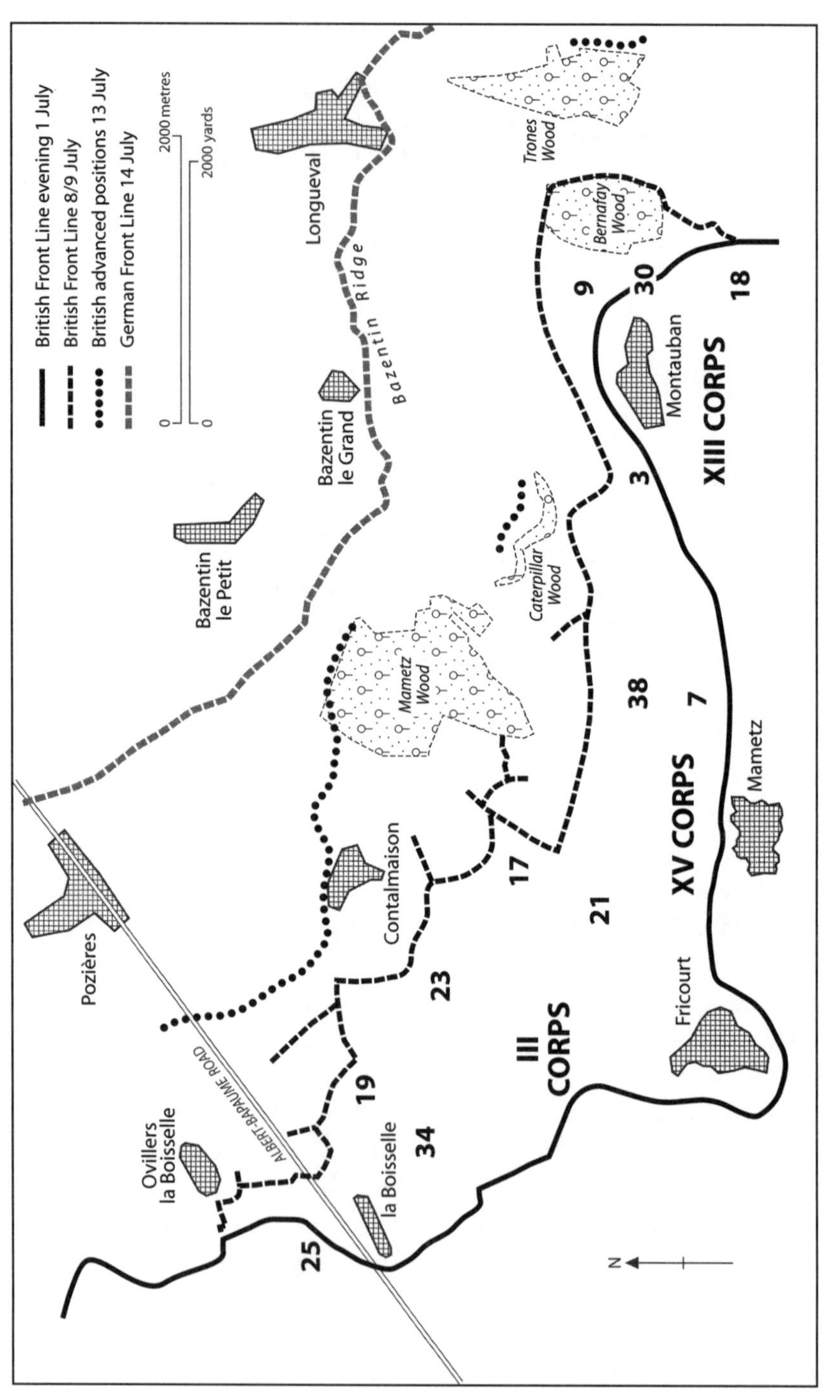
British Front Line evening 1 July
British Front Line 8/9 July
British advanced positions 13 July
German Front Line 14 July
0
2000 metres
0
2000 yards
Longueval
Bazentin le Grand
Bazentin le Petit
Bazentin Ridge
Trones Wood
Bernafay Wood
Caterpillar Wood
Mametz Wood
Pozières
Contalmaison
Montauban
Mametz
Fricourt
Ovillers la Boisselle
la Boisselle
ALBERT–BAPAUME ROAD
XIII CORPS
XV CORPS
III CORPS
9
30
18
3
38
7
17
21
23
19
34
25
N
2–13 July

On reflection the three commanders soon realised that there was no choice to be made. The line around Thiepval could not be assailed. As reported by Gough, whom Rawlinson had placed in command of the Northern Corps, the VIII Corps dead and wounded were still choking all communication trenches. To remove them and bring in fresh units would have meant a suspension of operations for some days, a situation no commander was prepared to contemplate. On closer inspection most of the X Corps area was found to be little better.[8] So it was decided by Haig and Rawlinson that operations must be confined to securing the southern sector, from Ovillers to Bernafay Wood, where some progress had been made.[9]

## II

These operations commenced promisingly. On the 2nd, a patrol from 7 Division found that the Germans had evacuated the Fricourt Salient. In short order the 7, the newly introduced 17, and the 21 Divisions linked up behind the village and wood, in the process considerably shortening the British line.

The advance in the south was not accompanied by any progress to its immediate left. Here the main effort consisted of an attempt by III Corps to capture Ovillers and La Boisselle.[10] This operation was to be undertaken by two new formations, the 19 Division which had taken over much of the front of 34 Division on the night of 1 July and the 12 Division which had relieved the shattered 8 Division on the night of 2 July.[11] The X Corps were to provide flank support by attacking just south of Thiepval.[12]

This attack, it may be noted, was to be carried out over the same ground which had brought disaster to III Corps on 1 July. However, a minor operation by 19 Division on the afternoon of the 2nd had captured the southern tip of La Boisselle and this raised expectations that the German defence in the areas had been affected by the events on the first day more than was apparent.[13] Perhaps for this reason, it was decided by III Corps that the major operation should be immediate. But because of the great width of no man's land along this section of the front it was clear that the main attack must take place by night. However, neither the 12 nor the 19 Division had made a major attack even in daytime. Moreover they were so new to the area that detailed reconnaissance was required to acquaint the divisions with the German defences. Instead, a rushed offensive was ordered. So there was no time for reconnaissance and the preliminary bombardment consisted of desultory artillery fire for only one hour.

The attack commenced on 3 July with the 19 Division advancing on La Boisselle from the north and south. At first the battle developed promisingly for the British with the troops entering the village, bombing their way through the rubble and reaching its eastern end. But, as one of the battalion accounts acknowledges, success was brief. The numerous dug-outs in the ruins held many snipers who had to be bombed out and as a result hand grenades soon ran short. Coherence between units proved hard to maintain in the dark and for reinforcements the location of the forward units was hard to find. Further, the whole scheme was too hurried, no time being allowed to explain to the men what was required of them.[14] Hence rapid advance on both sides of the village was followed by rapid retreat as bombs ran out, small groups of men found themselves unsupported on the flanks, and local counter-attacks by the German garrison developed.[15] Soon the whole of the 19 Division was pushed back to within 100 yards of their start line. The cost cannot have been fewer than 1,000 men.[16]

Meanwhile events further north were proceeding with even greater confusion. In the first place the flanking support from X Corps failed to develop because their trenches were still blocked with the dead and wounded from the first day.[17] So when 12 Division attacked they were unsupported on the left and had not proceeded far across no man's land when they were met by heavy enfilade fire from that direction.[18] Some troops penetrated the first and second German trenches but by then the enemy was firing such a strong artillery barrage on no man's land and the British assembly trenches that no reinforcement was possible. One of the leading battalions which had suffered over 400 casualties noted with some bitterness that they had received no assistance from their supporting unit, but the fact was that the latter formation had lost 275 men in trying to leave its own trenches.[19] Wisely, the commander had cancelled further plans to advance.

On the right, even without being subjected to enfilade fire, things were no better. The front units entered the German trenches, but then the enemy artillery barrage came down, reinforcements either lost their way in the dark or were wiped out, and ammunition for the front troops ran low. Consequently they were forced to withdraw.[20] In all, 12 Division in its introduction to Somme fighting lost 2,375 casualties for no ground gained.[21] In his report the divisional commander listed the reasons for failure. They are well summarised in the divisional history:

> The capture of the position had failed, and the failure was un-doubtedly affected by the flanking machine gun fire, which was unmolested, and raked the excessive distance between the opposing front lines over which supports

> had to cross. Also by the attack being carried out in the dark by troops who were hurried into the fight without being well acquainted with the terrain, leading to loss of cohesion; by the artillery bombardment destroying the wire and trenches, yet failing to reach the deep dug-outs, which remained unharmed; and the recent storms making shell holes and trenches in places almost unpassable.[22]

## III

Despite this setback on the 3rd, Haig and Rawlinson were determined to push on. Later that day the Fourth Army commander expressed his intensions. His goal was to push within striking distance of the German second line between the Bazentin Ridge and Longueval, and then make an all-out assault. To this end three things were required. The III Corps were to capture Bailiff Wood and Contalmaison, XV Corps was to secure Mametz Wood, and XIII Corps was to occupy in the first instance Caterpillar and Bernafay Woods, and then Trones Wood.[23]

In the following days the only action of the command was to reiterate these orders, exhorting that operations be vigorous, so as to take advantage of the disarray into which the Germans had allegedly fallen. For example, on the 4th Haig stated that the enemy's strength was diminishing and his reserves were worn down. Hence he ordered Rawlinson to 'continue the operations relentlessly and allow the enemy no respite'.[24] Two days later GHQ had reached the conclusion that the enemy was on the brink of collapse. Rawlinson was told that Intelligence indicated the Germans had few reserves with which to reinforce the 15 battered battalions in the line, and

> in view of the conclusive evidence of considerable loss of morale and confusion on the enemy's side you will realise that successes gained can and should be followed up more boldly than would be wise under conditions less favourable to us.... There is good evidence that we have reached a stage where serious demoralization may set in at any time, possibly tomorrow.[25]

Similar missives (despite the enemy's refusal to adhere to GHQ's demoralisation schedule) followed in the next few days.

Rawlinson, for his part, apparently saw no role for himself other than to act as a conduit passing GHQ's euphoric predictions on to his corps commanders. He certainly saw no need for Fourth Army headquarters to act as a co-ordinating body to ensure that corps attacks were simultaneous, supported by as much artillery as possible and assailing objectives with appropriate strength.

The results of this *laissez-faire* approach to command need to be grasped. In one section of the front between 5 and 10 July, the 23 Division of III Corps launched eight attacks against Contalmaison and the trenches that guarded its approaches.[26] On its immediate right 17 Division of XV Corps launched at least 11 attacks against the trenches contiguous with those attacked by 23 Division.[27] Yet on not one occasion were these operations delivered simultaneously, and only once did the artillery of a corps assist in the attack of the other.[28] As a consequence, both divisions suffered something of the order of 3,500 casualties.[29] And these losses yielded very small advances.

If the operations of units from different corps were conspicuously lacking in co-ordination, operations within corps were hardly better managed. For example, while the 23 Division of III Corps was struggling towards Contalmaison, on its left the 19 and 34 Divisions from the same corps only once attacked simultaneously. For the most part these units confined themselves to minor bombing operations, which were often intense and bloody but hardly distracted German attention from the main action around Contalmaison.[30]

A comprehensive report from an officer who took part in some of these disastrous attacks gives some of the flavour of the prevailing chaos. He noted that the failure to capture Contalmaison resulted from:

(1) Insufficient preliminary Reconnaissance by those responsible for executing the attack
(2) Lack of co-ordination between neighbouring units as regards time of attacks, that were disjointed and should have been simultaneous
(3) No proper liaison between units and those on their flanks
(4) Too many attempts to gain vital ground by bombing attacks up trenches, instead of well mounted, well gunned, simultaneous attack in strength and numbers across the open
(5) Lack of properly regulated and well timed Artillery support, and no proper liaison between front line troops and Artillery by means of Artillery liaison officers attached to attacking units, by which Artillery fire could have been brought to bear at vital moments.
There was further[,] no co-ordination between the first Artillery Barrage and the attack of the Infantry.
(6) False reports from Observation Balloons.[31]

For good measure he added that Contalmaison was attacked from the wrong direction, that brigade headquarters was too far back to appreciate the situation at the front and that the commander in charge of the battalion which attacked Contalmaison did not know his job.[32]

The artillery found this situation just as frustrating as the infantry. The 12 Divisional artillery which tried to support various divisions in this period commented:

> Owing to the confused situation, uncertainty as to where exactly the enemy and our own troops were at any moment , and observation difficulties, our fire must have been ... of little assistance in comparison to the expenditure of ammunition. It was the general opinion in 12th D.A. that these suddenly staged, ill coordinated attacks on a small front were futile. R.A. had no chance to afford real Support, while unlocated hostile M.G.s on the flanks of the attacks were left free to inflict very heavy casualties on the infantry.[33]

## IV

On the left, therefore, fragmented attempts to capture Contalmaison proceeded unavailingly. Meanwhile in the centre an operation was launched to clear one of the most formidable obstacles between the British and the German second line. This was Mametz Wood: a mile long and a mile wide, it was the largest of all the woods to figure in the Somme fighting. The undergrowth was 'wild and thick', and the British shelling had added to its impenetrability by bringing down many trees in full growth.[34] Into the wilderness was thrown a division yet to see battle, the 38 Welsh, which had taken over from the 7 Division on 5 July.[35] It was directed to attack Mametz Wood early the following day. This illustrates the haste with which operations during this period of the battle were being made. But haste was not the only disadvantage under which the Welshmen would labour. One of the reasons XV Corps (and particularly 7 Division) had done well on 1 July was the employment of the creeping barrage to protect the advancing infantry. The 7 Division was well aware of this factor, having noted it specifically as a reason for success.[36] Yet no one chose to pass this information on to 38 Division, which consequently had to deliver its first operation without it.

The endeavours of the 38 Division in the wood lasted from 7 to 11 July. During this time it attacked on seven occasions. It acted, in all but rare instances, without support on either flank. No operations were carried out in this period by 3 Division (XIII Corps) on its right, and the few attempts to co-ordinate attacks with 17 Division (also from XV Corps) on its left largely failed.[37] The attacks failed for a combination of reasons. Usually the brief bombardments which accompanied them were insufficient to subdue the machine-guns in the wood; the attacking forces were subject to fire from both flanks; untoward haste meant that orders reached troops just moments before an attack or that the men were still struggling forward to their start lines at zero hour. In addition, their own artillery often hit the men because insufficient time had been taken to ascertain their exact position within the wood. Moreover the command was so out of touch that it ordered incessant attacks without regard to the situation facing the troops. Circumstances improved somewhat on the 8th. On that date the divisional commander (Philips) was sacked and Watts from 7 Division took over command. The new commander at least knew the secret of the creeping barrage and from the 10th onwards the troops had the benefit of this form of protection.[38] Nevertheless, the fighting for Mametz Wood wrecked the division. In just five days it suffered 4,000 casualties, including 7 of its 12 battalion commanders.[39] It took no further part in the Somme Campaign.

## V

Meanwhile on the far right of the Fourth Army a portion of XIII Corps was involved in an operation entirely separate from those of the rest of its divisions – the clearing of Trones Wood as a preliminary to the great attack on the 14th. This task had first fallen to 30 Division which had been briefly out of the line following its exertions of the first two days. It was ordered to capture the long triangular-shaped Trones Wood on the 8th. As with Mametz Wood, all did not go according to plan. From the 8th to the early hours of the 14th the wood was assaulted on eight occasions, as shown below.

| *Date* | *Time* | *Strength of attack* | *Unit* | *Result* |
|---|---|---|---|---|
| 8 th | 7.15 a.m. | 1 Bn | 30 Div. | Failure |
| 8 th | 1.00 p.m. | 1 Bn | 30 Div. | Failure |
| 9 th | 6.40 a.m. | 1 Bn | 30 Div. | Failure |
| 9 th | 6.40 a.m. | 1 Bn | 30 Div. | Failure |
| 11 th | ? | 2 Bn | 30 Div. | Failure |
| 11 th | 10.30 p.m. | 1 Bn | 30 Div. | Failure |
| 13 th | 7.00 p.m. | 2 Bn | 18 Div. | Failure |
| 14 th | 4 .00 a.m. | 2 Bn | 18 Div. | Success |

Table compiled from XIII Corps, 'Narrative of events 1st July–15 August 1916', WO 95/895; 21 Brigade, '30 Division Account of Operations from July 1st–2nd', WO 95/2327; Maxse, 'Battle of the Somme: Capture of Trones Wood', WO 95/2015; 'Account of the Operations of the 54 Brigade', Maxse Papers 63/53/7, IWM.

The first seven attacks failed for the same reason: enfilade fire from three strongpoints along a railway line which bisected the wood. Only on the eighth occasion was the location of these strongpoints identified and an attack directed against them. As a result, the wood was cleared.

## VI

How do these three snapshots of the front at Contalmaison, Mametz Wood, and Trones Wood fit into the overall picture of operations between 2 and 13 July? During this period 86 battalions of the Fourth Army launched 46 attacks against the German positions. These actions were costly. Overall, Rawlinson's forces suffered 25,000 casualties, which took the total for thirteen days of operations to 85,000.[40] As should be clear from the examples given, these operations were carried out in sporadic fashion and on narrow fronts. On an average day just 14 per cent of the Fourth Army battalions attacked the enemy while the rest remained quiescent. During the most extensive attack in this period, that of 7 July, just 26 per cent (19) of available battalions (72) engaged the enemy. Yet even on that day the forces were not taking part in a co-ordinated attack. In the main they fought the enemy in piecemeal fashion, two or three battalions at a time. The maximum number that were in action at any one time was eight, and even then the attacks were not contiguous.[41]

The artillery support for these fragmented operations was no better coordinated. In most cases nothing approaching the available artillery resources of the Fourth Army was employed. For example on 7 July when 17 and 38 Divisions were attacking Mametz Wood the artillery of XIII Corps on the right flank – which was not attacking that day – remained silent.[42]

What we are observing, then, is a succession of narrow front attacks usually launched without adequate artillery preparation. This enabled the Germans to concentrate all their available artillery and infantry reserves against the particular section of the front which was being assailed. And what this ensured was that British troops had to advance through a greater weight of shell and machine-gun fire than if the Germans had been forced to spread their resources more thinly to meet wide-front operations.

Yet there was another side to this. Formidable fortified areas such as La Boisselle, Contalmaison, Mametz Wood, and Trones Wood were captured by the British in the relatively short period of 12 days. That is, where only 3 square miles had been captured on 1 July, the days between 2 and 13 July saw 20 square miles of German-held territory pass into British hands. As long as the command were prepared to disregard the prodigious casualties of these 13 days (and Haig's reaction to the casualties for the first day hardly suggested that he would respond otherwise), the British could regard the period as one of steady achievement.

This optimistic view could only be reinforced by the fact that British operations had indeed reduced the Germans in the area of La Boisselle to Trones Wood to a state of considerable disorganisation. We do not have to take the wildly exaggerated forecasts from GHQ Intelligence about the enemy's imminent collapse at face value to acknowledge that there was at least some basis for their hopeful reports. If not actually on the brink of collapse, the Germans were indeed in a state of disarray. There are a number of reasons for this. First, the British operations from 2 to 13 July (along with French operations north and south of the Somme) were being delivered in the one area where the large offensive of 1 July had dealt heavy blows to the Germans and overrun their well-prepared front system of defences along with its garrisons. Second, a significant proportion of German batteries in this region had fallen victim to British and French bombardments. Third, the German position in this area was being made worse by the determination of their high command to recover immediately every fragment of territory captured by the British on 1 July. This meant that the Germans threw reserves into the battle helter skelter rather than holding them back for subsequent concerted action. As a consequence all the German reserves in the immediate area had been expended.

There was a clear alternative to this proceeding, that of tactical withdrawal which husbanded reserves and shortened the line. Some German commanders recognised this wisdom. On 2 July, a subordinate commander south of the Somme sanctioned a local withdrawal just for the purpose of straightening the line. This brought down on him the wrath of Falkenhayn. The local commander was sacked and a stern warning issued by the commander-in-chief:

> The first principle in positional warfare must be not to give up an inch of territory and when an inch is lost to launch a counter-attack until the last man.[43]

It is important to take note of this directive. We have witnessed so many examples of ineptitude on the part of the British command that it is important to remember that they could be equalled or exceeded by the Germans whenever the opportunity presented.

## VII

It seems certain that the British command derived great comfort from the reasonably rapid gain of ground made in the period from 2 to 13 July. But in doing this they were ignoring two factors. The first was the fact that in proceeding with unrelenting, poorly planned and uncoordinated attacks, they were incurring very heavy casualties. The second was that such a method was only having success because of the shaken German defence. The same methods employed against resolute Germans manning intact defences around Ovillers and La Boisselle had brought disaster. In other words, the circumstances which made progress possible in this period would have to be replicated if such ill-prepared and costly methods were to lead to progress in the future.

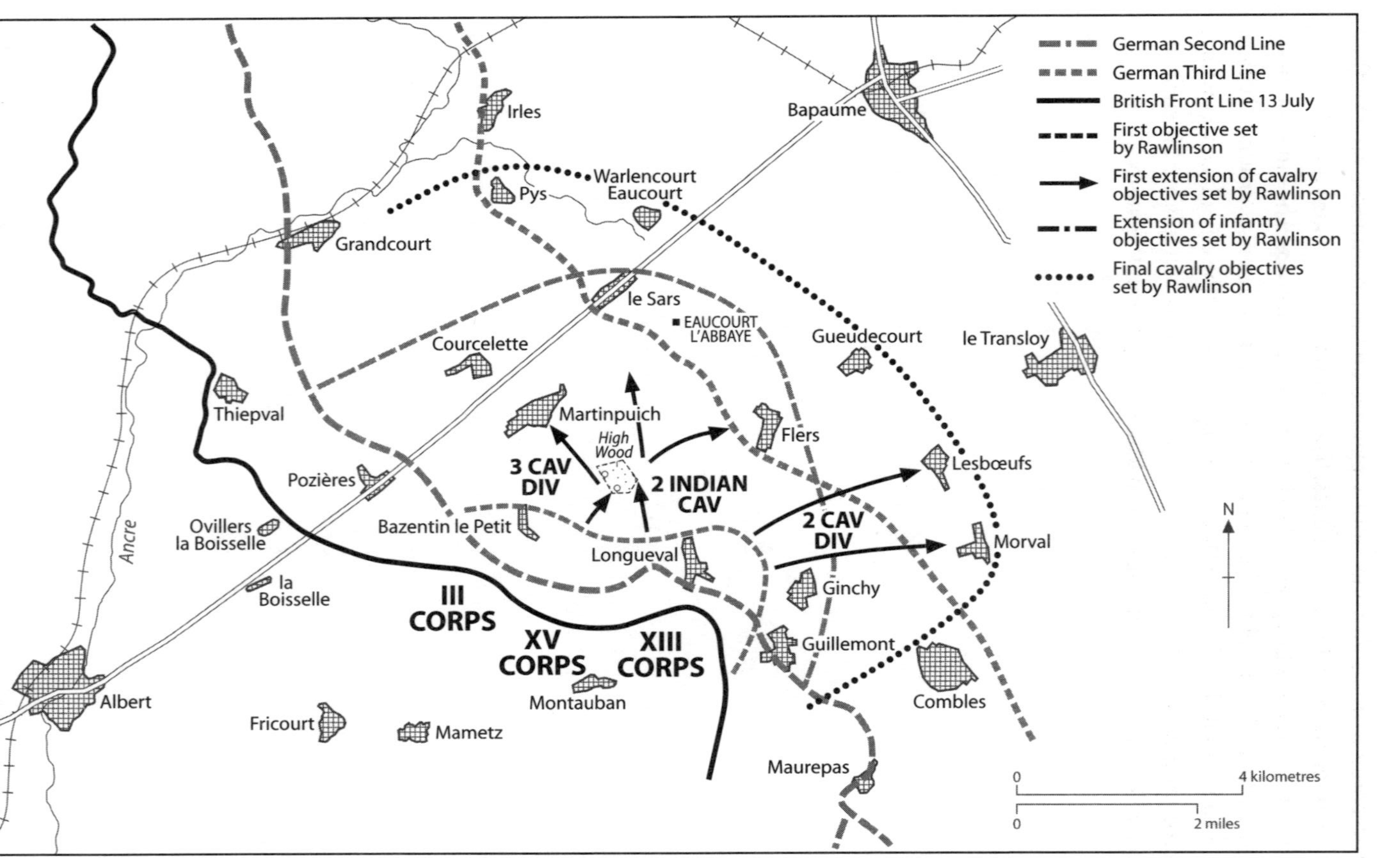
German Second Line
German Third Line
British Front Line 13 July
First objective set by Rawlinson
First extension of cavalry objectives set by Rawlinson
Extension of infantry objectives set by Rawlinson
Final cavalry objectives set by Rawlinson
Irles
Bapaume
Warlencourt
Eaucourt
Pys
Grandcourt
le Sars
EAUCOURT L'ABBAYE
Gueudecourt
le Transloy
Courcelette
Thiepval
Martinpuich
High Wood
Flers
Lesbœufs
3 CAV DIV
2 INDIAN CAV
2 CAV DIV
Pozières
Ovillers la Boisselle
Bazentin le Petit
Longueval
Morval
Ancre
la Boisselle
Ginchy
III CORPS
XV CORPS
XIII CORPS
Guillemont
Albert
Fricourt
Mametz
Montauban
Combles
Maurepas
N
0
4 kilometres
0
2 miles

The Plans, 14 July

# 13 'Cavalry Sharpening Their Swords', 14 July

## I

Preparations for a major new attack by Fourth Army had been under way from the second day of the campaign. On that day Haig had pointed out that if a modest advance in the south could be accomplished, it would open the way for an attack on the German second line from Bazentin-le-Grand to Longueval. If this attack coincided with an assault further south by the French, 'very considerable results could be achieved'.[1] The prerequisites for the operation were that Mametz Wood and Trones Wood should be in British hands to secure the flanks of the new endeavour.[2]

As noted earlier, Rawlinson had briefly considered renewing the attack in the north. But by 4 July he had accepted that this was impractical and was prepared to go along with Haig's scheme. On the 8th he had issued his first operation order for an assault by four divisions on 'the enemy's second line between Longueval and Bazentin-le-Petit Wood'.[3]

On a first reading, Haig seemed quite satisfied with this plan. Nevertheless in one important respect the two commanders were working on different assumptions. Haig thought that before attacking the German second line, Rawlinson would undertake preliminary action which would advance his front to within a few hundred yards of the German second position.[4] Rawlinson considered this impractical along the whole line of his front. The most he could do was to get forward on the flanks. But this would mean that in the centre there would remain a no man's land 1,500 yards wide and entirely devoid of cover – just the kind of scenario which had led to the destruction of III Corps on 1 July. To resolve this problem, Rawlinson was proposing to undertake an operation commencing at night in which the two divisions from XV Corps (3 and 9) to be employed in this area would form up in no man's land in the dark and close on the German front line. As soon as dawn broke these divisions, along with the two from XIII Corps on the right, would attack.[5]

Haig first heard of Rawlinson's plan on the 10th.[6] Initially he made no comment on it.[7] But by the next day he had formed a strongly negative opinion. He now refused to sanction the night attack, informing Rawlinson:

> Our troops are not highly trained and disciplined, nor are many of the staff experienced in such work, and to move two divisions in the dark over such a distance, form them up, and deliver an attack in good order and in the right direction at dawn, as proposed, would hardly be considered possible even in a peace manoeuvre.[8]

Instead, Haig proposed an attack by XV Corps on the left of Rawlinson's proposed operational front, from around Mametz Wood, which would then turn eastwards to roll up the German line around Longueval. If this attack was successful, XIII Corps would then attack Longueval next day. Haig's proposal had little to recommend it. XV Corps' attack was to take place on a narrow front and involved a highly complicated turning manoeuvre. The eastward attack towards Longueval also risked being taken in flank by a German counter-attack from High Wood. Finally, as Congreve (XIII Corps commander) pointed out, Haig was embarking on a two-stage attack which invited defeat in detail.[9]

Presumably most of these arguments were levelled against Haig's plan at a meeting between Rawlinson and his corps commanders (Horne and Congreve) at 2 p.m. on the 11th. Certainly Horne noted that 'some modification of plans [was] suggested'.[10] In any case, as a result of that meeting Rawlinson told Kiggell that the corps commanders were both strongly in favour of the original (Rawlinson) plan. He added that Horne was 'much averse' to attacking without the support of XIII Corps. Kiggell relayed these views to Haig and then spoke to Horne who reiterated his objections to Haig's plan. Haig refused to budge. Rawlinson was instructed to prepare the attack along the lines stipulated by the commander-in-chief.[11]

Rawlinson passed on this message to his corps commanders. But after a further talk with General Montgomery, his Chief of Staff and Horne, he decided to press Haig once more to countenance a night attack.[12]

Haig called a meeting of his own staff on the 12th to discuss what he called Rawlinson's 'amended plan'.[13] (It was in fact the same plan.) Birch, Haig's artillery adviser, who had been in touch with Congreve, assured the Commander-in-Chief that the British could dominate the German guns, and after some discussion Haig agreed that Rawlinson's plan should be tried.[14] He insisted, however, that Rawlinson re-examine his counter-battery programme, that a contingency plan in case of failure be worked out and that, if available, the use of motorised machine-guns be considered. But on the main issue there would be no further discussion: the night attack would take place.

As long as it remained undetected, the attack by night would certainly solve one of the problems that had doomed the attempted advance on 1 July – the crossing of no man's land in full view of the enemy machine-gunners and artillerymen. Preventing detection was therefore a crucial matter. Although many historians appear unaware of the fact, night operations had been attempted already and had not proved successful. They had been detected by alert machine-gunners and had also run into uncut wire. We have already noted the failure of such a night attack by 12 Division on 3 July. The key factors for a successful night attack were stealth and the ability of the artillery to eliminate or suppress sufficient of the German machine-gunners and hostile guns to give the troops a reasonable chance.

With the decision to undertake a night attack in place, other aspects of planning for the new operation could commence. In one respect the process seemed to indicate that the command had absorbed an important lesson from 1 July. If we compare the bombardment on 1 July with that of 14 July we find that – for the length of trench attacked – the new operation would deliver an intensity of shell five times that of the disastrous first day. Yet there was a singular aspect to the new artillery plan: on this occasion all the shell would be concentrated against the German front system, instead of, as previously in any Rawlinson–Haig operation, spreading the fire across all the German defensive systems within range.[15]

One other aspect of the planning for the 14 July operation depressingly paralleled that for 1 July. As the day of battle drew closer the objectives to be aimed for by the Fourth Army were further and further extended. But there was a bizarre difference between the two occasions. In the second instance, it was Rawlinson who kept extending the objectives while Haig tried (unsuccessfully) to rein them in.

Rawlinson's plan began modestly enough. Initially, there was little mention of any objective beyond the line running through the Bazentins to Delville Wood. Some elements of the 2 Indian Cavalry Division were to be on hand to seize High Wood, but that was all.[16] Three days later, however, at a conference with the cavalry commanders, we find Rawlinson – while entering the usual caveats about the cavalry being held back until infantry operations had succeeded – considerably enlarging the cavalry aspect of the plan. The 2 Indian Cavalry Division was not only to seize High Wood but push out patrols to Flers and Le Sars, some two and three miles beyond. Then the 1 Cavalry Division would be sent through to hold Morval and Les Boeufs until relieved by the infantry of XV Corps. Meanwhile, the 3 Cavalry Division would operate towards Martinpuich and Le Sars.[17]

What Rawlinson was trying to accomplish was not merely the capture of the German second line. He was aiming to seize a third line between Le Sars and Morval, which aerial reconnaissance had only just revealed to him.[18] This third line was continuous but the aerial photographs had revealed some gaps in the wire, and anyway Rawlinson did not consider that the Germans had enough troops to hold it in strength.[19] Whether there might be the odd machine gunner or reserve infantry division in the German rear areas over which the cavalry were to roam was not discussed. Nevertheless, the intent of Rawlinson's orders was clear – the objectives of the operation had been extended from the capture of the German second position (a depth of advance of a few hundred yards on a 6,000-yard front) to an advance of roughly four miles on a front of 10,000 yards.

Surprisingly, given his hankering after distant objectives before 1 July, this plan did not find favour with Sir Douglas Haig. At a conference with Rawlinson on the 12th he stated that he

> [did] not consider that large forces of cavalry should be pushed through at once as there would not be sufficient room for their action at first and they might be thrown back and cause confusion. A few squadrons could probably, however, be used in the circumstances without the danger alluded to and probably with good effect.[20]

And just in case Rawlinson had not got the point, later in the day Haig had Kiggell write to Archie Montgomery to repeat his doubts about the cavalry and to make the additional point that 'there would be too much danger of their [the cavalry] coming unexpectedly under heavy fire from the enemy's rallying points'.[21] Kiggell added for good measure that Haig wanted the 3 Cavalry Division withdrawn into reserve.[22]

Nothing followed from this. Far from changing his plan, Rawlinson on the following day (the 12th) issued a new set of orders for the cavalry which gave them precisely the same objectives as he had stipulated before Haig's intervention.[23]

Perhaps as a result of these orders Rawlinson received a visit from Haig on the 13th. Haig noted in his diary:

> I visited Sir H Rawlinson after lunch. I spoke about the use of cavalry. The divisions were not to go forward until we had got through the Enemy's fortifications, except a few squadrons to take "High Wood" … I also stated his objectives as follows:–

(1) Occupy position Longueval–Bazentin-le-Petit, and consolidate it.
(2) Take High Wood, and establish right flank on Ginchy and Guillemont.
(3) At the same time (if possible, as there are ample troops) extend left and take Pozieres ridge and village of Martinpuich.[24]

Only in the last aspect did Haig's instructions induce Rawlinson to modify his plan. He now incorporated III Corps into his operation and instructed them to take Pozières, Courcelette, Martinpuich, and Le Sars as soon as XV Corps had secured the Bazentins. As for the rest, he not only ignored Haig's instructions a second time but incorporated distant objectives into his infantry plan and gave the cavalry yet wider horizons beyond even the third German line. So, if operations succeeded, the infantry would occupy a line through Mouquet Farm to Guillemont (as indicated on the map) while the cavalry would proceed about seven miles further east to the dotted black line.[25] This would entail an infantry advance of about 2–5 miles on a 15,000-yard front, and a cavalry advance of 7–8 miles on a 20,000-yard front. The German second line would have fallen into British hands from Mouquet Farm to Guillemont and sections of it north of Thiepval would have been outflanked; and the third German line would have been captured from Pys to Leuze Wood.

Quite apart from Rawlinson's apparent disregard for his commander's strictures, this was an extraordinary exchange between the two men. In substance it was almost a mirror image of what had passed between them in the planning stage before 1 July. Then Rawlinson's preference had been for a modest operation, while Haig had opted for more distant objectives. Now the reverse was largely the case.

How do we explain this turnabout? Apparently Haig was no longer as optimistic about imminent German collapse as he had been before 1 July and in the aftermath of that day's endeavours. Whereas GHQ had written on 6 July about the enemy's waning morale leading to 'serious demoralisation [which] may set in at any time, possibly tomorrow', Haig only two days later was taking a more sober view. So he wrote to Robertson, the CIGS, that 'much remains to be done' before the Germans were defeated.[26] And three days later he warned Rawlinson that the enemy would rally at their strongpoints behind the front and offer much resistance.

Rawlinson to all appearances was oblivious to these changes in Haig's appreciation. His plans for 14 July seem to be based on the view that once the German front had been breached by the devastating bombardment, no serious resistance was to be anticipated, only a thoroughly demoralised enemy. Hence, he could plan to devote all of his artillery bombardment to the German forward position and yet still anticipate a sustained advance over several miles of unbombarded ground.

This failure of Rawlinson to take note of Haig's increasingly realistic assessments set the scene for a paradoxical operation. In it a strikingly successful first phase resulted from a considerable underestimation of enemy strength. But it led not to further triumphs, only to a restoration of futile operations and deadlock.

This point needs to be stressed, on account of the many occasions when commentators have hailed the plan for 14 July as being a great advance in tactical sophistication over that for 1 July. It must be emphasised that a night attack in itself did not guarantee success (as the failure of 3 July had made clear). And the aspects of the 14 July scheme envisaging wide-ranging exploitation by both cavalry and infantry were in themselves no more soundly based than similar plans before 1 July. Only one facet of Rawlinson's 14 July plan shows any improvement on the first day, namely the execution of a bombardment on the front German system of far greater intensity than anything delivered on 1 July. Here Rawlinson may have revealed a measure of insight, a learning curve perhaps. But two things tell firmly against any such notion. First is the fact that fundamental to the proceedings of 14 July was the delusion that the bombardment would not only overwhelm the German front defences but lead to a decisive collapse in German morale, opening the way for a wide-ranging cavalry sweep. The second is that Rawlinson, in his subsequent operations on the Somme, never again employed a bombardment of the intensity of 14 July against the enemy's foremost defences. In short, Rawlinson's delivery of a devastating bombardment on 14 July was based on delusion, not judgement – the operation was not planned as an example of bite and hold, but as the prelude to a Haig-like cavalry advance.

## II

The German second line had been under attack by the Fourth Army artillery since 11 July.[27] This line was in general much weaker than those sections of the first line captured on 1 July – the dug-outs were not so frequent or formidable and the trenches were not nearly as extensive. The line was well-wired however, with two belts of wire each five yards wide.[28]

In the early hours of 14 July the troops from the four assaulting divisions (from left to right 21 and 7 Divisions from XV Corps and 3 and 9 of XIII Corps) moved into position. For the men of XV Corps this presented no difficulty. The distance between the front lines in their area was small and the remains of

Mametz Wood still offered some cover for the assembling troops. The situation facing XIII Corps was quite different and provided Rawlinson's justification for a night attack. Here the British line was 1,000 to 1,500 yards from the German front position and in between the bare ground sloped gently up to the Bazentin Ridge. So in this area very careful preparations had to be made to get the troops within close proximity to the German line by zero hour (3.25 a.m.).

In the 9 Division this was done by sending forward small parties equipped with Lewis guns to form a screen at the crest of the ridge. Then even smaller parties crept forward to place marker tapes within 500 yards of the German front line. When these were in place the bulk of the assault battalions moved up by companies in single file until they reached the tapes. From there they slowly crawled forward until the enemy line was just 50 yards away.[29] This last phase could be a slow business. The 3 Division, which had moved forward in similar manner to the 9, started creeping forward at 2 a.m., gaining just 20 yards every quarter of an hour, so that by 3.15 a.m. they were 120 yards from the German trenches.[30] In what was a remarkable piece of staff work, these divisions were in place at zero without the Germans being aware that a major attack was imminent.

Despite the crushing intensity of the bombardment – by far the heaviest weight of shell fired by the British so far for the length of trench attacked- its effect varied along the front. On the left, 21 Division found the enemy front line obliterated and the wire well cut. Still, some units suffered heavy casualties from machine-guns in the rear of the German front system which had been left untouched by the artillery.[31]

The 7 Division generally fared better. The men found the trenches completely destroyed, the wire gone, few dug-outs to clear, and resistance slight. By 4 a.m. the German second line and its support trenches were entirely in their hands.[32]

Further right, 3 Division met with varying fortune. Their left brigade had little difficulty with wire or trench-defenders but on the right the 8 Brigade ran into belts of uncut wire and could make no progress. Only when their successful brigade could spare troops to fight along the German front line towards their beleaguered comrades did the situation improve. So in this area it was 1 p.m. before the German front line was finally secured by the British.[33]

On the very right of the attack, 9 Division had an easier time. Both of its attacking brigades stormed through the German positions and within a few minutes had entered the ruins of Longueval and Delville Wood and were approaching Waterlot Farm.[34]

Shortly after zero, therefore, with the exception of the area opposite 8 Brigade, the entire German front system had fallen. This was a considerable achievement, but significant obstacles to further progress lay ahead. In the immediate rear of the German position lay three woods and three villages in which the Germans had constructed defences and which barred the progress of Rawlinson's troops almost all along their front of attack. From left to right these defended localities were Bazentin-le-Petit Wood and village, Bazentin-le-Grand Wood and village, and Longueval and Delville Wood. The widest gap between any of these positions was the 2,000 yards between Bazentin-le-Grand and Longueval but this distance could easily be traversed by machine-guns. And even when these positions fell, High Wood, on the very crest of the ridge and able to dominate approaches from left and right, provided a further barrier. In fact the triangle of ground formed by the Bazentins–Longueval–High Wood could everywhere be covered by hostile machine-gun fire from one of these points or the other.

So by midday Rawlinson's troops had achieved their first objective – the capture of the German second line. But the purpose of the operation was much greater: to overrun in short order the three villages and woods in rear of this second line, and thereby unleash the cavalry towards distant objectives. Had GHQ predictions of collapsing German morale been at all warranted, and had Rawlinson's artillery plan reduced that morale further, then the next phase of the 14 July operation would have been a relatively straightforward matter. But none of it was warranted. German morale did not collapse. The bombardment which was to follow on the first phase proved difficult to arrange and when delivered proved hopelessly inadequate Opportunities for a great cavalry movement never presented themselves (even if the British command in some instances acted as if they had). As a consequence, the attack on 14 July, after such a hopeful beginning, became bogged down into a protracted, costly, and ill-rewarded endeavour. This negative aspect is little remembered.

What after the initial success the British found themselves facing was not the predicted demoralised enemy in precipitate flight, but a succession of heavily defended positions manned by well dug in infantry, lavishly supplied with machine-guns. So for most of the day the attacking forces could at best struggle forward against fierce resistance towards some of their more proximate objectives.[35] In the area of the Bazentins, the woods and villages did not fall into British hands until late afternoon.[36] Further right, only the southern section of Longueval village was captured, along with a small area of Delville Wood.[37] Casualties were heavy, some battalions losing half their number – a scale of loss on a par with that of 1 July.[38]

Prospects for further advance by Rawlinson's infantry were not good. And prospects for cavalry action were plainly non-existent. Nevertheless, there was a growing impression as the day wore on that German resistance in the Longueval area might be collapsing. So some units of the 2nd Indian Cavalry Division were ordered forward. With scant justification, Rawlinson became enthusiastic about their prospects. At 7.35 p.m., he sent to Haig the (surely astonishing) message, 'Indian Cavalry sharpening their swords.'[39] By then, as it happened, the horsed soldiers were already in action. Some squadrons of the Secunderabad Cavalry Brigade charged through the wheatfields between High Wood and Longueval. They immediately ran into machine-gun fire from Delville Wood and High Wood and were struck by an artillery barrage fired from around Flers. Nevertheless, they actually managed to spear sixteen Germans with their lances (certainly one of the strangest episodes in all of the fighting on the Western Front, and sixteen of the unluckiest victims) before being forced to dismount and take up defensive infantry positions.[40] This episode cost them ten men killed and wounded and 138 horses.[41] Thus ended cavalry participation, on which such hopes had been placed, in the 1916 Somme campaign.

The striking opening of the 14 July operation and the meagre achievements which followed have given rise to the notion that 14 July was a day of unfulfilled promise and lost opportunities. So it has been claimed that only tardiness and ill-organisation prevented the cavalry from getting forward in time to accomplish a great success, and that lack of initiative robbed the infantry of the uncontested occupation of High Wood. These views disregard the essential fact of the fighting on that day: that the initial successes of the British did not result in the collapse of German resistance on which the rest of the attack had been predicated. To the rear of their front positions, the Germans maintained an intact defence. So the cavalry would have suffered the fate awaiting the Indian horsemen whenever they attacked. And although an officer, Brigadier-General Potter, managed to walk to the edge of High Wood without encountering German defenders, any attempt by Rawlinson's forces to enter the wood would certainly have found key areas of it occupied.[42] Throughout the day, High Wood was garrisoned by rather more than a battalion of German troops, supported by heavy machine-guns and occupying a strong defensive position (later known as the Switch Line) within the wood.[43] Although it is true that a series of mishaps caused the attack on the wood to be delayed, there is no reason to believe that any earlier action would have been better rewarded.[44]

A summing up is in order.

The capture of the German second line by the Fourth Army was a considerable achievement. It demonstrated that if enough artillery shells could be brought to bear against a discrete objective, that objective could be overcome. The problem was that this accomplishment was only the preliminary stage of what Rawlinson had set out to achieve. His other aims had nothing to do with firing great quantities of shells at a limited objective. They envisaged an advance over a vast area – beyond the range of even the heaviest guns – an advance to be made by foot soldiers and the cavalry. None of this made sense in terms of what had been accomplished in the opening stage of 14 July. He had proved that weight of artillery could secure for his army the enemy front position. He had definitely not proved that anything more grandiose was on offer.

Rawlinson at least managed to identify the source of his limited success. After the battle he noted:

> There is no doubt that the success of the enterprise must be attributed in a very large measure to the accuracy and volume of the artillery bombardment. The enemy's wire, as well as his front and second line trenches were smashed to pieces. The morale of the defenders had been greatly reduced by the din and concussion of the constant explosions, and it was clear from the number of dead that were found in the trenches that he had likewise suffered heavy casualties from the artillery bombardment.[45]

What this passage fails to acknowledge is that the 'enterprise' of whose success he wrote was something quite different from that on which he had embarked. This remark is not intended to reflect on Rawlinson's failure to capture his larger objectives or on the inability of his infantry to advance into areas which had not been assailed by a devastating bombardment. Nor does it amount to a reflection on the inability of the cavalry (whatever the condition of their swords) to make any progress whatever.

The flaw in this analysis was to be an enduring feature of all British battle-analyses on the Somme – that is, in making the most of what had been achieved, the command failed to analyse the reasons why these achievements fell short of their original intentions. This proceeding might have provided Rawlinson and Haig with some comfort but it denied them the chance to learn from their mistakes. At this rate any learning curve would be very flat indeed.

# 14 'We Are a Bit Stuck', 15–31 July

## I

The atmosphere at Rawlinson's headquarters on 15 July was euphoric. In fourteen days the German first and second lines had been captured, admittedly at brutal cost, on a front of 6,000 yards. The units of the German Second Army defending the area had, in some cases, been wiped out, and in others been reduced to a chaotic shambles as they were thrown in piecemeal in an attempt to stabilise the line. Moreover, from just south of Pozières on the left to Delville Wood on the right, Haig's armies were within a short distance of the heights of the Thiepval–Ginchy ridge, a position which dominated the high ground behind the German front line for some miles.

Yet this optimism did not last 24 hours. Next day Rawlinson noted in his diary that things 'had not gone well'.[1] While XIII Corps had gained a little ground, the XV had been repulsed at the Switch Line and III Corps had been driven back from the outskirts of Pozières. His conclusion was that the enemy had evidently brought up fresh troops and were fighting better. In addition there was news that further German reserves had arrived at Bapaume and therefore could be expected on the battlefield at any moment.[2]

The trouble was this. The Germans were not only recovering from 14 July, but the British successes on that day had left Rawlinson's force in an awkward tactical situation. The German positions they now faced were divided into two distinct sections by a right angle at Delville Wood. To the left of this position the front faced north; to the right it faced east. So an advance along the whole front would result in the attacking forces diverging from each other the further they progressed. And operations around Delville Wood would be faced with German artillery concentrations from three sides,

The British tactical difficulties did not cease there. Pozières, the high ground around Mouquet Farm and High Wood, Longueval, Delville Wood and the

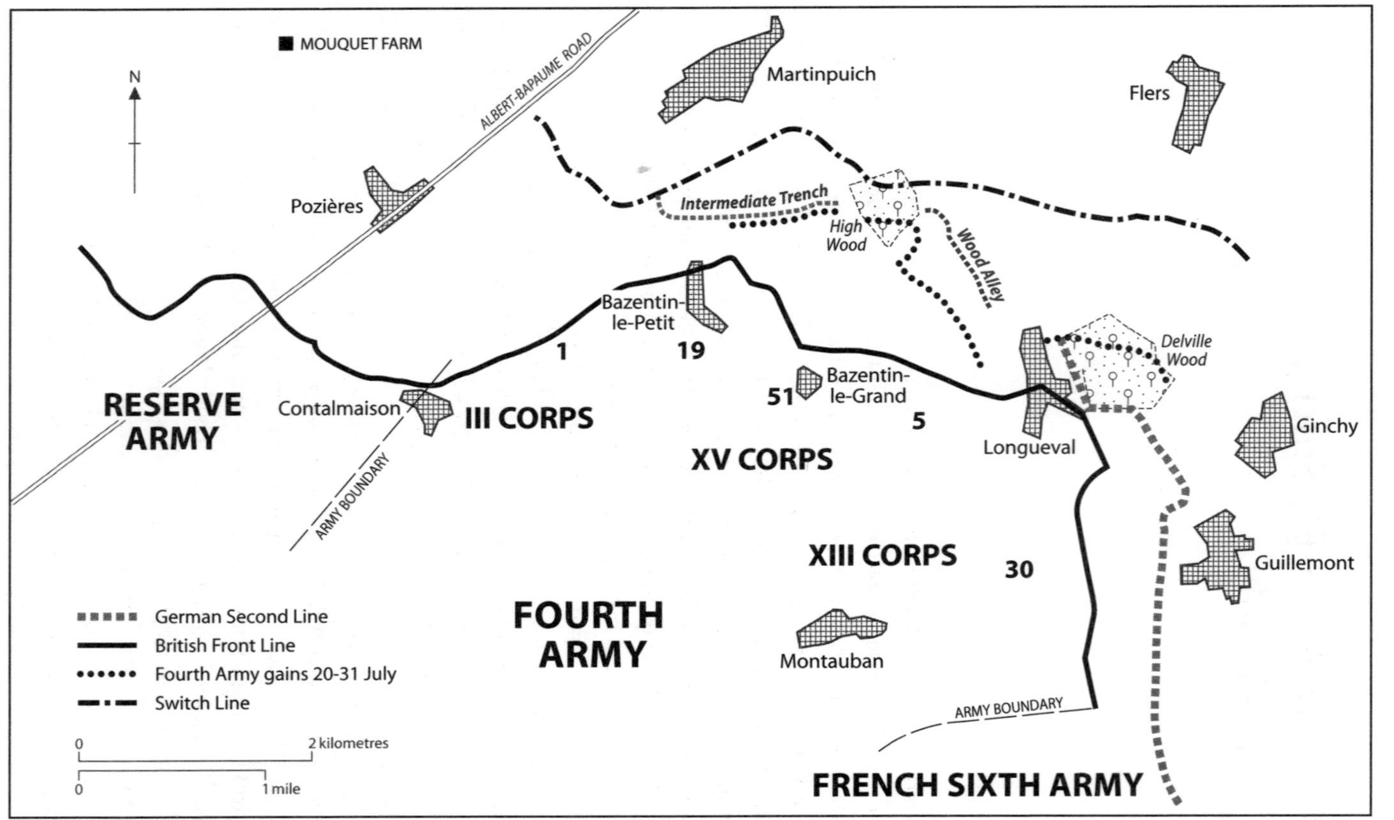

MOUQUET FARM
N
ALBERT-BAPAUME ROAD
Pozières
Martinpuich
Flers
Intermediate Trench
High Wood
Wood Alley
Bazentin-le-Petit
1
19
Bazentin-le-Grand
51
5
Delville Wood
Longueval
Ginchy
RESERVE ARMY
Contalmaison
III CORPS
XV CORPS
ARMY BOUNDARY
XIII CORPS
30
Guillemont
German Second Line
British Front Line
Fourth Army gains 20-31 July
Switch Line
FOURTH ARMY
Montauban
ARMY BOUNDARY
0
2 kilometres
0
1 mile
FRENCH SIXTH ARMY


15–31 July

second German line to its south remained to be captured. Each of these positions was a formidable obstacle in its own right; in combination they presented great challenges to the British command.

All this led Rawlinson to call a conference with his corps commanders on the 16th. He told them that because of enemy resistance 'the time for isolated attacks had now finished and an organised attack on a broad front was now necessary'.[3] There was much wisdom in this. As the British had already experienced between 2 and 13 July, narrow-front attacks against individual woods and villages could be subjected to murderous flanking fire. This method of attack enabled the enemy to concentrate great amounts of artillery fire against relatively small targets. A broader front attack would deprive them of both these advantages. Yet even a broad-front attack would need careful thought because the awkward nature of the front might mean that a success would see British troops diverging from each other on either side of the Delville Wood right angle.

In the event the organisation of any broad-front attack, well thought-out or ill, proved beyond Rawlinson. Three factors told against him. In the first instance he had set an overly optimistic timetable. He told his commanders that the new attack must begin within 24 hours – that is on 17 July. Later he conceded that the 18th was more propitious.[4] In fact both dates were impracticable. They gave a quite inadequate amount of time in which to distribute orders, and to organise a thoroughly planned, intense artillery bombardment.

The second factor was the weather. The 16th was dull and overcast. So was the 17th and, as it happened, the 18th and 19th.[5] This made aerial spotting for the artillery extremely difficult in circumstances where such observation was vital because some sections of the German line (from the east of Pozières to Delville Wood) were on a reverse slope and therefore out of direct sight of British forward observers in their own front line.

The third factor was the matter of co-ordination with the French. Rawlinson first mooted a combined operation with the French VI Army for the 18th. This seemed propitious because Foch had indicated that he would be launching a large-scale attack to the north and south of the Somme River on that date.[6] Then Foch postponed the French attack because of the weather. As the British also were not ready, the combined operation was amicably moved to the 20th.[7] But on the 19th an embarrassed Rawlinson had to admit to the French that his own preparations would not now be completed until the 22nd.[8] So the French, impatient with what they saw as unreasonable British delay, attacked alone on the 20th. Their operation did not prosper, whereupon Foch proposed to the British a joint attack on the 23rd confined to the area north of the Somme. This date was accepted by Rawlinson, only for him to find on the 22nd that

Balfourier, the French Corps Commander adjacent to them, would not be ready until the 24th.[9] This time the British lost patience. Rawlinson announced he would attack alone on the 23rd. Even this did not quite settle the matter. At the last moment and under pressure from Foch, Balfourier agreed to allow a small force on the right flank of the British to take part in the attack.

It might be thought that this enforced delay would have given the Fourth Army staff time to develop a measured response to the difficult tactical situation in which their forces were now placed. This was not the case. The front of attack would extend from just east of Pozières to Guillemont. If it succeeded all along the front, the right angle would merely have been moved to another location, or (more dangerously) the attacks to the left and right of the angle would diverge. In the latter case a gap might be created through which a strong German counter-attack might roll up their entire position.

What meanwhile was occurring on the front of the Fourth Army during the interval between 15 July when Rawlinson conceived his night attack and 23 July when he carried it out? Having acknowledged in his diary on the 15th and to his Corps Commanders on the 16th that the time for isolated attacks was now over, did Rawlinson maintain a quiescent front and rest his troops for the coming battle? Puzzlingly, he did not. The incessant attacks which Rawlinson had ordered in the flush of victory on 14 July proceeded as if his rethink on the 15th had never occurred. Between the 15th and the 22nd, *in quite separate operations*, XIII Corps attacked in the Longueval–Delville Wood sector on six occasions and against Guillemont once, XV Corps carried out two attacks against High Wood, and III Corps attacked to the east of Pozières five times. Hardly any of these operations gained more than derisory amounts of ground. Yet they were not cheap. Rather than chronicle each of these blighted, futile operations, let us turn our attention to just one set, those around Longueval and Delville Wood.

This was the most difficult part of the front, the very apex of the right angle. Here it was essential that German forces and batteries to left and right be distracted by simultaneous attacks so they could not bring murderous fire on the attacking troops from three directions. Yet on most occasions, no such supporting operations were mounted. This meant that even when some progress was made, as it was by the South African Brigade on the 15th, retention of the captured ground proved impossible. Great groups of German batteries on the three sides of the wood poured a deluge of shells into the newly won areas, followed by German counter-attacks (delivered by fresh troops) which forced the South Africans back to their original positions.[10]

Between 18 and 23 July repeated attempts were made to capture the wood and village. Troops from four divisions were consumed in these attacks. Yet these operations were not taking place in defiance of the wishes of the command. On the same day that Congreve, who had been present at Rawlinson's conference of corps commanders, heard his chief announce that the time for isolated attacks was now over, he received instructions from Fourth Army headquarters ordering him to capture Delville Wood at all costs and without delay.[11] In other words, isolated attacks were being ordered by the same commander who earlier had announced that they should cease.

Haig contributed nothing meaningful in this period. To start with he seemed to favour operations against Delville Wood, on the grounds that it commanded the German line around Guillemont to the south. Then he changed his mind and decided that operations against Guillemont could proceed without the capture of Delville Wood. After that he then instructed Rawlinson to broaden his front and include High Wood in any future attacks.[12] In the end nothing of this signified. Rawlinson continued to blast away at Delville Wood and Guillemont and High Wood as though Haig had never spoken.

The lower-order commanders who participated in these operations were quite aware of the futility of their endeavours. General Higginson's 53 Brigade (18 Division) suffered severely in Delville Wood on 17 July and he wrote a bitter report in which he compared this operation unfavourably with his brigade's successful operation on 1 July. The attack on the first day of campaigning, he noted, was characterised by: careful attention to all details of the attack; artillery preparation and wire-cutting; and co-operation of the artillery with the infantry in the attack. The latter operation, by contrast, was characterised by: insufficient time for careful consideration of plans; insufficient time for artillery preparation; difficulty of communication with battalions; lack of co-operation between artillery and infantry; difficulty of obtaining accurate information about the situation; intense hostile artillery bombardment and machine-gun fire; lack of co-operation with neighbouring units; and (perhaps most damningly) the fact that the attack was not launched until 45 minutes *after* the artillery bombardment had ceased.[13]

Eighteen years later Higginson's indignation is still manifest in a letter he wrote to Edmonds complaining about the description of this attack in the draft Official History:

> The account ... does not bring out a very important point, namely that this attack was carried out at such short notice that no previous reconnaissance or adequate preparations were possible and there was no time to arrange any effective fire plan. When it received orders to move the Bde was in bivouac at Talus Bois and was not expecting to be engaged immediately. In my opinion

> this attack demonstrated the futility of such hastily considered and ill-prepared attacks. At the time I thought that XIII Corps made a grave mistake in not allowing sufficient time for its preparation and I am even more firmly of that opinion today .... I notice that the Official History does not comment on the wisdom or otherwise of attacks such as this .... The failure of these attacks was not due to lack of determination on the part of the troops: the units of the 53rd Bde were in great form after their successes of the 1st July and their moral[e] was high ... I know it is extremely difficult in an account of operations of so great magnitude ... to give more than a bare outline ... but if you can bring to light the hasty nature of the attack I will feel that the official account does justice to my old Brigade.[14]

It seems certain that Higginson would have been disappointed with Edmonds' efforts. While mentioning that the brigade was brought forward 'hurriedly' and 'with no time for reconnaissance' the Official History gives no prominence to the botched preparations either for this attack or for the countless others made in this period of the Somme fighting. Neither Higginson nor his brigade got their due.[15]

## II

Final orders for Rawlinson's much-postponed and tactically dubious broad-front attack were issued on 21 July. At the strong urging of Haig, but with Rawlinson's full agreement, it was decided once more to employ the ruse of a night attack.[16] Six divisions in all were to be employed – from left to right, 1, 19, 51, 5, 3, 30. The main part of the attack was to commence at 1.30 a.m. on 23 July. On the right, however, the joint action with the small French component would be at an hour which suited the respective corps commanders, Congreve and Fayolle. For reasons that are not at all clear they decided on 3.40 a.m., 2 hours and ten minutes after the main attack.

The preliminary bombardment began at 7 p.m. on 22 July. Only hours earlier the Fourth Army commander had learned of two disturbing developments. First, at 2 p.m. he was told that the token contribution of the French would not now be ready until some time on the 24th. Given the insignificant nature of French support, Rawlinson was not prepared to alter his main start time. But he did not bring the zero hour for Congreve's XIII Corps into line with his major attack, even though its later hour had no justification except co-operation with the French.[17] So 3 and 30 Divisions were, in short order, divorced from the main attack.

Then, aerial reconnaissance revealed a newly dug trench (later called Intermediate Trench) across the line of advance of the 19 and 51 Divisions. Rawlinson therefore determined that these divisions would attack this objective at 12.30 a.m. and then proceed to attack their main objective, the Switch Line, at 1.30 a.m.[18]

In fact Rawlinson should already have been alerted to this. On the 21st the new trench was discovered by patrols of 19 Division but their reports were not passed on to Fourth Army headquarters by the divisional command.[19]

So now only 1 and 5 Divisions were to adhere to the original 1.30 a.m. zero hour, 19 and 51 were to go forward at 12.30 a.m., and 3 and 30 at 3.40 a.m.

The proliferation of start times, however, did not end there: 5 Division also found itself confronting a new German trench line (Wood Lane) between it and its main objective (the Switch Line). It was therefore decided by the divisional command, apparently without reference to the corps or army commanders, that Wood Lane would also be captured in a preliminary operation.[20] For reasons that are obscure, this attack would commence not at 12.30 a.m. as for the division on its left, but at 10 p.m. the previous night. And to further compound the obscurity, it was decided that the amended start time would only apply to the left of this division. The other brigade would conform to the start times of the divisions to its right (3 and 30), that is 3.40 a.m.[21]

Failures of communication, and unilateral actions by divisional commanders, occasioned yet further variety in the start times of this operation. On the left flank of the attack 1 Division had been told by the Australians in the Reserve Army that they intended to assault Pozières at 12.30 a.m. As 1 Division's advance would take them just to the right of this village they decided to conform to the Australians' start time instead of 1.30 a.m., as ordered by Rawlinson.

This brought about a bizarre situation. Not one of the Fourth Army divisions was now adhering to the initial start time of 1.30 a.m. On the right the 30, 3, and half of 5 Division would go over at 3.40 a.m., the other half of 5 Division would already have attacked at 10 p.m. the previous night, while on the left the 1, 19, and 51 Divisions would attack at 12.30 a.m., although the synchronicity obtained by 1 Division was accidental.

However, by another mischance one division *would* move to the attack at 1.30 a.m. Neither Fourth Army headquarters nor 19 Division had informed 51 Division of the discovery of Intermediate Trench or of the new start time of 12.30 a.m. The 51 Division therefore would advance at 1.30 a.m. as planned, but against an objective of which it was not aware and deprived of support on either flank.

What we are observing is a process by which an operation intended as a 'concerted' major attack degenerated into a series of distinct and uncoordinated minor attacks. All told, the attacking divisions of the Fourth Army had not one but four separate zero hours: 10 p.m. on the 22nd, 12.30 a.m., 1.30 a.m., and 3.40 a.m. on the 23rd. There was no reason to doubt that the first of these attacks would alert the whole German line and so eliminate any possible element of surprise from the assault. Clearly this was reason enough either to rethink the entire operation or anyway to delay it until its various elements could be synchronised – with the additional prospect that the French might also participate. Yet nothing of the kind happened. Rawlinson's 'concerted' attack proceeded in a palpably uncoordinated fashion.

Nor were the shortcomings in the planning of the attack confined to the matter of timing. In most respects the artillery preparations compare very unfavourably with those of 14 July. On that occasion, it has to be said, the task of the artillery had been relatively simple. Its task for the 23 July operation was anything but simple. On the left flank and in the area of Wood Lane the British divisions were attempting to advance into areas where fire could be directed against them from three sides: straight ahead and on both flanks. These flanking positions were so proximate to the forces attempting to advance that it was difficult for the British gunners to engage them without placing their own troops at risk.

The British artillerymen had a further problem. Intermediate Trench, the Switch Line, and Wood Lane were all concealed behind a reverse slope. The gunners therefore had to rely on aerial observation to ensure accurate registration and this could only occur in fine weather. In the days before the attack the weather was rainy and overcast. Moreover, on the right where there were areas of the German line which could be directly observed by the British, the defences being attacked were part of the old German second line and therefore lavishly supplied with deep dug-outs which could often resist all but a direct hit.

Furthermore, as noted, the bombardment only commenced on the evening of the 22nd. This gave the British artillerymen just a few hours of daylight in which to subdue the enemy defences. This may be compared to the three days allowed for the bombardment which proceeded the attack on 14 July.

Given all these adverse factors, it can hardly be deemed remarkable that the operation of 22/23 July failed dismally. Quite apart from Rawlinson's decision to send different units forward at a succession of times, there was no reason for the Germans – given their experiences of 14 July – to be taken by surprise by a night attack. And the inadequacy of the bombardment in most sectors left the enemy's trenches and their occupants intact. Consequently even the first of the attacking divisions, the left of the 5, which went forward at 10 p.m. on the 22nd, found itself up against an enemy alert and unimpaired. These defenders poured a hail of fire into the advancing British. On the left just fifty men from an assaulting battalion entered the enemy's front trench; on the right none got within bombing distance. Faced, as one of the war diaries comments indignantly, 'with an impossible situation', all further attacks were cancelled. By 2 a.m. all the survivors had retired to their own line.[22]

The next set of divisions to attack were the 1 and 19, two and a half hours later at 12.30 a.m. Even before it had managed to deploy, 1 Division was immediately deluged by shells, machine-gun fire, and rifle bullets from directly ahead and then, as a result of the failure of the British artillery to engage positions in such proximity to its own troops – from the flanks as well. They retired to their own line but were ordered forward again at 1.20 a.m., with similar results. At the end of the day there was nothing to show for over 1,000 casualties.[23]

The 19 Division on the right of this débâcle fared no better. They too were heavily shelled and machine-gunned as they left their trenches and were back in their own front line by 4 a.m.[24]

Further right, and still unaware of the existence of Intermediate Trench, 51 Division attacked an hour later. They first suffered flanking fire from the unexpected obstacle and then ran into the fire from the unscathed and alerted defenders of High Wood. Any survivors were then confronted by uncut wire and lost their way in the tangled ruins of the wood. They failed even to come within hailing distance of the Switch Line.[25]

The defenders of High Wood had of course been alerted by the left brigade of 5 Division which had attacked two and a half hours earlier. The battalions here were met by withering fire from Wood Lane and were soon back in their own trenches.

To the right of Wood Lane, and 5 hours and 40 minutes after the attack had commenced, the last of the strangely staggered attacks began their advance. Around Longueval and Delville Wood the attack was an immediate failure. In the maze of Delville Wood events bordered on the farcical. First, notwithstanding the delayed start time, the orders for the attack only arrived just before zero hour. Then it was discovered that just one operational map of the area was available. During the approach march in dim light troops soon became lost in the maze of trenches and shattered trees that by this time constituted the remains of the wood. Soon the attack disintegrated, with small groups stumbling around the tree trunks in the dark. The German defenders, untouched by the bombardment, had little difficulty in stopping the attack with machine-gun fire alone. Not a yard of ground was gained.[26]

On the far right of the Fourth Army's operations the 30 Division failed in its attack against Guillemont but for rather different reasons. These need to be noted because they were to have important implications for subsequent operations in the Somme campaign. In the sector around Guillemont the British artillery had good observation over the German defences. Consequently their bombardment wrought great damage on the German trench lines.[27]

However, in this particular area it no longer proved sufficient to target just the enemy line. For, in response to previous well-directed British bombardments the German machine-gunners had changed their tactics. Rather than remain in trench lines which were inevitably subjected to bombardment they had redeployed in shell holes, well clear of their trenches. As G. C. Wynne points out, this development converted a series of trenches into a 'zone or defended area, within which the front units moved as the situation demanded'. This change in German tactics meant that the British artillery now had 'no known and easily located trench line' on which to direct their fire. Instead they 'had to batter down a whole area of ground, using an immense quantity of ammunition' to ensure the destruction of the German defenders.[28] The amount of ammunition required and the guns to fire it were not available to the British at this stage of the battle.

So when Guillemont was assaulted, the British initially made good progress against the thinned-out German defence. Troops soon entered the village and penetrated to its far side. It was at this point that the machine-guns in shell holes on the flanks of the attack opened up. Many troops were prevented by the hail of bullets from pulling back and a company of the 19 Manchesters was never seen again. Soon those troops who could withdraw were back in their own lines. It is clear from their accounts that they had little idea of the cause of either their sudden success or their ultimate failure.[29]

On the morning of the 23rd both Haig and Rawlinson recorded the failure of the previous night's attack in meticulous detail.[30] Neither pondered the inappropriate nature of the disjointed start times but Rawlinson at least reflected on the paucity of artillery support. In a subsequent attempt to capture Delville Wood and Longueval he ensured that he had the guns to give his troops a decent chance of success. And on this occasion the attack was not to go in until there had been 24 hours of fine weather to allow the aerial spotters to give accurate directions to the guns.[31]

To carry out this attack a fresh division (2) was introduced into the line and an enormous amount of artillery assembled. The troops would be supported by the entire artillery of XV and XIII Corps, the 35 Divisional artillery, the guns of the French XX Corps, with some assistance provided by the largest-calibre guns of III Corps.[32] In all, 368 guns were to support the attack of a single division.[33]

The attack went in on 27 July after a furious bombardment during which 125,000 shells weighing 4.5 million pounds were fired.[34] Nothing in the wood and village could survive this storm. The troops pressed forward and within two hours had occupied most of the formidable objectives which had previously defied two weeks of assault.[35]

Many German attempts to drive the British from their newly won positions failed and for a time Rawlinson's troops were in sure possession of Longueval and Delville Wood. Nevertheless, their line was still most awkwardly placed. In truth, what the fighting from 15 to 29 July in this area had accomplished was to move forward the sharp angle of the British line from the near side of Delville Wood to the far.

# III

During this period of the Somme fighting a corps commander was sending home his thoughts on the battle in daily letters to his wife. General Horne, commander of XV Corps which was opposite High Wood and Wood Lane, had, in Somme terms, experienced a reasonable battle. His corps had gained ground on the generally disastrous first day, gone on to capture Mametz Wood, and then taken the second German line on 14 July. Now he found himself unable to make any progress at all. In his letters he reflected on his difficulties. His reflections are a combination of insight and obtuseness but they also reveal a distressing inability to translate any of his insights into action or to impress them upon his chiefs. The extracts from Horne's letters are best read as a block and then subjected to analysis.

> *16 July:* Yesterday I failed to make any progress as the German has [recovered? ] & I could not get on with-out a regular artillery preparation. I [drew?] my men back from High Wood where they were being too much exposed in order that I might be able to shell it. I thought that we had got the whole of it, but we only had half of it & it is so placed on a slope that the Hun's artillery can see into it and we cannot. The clouds are low ... which makes it difficult for aeroplanes to see well to direct our artillery on to the Hun trenches. He has succeeded in digging a line in front of us [the Switch Line] ... and we can only get the guns put on by aeroplane.

> *17 July:* The weather is sadly against us thick heavy weather with occasional drizzle, this is all in favour of the Hun, as we cannot get full use out of our aeroplanes.

*18 July:* Not fighting today .... There must be pauses in a great battle in order to arrange matters, as you can imagine.

*19 July:* The last few overcast days have prevented our air work, and the Hun has been able to place guns and bring up troops out of sight.

*20 July:* I attacked High Wood again this morning and we got in all right, but there is a great deal of confusion there now ... once we get to close quarters it is difficult to assist with the guns because the gunners cannot tell where our men are.

*21 July:* We got the whole of High Wood yesterday by evening time ... but about 11.30 I was woken up to [the news?] that the Hun had shelled it very heavily & counter-attacked and that we had lost the wood! I could not know whether we had lost the whole or only part so I could not get the guns on & had to wait until morning when I found that we were still holding a portion of it .... The Huns have fallen back to ... very cleverly sited positions where it is not possible or at any rate easy to get observed artillery fire & the approaches are very open .... However we must press on & see what we can do.

*22 July:* We had a nice bright day yesterday and our aeroplanes were able to do some work, but today it is overcast & dull again and I particularly wanted it to be bright for we are going for High Wood again tonight. We are in possession of half of it, but we want the rest badly. The German has brought up much more artillery during the last few days. I hope anyway to be able to make a good job of our next attempt, but it is very difficult and I am not ... too certain. However it is [not?] any good fretting. 'Do the best you can and trust in God' is the best way, I think.

*23 July:* The weather here is dry but overcast all day ... annoying as I cannot get full value out of the aeroplanes – it leaves us in the dark as to what the Hun is doing. Today has been dull & overcast all day. We have got a portion of High Wood but not all of it, and as things are now it is very difficult to get on any further. I puzzle my brains how to do it. We attacked again last night but it was not successful – The Hun has been reinforced to a certain degree and has a strong position.

*24 July:* Only one bright day for a long time. It handicaps me because we cannot get the use out of our aeroplanes. Still fighting away but nothing very violent at the moment.... I do not want to give up pressing the Germans as hard as I can. The longer we can go on doing that the better.

*25 July:* All goes well – The Germans counterattacked last evening but in a very half hearted way & did not press home. I do not think they could face the heavy artillery fire we put on them. They have brought up a good deal more artillery themselves and the shelling is much heavier. I hate seeing the German shells falling amongst our batteries … but the continuous overcast sky & ground haze prevents our aeroplanes from directing our fire on to the German batteries. A couple of clear days would allow us to make a great difference.

*26 July:* I have not got the whole of High Wood yet. I had another try for a corner of it last evening but it did not come off. We are a bit stuck here. The overcast weather has been favourable to the Germans. We have not had a clear day for a long time. Today is very thick again.... The German artillery has much increased and the thick weather prevents us dealing with it by aeroplane observation. The German digs away like a mole & his trenches are getting much stronger .... We keep pressing away and some progress has been made at Pozières. We cannot expect to keep on going the pace we did at first.[36]

These letters are a curious mixture. Horne is quick to appreciate that the Germans have recovered from the disorganisation of early July, that their new positions are strong, that the reverse slope on which they are situated has made aerial direction of his guns a crucial factor, that no such direction can be obtained in overcast weather, that some days of bright weather are required to get full value out of the air observation, and that a pause might be essential in the battle until this happy event occurs. At the same time he is hammering away at High Wood almost daily despite the adverse factors which are thwarting his efforts. His only comment is that this constant 'pressing' is essential and that he must do the best he can and trust in God. In other words his considerable tactical insights make not a jot of difference to the way in which he is conducting the battle. He is, in truth, the corps equivalent of Rawlinson and Haig. Of course it may have been that orders from above required the constant, futile attacks which he was undertaking. Yet there is not the slightest sign in his letters that he is under such pressure or that left to his own devices he would be doing things differently.

## IV

While Horne was cogitating on his difficulties with High Wood and the operation at Delville Wood was being planned and executed, the British command was deciding on what to do next. Haig seemed reasonably certain of the way forward. On the 23rd he told Rawlinson that he should consolidate his left and concentrate on his right to try to capture Guillemont in co-operation with the French.[37] There was much wisdom in this. Quite apart from the fractured start times which blighted the 23 July operation, Rawlinson's plan had made little tactical sense anyway. For if any advance had been accomplished, his rightward and leftward troops would have diverged. By concentrating on the right he would straighten out the angle around Delville Wood, which would make that position easier to hold and the planning of future operations more straightforward.

But as so often with Haig, he then went on to muddy the waters. As if unaware of what he had just written, he told Rawlinson that 'We must press the enemy in the way we have been doing' and that there must be no 'delay to organise a great attack which will take time to prepare'.[38]

This made the overall intent of Haig's instructions quite obscure. Was the Fourth Army commander to concentrate on operations with the French, which would certainly take time to co-ordinate, thus negating one of Haig's imperatives: that there be no delay while great attacks were organised? Or was Rawlinson to continue to operate in the way he had been doing – which rather begged the question of what that was. It might be the large-scale broad-front attacks of 14 and 22/23 July. Or it might be the narrow-front attacks which characterised the intervals between them. What Haig's later statement would certainly not do was to confine operations to the right. Attacks were going on across the entire front, be they small or large in scale.

Rawlinson's interpretation of the Commander-in-Chief's views needs to be noted. He seems to have endeavoured to meet all of Haig's wishes. So he engaged in whatever joint actions could be arranged in short order with the French, but at the same time he delivered a handful of tiny operations designed to gain ground on the left. The latter certainly ran counter to one of his chief's wishes (concentrate on the right) but no doubt seemed to Rawlinson to be in accordance with another ('to press the enemy in the way we have been doing').

The largest operation in the period following the débâcle of 22/23 July was certainly on the right flank in co-operation with the French. Its main target was Guillemont, which had been captured briefly by the British before the flanking machine-guns drove them out. The threat to this operation posed by the new tactics employed by the enemy machine-gunners remained unrecognised by the British command, with the result that they merely repeated on the 30th their mistakes of a week before. That is, the British troops advanced into Guillemont, assisted on this occasion by heavy mist, and were driven out by flanking machine-gun fire when the mist lifted. The cost was high. In one leading unit (2 Royal Scots Fusiliers), of the 770 officers and men who went in just 120 returned.[39]

Of the other operations on the left carried out on the 30th little need be said. A few battalions went forward against Intermediate Trench and High Wood with a general lack of success, except in one singular instance. A section of Intermediate Trench was captured by a unit advancing close behind a creeping barrage.[40] Although of no great significance in the day's operations, the artillery aspect of this small success deserves attention.

As early as 16 July GHQ had issued an instruction regarding the creeping barrage. It enjoined all units to adopt it, noting:

> It is ... of the first importance that in all cases infantry should be instructed to advance right under the field artillery barrage, which should not uncover the first objective until the infantry are close to it (even within fifty or sixty yards.[41]

Yet it is clear from the barrage maps that even on 30 July most units did not adopt the creeping barrage. Why was this? Perhaps the answer can be found in the comments of a 35 Division artilleryman whose guns were supporting the 30 Division that day. He noted that the French on his right were using a creeping barrage which he contrasted favourably with the jumping barrage used in the British area. Although relatively new to the front, this gunner appreciated the advantages of this form of infantry protection.

> I favour the creeping method .... The bursts on percussion act as a guide to the advancing Infantry and the depth of the barrage screens them and ... may enable the infantry to get so close up to the hostile line that the final assault interval under rifle and machine gun fire is reduced to a minimum.[42]

However, he went on, 'the limitations to our own equipment at the moment, namely worn guns and difficulties in ammunition supply', prevented the British from adopting the creeping barrage.[43]

This perceptive comment draws attention to an important fact. Haig's insistence on large-scale attacks in the immediate future was simply not appropriate. GHQ was pressing for the artillery to fire the creeping barrage, yet for the moment Haig's army did not possess the unworn guns or quantities of ammunition (or, it may be speculated, the required expertise on the part of many of the gunners) to fire the sort of barrage which alone might fulfil his purpose. The imperative was therefore to call a halt to all but the smallest probing operations or trench raids until the artillery position improved. But Haig had a different imperative, namely to attack and keep on attacking without regard to whether the infantry could be adequately protected. In the next few weeks the British soldiers would pay a high price for this orientation.

The two weeks between the success of the night attack and the failure at Guillemont is a curious episode in the Battle of the Somme. What seems clear is that the British command could not decide on the best way of proceeding. Would they conduct wide-front attacks and pay the price of delay while these operations were prepared? Or would they perpetuate the disjointed attacks which characterised the period between 2 and 13 July? Or would they hold on the left and eliminate the awkward angle around Delville Wood by advancing arm in arm with the French on the right? In the end they attempted all of these things and consequently failed everywhere.

What the command never grasped was that it was facing a different situation both from that prevailing between 2 and 13 July and from that on 14 July. The small, high-cost, bludgeoning attacks of the first period would no longer gain ground, because the German defence had recovered from the shock inflicted upon it in the south on 1 July. The Germans were now well organised into their divisional units and able to offer a coherent and stubborn defence. Moreover, many of the localities they were defending, such as the Switch Line and Wood Lane, were – unlike the objectives attacked in the first two weeks of July – out of direct British artillery observation. And on account of generally poor weather, the British could not use their aerial superiority. Nor, because of the wear on the guns, could creeping barrages be fired across a wide front or the heavy artillery maintain the accuracy needed to hit the German defences with any reliability.

Finally, the British command had not yet grasped the import of the change in German machine-gun tactics around Guillemont and did not realise that they lacked the artillery resources to deal with them. All of this added up to a complete inability of the command to cope with the situation which confronted their soldiers. The auguries for August did not look promising on the Somme.

# 15 'Something Wanting in the Methods Employed', 1 August–12 September

## I

In the last two weeks of July British operations on the Somme failed comprehensively, save for the precarious hold on Delville Wood. Even Haig's optimism was momentarily dented by this period of non-achievement. So on 2 August he responded with a long memorandum designed to give direction to the future conduct of the battle.

The paper began sensibly with the observation that the Germans had recovered from their disorganised state and were now 'too formidable to be rushed without careful and methodical preparation'.[1] The Germans, he opined, might even be capable of mounting strong and well-organised counter-attacks.

What, in his view, was the consequence of the enemy recovery for the future conduct of the battle? Haig wrote:

> To enable us to bring the present operations (the existing phase of which may be regarded as a 'wearing out' battle) to a successful termination, we must practise such economy of men and materiel as will ensure us having the 'last reserves' at our disposal when the crisis of the fight is reached, which may – and probably will – not be sooner than the last half of September.[2]

This represents something of a transition from the optimism of early July, when Haig imagined that the Germans were already down to their last reserves and that their collapse was imminent. He now acknowledged that it would require both time and caution to reach a situation where the Germans had indeed expended their forces for the Somme battle, opening the way for a climactic action in late September. Breakthrough remained his ultimate goal, but its occurrence would now be delayed.

What, then, of the operations in August and September which would precede the climax of the battle? Here, Haig's instructions degenerated into such a

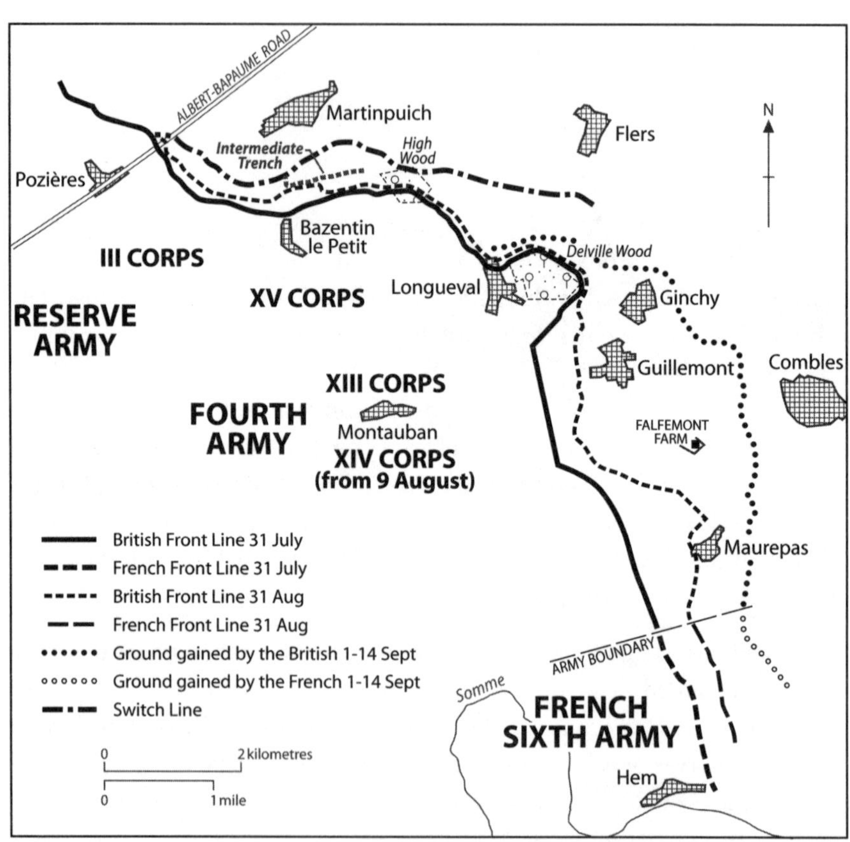

ALBERT-BAPAUME ROAD
Martinpuich
Flers
N
Intermediate Trench
High Wood
Pozières
Bazentin le Petit
III CORPS
Delville Wood
Longueval
XV CORPS
Ginchy
RESERVE ARMY
Guillemont
Combles
XIII CORPS
FOURTH ARMY
Montauban
FALFEMONT FARM
XIV CORPS (from 9 August)
Maurepas
British Front Line 31 July
French Front Line 31 July
British Front Line 31 Aug
French Front Line 31 Aug
Ground gained by the British 1-14 Sept
Ground gained by the French 1-14 Sept
Switch Line
ARMY BOUNDARY
Somme
FRENCH SIXTH ARMY
0
2 kilometres
0
1 mile
Hem


August

welter of contradiction and muddle that it must have been difficult for Rawlinson and Gough to appreciate what was required of them.

Haig stated that the 'first necessity' was to swing the right flank forward in co-operation with the French, while making 'no serious attack' on the left (defined as running from Munster Alley to Delville Wood). Haig had said this earlier and it made sense now for the same reason as it had then: it would eliminate the right angle around Delville Wood and make subsequent operations easier to stage. However, as he had also done earlier, he now proceeded to qualify this good sense out of existence. The trouble started when Haig expanded on what he meant by the statement that no 'serious attack' should be conducted on the left. He said that this statement was not to be taken to mean that no operations at all should be carried out in that area. He merely wanted them confined to the capture of 'important posts held by the enemy within easy reach'. With this qualification, disaster beckoned. The 'important posts' held by the enemy on the left were Intermediate Trench, the Switch Line, High Wood, and Wood Lane. While all were close to the British front line, they could hardly be said to be within 'easy reach', as two weeks of futile and expensive operations against them had already demonstrated. What Haig was doing therefore, was giving licence for operations to be carried out on the right *and* on the left, that is for a repetition of the formula which had failed so badly in the last weeks of July.

But this was not the end of confusion. In the document quoted above Haig had called for 'careful and methodical preparation' for any attacks against the strengthened German defences. He reiterated this point later in the document, even repeating the phrase 'careful and methodical'. Yet he then went on to insist that preparations 'be pushed forward without delay', thus ensuring that they would be anything but careful and methodical. Here too was a blueprint for continuation of the hastily planned and poorly executed attacks of late July.

Worse was to follow. In one of the most starkly contradictory statements in the entire document, Haig laid down that *all* operations were to be conducted with a wise 'economy of men and materials'. This dictum, which was stated no fewer than three times in the course of the memorandum, was designed to give the British the 'last reserves' which would carry out the breakthrough in late September. But it made no sense. The only way of economising on men and munitions was not to attack at all or to attack infrequently. To conduct attacks in which munitions were husbanded was to deny to the troops the only method of protecting them against enemy machine-guns and artillery.

As to what might constitute a 'wise economy of men and munitions' Haig offered the following: 'operations ... are to be carried out with as little expenditure of fresh troops and munitions as circumstances will admit of, but in each attack a sufficient force must be employed to make success as certain as possible'.[3]

So to summarise, Haig was asking for careful and methodical operations to be conducted in haste: to concentrate on the right flank but to attack on the left as well; to use as few troops as possible but in sufficient numbers to succeed; and to economise in munitions which would result, as Western Front fighting had demonstrated over the course of two years, in a prodigality of casualties.

Of course, Haig's document could merely be written off as an exhortation unrelated to any consequent action. After all, it might be thought unlikely that his subordinate army commanders would subject it to the detail of analysis given above. Unfortunately for the troops, this speculation seems ungrounded. There is good evidence that the army commanders did at least attempt to make sense of Haig's missive, and – to the extent that they could understand it – put its wishes into effect.

So Rawlinson's operations in the wake of this document were not at all at odds with Haig's directions. The weight of attacks made on the right flank exceeded those made on the left, which seemed to be in accord with the directions to concentrate on bringing this flank into line. But in number, attacks on the left flank exceeded those on the right, which was in accord with the instruction to seize posts 'within easy reach' in that area. As regards munitions, many fewer shells were fired in August than in July, even if the huge quantities fired on 1 July are discounted.[4]

## II

The actual operations conducted in this period cannot be described in detail. However, a typical example carried out on the left flank will suffice to illustrate what Haig's instructions meant for the troops.

On the night of 4/5 August the 13 Durham Light Infantry from 23 Division were ordered to attack Torr Trench, just to the east of Pozières. The enemy trench was 200 yards from their own front line and certainly fell within the definition of a post 'within easy reach'. Their attack was unsupported on the right and left flanks, perhaps in line with the need to economise on men. It was supported by a derisory amount of artillery fire, possibly to economise on ammunition. In any case the small number of shells that were fired missed their targets comprehensively while areas outside the immediate attack zone were not subjected to any bombardment at all.

As a consequence, the leading waves were raked with machine-gun fire from the undisturbed defenders in Torr Trench, while fire from the unbombarded Munster Alley on the left hit the attackers in flank. The follow-up waves had the same reception. Remarkably, a few men actually entered Torr Trench but they could not be supported and were eventually captured or killed. Meanwhile a third contingent tried to bomb up Munster Alley towards their objective and so avoid the open ground where their comrades had been cut down. Machine-guns in the Alley stopped this attack before it had proceeded 30 yards.

Eventually, the commanding officer of the battalion made his way to the front and cancelled any further frontal attacks. Instead he tried to outflank the Germans in Munster Alley by ordering a bombing party to swing around this trench from the right. Most of this party were immediately hit by defenders on the unattacked portion of this part of the front. A second attempt at this type of manoeuvre was thwarted by the British artillery which, while failing to inflict any serious damage on the enemy, on this occasion hit the Durhams with great accuracy. Yet another attack was ordered, but most men from the designated unit failed to appear and those who did had to be prevented from fleeing by officers with drawn revolvers. Finally the attack was cancelled and the battalion relieved. So for no result, in an operation that even if successful could have gained only 200 yards, the 13 Durhams lost four officers killed, four wounded, 10 other ranks killed, 91 wounded, 11 missing, 12 suffering from shell-shock, and one with a self-inflicted wound. In short, 132 casualties had been suffered and a platoon reduced to mutiny.[5]

While futile, penny-packet, but costly attacks of the type described were being conducted on the left flank, a larger operation to capture Guillemont was being planned for the right. Even then this operation was not to be that large. In all, just four battalions from 55 Division would attack the village direct while two battalions from 2 Division would advance on it from the north. There would be no flanking support from neighbouring divisions. To the north the entire XV Corps would be quiescent and to the south, for reasons that are incomprehensible, the French would advance but on the Hem Plateau near the River Somme, not in an area contiguous with the British.[6]

In the event, Rawlinson had to postpone his attack until 8 August. As was becoming customary, the French went ahead on the 7th anyway, to very little effect. This now meant that on their right flank the British would not even have the support of the distant French on the Hem Plateau.

The attack on the 8th was almost a total failure, although a small amount of ground south of Guillemont was gained by 55 Division. Explanations for the failure are not wanting. First there was the unimaginative nature of the plan –

zero hour was at exactly the same time (4.20 a.m.) as all previous attacks on the village. Second, the heavy guns lifted from the German front line 15 minutes before zero, thus giving the defenders ample warning of the impending attack and sufficient time to bring their weapons to the parapet in complete safety. Third, the jumping barrage fired by the field artillery gave the troops no protection. Fourth, the British had still not grasped that the main defences of Guillemont were not the trench lines in front of the village, which were either lightly manned or evacuated completely before an attack, but the flanking fire from defenders in shell holes and occupants of the cellars in the village itself. Once again therefore, the troops swept through the village only to be cut down by fire from the flanks and rear.[7]

Finally, as always, there were local factors. In some areas smoke and haze caused the troops to lose direction; in others the artillery had not cut any of the belts of wire in front of the German line.[8]

The ordeal of the troops facing Guillemont was not yet over. Haig was convinced that some British troops were holding out in the ruins of the village and that insufficient effort was being made by Rawlinson or the divisional command to support them. He therefore demanded that the attack be renewed on the 9th.[9]

So once again the hapless troops, supported by even less artillery than the inadequate amount that had failed them on the previous day, were committed to a repetition of the attack on the 8th. The result is best described in the War Diary of one of the participating units:

> 3am Company officers warned of ... changes [to] scheme of attack. No time to go into detail, or for Coy Comndrs to explain to Coy officers and N.C.O's as attack was timed for 4.20 a.m. Owing to all N.C.O's and Btn and Coy runners having no idea of the country, and the sunken road being crowded with men from [a neighbouring battalion], great delay was caused in getting the Coys out in position.
>
> 3.55 North Lancs just arriving and officer in command said he had only just heard they were going to attack.
>
> 4.15 Our guns opened a heavy Barrage and the Germans dropped their Barrage [i.e. retaliated] within 3 minutes. Their back barrage line being on sunken road. Companies not all in position had to move thro barrage. Those in position moved forward behind assaulting waves but whole line was unable to make headway owing to machine gun fire and heavy barrage. Whole line fell back and manned our original front line, Coys hopelessly intermixed with men of other attacking Battalions.[10]

Not surprisingly, soon after this fiasco, the battalion was withdrawn. It had suffered 138 casualties and had hardly taken part in anything that could be dignified as an attack.[11]

It was clear to some close to the action why these attacks continually failed. As one observer later remarked:

> Their [that is the German] guns were located on the flanks away from the trench systems, and consequently in positions impossible to locate and destroy before an attack.[12]

Rawlinson took a different view – he blamed the troops. In his diary on the 8th he remarked that 'failure was mainly due to the want of go and inferior training of the infantry'.[13] Next day he was still blaming them, noting: 'I don't think the Infantry were for it'.[14]

For once, Haig disagreed. He was becoming convinced that the responsibility for failure did not lie with the foot soldiers but with the plan. And he was not hesitant in blaming Rawlinson for slipshod planning.

After the failure on the 9th he dispatched Kiggell and another staff officer, General Davidson to Fourth Army headquarters with a stern message:

> repeated failures to capture Guillemont have convinced the Commander-in-Chief that the method of attack adopted requires careful and full reconsideration.[15]

Haig insisted that Rawlinson should do two things. He should discuss the problem of capturing Guillemont with officers – down to brigade level if necessary – who had already been involved in attacking it. And he should then, after careful consideration, *himself* draw up a plan for the next attack. Haig even gave Rawlinson a strong indication of the form the operation should take. It should consist of an attack 'on a very wide front', in conjunction with the French from the River Somme on the right to High Wood on the left, 'so as to prevent the enemy from placing a barrage which might stop us if we attacked on a small front'.[16]

After this *démarche* Rawlinson set about preparing to attack Guillemont in some force. He determined to attack immediately, which seemed contrary to Haig's statement that the plan should be given careful consideration but was in line with the general intention of the Commander-in-Chief as outlined in his memorandum of 2 August.

As it happened, no operations took place for ten days. The cause was force of circumstances rather than Rawlinson imposing a delay in order to develop a sensible plan. On 10 August Congreve, the Corps Commander in the Guillemont area, became seriously ill.[17] Haig ordered that he be replaced by General Cavan, the commander of XIV Corps, which was at the time operating on the front of the Reserve Army. Cavan too then became ill and his recuperation and the need to familiarise himself with the situation delayed the operation until 18 August.[18]

In the interval, of course, operations did not entirely cease. On the left one battalion of 34 Division attacked the Switch Line on the 11th. Next day three battalions from 15 Division assaulted the same line. All failed. Also on the 12th one battalion from 55 Division tried unsuccessfully to gain ground south of Guillemont. Then the 16th and the 17th saw more attacks on the Switch Line and more attempts to advance closer to Guillemont. These last must have had the effect of alerting the Germans to the impending large-scale assault on the village but no one in authority seems to have considered this point.

Though none of these operations had a scintilla of success it would be wrong to leave the impression that all attacks were poorly planned and executed. On 12 August, a batallion of Cameron Highlanders from 15 Division assaulted the Switch Line from a position called the Elbow. The artillery support was excellent, 'a wall of flame' (according to the battalion report), and the men advanced close under it and captured 300 yards of their objective.[19]

More characteristic however, was the attempt of the East Surreys to capture a stongpoint south-west of Guillemont. One quarter of the battalion became casualties and precisely nothing was gained. The East Surreys' War Diary lists the following reasons for failure:

(1) the bombardment of the strongpoint by 9.2″ howitzers did not take place.
(2) the barrage plan was too complicated, the barrage being fired at an angle to the front line.
(3) as a consequence of (2) the barrage commenced so distant from the British line that most of the men were not even aware that it had been fired.
(4) the infantry plan was too rushed and resulted in the units commencing at different times.
(5) machine guns to the south of the operation were left unattacked.[20]

Rawlinson's large-scale attack was scheduled to commence on the 18th. But even as the date was being decided, the plan for the vital right flank began to unravel. Fayolle, the commander of the French VI Army, decided unilaterally that his troops were too exhausted to launch a major offensive. He therefore reduced his participation in the battle to just one division. As a consequence Rawlinson considered that Guillemont was too tough a proposition to capture in one bound. He ordered XIV Corps merely to gain ground towards the village on the 18th and to effect its capture the next day.[21]

So the British, deprived of significant French support on the right, would attack the Germans with five divisions along a front from Intermediate Trench on the left to just south of Guillemont on the right, a distance of 12,000 yards. This was a much more extensive front of attack than on 14 July and some comparisons between the two battles are instructive. On the previous occasion four British divisions attacked on a front of 6,000 yards – i.e. 1,500 yards per division. Now five British divisions were attacking on a 12,000-yard front, a ratio of 2,400 yards per division, a 60 per cent increase from that of 14 July. More significantly, artillery devoted to the wider front had not risen commensurately – in fact it had diminished. On 14 July the 6,000 yards of front had been subjected to a bombardment of 491,804 shells; for 18 August the figure was 396,912.[22] In other words, while the width of front had more than doubled, the number of shells to be fired at it had decreased by 20 per cent.

In fact the situation was even less favourable than these figures reveal. On 14 July all the shells had been directed against the German front system, owing to Rawlinson's erroneous belief that there were no formidable German defences behind the front, and almost all of this front lay within clear view of the British gunners. None of this applied on 18 August. As the British command was finally aware, German defensive arrangements around Guillemont had transmuted from a series of lines into a chequerboard arrangement situated in shell holes. This required many more shells to subdue. Moreover, from Delville Wood through High Wood to Intermediate Trench, the German positions were located on a reverse slope, also requiring a greater bombardment because of the need for aerial spotters continually to adjust the range of the guns. In every way, therefore, the British bombardment before the attack on the 18th was woefully inadequate. And Rawlinson, had he reflected for a moment on the figures he produced for his conference, should have been well aware of this.

Command failures did not cease with the artillery arrangements. The divisions chosen to conduct the attack (1, 33, 14, 24, 3) were in some ways a decidedly peculiar choice. In the case of 1 and 3 Divisions, the fact that they had been in the line for so long made their choice questionable. In addition 3 Division faced the most unenviable task. It had been selected to capture Guillemont. Yet in its period at the front it had consumed half of its infantry strength (6,000 men), and had received as reinforcements just 3,000.[23] What this amounted to is described by the commander of the division:

> All battalions were short of officers, many of them very short, whilst the reinforcements both of officers and men which had arrived had received but little training, and were quite inexperienced in war.[24]

The broad-front attack went in at 2.45 p.m. on 18 August. The resulting gains varied from the non-existent or derisory on the left to extremely modest on the right.

On the extreme left, the artillery had in the main missed Intermediate Trench, with the result that the left of 1 Division was driven back with heavy casualties. On the right of the divisional front near High Wood a more accurate bombardment and a creeping barrage enabled them to occupy a few hundred yards of the enemy front line.[25]

On its right, the attack of 33 Division in High Wood was a complete fiasco. In this area the British had tried to innovate. They had brought forward two large flame-throwers. In addition pipes full of explosive were to be pushed under the German front line and detonated. And because the trench lines in the wood were so close together the forward troops were withdrawn and the wood subjected to a bombardment by the heavy artillery for 48 hours before the attack.[26]

Nothing went according to plan. The heavy artillery comprehensively missed the German positions but succeeded in eliminating its own flame-throwers in the first few minutes of the bombardment. Then, the 'push-pipes' failed to explode. Moreover, the troops who had been withdrawn from the front line so as to facilitate the bombardment were moved back into it ahead of zero hour, which meant that no creeping barrage could be fired because once more they were too close to the German line to permit it. At zero these troops emerged from their trenches to find that not even the wire protecting the German front trench had been cut. Consequently they gained no ground and suffered heavy casualties. Outside the wood affairs went no better. Troops were shot down in numbers by fire from strongpoints in the north-eastern corner of the wood which had also escaped the attention of the British artillery.[27]

The 14 Division immediately to the right also fell victim to the fire from the German strongpoint in the corner of the wood. Further right, however, beyond the range of the German guns in that strongpoint, British troops following closely behind an accurately fired creeping barrage succeeded in gaining ground on either side of Delville Wood. These gains made the wood vulnerable to converging attacks.[28]

The most important gains of the day were made by 24 Division to the north and east of Guillemont in an attack which apparently caught the Germans unawares. It advanced the British line some 500 yards. In addition, all units speak of the accuracy of the creeping barrage. Nevertheless, the division sustained heavy casualties, probably from machine-guns in Ginchy and Guillemont which were beyond the range of the creeping barrage and untouched by the feeble preliminary bombardment.[29]

Failure was most comprehensive on the front of 3 Division, the unit directly in front of Guillemont. Some ground was gained by the troops well south of the village and therefore furthest away from the flanking machine-gunners. Further north, the battalions had not gone 20 yards when they were met with heavy machine-gun fire and an artillery barrage. The machine-gunners were located in cellars in the ruined village and in Wedge Wood and Falfemont Farm, beyond the range of the creeping barrage and left untouched by the bombardment. An attempt to bombard some of the German positions with trench mortars failed because the mortar crews consisted of raw recruits from Britain. At the end of the day the troops had gained no ground at all.[30]

The attack on the 18th was therefore a failure except where ground was gained around Delville Wood and to the north and south of Guillemont. The anchors of the German defence, the Switch Line, High Wood, Delville Wood, and Guillemont, remained in enemy hands.

There was no question of resuming the offensive on the 19th. The 3 Division was shattered, destroyed for the moment as a fighting unit. It would not reappear at the Somme until the very last days of the battle in November. Haig therefore arranged for the division to be relieved and for Guillemont to be attacked on the 21st by the successful 24 Division. After that, there would be another attempt at a joint operation with the French on the 24th.[31]

These operations were largely unsuccessful. They were made in insufficient strength and with inadequate artillery support against a German defence that, although shaken by the experiences of the 18th, was still intact and thoroughly alert. Guillemont remained in German hands.

For Haig this seemed to be the last straw. He was expecting at any moment the delivery of a new weapon in the form of the tank and he was determined to use it in mid-September in a large-scale operation to break the enemy line. But to give this operation every chance of success a reasonable start line had to be established, and this meant eliminating the awkward right angle by capturing such obstacles as High Wood, Ginchy, and, above all, Guillemont.[32] Rawlinson, in his nibbling, poorly thought out attacks, showed no sign of being able to achieve Haig's desired start line. So on 24 August Haig penned him his strongest note yet. Regarding recent operations he told Rawlinson that 'The only conclusion that can be drawn from the repeated attacks on Guillemont is that something is wanting in the methods employed.'[33] He then went on to make crystal clear what this 'something' was. Rawlinson's attacks had been delivered on excessively narrow frontages, had employed insufficient forces, and had lacked the kind of oversight Haig had already suggested that Rawlinson employ. For the next endeavour, Haig wrote:

> The attack must be a general one, engaging the enemy simultaneously along the whole front to be captured, and a sufficient force must be employed, in proper proportion to the extent of front, to beat down all opposition.[34]

He suggested to Rawlinson that two and a half divisions be used to attack Guillemont, a force sufficient to deliver a continuous attack along the whole front.

But Haig's attempt to educate his army commander did not stop there. He reminded Rawlinson that his directive of 9 August had not been sufficiently taken to heart and proceeded to spell out in detail what was required.

> In actual *execution* of plans, when control by higher Commanders is impossible, subordinates on the spot must act on their own initiative, and they must be trained to [do] so. [However] in *preparation* for battle, close supervision by higher Commanders is not only possible, but is their duty, to such extent as they find necessary to ensure that everything is done that can be done to ensure success. [This did not constitute 'interference'] but [is] a legitimate and necessary exercise of the functions of a Commander on whom ultimate responsibility for success or failure lies .... It appears to the Commander-in-Chief that some misconception exists in the Army as to the object and the limitations of the principle of the initiative of subordinates, and it is essential that this misconception should be corrected at once, where it does exist.[35]

So far, in this boys' own guide on how to command an army, Haig had been making good sense. But almost characteristically, he then put all this useful instruction at risk by seeking to deny Rawlinson sufficient time to implement the necessary changes. 'Not a moment must be lost', he told the Fourth Army commander, in carrying out the new 'general' attack.[36] This was an invitation to disaster. Undue haste was simply incompatible with the changes in Fourth Army practice desired by Haig.

At this point the realities of the battlefield, the weather and the perennial difficulties in arranging an attack with the French intervened to impose delay. The three divisions opposite Guillemont were too worn down to attack and one of them (the 35 Bantam Division) was physically inadequate for the task. It was therefore decided to replace these divisions with the relatively fresh 5, 20, and 7 Divisions, a transition that was bound to take time.[37] Then on 25 August it began to rain and the rain's continuing for a number of days made immediate operations impossible.[38] Finally, there was the matter of co-ordinating operations with the French. After a number of tentative dates had been set and then abandoned, 3 September was finally chosen as the day of the combined attack.

**1** The 10th East Yorkshire Battalion marching to the trenches, 28 June. Luckily for these men they were in reserve on 1 July and, because of the efforts of General Rees, were spared the carnage that befell their comrades in the other battalions of 31 Division.

**2** Dump of empty 18-pounder shell cases. This enormous pile represents shells fired by the artillery of just one British division during the preliminary bombardment before 1 July.

**3** The explosion of the mine at the Hawthorn Redoubt. The inexplicable decision to detonate this mine ten minutes before zero hour alerted the German defence and disrupted the artillery programme.

**4** 'The determinant of victory'. An 8-inch Howitzer in a camouflaged emplacement. If such guns as these could destroy the German defences the British infantry might gain ground. If they missed, no infantry gains were possible.

**5** Ration party of the Royal Irish Rifles resting in a communication trench, 1 July. This familiar image is often concentrated on the face of the second man on the left to indicate the effects of shell-shock. Whatever the condition of this man, the party as a whole seem in good health and have, in fact, not yet entered the battle in a combat role.

**6** Fricourt, 2 July, showing the effect of the massive British bombardment in the southern section of the front.

7 A Lewis gun in action in a front-line trench near Ovillers, July. This light machine-gun gave the infantry some fire support as they endeavored to move forward.

**8** Battle of Pozières. 18-pounders firing a barrage, 30 July. As evidenced on page 181, below, such barrages could be quite inaccurate at this stage of the war.

**9** The toll of battle: Guillemont, August.

**10** Sir Douglas Haig with General Joffre and Marshall Foch, leaving the Commander-in-Chief's Château Beauquesne, 12 August. Joffre was worried, rightly, that Haig had lost his grip on the battle during this period.

**11** Men of the 16th (Irish) Division going back for a rest after the taking of Guillemont, 3 September.

**12** 15 September. The cavalry moving forward. These men were, in Haig's plan, to attack the Germans from the rear around Arras some 70 miles distant. In the event and as with most cavalry on the Somme they did not cross their own front line.

**13** Flers, 15 September. The capture of these ruins marked the greatest advance achieved on that day.

**14** The ruins of Morval, captured on 25 September. Its capture led to expectations of great successes which were to be blighted in the next six weeks.

**15** This obviously posed photograph shows troops well behind the front line on 25 September. Note the soldier looking at the camera.

**16** The battlefield in late September. Note the lack of features and the dispersed formations of the soldiers moving forward to the attack.

**17** Mr Balfour and General Sir Henry Rawlinson at Château de Querrieu, headquarters of Fourth Army, October. The men had two things in common. Both were uneasy about the course of the campaign and neither did anything to stop it.

**18** By November even supplying the troops by horse-drawn wagon was an ordeal.

While planning for this large operation was proceeding, the Germans seized the initiative. On 29 August Haig was offering the judgement that the enemy troops were suffering 'an all-round loss of morale'.[39] Two days later, they launched their largest counter-attack of the Somme campaign. On the salient around Delville Wood, the newly arrived 7 and the recently positioned 24 Divisions were subjected to a shattering bombardment.[40] The 4 Bavarian and 56 German Infantry Divisions, whose morale seemed quite intact, then advanced, pushing the British back into the ruins of the wood.[41] Within a few hours, all ground gained in the area in the latter half of August by the British had been lost.

Undeterred, the British command pushed ahead with preparations for the large operation on 3 September. From right to left, the French would attack north and south of the Somme, the British Fourth Army would employ five divisions to assault from the south of Guillemont to High Wood, and four divisions from the Reserve Army would launch a major effort from Pozières to the Ancre Valley.

But in many respects this operation promised no more than those which had preceded it. The artillery bombardment was no heavier than that of 18 August, and so was again well below that of the successful 14 July operation.[42] And an attempt to take the strongpoint of Falfemont Farm in a preliminary operation served no purpose but to alert the enemy that a major attack was imminent.

This preliminary attack started at 9 a.m. on 3 September and was a predictable disaster. The bombardment missed the target and the creeping barrage failed equally. Seeing this the French refused to attack, but the British went ahead. The contrast is well demonstrated in a letter quoted in the 2 King's Own Scottish Borderers War Diary:

> I don't think a man of any regiment would have gone to certain death the way ours did – having seen as they did the failure of both preliminary bombardment and creeping barrage. The beautiful [!!!] thing about it is that they all knew when they went over that this would happen and not a man flinched.[43]

In the main attack to the left of Falfemont Farm affairs went much more smoothly for the British. There the left brigade of 5 Division (95) made a surprisingly swift advance. They were soon 3,500 yards deep into enemy territory. Where other divisions in the same area had hardly managed to get further than their own front line, this unit had outflanked Guillemont and joined hands with 20 Division on its eastern side.[44]

Three factors appear to have contributed to this success. First, the German machine-gunners in the ruins of the village who had previously taken such a toll on attacks from this direction were now pinned down by the assault of 20 Division to their north. Second, a gap existed in the German defences, probably as a result of one German division being in the process of relieving another just as 95 Brigade happened to attack.[45] Third, the bombardment this time managed to create havoc among those German defenders still clinging to trench lines.[46]

To the north, meanwhile, 20 Division had at long last captured Guillemont. Again there were three reasons for this success. First, to the north the attacking forces constructed a series of trenches within a few hundred yards of the village. Not having attacked from this direction before, they did not arouse the suspicions of the Germans and covered the short distance to their objectives before the German machine-guns could become engaged.[47] Second, the British had finally accounted for most of the deep dug-outs beneath the village.[48] Third, the Germans, accustomed to small-scale attacks, had thinned out their defences. Hence they were not equipped to withstand a concentrated attack by three brigades delivered in depth and with powerful artillery support.[49]

Success on this flank was not confined to the capture of Guillemont. The few Germans in the area were so disorganised that they were unable to prevent further advances by Rawlinson's troops. In short order Falfemont Farm and Leuze Wood fell.[50] All told, the advance in this area amounted to 4,500 yards on a 2,000 yard front.

This success resulted in a considerable improvement in the tactical position of the Fourth Army. The right angle around Delville Wood had at last been eliminated and the wood itself would soon fall as out-flanking operations forced the Germans to evacuate it. Thereby the German artillery was denied the advantage of converging fire, sometimes in enfilade, on exposed British troops. It would also make any infantry advances from this area less complicated because the attacks now need not diverge. As a result, artillery support would be a relatively straightforward matter.

To the north of Guillemont, the 7 Division was to capture Ginchy. But the change in tactics which were in evidence in the last assault on Guillemont were not to be found here. The attack did not possess weight, and it was lacking in depth in the form of moppers-up to deal with the unsubdued machine-gunners and survivors in cellars. Nor had the artillery paid sufficient attention to the threat from enemy machine-guns on the flank of the attack.[51] As a consequence the attack failed.

But the command of 7 Division persisted. Over the next three days they launched a series of small attacks of the sort which had already failed against Guillemont: 3,600 casualties were suffered without reward.[52] The 7 Division was then withdrawn.

Further left, few advances were made. The 1 Division was directed against a key target, High Wood, yet the scale of attack was quite inadequate.[53] As a result, High Wood remained in German hands. So this considerable obstacle, intended to be eliminated ahead of Haig's major battle, remained as an objective which would require much endeavour in the coming operation.

No further attempt would be made on High Wood in advance of the new operation but Haig was determined to seize Ginchy. So a new division, the 16 (Irish) was given the job. The omens were not good. Rain was now falling and many battalions in the division were under strength. But their plan of attack possessed some originality. So far, all the attacks against Ginchy had come from the direction of Delville Wood. The new endeavour was to be made from the south, around the newly won ground near Guillemont. And the attack was to be made in greater strength this time – six battalions as against only two employed by 7 Division. Good fortune also favoured the Irish. Just before the attack the Germans brought into this sector two new divisions who somehow did not manage to establish contact with each other, so leaving the defenders in Ginchy village entirely unsupported. So when, on 9 September, the Irish assaulted in some weight from an unexpected direction, and with the support of a particularly heavy creeping barrage (fired by the field artillery of no less than two divisions) they overran their objectives.[54] In two hours the ruins of Ginchy were securely in the hands of the Fourth Army.

## III

The British command does not emerge well from the operations in August. Haig is the main culprit. His memorandum of 2 August, which was intended to set the scene for what was to come, was so riddled with ambiguities as to render it almost incomprehensible. Rawlinson certainly endeavoured to put what he took to be the gist of Haig's instructions into effect. But muddled thinking translated into action can hardly result in anything but muddle. So the source of the confused operations which characterise this intermediate period of the Somme was not Rawlinson but the Commander-in-Chief.

Rawlinson, however, hardly emerges with great credit. When, for one section of the front at least (around Guillemont) Haig eventually divined what was required, Rawlinson proved incapable of translating his chief's orders into action. In the end even Haig's boys' own guide to fighting a battle' did not redeem Rawlinson's command. What did was only a series of accidents (sickness, weather), which delayed the operation long enough for a thorough plan to be developed.

As for the concept of the 'last reserves', applied by Haig to the enemy, this was always pure fantasy. The German manpower position in the autumn of 1916 was hardly so perilous that Haig could materially affect it in the course of six weeks' fighting on the Somme. Had by some miracle the enemy line been breached in mid-September the Germans could have sealed it in short order with troops taken from unattacked sections of the Western Front and then moved troops from other less critical fronts to make up for any deficiencies. Haig's plans for a climactic battle in September with his new weapon required an enemy down to its last reserves of manpower. The reality would prove very different.

# 16 'A Hell of a Time': Pozières and Mouquet Farm, July–August

## I

It will be recalled that on 2 July the two northern corps of the Fourth Army (VIII and X) had been placed under the command of General Gough and designated the Reserve Army. These formations would play little role in the fighting in late July and August. The VIII Corps facing Serre was too shattered to undertake anything but patrolling for some time. And, in any case, 1 July had demonstrated that the German defences in that area were too formidable to be attacked frontally. Much the same could be said of the X Corps and the defences around Thiepval. Moreover, most of the heavy artillery was now supporting Rawlinson's efforts further south. The artillery position of the Reserve Army improved somewhat in the following weeks but never to the extent of placing it on an equal footing with the Fourth. So, for most of the period 15 July to 4 September, Gough's operations were confined to attacks by just two divisions from the southern section of X Corps and then from II Corps. It is much more accurate, therefore, to consider the Reserve Army as a corps operating on the flank of the Fourth Army.

If this is so why should we not consider the operations of the Reserve Army in conjunction with the Fourth? The answer is both straightforward and melancholy. Hardly ever were major attacks by the two forces co-ordinated. Only twice in the period under discussion were substantial operations conducted by the two armies simultaneously, and in one case (22/23 July) this came about by accident. On other occasions operations between adjoining battalions might be co-ordinated by the actions of their respective commanders but that was all. It was not until 3 September that the two forces planned and conducted a major attack on the same day. To all intents and purposes then, the Reserve Army in this period fought its own battles and can be considered separately.

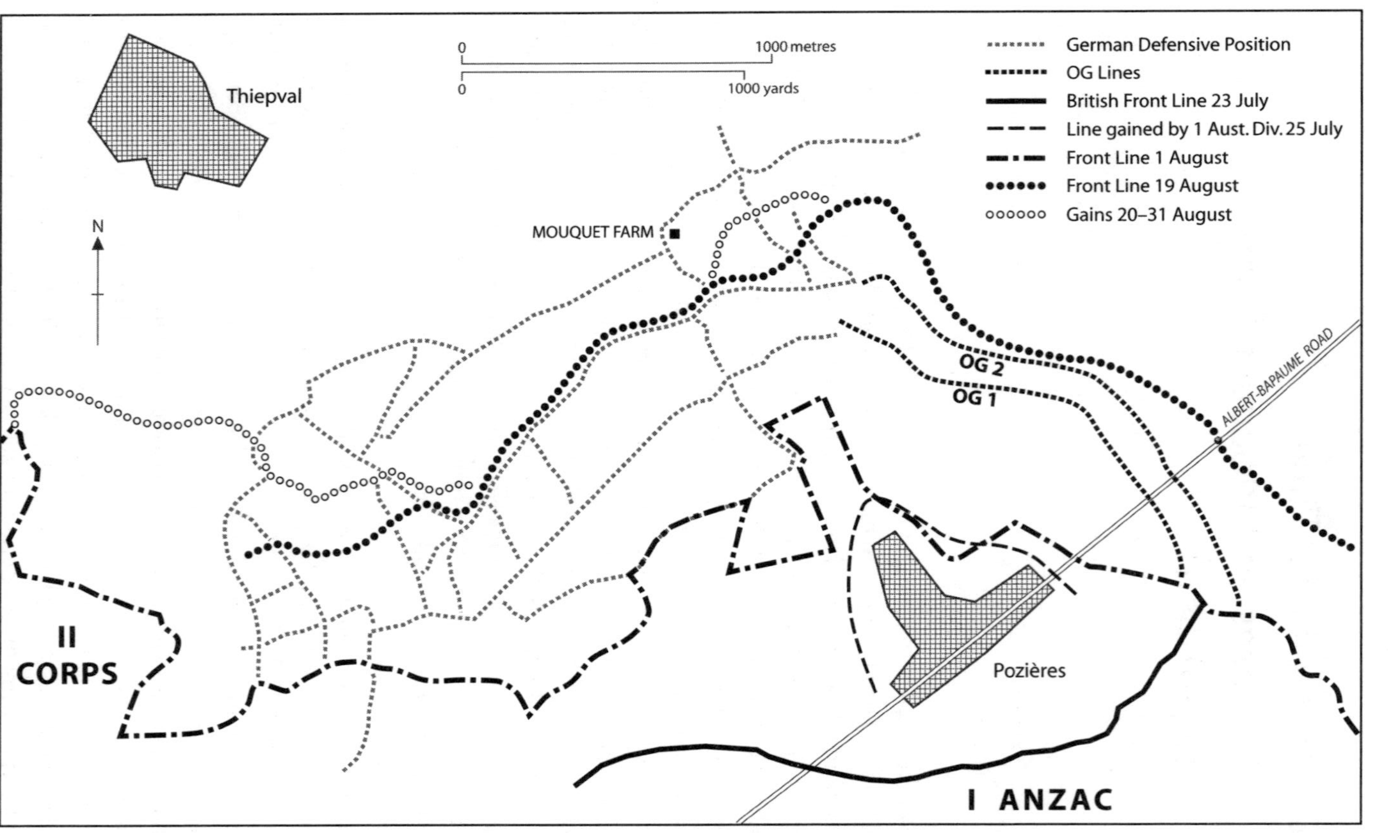


From Pozières to Mouquet Farm, 23 July–31 August

So, for most of the middle period on the Somme, the Reserve Army confined its attacks to one or two divisions operating on but not with the left flank of the Fourth Army. The main area of these operations was around Pozières, a fortified village standing high on the Thiepval Ridge and behind which ran the German second line. Rawlinson's forces had gained some ground towards Pozières in the first two weeks of July but then Haig adjusted the boundaries between his two armies and on 15 July the area was handed over to Gough.

Haig's instructions to Gough were sketchy in the extreme. He merely stated that

> Reserve Army will carry out methodical operations against Pozières with a view to capturing that important position with as little delay as possible.[1]

Note that once more there was the usual contradiction at the heart of Haig's instructions. Gough was to conduct 'methodical operations' but with 'as little delay as possible'. To conduct them Haig assigned to Gough the newly arrived Australian Corps while X Corps, which was already in the line, was given some fresh divisions.

Why was the capture of Pozières important? There were three reasons. First, it stood in the path of any force attempting the capture of the German second line in this area. Second, the ground to the immediate rear of the village stood on the very summit of the Thiepval–Ginchy Ridge, so that possession of this ground would secure the flank of any major advance by Fourth Army. Third, the possession of this ground, and especially that around Mouquet Farm, would allow observation over the German positions around Thiepval from the rear.

As was his wont, Gough seized on the section of Haig's instructions urging that there be no delay in attacking Pozières. On the same day that he received the Commander-in-Chief's letter, he summoned General Walker, the Commander of 1 Australian Division, to his headquarters, told him that his unit was now under the direct command of Reserve Army (thus bypassing the corps commander, General Birdwood), and ordered him to attack Pozières at once.[2]

Walker, a British Regular officer and a veteran of eight months' fighting at Gallipoli, was too cautious to be rushed. He asked for time to reconnoitre the position to establish from which direction it might be best attacked. His reconnaissances revealed that he faced an unenviable situation. If he attacked Pozières from the south-west, his left flank would be open and vulnerable to flanking fire from the high ground around Thiepval and he would be attacking directly up a steep hill. On the other hand, if he attacked from the south-east, his assembly area would crowd into the area on the left of Fourth Army and as his troops advanced they would face flanking fire from trenches just to the north of Pozières, called OG1 and OG2. Nevertheless, the terrain to the south-east of the village avoided an uphill attack and the flanks of the Australian advance, left and right, could be covered by British troops. For these reasons Walker decided on the south-east.[3]

It was immediately obvious to Walker that some basic information needed to be collected before attack could commence. So he sent his staff officer, Lt-Col. Blamey, to discuss the problem of Pozières with some units (7 and 19 Divisions) who had already unsuccessfully attacked it. What Blamey returned with formed the basis of the Australian attack.[4] First, as no man's land in the area of attack was 600 yards wide Walker required that new trenches be dug forward to reduce this killing zone to 200 yards.[5] Second, and most importantly, was the artillery. Walker insisted on the maximum support available, with the result that his troops would be assisted by their own divisional artillery, the 25 Divisional artillery, and the entire heavy guns of X Corps.[6]

All this meant delay, so instead of attacking on the 19th as Gough had wanted, the Australians would assault Pozières on the night of the 22nd/23rd. By chance this brought it in line with the operations of the Fourth Army.

The infantry plan for the capture of Pozières was simple. The troops would advance in three stages to capture the three lines of trenches guarding the village and the bombardment would lift from each line as the attack went in. Then, while the infantry consolidated their hold on the Pozières–Bapaume road, a standing barrage falling some 200 yards ahead of them would protect then from counter-attack. Meanwhile a battalion would advance to the right of the main attack to capture the OG lines and thus protect the main body from flanking fire. And on their left flank the British 48 Division from X Corps would launch an attack to keep down fire from that direction.[7]

The bombardment opened on the 19th and was one of the heaviest yet seen on the British front in support of an attack by a single division. At 12.30 a.m. on the 23rd it lifted from the first German trench line and the infantry assault began. Most troops had crawled to within 60 yards of their objective and when the artillery lifted they rushed forward, 'meeting opposition', in the words of one account, 'but taking no prisoners'.[8] The remaining two lines were soon captured in similar fashion. By 2.30 a.m. the Australians were digging in along what was thought to be the Pozières–Bapaume road.[9] Pozières, one of the strongest positions in the German second line, had certainly been captured.

The success was due to the meticulous infantry plan devised by Walker and the stunning effect of the heavy bombardment on the defending troops. But there had also been an element of luck. At the time of the attack the German command was in the process of replacing the division which had held Pozières from the beginning of the Somme offensive with a fresh unit brought south from Ypres. The tired troops were still in occupation of the south-eastern section of the village when the Australians struck. They immediately gave way.[10]

There was no such collapse in the OG lines to the north of the village. Here the German dug-outs had survived the bombardment intact. The attacking Australian battalion ran into heavy machine-gun fire and could make little progress. A reinforcing battalion had no more success. A few hundred yards of trenches were captured, but that was all.[11]

On the left, the 48 Division attack in the area of the Reserve Army failed. The bombardment in this area was described by one unit as 'quite useless [as] not a single shell burst along the front to be attacked'.[12] The account continued: 'the result of this was that the enemy M.G.s had nothing to worry them & were able to fire on the assaulting troops as they pleased'.[13] By the end of the day contact had not been made with the Australians, so leaving a gap in the front to the south of the village.[14]

Despite these setbacks, and considering the lack of success on the front of Fourth Army on 22/23 July, the capture of Pozières could be counted as a success. Yet it was at this point that events turned Pozières into a nightmare for the troops and did much to negate its easy capture.

Ironically, these events were brought about by the failure of German attempts to recapture the village by counter-attack. In line with German policy during this phase of the Somme battle, immediate orders were given to retake the village. The first attempt was made at 5.30 a.m. on the 23rd but was beaten back by the already entrenched Australian machine-gunners on the Pozières–Bapaume road.[15] A second was then stopped by the 48 Division.[16] The Germans decided to postpone any further action until the 24th and bring forward a fresh division to carry it out. The 18 German Reserve Division was the unit selected and its 86 Regiment was designated to carry out the attack. But as each battalion of this regiment was sent forward it was caught in a murderous crossfire by troops from the Fourth Army on its flank and from the Australian troops in Pozières itself. Three German battalions ceased to exist before they had even come within rifle shot of their objective. Hearing of the fate of these troops the army commander (von Boehm) instructed that further attempts to retake Pozières were to cease and that the village was to be rendered uninhabitable by constant heavy shelling. It was this decision that would prove so costly to the Australian troops occupying the village in the subsequent days and weeks.[17]

Meanwhile back at Reserve Army headquarters Gough was also issuing orders. He instructed the Australians to capture the OG lines to the north of the village to remove the threat of counter-attack from that direction. Then he ordered that operations by X Corps and 1 Anzac Corps should be directed northwards to Mouquet Farm, so threatening Thiepval from the rear. As always, the first of these objectives was to be captured immediately.[18]

The first attempt to take the OG lines need not detain us. It was made in haste and in the dark by tired troops who had extreme difficulty in identifying any of their objectives in the moonscape battlefield.[19] In truth the First Australian Division was exhausted. Since 23 July it had suffered 5,283 casualties, most caused by enemy shelling of Pozières after its capture. The men were described as 'drawn and haggard and so dazed that they seemed to be walking in a dream'.[20] They were withdrawn on the 25th and replaced by 2 Australian Division.[21]

The new operation proved that fresh troops in themselves would make little difference if other aspects of planning went awry. First there was the artillery factor. Certainly, given that the attack was to take place at night, no close support from the guns could be expected. Even so, the expedient adopted to support the night attack defied common sense. The OG lines were to be subjected to an intense bombardment immediately before they were attacked. But before the bombardment commenced the assault troops were to leave their trenches and move to within striking distance of their objective. This movement would take place across open ground and occupy 12 minutes, during which period not one gun would be firing on the German defences.[22]

Moreover, the OG lines were on a reverse slope, so no direct observation could be obtained of the effect of the bombardment on the German wire and trenches. Patrols did send in reports which indicated that the German wire still represented a formidable obstacle but these seem to have been ignored.[23]

Under these conditions the results of the attack could have been predicted. As the attacking troops left their trenches and proceeded into no man's land they were mowed down by the as yet unbombarded German machine-gunners.[24] Those small groups who did get close enough to the German line to deploy for an attack ran into uncut wire and were killed, wounded, or forced back. One very small group actually captured a section of the first German line, but without support they too were forced to withdraw. In all, 2,000 casualties were suffered and no ground gained.[25]

At least some important lessons were drawn from this fiasco by the divisional staff. They insisted that before another attack approach trenches must be dug across no man's land to bring the attacking troops within striking distance of their objective. They also decreed that the next attack should take place in daylight to enable the troops to be 'under cover of intense Artillery bombardment and smoke barrages' and so that the state of the enemy wire could be clearly seen.[26] Above all, they insisted that time be taken so that arrangements could be made thoroughly.

Time was certainly needed. The working parties engaged in digging trenches across no man's land had to carry out this hazardous work at night. Even then,

> Work was delayed and hampered each night by severe hostile artillery bombardment and barrages and many casualties were incurred by the working parties – partly while getting up the communication trenches to the site of the work and partly while doing the work. Much of the work too was broken down by the enemy fire and had to be done again.[27]

The attack had to be postponed again and again while this work was completed.

Gough did not contemplate these delays with equanimity. He wrote to the corps commander (Birdwood) demanding an explanation. In the usual double-speak of the high command he insisted that he did not 'wish to unduly hurry on any attack', while at the same time inquiring if the delay could have been avoided 'by greater energy and foresight on the part of the higher commanders'.[28]

The reply from Birdwood was surprisingly blunt. He informed the army commander that he had not passed on the note to the divisional commander (Legge) because he did not want him to be 'disturbed during his operation' and said that to retain the confidence of senior officers it was 'essential to give them a fair trial'.[29]

So the attack was delayed until Legge was ready. It went in at dusk on 4 August and was a complete success. Most of the wire had been cut and the troops followed what seems to have been a creeping barrage into the OG lines. After their newly won positions were consolidated they were replaced by 4 Australian Division. The 2 Division had suffered 6,846 casualties, or half their infantry strength in a fortnight.[30]

## II

Gough had now achieved the first of Haig's objectives – the capture of the high ground to the north of Pozières. Haig's second objective lay ahead – Mouquet Farm just 1,000 yards from Pozières. Gough now defined the purpose of capturing this objective as 'cutting off Thiepval and getting observation over Courcelette and Grandcourt'.[31] Later he amplified this order. The object of operations was to be the capture of Thiepval – by converging attacks by the Anzacs to the north-east and by the newly arrived II Corps to the south-west.[32]

The operation against Mouquet Farm was fraught with danger, both for the Australian troops and for those of II Corps. The advance they would be making would take place on an exceedingly narrow front. Moreover, the Australians on the right would attempt the advance along the very crest of the ridge. All their troop movements would be easily observable by German forces around Courcelette, who would be able to direct machine-gun and artillery fire against them. In addition the advance would create a salient which could be brought under fire from many directions – from Courcelette on the right, from Thiepval almost directly ahead, from Grandcourt to the north, and even from Martinpuich to the south-east. And most dangerous of all for the attackers, enemy artillery could not only fire in enfilade but directly along the trench lines which led to Mouquet Farm. Of all the tactical nightmares on the Somme this has some claim to be considered the worst.

There is also another issue to consider. It is extremely hard to see how such an operation could contribute to the 'wise economy in men' that Haig was trying to practise in order that he should have the 'last reserves' at the climax of the battle.[33] Moreover, the further Gough's troops advanced, the more remote they would become from the scene of the main advance – which Haig had dictated would take place from Courcelette to Delville Wood. In short, while Gough would be advancing north-west, the remainder of the British armies would be advancing north-east.

So, from the first week in August to the second week of September, the men of the Anzac and II Corps battered their way towards Mouquet Farm. Because of their depressing similarity these operations need not be described in detail. They did however have some noteworthy features. Because of the confined front, all attacks were small in scale. In fact, because the Reserve Army showed the same chronic inability to co-ordinate their operations as the Fourth, the attacks were even smaller in scale than was necessary. So when the Australian troops were attempting to advance, those of II Corps were often quiescent, and when II Corps attacked the Anzacs did not. What this meant was that on most occasions the German artillery could concentrate all their fire on a very small front and as their fire was coming from all directions most attempts to advance were stopped dead. Such was the intensity of the fighting that exhausted divisions had to be relieved frequently, so for some periods no attacks at all could be made, thus allowing the German defence time to recover. To compound all these problems, the advance on Mouquet Farm was taking place at a time when the Fourth Army on their flank were making only sporadic attacks and this gave the Germans the opportunity to direct some of their batteries opposite Rawlinson's troops on to the hapless men of the Reserve Army.

The Germans possessed yet another advantage. Early in August they had captured some British documents which revealed Mouquet Farm as the objective of their operations.[34] They were consequently able to concentrate most of their artillery fire in the area to the south of the farm, dig further trench lines to impede the enemy advance and thin out their own troops within British artillery range while keeping reserves on hand which could intervene if Gough's troops looked like breaking through.[35]

All this gave the advance on Mouquet Farm a grim aspect. When Gough's artillery fire was accurate, the British and Anzac forces might seize a trench line. And when casualties had not been excessive they might hold it against counter-attack. If the guns missed their targets, failure was certain.

In the event the guns often did fail to support the infantry. One reason for this can be gleaned from a report made by the officer commanding 1 Anzac Corps' artillery. After a singularly egregious failure by the guns he sent a staff officer forward to the batteries to seek an explanation. The first action this officer took was to check the synchronisation of the watches of adjoining batteries, He found that

> in not one case were they right, and the time given to him differed as much as a quarter of an hour. It is useless to expect good results under these circumstances, and it should be impressed on all officers that the greatest care should be taken at all times to get the time accurately , even to seconds, and that at all times any fire which has been ordered for a particular time shall commence to the second at that time. [36]

To make matters even worse he found that

> battery officers have said that they do not always fire exactly at the points ordered.[37]

Gough's lame response to this remarkable piece of information was that he 'hoped and believed' that there was 'some mistake about this'.[38]

The flavour of the Mouquet Farm operations can be gauged by the experiences of some units involved. On the night of 12/13 August the 7 East Surreys (12 Division) were ordered to capture a section of the enemy front line. The attack was carried out by just two companies. The left company was brought to a halt by heavy machine-gun fire as they left their trenches. The right company advanced a small distance until machine-gun fire forced the survivors to shelter in some shell holes in no man's land. One of the officers in this group attempted to return to his own lines in order to summon reinforcements. After an hour of wandering around the featureless battlefield he found himself back in the shell hole from where he had started. And this when his own front line had been less than 100 yards away.[39]

Then there was the experience of the 1/8 Royal Warwickshires (48 Division) on 27 August. They were assembled for the assault around midnight. It was then discovered that there were no scaling ladders to allow them to exit the trench. A ten-hour search for ladders ensued. When some were located it was broad daylight and they were placed in position under the watch of German sentries in their own front line just 100 yards away. Their attack therefore ran into withering machine-gun fire, which was compounded by the fire from their own guns dropping short. Miraculously a few men reached their objective, but failed to recognise it and advanced beyond, only to run into their own barrage a second time. The remnants of the battalion were forced to withdraw. Losses constituted 50 per cent of the battalion's strength.[40]

If anything conditions were worse on the Australian section of the front because of their exposed position on the very crest of the ridge. On 14 August an ambitious plan was devised by 4 Australian Division to capture Mouquet Farm itself. The battalions which were to carry it out were (from right to left) the 50, 13, and 51. The 50 in particular was in a much reduced condition before the attack was ordered. Two days previously, as it had moved into the line, it had suffered heavy losses from incessant German shelling which fell on all its approach roads to the front. The battalion then took part in a combined operation with British troops which failed with heavy casualties. Another of the battalions earmarked for the operation, the 13th, had also suffered heavy casualties before zero.

The operation to capture Mouquet Farm was due to go in at 10 p.m. on the 14th. But some hours before this there was an indication that all was not well with 50 Battalion. One of the company commanders, Lt Rhodes, sent a message back to brigade headquarters indicating that they were running short of hand grenades. He then added: 'Have had a hell of a time – enfiladed. Suffering from slight shell-shock.'[41] Then at 7.55 p.m. an even more startling message was received from another company of the 50:

> We cannot move. We have few tools, few bombs, no water, and the men are badly shaken. At present we are digging a number out .... After consulting the company commanders have decided to remain fast.[42]

The import of these messages was quite clear – 50 Battalion would not be taking part in the attack. Just as brigade staff were digesting this information, 13 Battalion reported that one of their companies was 'rattled' and down to just 38 men (from a nominal 200),[43] which suggested that this unit was hardly in optimum shape for an attack either.

Two of the assault battalions had now announced that they were in a seriously depleted state. At this moment the third (51 Battalion), which had been in touch with the CO of 13 Battalion, sent the following message:

> Both 13th CO thinks, and it is my genuine (not depressed) opinion that it would be a mistake to press the offensive further locally in this salient. We are heavily shelled from due E right round to N W and the communications are simply awful .... Our artillery are bombarding our own front trenches (heavies!!!).[44]

So by this time all three of the attacking battalions had revealed themselves as unfit for an assault and one of the three had announced that it would not attack.

Undeterred, brigade headquarters ignored all of this. They deemed the claim that one of the companies of 13 Battalion had been reduced to 38 men 'ridiculous' (it was in fact quite true) and sent their staff forward to organise the attack as planned.[45] Thus on the morning of the 14th the three hapless battalions were forced over the top. The result was deplorable. The 50 was immediately hit by a German barrage and 'broke in all directions', the panic being stemmed only by the (unspecified) action of a number of officers. In short order they were back in their own trenches.[46] On the other flank the 51 was detected assembling for the attack by the German defenders in a strongpoint called Fabeck Graben. Withering machine-gun fire opened on the troops as they endeavoured to cross no man's land and soon shouts of 'retire' could be heard up and down the line. In the understated words of the Official Historian, 'there followed much confusion', during which the survivors of the attack returned to their starting point.[47]

The centre battalion (13), out of touch with events on either flank, by good fortune advanced through a gap in the German defences past Mouquet Farm and was approaching Fabeck Graben when it became obvious that it had advanced alone. The commander, Colonel Murray, instituted a fighting withdrawal, 'one of the most skilfully conducted fights in the history of the A.I.F.', and returned his men to the start line.[48] Much was made of this action by Australia's official military historian,but the fact remains that battles are not won by fighting withdrawals, however skilfully conducted. And the melancholy fact is that the three battalions which were in no shape to attack at all suffered some 1,100 casualties for precisely no gain of ground.[49] The husks of the three battalions had been reduced to a state of rebellion by the incompetence of their superiors. In truth the operation should never have taken place. But then, as we shall see, that could be said about the whole Mouquet Farm episode.

# III

By early September the Australian Corps was exhausted and the Canadians were brought in to complete their task. They too failed. The casualties incurred in attempting the capture of Mouquet Farm can be given with reasonable accuracy:

| | |
|---|---|
| 1 Australian Division | 2,650 |
| 2 Australian Division | 1,300 |
| 4 Australian Division | 4,650 |
| 12 Division | 1,450 |
| 25 Division | 1,700 |
| 48 Division | 3,650 |
| Canadian Corps | 2,800 |
| Total | 18,200 |

If other sundry units are added, the total casualties incurred in attempting to take the farm in the period 7 August to 12 September cannot have been much short of 20,000 – the better part of the infantry strength of two divisions.

In the plainest sense this terrible toll was taken for no purpose. Some time in September Gough had abandoned the idea of capturing Thiepval by converging attacks and determined to assault it frontally. Exactly when this decision was made, and why, is not revealed by the documents. What can be said with some certainty is that the possession of Mouquet Farm had ceased to be regarded as the key to the capture of Thiepval (which, as it happened, fell before the farm had been taken).

Gough and Haig bear a heavy responsibility for the Mouquet Farm fiasco. Gough drove his troops into a narrowing salient, a circumstance which was bound to give the German artillery the maximum chance to inflict heavy losses. And at the same time he abandoned the idea of using Mouquet Farm as a staging point for the capture of Thiepval, yet persisted in operations as though he had not.

Haig has a wider responsibility. First, he played no co-ordinating role between the actions of the Fourth and Reserve Armies to the point of not seeming to notice how little support Rawlinson's men were providing for Gough. More importantly, while the struggle for Mouquet Farm was taking place, Haig was preparing what he considered to be a war-winning operation with the first tanks in another sector of the Somme front. And as a necessary precondition for success in this endeavour he had decreed back in early August that men and munitions must be conserved in order that he should have the last reserves with which to exploit the victory. Yet at the same time he was allowing Gough to cast away 20,000 of these reserves in an operation that was always tactically dubious and eventually became completely irrelevant.

# 17 Summary, 15 July–12 September

What was the effect of operations from 15 July to 12 September and what does this period tell us about the overall competence or otherwise of the British command?

On 15 July British forces were occupying a section of Delville Wood, Longueval, and High Wood. Sixty days later this was still the case. In those areas hardly an inch of ground had been gained. Moreover, those gains which had been made in other areas (particularly around Guillemont and Ginchy) had taken until the last few days of the period to accomplish. So over a period of 60 days the British line had advanced just 1,000 to 1,500 yards on a 12,000-yard front (an area of 6 square miles). And the cost of these tiny advances had not been cheap. In all, 32 divisions of the British army had attacked on the Somme during this period. The casualty bill was approximately 126,000 – or about 4,000 per division,[1] that is one third of the strength of every division engaged. But even this conceals yet greater disasters. The 5 Division, in a series of attacks around Delville Wood, lost the equivalent of its entire infantry strength, some 11,000 men. The 1 Division in fourteen attacks lost 10,000. Two other divisions (3 and 33) lost over 8,000. Six others lost between 5,500 and 7,500.[2]

The import of these figures needs to be grasped. On the first day of the Somme 60,000 casualties were incurred in securing 3 square miles of territory. From 15 July to 12 September 126,000 were suffered in gaining 6 square miles. In other words, in terms of casualties for ground gained, the middle battles on the Somme are no less of a tragedy than the first day. Only the fact that the slaughter was not encompassed within a single day has concealed its dramatic impact, both at the time and from historians since.

Clearly something had gone terribly wrong since the optimistic forecasts had emanated from Rawlinson's and Haig's headquarters following the achievements of 14 July. In general terms the command failed to exercise any real grip on the battle, a deficiency which manifested itself in a number of ways.

The first of these command failures is revealed in the nature of operations conducted in the period. On 50 of the 60 days under scrutiny, the Fourth or the Reserve Army launched at least some action against the German defences. The number of troops available for an attack throughout this period was remarkably consistent. The Fourth Army always consisted of three army corps, with at least six and occasionally seven divisions in the front line. The active portion of the Reserve Army usually comprised two army corps with just two divisions in the line. That is, the British armies on the Somme had on average eight divisions available for attack on almost every day of our period. Yet when we look at the figures for the number of battalions within divisions which actually did attack we discover that nothing like the full complement of troops was being employed. For example:

1. On just two occasions (22/23 July and 3 September) were more than 50 per cent of the available battalions committed to the attack.
2. On only two other occasions (30 July and 18 August) were more than 24 per cent of the available battalions committed to the attack.
3. On just two occasions (22/23 July and 3 September) was a major attack by Fourth Army made to coincide with a major effort by the Reserve Army, and on the second of these occasions the attack by the left of the Fourth Army diverged by seven hours.
4. On an average day just under six battalions (less than 10 per cent of the total available) engaged the enemy.
5. On 37 occasions the Fourth Army attacked with less than 10 battalions, including 22 attacks that were made with less than five.
6. In the Reserve Army area, only once did the strength of attack exceed 10 battalions.
7. On 10 days out of the 60, British attacks were made by only one or two battalions.

The overwhelming chacteristics of the attacks were that they were constant, small-scale, and narrow-front. This method of proceeding allowed the German troops to concentrate the maximum artillery resources against the small number of attacking troops and on each occasion inflict on the attackers a high percentage of casualties.

The second command failure is the random way in which the available divisions were used. For example the length of time divisions were in the line varied widely – two days in the case of 30 Division; eight days in the case of 56; 16 days for 51; 24 days for 5; and 42 days for 1 Division.[3] Casualties also varied, from a staggering 500 per day for 5 Division to less than 100 per day for 23 Division.

The number of operations launched by these divisions was also random. The much-used 1 Division attacked on 14 occasions, the 5 attacked on nine, the 3, 7, 24, 25, 2 Australian, and 4 Australian attacked on seven. Others such as the 16, 17, 18, 30, 35 and 39 attacked just once.[4]

In some instances this disparity has a simple explanation. The 18 and 30 Divisions were used sparingly in this period because they had been heavily engaged between 1 and 14 July. In most cases, however, there is no such obvious explanation. Divisions were kept in the line, and used repeatedly or sparingly in attacks, apparently at whim.

The third command failure relates to the objectives chosen for attacks. At the end of the fighting on 14 July, the British line resembled a right angle with the apex around Delville Wood. This left the Germans in an ideal situation to concentrate artillery fire on the angle and to enfilade it from the north and east. Fourth Army Command was not unaware of this situation as their aerial superiority allowed them to locate the major groupings of the German batteries with some accuracy.[5]

Common sense required that some effort be made to flatten out this right angle. The evident way of accomplishing this was by concentrating major attacks on the southern section of the British battlefront. On several occasions Haig tried to induce Rawlinson to do this. Yet when we look at the locations of attacks in this period, we find that 29 were made on the left of the right angle, 21 at its apex, and 20 on its right. So it is not only the small scale of the attacks that makes no sense but the direction in which they were pointed.

Nor does the picture become any less random when we go down a further step in the structure of divisions. Each division on the Somme contained 12 battalions. When we look at the way in which they were used we find the following:

164 battalions attacked once
46 battalions attacked twice
24 battalions attacked three times
7 battalions attacked four times
1 battalion attacked five times
1 battalion attacked six times

That is, no sort of investigation makes sense of the middle period of the Battle of the Somme. There was no pattern in the direction of the attacks, no pattern in the time that divisions spent in the line, no pattern in the frequency or infrequency with which divisions (or battalions within divisions) were called upon to attack. In these circumstances it is difficult to argue that the commanders were fulfilling their clear duty to impose some order on what is of necessity the disordered occupation of waging war. There is another duty required of command: to ensure that the troops under them are being husbanded in a manner that will allow them to be used to optimum efficiency. A well-thought-out battle of attrition (such as Haig in his memorandum of 2 August claimed to be fighting) demands that these matters are given the utmost consideration to ensure that the enemy is worn down more than a commander's own armies. Yet in the welter of small, disjointed attacks into which divisions and battalions were being thrown willy-nilly no one at the higher levels of command appeared to be keeping a check on these matters. The vital question in attritional warfare, namely which army will finish the stronger at the end of battle, was being left to chance. No one in authority on the British side, evidently, was keeping careful watch upon how the divisions of their army were being used, or assessing whether at the end of the day they would emerge stronger or weaker than their opponents. As an officer commented later after receiving a draft copy of the Official History:

> It is all very sad reading with the hundreds of little disjointed attacks by Battalion[s] and even Companies repeated day after day to try to capture some small feature or 50 yards of trench with appalling casualties. I am afraid History must condemn the battle of the Somme as a ghastly waste of men and material.[6]

Exactly why the command failed to 'grip' the battle in this period and allowed it to drift in the ways specified does not admit of an easy answer. Perhaps it is simply that a battle on the scale of the Somme was so far from the experience of Haig (a commander of a small army in 1914) or Rawlinson (a divisional commander in the same period) or Gough (the commander of a cavalry division of just 6,000 men at the outbreak of the war) that executing a battle with a force 10 times that of the peacetime army was beyond them.

The British army's 'philosophy of battle' in the form of Field Service Regulations was of little use. No doctrine written in 1909 (which anyway amounted to little more than a series of platitudes) could have anticipated the nature of warfare to be found on the Western Front in 1916. The only section of FSR that was remotely relevant to their situation was Section 99. It offered contradictory advice. On the one hand it advocated persistent attacks while on the other hand it suggested a more deliberate approach may be needed 'on occasion'. Such woolly thinking in fact sanctioned any and every approach to battle.[7]

There is of course another side to all this. The incessant attacks made by Haig's forces, however ill conceived, could not but have a considerable effect on the German army. The 32 British divisions engaged in this period fought 28

German divisions, some more than once. It is extremely difficult to obtain precise casualty statistics for individual German divisions from this period but of the 28 engaged we have 20 that at least reported on the scale of their casualties. Only one described them as 'light'. The others range from percentages (none less than 50 per cent), to such generalisations as 'terrible losses', 'very heavy losses', 'considerable losses', and 'exhausted'.[8] These comments are hardly surprising when we consider the number of shells the British were throwing at the Germans. From 15 July to 12 September they amounted to 7.8 million.[9] The German Official History does not seek to conceal the fact that such a weight of shelling was wearing down the German forces to a significant degree.[10]

Further, it is not only on the British side that we witness inadequacies of command. For most of this period the German command held to a policy of seeking to regain by counter-attack every yard of ground lost to the British, no matter whether the ground was of any tactical value. So while the British during these weeks carried out some 150 attacks in battalion strength and above, the Germans counter-attacked on no fewer than 90 occasions. We have no way of calculating the cost of these endeavours but it cannot have been small.[11] So if there was any factor which helped balance the enormous casualties Haig was causing to his own forces, it was the actions of his counterparts on the other side of the hill. Attrition may have been the outcome but it was a form of attrition over which the commanders of neither side were exercising any real control.

# 18 The Politicians and the Somme Campaign, July–August

## I

In the weeks following the inception of the battle, the nation's leaders found themselves in a dilemma. The central issue of strategy was now settled. A great Western Front campaign was now under way and was expected to deliver large results. The civilian leaders, apparently, would have no deciding to do until the extent and nature of these results expressed themselves.

Yet certain realities intruded. Almost from the outset it became evident that the Somme campaign was not, at least in the short run, transforming the military situation. As early as 3 July, the Secretary of the Committee, Sir Maurice Hankey, reported a meeting between Lloyd George and Balfour where concern had been expressed at the high level of casualties.[1] Robertson was also worried, although there is no evidence that he shared his anxieties with the War Committee. On the 5th he cautioned Haig to limit his ambitions to 'moderate objectives, and to forbid going beyond those objectives until all have been reached by the troops engaged' and said that even this could only be accomplished by powerful artillery action.[2]

Then at a meeting on 11 July, the War Committee was informed that British forces had sustained casualties of 80,000, and that the Germans had more than doubled their military personnel in the area of the offensive. Such hopeful news as the War Committee received – for example that British forces had occupied two-thirds of Mametz Wood and that the supply of ammunition was 'holding out very well' – was hardly of an order to suggest that a mighty Allied victory was at hand.[3]

A missive sent to this meeting by the Commander-in-Chief provided aspirations and expectations, but few concrete achievements:

> He considered that when the present offensive had been developed and exploited they would be in a good position[;] it was as important to the

> French as to ourselves, as it would enable them to cross the Somme and would place us and the French in a good position for a considerable further advance.[4]

Haig was anticipating an advance to the Thiepval Ridge, and expecting strong German counter-attacks for which he hoped to make the enemy pay dearly. '[The British] have inflicted heavy casualties on the Germans, and signs of demoralization were evident' – signs which, it might be noted, Haig, with less than compelling cause, would manage to detect many times thereafter. His conclusion was anything but specific:

> So much had been done already, but they must be prepared to carry on for some weeks, therefore they must have reserves and the necessary flow of drafts.[5]

The War Committee, evidently, was expected to wait and see.

Quite apart from the fact that the offensive was scarcely fulfilling large expectations, there were other developments requiring consideration. These were occurring in the Balkans. Certainly the War Committee, in endorsing the offensive on the Somme, had decided firmly against anything but a defensive stance at Salonika. But the situation there appeared to be changing in ways warranting a reconsideration of strategy. The striking successes of the Russians, admittedly not against the Germans on their northern sector (where any advance would have amounted to a lot), but anyway against the Austro-Hungarians in the south, were having a positive effect. The government of Romania was reconsidering its position of strict neutrality.

To all appearances, Austria-Hungary might, in face of the Russian assault, soon collapse utterly. If Romania was to share in the spoils of dismemberment, it would have to act swiftly. But, the Romanian government was reluctant to proceed without double assurance. It required, as the price of its entry into the war, offensive action not just by the Russians against Austria-Hungary but by the French and British against Bulgaria. (As a result of the outcome of the Second Balkan War of 1913, Bulgaria nursed severe animosity towards Romania.) So, within days of the initiation of the Somme campaign, Britain's leaders found themselves under pressure to reconsider their decision against an offensive out of Salonika.

The War Committee approached this matter warily. For one thing, the potential new ally was requiring action by the British and French against the Bulgarians in advance of any formal commitment by Romania. Britain's leaders harboured doubts about Romania's military competence and the state of its army's equipment. And they suspected that the Romanian authorities might, even yet, wriggle out of participation in the war. So on 6 July the War Committee reasserted, at least for the moment, its decisions for action on the Somme and inaction at Salonika. However, it acknowledged that a clear commitment by Romania to the Allied cause might create a new situation. Action out of Salonika, in short, must await Romania's 'effective entry into the field'.[6]

As July proceeded, differing opinions about these potentially rival offensives developed. On the one hand the War Committee was heartened by the British action on the Somme on 14 July, 'a wonderful performance for 4 divisions', according to Robertson. 'Such a force,' he observed, 'had never been moved by night before.' Also, munitions were holding up well, and captured documents showed 'how great the German losses had been'. On the other hand, 'The Germans had withdrawn only one division from Verdun, where they had gained ground lately, and were only three miles away.'[7]

Events on the Western Front, therefore, remained ambiguous, while developments in the Balkans seemed to be making large promises. The War Committee was informed that the Russians and Romanians had fixed upon a joint offensive against both Austria-Hungary and Bulgaria for 8 August, and that General Sarrail, who exercised principal command at Salonika, was planning an offensive against Bulgaria for a week earlier, 'to prevent hindrance to the Roumanian mobilization'. That seemed to constitute a strong case for British action in the Balkans.[8]

The issue that developed in the War Committee was how substantial that participation should be. As against the apparent conviction among Britain's allies that a great offensive should be launched on the Salonika front, Balfour argued that action there should only be sufficient to hold the Bulgarians in place and so enable the Romanians to devote their full attention to the Habsburg forces. And Robertson expressed disbelief that an Allied offensive from Salonika would actually pierce the Bulgarian lines. He also objected to the commander of British forces in Salonika being placed under Sarrail's authority, and doubted that Romania would be ready or equipped for intervention by the assigned date. More than that: 'We must keep our eye on the West, where we were doing very well.' He agreed to the proposal for action at Salonika, but warned: 'we must go very carefully or we should be depriving ourselves in France'.[9]

The most prominent voice raised in support of a serious commitment to Salonika was, perhaps predictably, Lloyd George's. No doubt recalling that he had once been enthusiastic for knocking the 'props' from under Germany rather than attacking it directly, he set out to present 'another side'. Would it not be an advantage, he asked, 'to cut out Bulgaria and clear a road to Romania. This would have the effect of cutting off the Turks.' Such a proposal, he urged, would 'prevent the supply of ammunition to the Turks and stop Germany from getting food supplies from the east'. It would 'open up a new road to Russia'.

Lloyd George's somewhat bizarre foray in both geography and the intentions of the opposing alliance did not carry the day. Opinion did firm around the notion that, as soon as Romania had unequivocally entered the war, British forces at Salonika would participate in an offensive there. But its object would be limited: to hold Bulgarian forces in place. If it accomplished that, Robertson asserted and no one contradicted, the British mission would be complete.[10]

Thereafter, Romania's decision to enter the struggle hung fire, and Robertson's attitude towards action out of Salonika grew more dismissive. (There would, he said, be no object in our taking the offensive against Bulgaria, 'as Bulgaria was stronger than us'.) Lloyd George, nevertheless, continued to press his case. He explained Romania's tardiness as springing from well-grounded suspicions regarding Russia's intentions. Russia, he said, might 'sell' Romania as it had done in the past (a rather curious form of advocacy for an alternative strategy to which Russia must be the principal contributor).[11]

One thing needs to be stressed. Lloyd George was advocating British action on behalf of Romania. He was not arguing for the cessation of action on the Somme. This he made explicit at a War Committee meeting on 28 July. Edwin Montagu, Lloyd George's successor as Minister of Munitions, stated that output of 6-inch howitzer ammunition had risen from 70,000 to 90,000 rounds a week. He inquired whether the entire complement should go to the battle in France, as the War Office was stipulating, or whether some part of it should be sent to Russia. Lloyd George, donning his hat as War Secretary, firmly opted for the former course. The Germans, he said, had as many guns at the Somme as their opponent, and would have more if they called off their offensive against Verdun. Further, it would be dangerous to send to Russia weapons required by British forces. Already the Russians had been supplied with 4.5-inch howitzers which they had never used, 'whereas Sir D. Haig used them very much, and was clamouring for more':

> Our people were using them, and the Russians were not using them.

Also, he added almost as an afterthought, some might be needed for an offensive at Salonika. Grey, the Foreign Minister chimed in, offering the by now axiomatic judgement that Germany could not act against Russia while its forces were being pinned down on the Somme.[12]

# II

Evidently, whatever the pressures for some British action elsewhere, the offensive on the Somme remained at the end of its first month the main element in the War Committee's strategy. Yet this endorsement was less than wholehearted. As Robertson, in a plea to Haig to provide more information about what was happening at the front, warned the C-in-C:

> The Powers that be are beginning to get a little uneasy in regard to the situation. The casualties are mounting up and they are wondering whether we are likely to get a proper return for them … they will persist in asking me whether I think a loss of say 300,000 men will lead to really great results, because if not we ought to be content with something less than what we are now doing …. It is thought that the primary object – relief of pressure on Verdun – has to some extent been achieved.[13]

Moeover, from outside the government a powerful voice protested strongly against continuation of the Somme campaign.

As First Lord of the Admiralty, Winston Churchill had been a principal figure in the government at the start of the war. But in May 1915 the setback in the Dardanelles had led to his demotion to a minor cabinet post, and when in November it became evident that the Gallipoli campaign was about to be abandoned he resigned from office. After serving for some months on the Western Front, he had assumed the position of an independently minded backbench MP. On 1 August 1916 he penned a critique of the first month of the Somme campaign. The document was not made public, but it was circulated to the cabinet and War Committee.

Churchill began with a bold statement of what had, and more particularly what had not, been accomplished on the Somme. The British army on the opening day had attacked on a front of 20,000–25,000 yards. On nearly three-fifths of that front it had been repulsed. On the remainder it had advanced 'about 2 miles'. British losses for the first two days had been 'not less than 60,000', of whom 40,000 constituted 'permanent loss'. By contrast, Germany's permanent loss he calculated as 12,000. The German front against the British 'is firmly held'.

> It has been tested at many points, and the enemy has himself shown enterprise and activity at many others.

The British had been attacking with 30 divisions, whereas 'the total German force successively or simultaneously engaged in the battle with us cannot exceed fourteen or fifteen divisions. It is probably less.'

The progress made since the opening day gave Churchill no satisfaction:

> We have not conquered in a month's fighting as much ground as we were expected to gain in the first two hours.

So narrow had been the front whatever advance had been made that it was 'quite useless for the purpose of breaking the line'.

> In four weeks we have progressed less than 1 mile. Unless a gap of at least 20 miles can be opened, no large force could be put through ....
>
> Nor are we making for any point of strategic or political consequence ... what are Péronne and Bapaume, even if we were likely to take them? The open country towards which we are struggling by inches is capable of entrenched defence at every step, and is utterly devoid of military significance. There is no question of breaking the line, of 'letting loose the cavalry in the open country behind', or of inducing a general withdrawal of the German armies in the West.

Churchill accepted that the British offensive had obliged the enemy, at least for the present, to suspend 'his costly attacks on Verdun'. ('This is the solitary advantage in the West.') But he denied that the action on the Somme had contributed to Russia's successes in the east, successes 'gained largely by surprise before we had begun'. And he believed that, with division after division of British forces being used up on the Somme, 'the enemy's anxiety is relieved, and he recovers his freedom of movement. This is the danger into which we are now drifting.'

Churchill's summing up of the first month of Somme campaign was devastating:

> In *personnel* the results of the operation have been disastrous; in *terrain* they have been absolutely barren .... From every point of view, therefore, the British offensive *per se* has been a great failure. With twenty times the shell, and five times the guns, and more than double the losses, the gains have but little exceeded those of Loos. And how was Loos viewed in retrospect?

Given that the Loos battle had been followed by the dismissal of Sir John French, the then British commander-in-chief, the question required no answer.

This document by Winston Churchill was marked by a high level of cogency and command of events. It appeared to constitute a powerful case for calling a halt to the Somme offensive. But it contained one glaring omission. At this stage of the war, no one appeared to doubt that Britain's great new army must be fiercely active somewhere, if its allies were not to lose heart and its enemies to take comfort. Churchill nowhere hinted in what other region that army ought to be engaged.[14]

## III

Churchill's memorandum – 'a damnable paper', in the judgement of Robertson – demanded a reply.[15] The nation's military spokesmen provided it.

On 1 August Robertson presented to the War Committee a survey of the military situation. On the Somme front, he said, the Germans now had 32 divisions, formed into two corps which constituted the German Second Army. The Allies had secured a copy of an order by von Below, commander of this Second Army, stating that the decisive outcome of the war depended on the victory of his forces there.

Robertson then presented an appreciation of the previous weeks of battle. Haig, he said (if with less than compelling precision), was doing all he could, he could not do more and he could not do less. British casualties had been heavy, but they included 56,000 sustained on the first day, whereas during the last week they had amounted to 18,000. He calculated (on what basis it is difficult to imagine) that German losses were at least 1.25 million, 'of which 600,000 were a dead loss', as against total losses 'on our side' of 160,000.[16] Joffre had spoken highly of the British contribution, saying that 'we had killed more Germans than the French'. (Four days later, Robertson provided supposed figures of total German losses since the beginning of the war. The figure was 3.575 million, including one million killed.)[17]

On the matter of what all these actual British and supposed German casualties had accomplished, Robertson offered the following: 'We had started operations to relieve Verdun, and to prevent the move of troops to Russia.' Since the opening of the campaign, 'there had been no large attacks against Verdun'. As for the Eastern Front, as a consequence of Russia's offensive the Austro-Hungarians 'were now in a bad way', whereas 'if we had not been fighting' on the Somme the Habsburg forces would have received great assistance from their German allies.[18]

A large issue was being neglected here. The War Committee had now before it a bewildering set of contradictory casualty statistics. Yet no one on the political side pointed to the discrepancies between the casualty balances given by Robertson and Churchill. Nor did they question whether Robertson's fantastical total of 1.25 million German casualties had been incurred against the British alone, or against the British and the French, or whether it applied to the entire Western Front. If the War Committee was to audit the battle with care it was desperately necessary that these discrepancies be resolved. Instead nothing happened. The meeting ended and the politicians dispersed.

On 5 August it met again, only to receive from Robertson a further counter to Churchill's memorandum in the form of a communication from Haig. This was designed to neutralise the views of the former minister. Its subject was 'the results of the offensive on the Somme'.

> First:
> The pressure on Verdun had been relieved, and the situation was no longer regarded as serious by the French authorities.
> Second:
> The Russian front would certainly have been reinforced [by the Germans] and Russia would not have got on as she had.
> Third:
> There was a general good moral[e] effect. The moral[e] and material results had brought the Allies forward on the way to victory. The Germans regarded the Somme operations as very serious.[19]

What followed from these sometimes hypothetical accomplishments was less enumeration than exploration. Haig wrote:

> Under no circumstances must we relax our effort, and we must retain the offensive. Our loss had been 120,000 in the last month more than if we had not attacked which could not be considered unduly heavy. Our troops were in excellent heart. We should maintain a vigorous offensive well into the autumn, and prepare for a further campaign next year.[20]

There was much here that seemed to require devoted probing. The extent of achievement after a month's severe endeavour, according to the nation's chief military spokesmen, appeared to be only that of holding the enemy in place. No significant advance, with all the disruption of enemy arrangements which that might generate, appeared either to have been accomplished or to be in sight. And the claim that the Allies were 'forward on the way to victory' accorded ill with the admitted need for 'a vigorous offensive well into the autumn' followed by 'a further campaign next year'.

Yet no one in the War Committee pressed these matters. Asquith considered Haig's missive 'very satisfactory'. And Curzon judged it 'the real rejoinder to Mr W. Churchill's letter'. So, at the Prime Minister's instigation, Robertson was instructed to send Haig a message 'assuring him that he might count on full support from home' – a message which, Robertson hastened to assure Haig, 'was *not* inserted by my suggestion, but was spontaneous on the part of the Committee after I had read your paper and explained things'.[21]

## IV

Yet in the weeks that followed, these expressions of satisfaction lost at least some of their substance. Misgivings expressed themselves in two ways. Some mildly probing questions, and some hints of disheartenment, appeared in references to the Somme battles. And proposals implying that the time was approaching to look elsewhere for substantial achievements received an airing.

Lloyd George figured in these matters. Certainly he did not espouse Churchill's judgement on the Somme campaign, but he was attracted to devising schemes for big victories elsewhere, although without diverting British forces from the main theatre. As ever, the situation in the Balkans attracted his attention. He pondered a scheme for persuading Bulgaria to pull out of the war in the near future, both by threatening serious military action and by offering territorial inducements (at the expense of Serbia). The additional forces required to accomplish this would, primarily, be provided by Russia.

The Tsar's forces, Lloyd George observed, were awaiting from their Western allies large numbers of heavy guns. Owing to the ice-bound condition of Russia's ports, these would not reach their destination before mid-1917. Lloyd George proposed holding out the bait to the Russians of delivering these weapons by the end of 1916. To gain this, Russia should agree to send an army of 150,000 men across the territory of its potential new ally, Romania, to the border between Romania and Bulgaria. Coupled with a simultaneous offensive out of Salonika by French and British forces, this action by Russia would confront Bulgaria with attack from two sides, north and south, and with hostile forces of 350,000. In these circumstances Bulgaria might withdraw from the war without a fight, especially if it was allowed to retain areas of Macedonia which it had recently annexed from Serbia – areas to which, in the opinon of many in the West, Serbia had no entitlement.[22] (Asquith had observed, in the course of a meeting of the War Committee, that of all the Balkan states Serbia had behaved the worst of the lot.)

On 10 August the War Committee – of course noting that the main operations would befall Russian, not British or French, troops – gave its endorsement to this scheme. Differences, nevertheless, underlay this appearance of agreement. Devotees of the Western strategy wanted to confine British participation to a holding action against the Bulgarians. (As long as the Bulgarians remained within their lines, Robertson argued, 'we should play about, as our guns were not there'.) By contrast Lloyd George, along with Curzon, wanted British forces to make a substantial effort and be prepared to exploit any breakthrough: in short, to do a good deal more than 'play about'.[23]

Events on the Somme, meanwhile, provided little ground for optimism. On 18 August, reference was made to 'the temporary standstill' there. And when Balfour pressed in the War Committee for good news from the Somme, Robertson had little to offer. Asked by Balfour whether he was satisfied by the level of German wastage, Robertson could only reply that he 'did not really know what it was'.

> It was his impression that [the Germans] were losing as many and more than we were. Our losses amounted to about 6000 or 7000 a week.[24]

Given that, very recently, Robertson had been suggesting that German casualties vastly exceeded those of the British, this admission was hardly reassuring.

Balfour, still seeking after hopeful developments, noted how many German divisions were now facing the British on the Somme, and 'suggested the possibility of our striking elsewhere at a thinner line'. Again, Robertson offered no comfort. He opined 'that it could not be done. With more guns they could do it.' Grey came up with an intervention that was hardly more comforting. He observed that the French were in good spirits at the moment 'because they cherished the great expectation of a big advance', but that should October arrive with no advance accomplished, 'there would be a reaction'.

> The French would not like the idea of another winter without a definite advance to our credit.[25]

Robertson's response was a stark demonstration of how expectations were being reined in to conform with the realities of the Somme battle: 'we should', he enjoined, 'be doing very well if we only held the Germans there, and let Russia get on'.

An Anglo-French offensive in the West, whose sole *raison d'être* had now become not its own forward progress but to allow for the accomplishments of the Tsar's forces, was clearly proceeding under a cloud. The Russian advance against the Austrians was slowing down, and against the Germans continued a non-event. Robertson tried to place the best construction on this, but it was less than reassuring:

> things were steady for the moment, but the Russians were getting on. Colonel Knox [British military attaché with the Russian army] did not send a very good report, but he was generally pessimistic.[26]

Events in the second half of August provided grounds for both hope and pessimism. Action on the Somme on 18 August seemed promising, but by the end of the month Joffre was again reported as complaining about the absence of progress. On 27 August, the much-delayed intervention of Romania on the Allied side, with their reported four armies of 600,000 men and their trained forces numbering one million, raised large hopes among Britain's leaders. But Lloyd George's scheme for a great movement of Russian and Romanian forces against Bulgaria, with promised weaponry from Britain, was turned down flat by the Russian command. And the War Committee was painfully oppressed at the end of the month by changes in the German high command. Falkenhayn, whose predilection had all along been for action on the Western Front, had been dismissed. His successors, Hindenburg and Ludendorff, were recognised as having a different orientation, at least for the present: the elimination of Russia and the closure of the Eastern Front, accompanied only by defensive action in the west.[27]

What was particularly ominous about this was the realisation that, after two months of a great Allied endeavour on the Somme, the Germans had still not been deprived of strategic initiative on all fronts. The principal justification for the Somme offensive had become its capacity to force the Germans on to the defensive in east and west. Now the fragility of this claim was becoming all too evident.

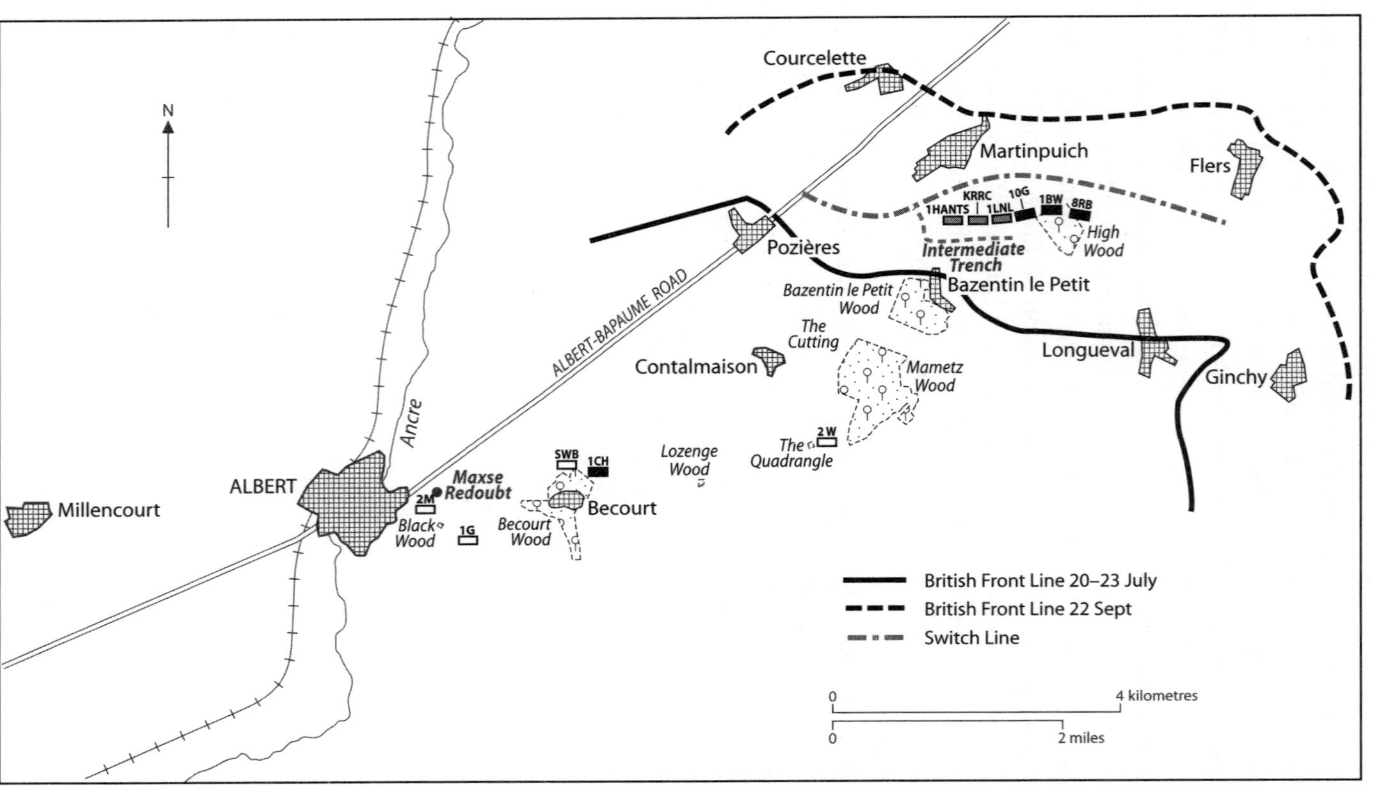


The I Division on the Somme, July–September

# 19 One Division's Somme: The First Division, July–September

## I

What was the experience of just a single British division in the Battle of the Somme? The earlier statistical discussion of Haig's armies in the period 15 July to 12 September indicated that no division could be said to have had a 'typical experience'. However it seems worthwhile to look in more detail at one of the British divisions to see exactly how it experienced the battle and coped with its effects.

The 1 British Division entered the line on 11 July and exited on 28 September – a period of 80 days. During this time it had three tours of duty in the line – 15 days from 11 to 25 July, 27 days from 16 August to 11 September, and 8 days from 21 to 28 September. Overall then the division was 'in the line' for 50 days and resting, refitting, or training for 30 days.[1]

During these tours of duty the division suffered the following casualties:[2]

| | *Officers* | | | *Other Ranks* | | | |
|---|---|---|---|---|---|---|---|
| | *killed* | *wounded* | *missing* | *killed* | *wounded* | *missing* | *Total* |
| 11–27 July | 21 | 92 | 17 | 395 | 2093 | 472 | 3090 |
| 14 Aug.–12 Sept. | 59 | 169 | 22 | 953 | 3744 | 969 | 5916 |
| 20–29 Sept. | 16 | 43 | 1 | 236 | 969 | 187 | 1452 |
| Totals | 96 | 304 | 40 | 1584 | 6806 | 1628 | 10458 |

Several aspects of these figures are remarkable. The first is that although the division almost entirely avoided the major encounters of 1 July, 14 July, 15 September, and 25 September, it still suffered almost 100 per cent infantry casualties while it was in battle, 200 on average for every day in the line. The second is that by the end of the battle the division must have been a quite different formation from that which had entered. About 3,000 of its officers and men were missing or killed[3] and just over 7,000 wounded. Although many in this last category would have suffered only light wounds and returned to their unit, many would not. It seems likely that at least 2,000 of the wounded would have been regarded as 'serious' and never returned. In other words no less than 50 per cent of the infantry of the division present on 11 July would not have been present on 28 September.

How did the 1 Division survive this kind of ordeal and still emerge as an effective fighting unit? A partial understanding might come from a closer investigation of the structure of an infantry division.

In 1916 a division consisted of approximately 17,000 men. Of these, 4,000 belonged to the divisional artillery (4 × 4 batteries of 18-pounder guns and 2 × 4 batteries of 4.5-inch howitzers) and an additional 1,000 men consisted of headquarters troops, machine-gun detachments, and miscellaneous troops. In general these men, who often operated well behind the front and, in the case of the artillery, often stayed in the line when the infantry moved out, will not be considered here. We will focus our attention on the 12,000 infantry, which constituted the backbone of the division. During the Somme a British infantry division was organised into three brigades of approximately 4,000 men and each brigade contained four battalions, nominally (although few were up to strength) of 1,000 men each. An organisational chart of the division as it entered the Somme fighting looked thus:

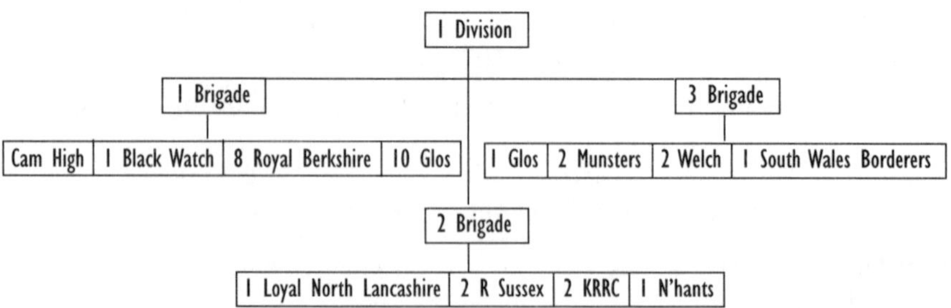


All modern European armies had adopted a similar structure, for the good reason it is were very flexible. So at the Somme when we say that the 1 Division was 'holding the line' what we often mean is that only one of its brigades was actually in the front trench system. A second brigade could be 1,000 to 2,000 yards behind in support and the third perhaps some 3,000 yards behind the second, in reserve. The brigade holding this front would be subjected to the most intense enemy fire and would be the unit that went 'over the top' in a battle. The brigade in support would still be under fire but probably of a less intense nature. It was so placed to reinforce the front brigade in case of a success in battle (hardly ever a factor at the Somme). Alternatively, it could be available to provide a quick replacement for units shattered in an attack (a very frequent occurrence) or to be on hand to stem an enemy attack (again hardly ever a factor during the Somme campaign). German attacks during the Somme fighting were frequent but usually only had the purpose of recapturing positions recently lost. Few penetrated (or tried to penetrate) so far as the area held by the support units. The reserve brigade would merely take the place of the support brigade if it had been called upon to fulfil any of the above roles. Of course these dispositions represent a typical situation. During a large offensive the front might be held by more than one brigade. This was the case on 18 August when both 1 and 2 Brigades of 1 Division took part in the offensive. A map showing 1 Division's dispositions on this occasion is given on p. 202.

Yet the picture could even be more complicated. If a brigade held the front line it might place just one of its four battalions in the front trench. This hardly meant that the other three battalions were not in danger. They were almost certainly located in the front 'system' of trenches, which might mean that even the rearward unit was within 500 yards of the front – well within the areas habitually shelled by the German artillery and swept by machine-guns.

It needs to be emphasised that no unit of a division holding the line was exempt from the risk of injury or death. All the battalions near the front were well within range of the German artillery, although the rearward groups would probably not experience much enemy machine-gun fire. Positions further back were not immune from fire. Heavy German guns could penetrate as far back as Albert during the 1 Division's tour of duty. Only the training area could be said to be truly safe.

## II

If we divide the battlefield into six 'areas of activity' from the rear to the front – training or resting; in reserve; in support; in close support; holding the front line; and attacking – we may depict the number of days spent on each by the battalions of 1 Division (see over).

This table can be taken as a reasonable representation of the experiences of the battalions of 1 Division on the Somme.[4] The first thing to notice about it is its apparent uniformity. It seems clear that each unit was rotated into the various areas for as even a period as the exigencies of battle would allow. Thus each battalion spent approximately 15 days of the 80 in the front line, 12 to 13 in close

| | *Attack* | *Front* | *Close support* | *Support* | *Reserve* | *Training* | *Total* |
|---|---|---|---|---|---|---|---|
| 10 Gloucester | 2.5 | 14 | 15.5 | 12 | 5 | 31 | 80 |
| 8 Royal Berks | 1.5 | 11.5 | 26 | 10 | 4 | 27 | 80 |
| 1 Camerons | 2 | 13 | 12 | 15 | 14 | 24 | 80 |
| 1 Black Watch | 3 | 13.5 | 11.5 | 14 | 8 | 30 | 80 |
| 2 Royal Sussex | 4 | 11 | 15 | 20 | 6 | 24 | 80 |
| 1 Loyal N Lancs | 3 | 7 | 13 | 15 | 17 | 25 | 80 |
| KRRC | 3 | 13 | 15 | 12 | 11 | 26 | 80 |
| 1 Northants | 4.5 | 11.5 | 10 | 12 | 15 | 27 | 80 |
| S Wales Borderers | 1.5 | 8.5 | 14 | 11 | 18 | 27 | 80 |
| 2 Welch | 4 | 10 | 11 | 8 | 19 | 28 | 80 |
| 2 Munster | 4 | 11 | 11 | 9 | 17 | 28 | 80 |
| 1 Gloucester | 2 | 11 | 9 | 11 | 19 | 28 | 80 |

reserve and about 28 in training. The number of attacks carried out during this period varies – from 1.5 to 4 – but this is often a reflection of the level of casualties suffered in particular battles. In some ways, however, this uniformity is deceptive. Units in support could suddenly be thrown into battle, and units in reserve could find themselves engaged in front-line duty. In other words, the actual experience of a unit could be much more chaotic than the table suggests.

A major point to note about the attacks is that they did not happen very often. On average, in this period, a battalion attacked three times – or once every four weeks. What this reveals is that for most divisions, fighting at the Somme was not a matter of incessant attacks until the unit was destroyed. Just 5 per cent of 1 Division's time was spent in going over the top. However, the time spent in the front line and close support could be just as dangerous as launching an attack – because of continual German machine-gunning and shelling. And no less than an additional 35–40 per cent of a unit's time could be spent in these areas. In short, a soldier could be in mortal danger for four days in ten spent in the battle, which for 1 Division soldiers meant a total of 32 days.

## III

We will now look at each of the six categories of activity in more detail so that we can establish as exactly as possible what the Somme experience meant for the infantrymen of 1 Division.

For example, what did it actually mean when a battalion was designated 'resting or training'? A typical battalion was the South Wales Borderers, which had two periods out of the battle: from 27 July to 14 August and from 11 to 17 September.[5]

The battalion came out of the line after a totally unsuccessful and ill-planned attack on Munster Alley which caused around 100 casualties. [6] It marched to billets in Millencourt, a small village two miles west of Albert where it would be based for the entire rest period. The first few days at Millencourt were spent 'as a holiday for rest and refuelling' and absorbing new drafts to make up for the casualties suffered.[7] This period came to an end on 31 July. From then until 14 August the battalion undertook a regular programme of drill, training, and recreational activities. Recreation took the form of sports, horse shows, and concert parties, all run by the officers on public school lines. The favourite sport was boxing, possibly because it was thought 'manly' and instilled the controlled aggression considered necessary for infantrymen. The main tournament was held between 1 and 4 August. The Borderers were quite successful in this competition, Drummer Jones winning the heavyweight division and Private Young winning the middleweight division.[8]

Other sports played were tug-of-war, sack racing, relay and sprint races and a battalion special, the V.C. Race. This event is best described by the War Diary:

> At a given signal the competitors had to leap on to the bare back horses, gallop the hundred yards between the flags, dismount and pick up a dummy corpse, mount again and gallop back to the tape. After several collisions, and much excitement, Sgt Freeman won on Minnie.[9]

Among the other activities were frequent horse shows, an indication of the dependence of armies in this period on the horse to transport guns, cart supplies from the railheads, and carry out many other tasks. Time was also spent at concert parties, although the only one mentioned in the 1 Division diaries is the 'Follies', which belonged to another division. There were also such bizarre activities as boot races, one of which caused a casualty when a boot was flung with 'unnecessary vigour'.[10] The absence of team games involving large numbers of men as participants, not just onlookers, can only be deemed surprising.

The main activity was of course training. At its most basic this consisted of PT, drill, and rifle and bayonet practice, all carried out on most mornings. An inordinate amount of time seems to have been spent on bayonet practice, considering the limited opportunities for using a bayonet in trench warfare. No doubt this was thought to instil the bloodthirstiness needed for a successful infantry attack. (Just 0.004 per cent of all casualties in the war were inflicted by bayonets.)

One other form of training consisted of rehearsing night attacks. The battalion practised this manoeuvre on four occasions. Twice the exercise was judged unsuccessful because there was 'too much talking and coughing'.[11] On the third occasion the attack was pronounced a success, the 'only fault being' a tendency among the men to stop when they were within a few yards of the trench, as if they were not quite sure what to do.[12] After this fiasco the battalion was taken to watch a night attack carried out by day, presumably to show them the correct procedure.[13] On their last experience of night fighting they had to advance behind a barrage 'represented by a big drum [which] raged for 3 minutes'.[14]

Attempts to practise with contact patrol aeroplanes fared no better. The watches carried by the airmen and the infantry were not synchronised, so that by the time the planes appeared the battalion had gone back to billets 'rendering' in the words of the War Diary, 'the whole scheme meaningless'.[15]

Regrettably no detail is given on this battalion's only incursion into wood fighting.[16]

In between such activities there were always the stirring speeches by higher commanders. These talks were no doubt intended to raise morale. On 1 August the Borderers were addressed by General Pulteney, GOC III Corps of which 1 Division was a part. After inspecting the troops Pulteney

> thanked the Brigade for their share in recent operations and hoped that the men clearly understood that they were now in open warfare and must use their own initiative without waiting for the commands of their superiors.[17]

As the battalion had just engaged in a period of particularly grim trench fighting in which every attempt to capture the German front line (on average just 50 yards from the British) had failed with heavy casualties and which in two weeks hardly gained a yard of ground, their reaction to the news that they had been engaged in 'open warfare' operations may well have been ribald.

The training areas were beyond the range of enemy machine-guns and artillery. The only danger posed to the men by the Germans came from aircraft, which could either machine-gun them or drop bombs. However, for most of the Somme campaign the British possessed air superiority and in any case targets favoured by enemy aircraft were headquarters, crossroads, known ammunition dumps, artillery concentrations, and troops entering or leaving the line. Training areas had a low priority and the 1 Division war diaries do not mention one instance of men in training being attacked by enemy planes.

Closer to the front were areas designated for units in reserve. For 1 Division these were around Albert (either in the town itself or nearby in Black Wood, Bécourt Wood, or Maxse Redoubt (see map, 'The 1 Division on the Somme', p. 202). The units in these areas were normally on standby to replace troops in the line, reinforce attacks, or to halt successful enemy counter-attacks. As noted, on the Somme the last two circumstances hardly ever occurred, so the reserve areas were usually staging posts for troops on their way to the front or to the rest areas in rear.

So what did troops 'in reserve' actually do and what danger were they in? The degree of danger varied enormously. Some units such as the Black Watch recorded heavy shelling for each of the days in July that they were in reserve.[18] Similarly, the 1 Gloucesters recalled that Albert 'was frequently hit by heavy stuff'.[19] They noted a direct hit on a house on 13 July which killed twelve gunners from the field artillery, a billet being demolished by a shell with a delayed action fuse on the 14th and a shell bursting (harmlessly, as it happened) among the headquarters staff as they sunned themselves in a garden on the 15th.[20]

The unluckiest of the battalions in reserve was perhaps the 2 Welch. They arrived in Albert on 10 July and almost at once were hit by a heavy shell which killed six troops and wounded twenty-one more.[21]

Being in reserve could be accompanied by other dangers. 'Reserve' troops were often regarded by the divisional command as being underutilised and they were liable to be used to carry stores up to the front. So on 19, 20, and 21 July, the 1 Gloucesters, who had just come out of the line, were required to provide 'large fatigue parties' for, among other things, repairing the wire which protected the front-line trench. These parties suffered twenty casualties while carrying out those duties.[22] Another battalion, 1 Northamptonshire, described its experience of these tasks in rather bitter terms:

> Working party of 400 under 2$^{nd}$ in cmnd marched to Lozenge Wood, and thence carried wire, stores etc thro Contalmaison to the front line – considerable shelling in the village, some casualties. Party carried back some 70 wounded, mostly German, from the cellars of Contalmaison – a work which would seem to have been the duty of the 2$^{nd}$ Field Ambulance, which was stationed at Fricourt for the purpose.[23]

Five days later the War Diary reported that they were still carrying wire, tools, and water to the front line.[24]

Closer to the front were the 'support' areas. These shifted slightly after the advances made on 14 July and 15 September but could broadly be defined as anywhere in advance of Bécourt Wood and short of the front system of trenches. The main areas inhabited by the support battalions of 1 Division were Lozenge Wood, the Quadrangle, Mametz Wood and, after 15 September, Bazentin-le-Petit Wood.

There were varying degrees of danger in these positions. All troops in these areas could be brought under artillery fire from almost all types of German gun. Closer to the front they could be targets of machine-gun fire as well.

In July a typical tour in the area was undertaken by the South Wales Borderers. On the 14th the battalion was ordered to move from Albert to Lozenge Wood with the rest of 3 Brigade. In this position they were to wait in general support of operations until they received more specific orders.[25] The position occupied at Lozenge was reasonably secure. The battalion was located in the old German front-line trenches and found shelter in 'several excellent deep dugouts'.[26] On the 15th however, further orders arrived – they were to move to Mametz Wood and be prepared to support an attack by 2 Welch on the following day.[27] While in the wood they experienced heavy shelling which included gas shells. The attack by the Welch failed but another was immediately scheduled and the carrying parties were now required to move bombs, tools, and barbed wire up to the front line. These carrying parties were heavily shelled and gassed and casualties began to mount.[28] On the 18th they were withdrawn to the relative safety of Lozenge Wood but were immediately ordered to provide small working parties to construct keeps in front of Contalmaison. These duties resulted in yet heavier casualties as the men came under machine-gun fire as well as shrapnel and gas.[29] Finally, on the 19th, they were withdrawn first to Bécourt Wood and then to Albert. They had been in support for seven days, and suffered intense shelling on six of these days, resulting in 50 casualties. Yet, apart from the working parties, they had not come within 500 yards of the front line.

There could be more gruesome tasks for troops in support than carrying ammunition and equipment. The War Diary of the 10 Gloucesters (a new army unit) recounts a five-day period it spent near Fricourt:

> moved up to the line (from Albert) at the dingle about a mile north of Fricourt and came into Brigade support. The ground occupied had only just been won from the enemy and was strewn with corpse's between four and five hundred of which we buried. On 11/7/16 Lt. J.W. Gray was hit in the hand and sent back .... Between 10/7/16 and 12/7/16 we had 5 killed and 24 wounded practically all from shellfire. The battalion was mainly employed in improving existing and digging fresh communication trenches to Contalmaison.[30]

There were even more dangerous aspects of 'support' than this. Troops in close support could in various ways be drawn into the actual fighting. On 20 July the 8 Royal Berkshires were in close support in the OG lines some 400 yards from the front. On the 21st they received orders to support an attack on the Switch Line on 22/23 July by the 10 Gloucesters and 1 Camerons. As the attack commenced, two companies of the Berkshires moved up to the front with the other two in reserve near the Cutting. The operation proved such a disaster (the three assaulting battalions suffered about 400 casualties) that the remaining

Berkshire companies were rushed forward to reinforce those in the front line in case the Germans counter-attacked. They were required to hold that line until relieved on the 25th.

Even units which had just been in battle could be sent back to the front from support positions. The 2 Royal Sussex were in the line at High Wood from 14 to 17 August during which time they had carried out two attacks, one successful, one not, both costly.[31] On the 18th the battalion was relieved and on the 19th bivouacked at Mametz Wood, on the way back to Albert. Then in the early morning news came from High Wood that a German counter-attack had driven in the British line. Orders to the Sussex were revised and they sent two companies forward to assist in re-establishing the position. That attack failed so the remaining two companies were sent forward for a second attempt. That too failed and finally the battalion, now reduced to four officers and 160 men from a strength of 20 officers and 650 men when it entered the battle, was withdrawn to reserve.[32]

Forward of the support positions of course lay the front line system of trenches – the area of the most acute danger. At the Somme these positions consisted of a front trench, usually protected by barbed-wire entanglements, and several lines of other trenches some 50 yards in rear of the front line and parallel to it. At right angles to these trenches ran interconnecting communication trenches to allow rearward troops relatively safe access to the front. Most trenches were zigzagged to confine the explosive force of a shell to a relatively small area.

There was danger for troops wherever they were in this system. Any attempt to leave the safety of a trench could produce a hail of machine-gun bullets from across no man's land, which could be as narrow as 50 yards. Even trenches did not protect from shells landing close by. Shell fragments ricocheting at high velocity around the narrow confines of a trench could wound or maim or dismember a soldier unlucky enough to be in the wrong place. Nor, as far as shelling was concerned, were the rear lines much safer. Artillery shells fired from the same gun on the same trajectory would not all land in the same place. What the spread of fire meant was that a soldier 100 yards behind the front had an equal chance of being hit by a shell as one in the front line.

The most dangerous activity was a tour of duty in the front line, even when the tour did not actually involve an attack.

An example of such a tour of duty is provided by the 2 Welch in the August phase of the Somme battle. Their progress to the front followed the usual pattern. On 17 August they were in Bécourt Wood. On the 18th they were ordered forward to support positions around the Quadrangle. On the 20th they moved into the front line, between High Wood and Bazentin-le-Petit. They were to remain in this position until the 27th. From the moment they arrived the War Diary comments on the severity of the shelling. It is described as 'heavy' on 20, 22, and 23 August, as 'very active' on the 24th, and as 'slackening' on the 26th and 27th. The erratic nature of the shelling was also noted:

> 22/8/16 Hostile artillery again kept up heavy barrage especially across the main communication trench, almost all day and night.... During the shelling the three companies in rear [of the front line] suffered rather heavily from many shells.

But the Welch troops required more than edurance under fire. For the eight days of their stay at the front they were obliged to dig trenches at right angles to the front line into no man's land. The idea of this 'sapping', as it was called, was to join up the 'saps' at a later date and thus advance the line by some tens of yards. It was a dangerous business, always likely to be interrupted by enemy patrols. In the case of the Welch there was an additional hazard. They had succeeded in pushing the line forward to such an extent that they came under enemy enfilade machine-gun fire from adjacent parts of the front. In addition they were required to undertake patrols into no man's land. From these they might glean information about the German defences to be passed back to the brigade intelligence officer and the artillery, or capture prisoners to help establish the enemy order of battle in that part of the line.

All this activity took its toll. On the 28th when the Welch were in billets in Albert, roll-call revealed that one officer had been killed and three wounded, while 41 other ranks died, 170 were wounded, four were missing, and 46 were suffering from shell-shock and incapable of further duties. In all, 265 men (or 30 per cent of their strength) had become casualties in a seven-day spell in the line which did not contain one major episode. One point to note about this is the relatively low officer casualties, a figure which would have been much higher if the battalion had attacked: junior officers invariably led these attacks making themselves conspicuous to their troops and, as an unhappy by-product, to the enemy.[33]

The most dangerous task of the infantry was actually to leave the shelter of their trenches and attack across no man's land

The experience of the troops conducting these attacks could be very different. Some idea of different experiences can be gleaned from the casualty statistics. For those attacks for which we have statistics, casualties for battalion attacks range from 28 for 1 Gloucesters on 17 July to 306 for 1 Cameron Highlanders on 3 September, though it is possible that even higher casualties were suffered in other operations.[34]

Moreover, the accounts show that most attacks failed. Of the 36 carried out by 1 Division in this period 22 gained not a single yard of ground. The causes of these failures were various.

Occasionally failure could be ascribed to the poor arrangements made for the attack at a higher level. On 9 September, 10 Gloucesters were loaned to 3 Brigade for an attack on High Wood. So little advance notice was given to the Gloucesters that their assaulting companies arrived in position just before zero. With no time to reconnoitre their objective, and attacking in the dark, the result was a predictable failure. The two companies participating lost 127 casualties for no result.

More often than not it was the failure of fire support which was the major factor. Sometimes this might not be the distant guns but the trench artillery under the command of the infantry. On 24 August the 2 Munster Fusiliers were ordered to attack a section of Intermediate Trench where the German defences were shaped like three sides of a rectangle. The furthest trench was to be bombarded by the field artillery but the flanking positions were left to the Stokes mortars. As an account of the action by the commanding officer of the Munsters states:

> On launching the attack it soon became evident that … [the Stokes mortars] had failed either to knock out the enemy, destroy his morale or injure his machine guns. The assaulting parties followed each other without hesitation but in both cases were met with very heavy machine gun & rifle fire at point blank range, the survivors being bombed on reaching bombing distance. It is doubtful if a single man actually reached the enemy trench in either case, tho several officers & men fell on the enemy parapet.[35]

Occasionally the artillery could be more foe than friend, as the 8 Royal Berkshires found on 18 August:

> At 12 noon the heavy artillery commenced a bombardment of the Intermediate Line. Unfortunately one gun was firing short and its shells fell on our own front line just at the time when the relief was taking place. The effect of these shells was that many of our men were buried and the trench was so badly blown in that inter-communication between our portion of the trench and another was impossible. This caused a good deal of confusion and the companies were scarcely in position by the time they had to attack.[36]

Nevertheless, despite the generally dismal aspect of the Somme campaign, and the infinitesimal amount of ground gained by 1 Division in 80 days, not all attacks were disastrous or ill-planned. On 17 July, just after they had entered the line, the 1 Gloucesters were required to take part in a night attack on a series of German trenches just to the south-east of Pozières, which stood between the British and the Switch Line. Before the attack started it was discovered by the divisional artillery that the German positions could be enfiladed by batteries located around Montauban. So all through the day the guns fired on the enemy trenches, cutting the wire, and it may be imagined, making the defences very difficult to inhabit for the German garrison.[37] The 1 Gloucester War Diary takes up the story close to zero hour at midnight:

> At 11.40 the Battalion advanced [into no man's land] and after 150 yards deployed .... At 11.50pm the artillery commenced an intense bombardment of enemy's front and support lines. The battalion continued to advance until within 150 yards of enemy line. At 12 midnight artillery lifted on to the support line and till 12.5 am intensely shelled it. B and D companies marched through the [cut] wire and over the German line, the enemy on our approach hastily retired. A Company coming up behind seized the line, bombed the dug-outs and at once commenced consolidating, and got into touch with Munsters on left.
>
> B & D Companies continued their advance and crossed the enemy's Support line. The enemy had by this time fled. At 12.50am a red flare was burnt to show that our objective had been gained.[38]

For their part in an operation, which due to careful artillery planning captured two lines of trenches some 1,200 yards long,[39] 1 Gloucester had suffered just two men killed, 25 wounded, and one missing.

It was the unfortunate lot of 1 Division to take part in many of the failures of the Somme campaign but none of its notable successes. This was a matter of bad luck and timing rather than lack of endeavour on its part. It was also bad fortune to be called on to attack three positions (Switch Line, High Wood, Wood Lane) which were out of direct observation of the British artillery. At this stage of the battle the gunners could very rarely hit such targets with any regularity. Accuracy depended on continual adjustments to the range of a gun telephoned back from a forward observation officer who was directly observing the fall of shot. When the artillery could not see the target, slow adjustments had to be made from directions given by aerial observers (when available) or they had to be attacked using map co-ordinates from maps which were often inaccurate. This last method was by far the most common and accounts for much of the inaccuracy of the guns during this period. Furthermore, as the campaign went on the incidents of short shooting (friendly fire, it would now be called) increased as the gun barrels wore out. The effect of wear on the barrels was not fully grasped at this time and so only crude attempts were made to correct it. It was also the misfortune of 1 Division to be engaged at a time when the determination of the command to launch incessant narrow-front attacks was at its height. As already noted, this gave the units involved minimum chance of success.

Yet despite its many misfortunes 1 Division remained a viable fighting unit, as the minor successes obtained by some of its battalions on 26 and 27 September demonstrate. How are we to account for this? Partly the reason can be found in the fairly lengthy periods spent resting and training out of the line. Despite the inadequate nature of much of the training, the rest and recreation did much for morale and ensured that some kind of *esprit de corps* was maintained.

Nevertheless, on average only one soldier in two who had been present at the commencement of the battle would have been present at the end. The remainder consisted of drafts received during the battle who had blended into the battalions in the rest periods. But if the South Wales Borderers are representative, the training of these recruits ranged from the elementary to the farcical. In the light of these facts it is hard to believe that training was a major determinant of success in battle. As the Battle of the Somme wore on it became obvious to many that it was the artillery which determined whether an action succeeded or not. There were two major ways in which the guns could achieve this end. The creeping barrage, which was fired by *all* the divisional artilleries from 15 September, could protect troops advancing across no man's land until they were close enough to overpower the defenders. And the larger guns could suppress or destroy enemy batteries and disorganise trench defenders by destroying either their dug-outs or their morale, or both. As we will see, this is what happened on 25 September. In other words what was required of the infantry was not so much the skill needed in manoeuvre warfare, which (General Pulteney notwithstanding), the 1 Division was not fighting, as the ability to stick close behind a barrage as it moved from trench to trench. This the men of 1 Division could do. The bravery required to carry out this task should not be underestimated. An artillery barrage, even a friendly one, could be terrifying, especially if some guns were shooting short. Moreover, the infantry always required that obedience to authority without which no attack could be made. This is a factor which is largely absent from the accounts, no doubt because it was taken for granted. Indeed, what Churchill described as the 'wonderful tenacity' of the British infantry at the Somme could always be taken for granted. It was this quality then rather than superior training which, we can surmise, saw 1 Division through its ordeal on the Somme.

# 20 'An Operation Planned on Bolder Lines': Tanks and the 15 September Plan

## I

In his memorandum of 2 August Haig had foreshadowed a major battle: perhaps the climactic episode of the Somme campaign if not of the entire war. He knew that by mid-September a new weapon of war, in the form of the tank, would be available to him. He was under the impression that the French would also have this novel instrument at their disposal until inquiry revealed Foch was completely unaware of its existence.[1] On the 16th Haig informed Rawlinson that the tanks would be on hand for the next battle and the Fourth Army might be called on to attack in mid-September with the objective of capturing the three German lines which faced them 'and possibly the gun positions beyond'.[2] He envisaged that Rawlinson, who had never seen a tank, might have between 36 and 42 machines and Gough, whose Reserve Army would act in a supporting role, should have between 18 and 24. Haig expected that the infantry would work close behind the tanks, that the manner of how tanks and artillery would work together required careful consideration, and that the tanks should be given simple objectives as they were very hard to manoeuvre.[3]

On 19 August Rawlinson was asked to submit plans to 'seize the last line of the prepared [German] defences between Morval and Le Sars with a view to opening the way for the Cavalry'.[4]

Before submitting his plan Rawlinson, along with Haig, Gough, and senior staff officers, visited the tank training ground at St Riquier. There the tanks demonstrated how they could cross trenches, climb parapets, and even knock down small trees. Haig thought the day 'encouraging'.[5] Rawlinson's impressions were mixed. He noted that two of the six tanks on show broke down and that an officer fainted while driving. He thought the crews green and in need of much practice. Nevertheless, overall he pronounced himself 'rather favourably impressed'.[6] So he agreed to incorporate the tanks into his plan but, as he wrote in his diary, 'I am in favour of using them cautiously and not doing too much in one bound .... If we attempt to do too much we run the risk of doing nothing'.[7] He added perceptively: 'D.H. won't like this'.[8]

Indeed, when Rawlinson's first plan arrived at GHQ on the 29th the Commander-in-Chief did not like it. Far from picking up on Haig's remarks that the Fourth Army should aim for the third German line and possibly the gun positions beyond to open the way for the cavalry, Rawlinson had discounted the third German line and the horsed soldiers. He observed that the enemy systems were less formidable than those which faced the Fourth Army on 1 July, but that nevertheless capturing all three would be impossible. All the lines had some dug-outs and were protected by belts of wire, some of which could not be seen by direct observation from the British front. Moreover the Germans had incorporated no fewer than five fortified villages – Martinpuich, Flers, Gueudecourt, Lesboeufs, Morval – into their defences. The first and second lines were in places some 2,000 yards apart, a formidable distance for attacking troops to traverse. Taking all this into consideration, he came up with a cautious plan that fell well short of Haig's expectations.

Rawlinson thought that the first line could be captured and the presence of tanks might make it possible to seize points of tactical importance, such as Flers and Martinpuich. A foothold in Flers in particular would enable the remainder of that line to be rolled up with the assistance of tanks directed towards Eaucourt l'Abbaye within 24 hours of the original attack. He gave no consideration to the capture of the third German line as it was 'out of range of the large majority of our guns and howitzers'.[9] The tanks, having operated entirely at night, would then be withdrawn, thus maintaining their mystery. The Fourth Army could then proceed to attack the final German line within a further 24 hours. In all, six divisions would be employed.[10]

This plan has a familiar ring. It resembles very closely Rawlinson's first thoughts for the first day of the Somme – the seizure of the enemy's front line and important tactical features beyond, then the rolling up of the second line, then further operations against the remaining defences. Unfortunately for Rawlinson, Haig's reply also has a familiar ring. After studying Rawlinson's plan he then noted in his diary:

> In my opinion he is not making enough of the situation with the deterioration and all-round loss of moral[e] of the enemy troops. I think we should make our attack as strong and as violent as possible, and plan to go as far as possible.[11]

To drive this point home Haig sent his Chief of Staff, General Kiggell, to Fourth Army headquarters with the following memorandum:

> With reference to your [plan] dated 28th August, 1916, the Commander-in-Chief considers that the situation is likely to be favourable for an operation planned on bolder lines. Accordingly he desires that the 'tanks' may be used boldly and success pressed in order to demoralize the enemy and, if possible, capture his guns.[12]

He added, in a blow that ended one aspect of Rawlinson's plan, that information from the tank experts indicated that the tanks could not be used at night.[13] And just in case Rawlinson had not got the point of Kiggell's message and the accompanying note, Haig penned an even longer set of instructions. He emphasised yet again that enemy morale was deteriorating, that they had suffered repeated defeats and that their resources were limited to very tired troops who had already suffered severely. Bold action now would perhaps yield 'decisive results', a point which must be stressed to all commanders. The slow methods of trench warfare were inappropriate. The cavalry available to Fourth Army would be increased to four or five divisions and their final objective extended. Now they were to aim first at establishing a flank guard along the line Morval–Le Transloy–Bapaume, then proceed north-west to roll up the entire enemy line.[14] So what all this meant was that in a matter of a few hours Haig's thoughts had advanced beyond the enemy gun line to Bapaume and points north-west.

What underlay Haig's optimism was his view that German morale was collapsing. The recent successes were being regarded not as fortunate incidents in a generally unrewarding period of fighting, but as proof that the German army had entered a decline possibly approaching terminal collapse which could be accelerated by a large offensive employing novel weaponry. What is to be made of this? Of course it is unlikely that the morale of German units facing the British on 15 September was universally good. Some of the Bavarian regiments in the line had been involved in the severe fighting around Ginchy, Delville Wood, and High Wood during the first two weeks of September. Three in particular had suffered heavy casualties.[15] On 10 September one of these regiments described the mood in the battalions as 'depressed'.[16] Yet the majority of the Bavarian regiments facing the British were fresh and their morale was good.[17] British Intelligence may once more have made the error of generalising about morale from a small sample of German prisoners.

But these considerations did not weigh with Haig. He required a strong reason to believe – despite the scanty evidence – that German morale was all but spent. For if the German guns were to be captured and the cavalry unleashed, it was essential that enemy morale be on the point of collapse. Only then could the employment of cavalry be justified. So for Haig to believe that a major British victory was anywhere in sight, he was bound to look about for indications that the prerequisite circumstances for a great triumph were now present.

## II

In the face of Haig's barrage of memoranda and messages. Rawlinson capitulated. He drew up a new plan. Perhaps Rawlinson was simply overwhelmed by the vigour, frequency, and imperious nature of Haig's memoranda. Perhaps also Rawlinson's position had been weakened by his lack of grip on the battle in August, a performance that had eventually earned him a stern lecture from Haig on his duties as an army commander.

Rawlinson's response was to call an immediate conference of his corps commanders and senior staff officers. He told them the Commander-in-Chief wanted to go 'all out' and push the cavalry through and to this end he was increasing the number of infantry divisions for the attack from six to nine. Nevertheless, Rawlinson was clearly unhappy. He told the corps commanders that ways would have to be found to push the artillery forward to enable it to bombard the third German line (a point Haig had ignored in all his memoranda) and then support the forces consolidating its capture. And when the corps commanders indicated that the roads behind the British front were in such bad repair that this might not be possible, he merely said that the roads '*must*' be improved. On the matter of tanks he expressed a 'reasonable hope' that they 'may' prove of some help and repeated Haig's assertion that the enemy, which would be subjected to the new weapon, was tired and demoralised. General Horne, commander of XV Corps, initiated a discussion on the still unresolved matter of how the tanks were to be integrated with the artillery. To appreciate this discussion it is necessary to say something about the capabilities and limitations of the Mark I tank, lest they be mistaken for anything resembling the modern equivalent.

The Mark I was a very cumbersome weapon. It weighed 27 to 28 tons depending on whether its armament was cannon or machine-guns. It was 8 feet high and 32 feet long. It could cross rough ground, crush barbed wire, and engage enemy trench-defenders. But its maximum speed over average going on the Western Front was just 2 miles per hour, which made it slower than a walking infantryman. It was also decidedly prone to mechanical failure and very vulnerable to artillery fire.[18] Moeover, the crews could not function for more than a few hours because they were breathing in 'noxious fumes [from the engine] at very high temperatures'.[19]

In the light of these considerations, Rawlinson's arrangements for the employment of tanks are open to question. He intended to employ the tanks against the most formidable objectives in the German line while denying them the artillery support they needed. He stated that

> the 'tanks' should go forward with the shrapnel barrage, that they should be concentrated in groups in trench junctions and strong points, and that the shrapnel barrage should be put on *between* the groups of 'tanks'.[20]

What this meant was that gaps would be introduced in the creeping barrage, so that it would fall in the areas where infantry were advancing but not in the areas where tanks would be operating.

The 'problem' Rawlinson was attempting to solve here was that if a continuous shrapnel barrage was fired along the whole front it might hit the tanks. Why this was thought to be a problem is unclear – the armour of a tank could withstand shrapnel. Nevertheless, Rawlinson was decreeing that lanes be left in the barrage and – since the tanks would proceed in groups – these would have to be at least 100 yards wide. As the tanks were intended to be used specifically against enemy strongpoints this meant that the artillery would at this stage not be employed in this phase of the battle precisely against the targets where it was most required. This arrangement may have seemed to Rawlinson to constitute a solution to the problem of protecting his tanks from his own artillery. But it did so only by causing a much larger problem. At best, the tanks would only manage to deal with the strongpoints when they got within close range of them. The strongpoints, by contrast – which would be spared the creeping barrage – could exact their toll on the attacking infantry from the moment the latter left their trenches. Further, it was even questionable whether the tanks would go ahead of the infantry. Given the derisory speed of which armoured vehicles were capable at this time, the infantry – unless they were prepared to dawdle across no man's land and endure all the resultant losses – were likely to precede the tanks in their progress towards the strongpoints. But they would do so in the absence of a creeping barrage.

So the appearance of the tank on 15 September did not provide a large body of British infantrymen with an additional form of protection and support. Ironically, it denied them the established sustenance of the creeping barrage and replaced it with a vulnerable substitute of doubtful efficacy.

# III

The purpose of the conference between Rawlinson and his corps commanders was not only to decide on arrangements for the tank but to produce a revised plan for the Commander-in-Chief. After the conference Rawlinson informed Haig that he now understood that given the 'undoubted' deterioration in enemy morale his first plan had not been 'sufficiently ambitious'. He now also realised the need to act boldly and to take every advantage of panic. He had therefore increased the infantry divisions from six to nine to give the attack the depth and weight needed to capture the third German line. As for the increased force of cavalry, the gap for them would probably occur between Lesboeufs and Gueudecourt and they would proceed from there to Bapaume. The tank lanes had also undergone some modification. Because of the vagaries in the flight of shells, it was realised that the lanes could not be maintained beyond the German second line. Once that point had been reached the creeping barrage would be reimposed across the entire front. So for the advance on the third German position the infantry and tanks would both follow the curtain of shells.

So far all of this was in line with Haig's wishes. But even now Rawlinson was not prepared to go further. There was no mention of what the cavalry might do after it had reached Bapaume. And he concluded his plan by emphasising to Haig the difficulty of constructing roads for the artillery and of supplying the large breakthrough force with food and ammunition.[21]

Rawlinson had now devised a plan in which the tank, along some sections of the front, would be substituted for the creeping barrage. This decision seemed to indicate that he saw the armoured vehicles as possessing the equivalence of his most powerful weapon – the artillery. Yet at the same time he also seemed to be having doubts about the tank. He saw them perform again on 2 September and again 'was not pleased with them'. He still considered the tank crews 'green' and 'raw' and felt that they did 'not understand fighting the Bosche'. In addition he thought the CO (Colonel Brough) was 'no sort of good'.[22] He passed his complaints on to GHQ but clearly was not reassured. A few days later, in conversation with the Prime Minister (who was visiting the Western Front), he stated that he was placing no 'great reliance' on the tanks.[23] In other words he was failing to notice that his plan, by expecting the tank to capture strongpoints in the absence of a creeping barrage, was placing every reliance on them.

While Rawlinson's enthusiasm for tanks was waning, Haig's enthusiasm for the operation as a whole was increasing exponentially. On the 7th he told Rawlinson that he had informed the commanders of the Third and First

Armies (Allenby and Monro) of the impending attack. He wanted them both to develop operations to seize points of tactical importance on their fronts (identified as Gommecourt and Monchy for the Third Army and Vimy Ridge for the First). These operations were to be launched by Allenby's forces on 20 September and Monro's on the 30th, so coinciding with the advance of the Fourth and Reserve Armies from the south.[24] Now the Third Army's front ran from the north of Gough's forces around Gommecourt to Arras, and the First Army northwards from that point to Aubers Ridge – a distance of some 60 miles as the crow flies or 90 to 100 miles as the cavalry trots. In other words Haig's ambitions for the new attack were now virtually unlimited. He was envisaging nothing less than the collapse of the entire German army facing the BEF. The disintegration of the Germans opposite the northernmost British army, the Second around Ypres, would presumably have been a bagatelle if all else succeeded. Indeed, even the Second Army was given a role to play. On 4 September Haig had broached a plan to Rawlinson to distract the enemy's attention from his main attack by threatening to land a force from Plumer's Second Army on the Belgian coast behind German lines.[25] Discussions with Admiral Bacon of the Dover Patrol and General Plumer followed.[26] By the 13th a brigade of infantry from 4 Division was in place at Nieuport and asked to display 'liveliness' on the day of the great attack.[27] Haig anticipated that if all went according to plan the Germans might abandon the Belgian coast, whereupon the threat of a landing would be converted into a reality.[28]

In the event none of these expectations regarding the northern sector were fulfilled. Perhaps not surprisingly, the appearance of a few thousand men at Nieuport, however 'lively' their disposition, did not distract the Germans' attention from an impending attack by 100,000 troops on the Somme.

It is important to reflect on the import of all this. Haig's conception was nothing less than the most grandiose vision for victory developed by any commander since Schlieffen. Ludendorff's subsequent conception for March 1918 can be compared to it, but even that lacks the audacity of Haig's operation. For to carry his plan through, Haig (unlike Ludendorff) had not assembled the largest number of guns seen on the Western Front. He had assembled the largest number of horses. Sharper eyes than ours have detected a 'learning curve' in the performance of the Commander-in-Chief during the Somme battle. Such an argument is scarcely applicable in this instance.

While Haig was inhabiting his own world of collapsing enemy morale and decisive victories, Rawlinson and his corps commanders were grappling with less fanciful matters such as how to capture the front line of an army whose morale was not conspicuously disintegrating.

A large difficulty presented itself: how to combine a new weapon, the tank, and an old weapon, the cavalry, with the main weapon that could ensure success, the artillery.

The first issue was to ensure that the tanks were on the start line at zero (6.20 a.m.) so that they could move forward as the preliminary bombardment reached its crescendo. It was decided to accomplish this by bringing the tanks forward under the cover of darkness. This would also ensure concealment. The main difficulty lay in the area of III Corps where the front line ran through High Wood, a treacherous enough place for the transit of men let alone for tanks at night. Should the tanks in this area begin their forward move earlier? Surprisingly the corps commander, General Pulteney thought not. He stated: 'The tanks will go quickly through High Wood because they will have cover all the way.'[29]

It is difficult to know what Pulteney had in mind here. There was no 'cover' in High Wood. By September there was only a scattering of trees standing and these certainly had no leaves attached. What High Wood did consist of in September 1916 was a tangle of tree stumps, fallen branches, trenches, dug-outs, and belts of rusting wire. It was doubtful whether tanks could even traverse this landscape let alone 'go quickly' through it. If the opportunity presented by tanks on this part of the front was not to be cast aside, it was desperately necessary that Pulteney's views be corrected. Colonel Ellis, a tank expert at GHQ, attempted to do this, but he dissipated his whole message by telling Pulteney that tanks could not get through Trones Wood, a position that had fallen two months previously. Yet more remarkably, he did not mention High Wood at all. The end result of this dialogue of the deaf was that Rawlinson decided it to be a 'matter of consideration' and left the decision to Pulteney. The results would be quite disastrous.

The discussion then turned to the matter of the formations to be used by the groups of tanks. Rawlinson wanted them deployed in groups of four in diamond formation. Horne, in an isolated burst of insight, pointed out that this would mask the inward guns of the two centre tanks. Rawlinson made the bizarre reply that it would not matter if they shot into each other, providing these tanks were only equipped with machine-guns! In this instance common sense eventually prevailed – most tanks would be used in groups of three in line ahead, thus giving them the ability to use all their guns against the enemy.

The next item covered was how the creeping barrage might affect the tanks. Rawlinson, it will be recalled, had produced an uneasy compromise whereby a creeping barrage was to be fired but not in the areas where the tanks were bunched. At this conference General Horne (XV Corps), who was an artilleryman, put his finger on the weakness of this plan. It will, he told Rawlinson, 'leave enormous unprotected places in the line'. Horne was making sense here, but he then went on to say that it would be better to have standing barrages on each of the enemy trench lines towards which the tanks and the infantry could work. This of course was the type of plan which had failed so disastrously in the north on 1 July. The barrages then missed the German trench lines and thus gave the German machine-gunners complete freedom to mow down the attacking infantry. Anyway by September it was clear that many German machine-gunners were located in shell holes well away from the main trench defences. So Horne was substituting for a scheme which gave only partial protection to the infantry one which, unless the guns fired with pinpoint accuracy, would give them no protection at all. Rawlinson recognised this. He told Horne that he 'was very reluctant to give up the creeping barrage. I would prefer to maintain it and have a hole for the "tanks"'. Horne replied that he was aware that a creeping barrage was useful to clear out men 'lying about in shell holes' but apart from that he 'could never follow what is the value of a creeping barrage'.

This exchange is extraordinary. Horne's characterisation of German machine-gunners situated outside the trench lines, who would present a deadly threat to his advancing infantry, as 'men lying about in shell holes' appears to show little appreciation of the reality of battle. Even more puzzling is his statement that he could not make sense of the creeping barrage, the surest method of artillery protection yet devised and one which, in the previous two months, had clearly established its effectiveness. Indeed the first group to fire a creeping barrage was Horne's own XV Corps artillery on 1 July. It had achieved decidedly favourable results on an occasion where instances of success were conspicuously absent

Rawlinson, for his part, was not noticing that the gaps that he was instituting in the barrage for the sake of the tanks were opposite strongpoints from which would emanate the most devastating German defensive fire. In the end, and in one sense not surprisingly given the incoherence of Horne's arguments, Rawlinson's plan remained. But what is remarkable about this is that no one questioned the wisdom of withholding the creeping barrage from areas in front of the tanks. For one thing the hulls even of the Mark I tank could well withstand a shrapnel barrage. For another, as long as the infantry were required, for good reason, to place their un-armoured bodies at hazard by clinging close to the advancing curtain of shrapnel it made no sense to deprive them of this protection. The arrival of the tank in this instance was causing confusion where none had existed before.

A further matter discussed at this conference was the difficulty of combining the cavalry with the artillery. After the German second line had fallen it would be necessary to move many of the guns forward to bombard the third line.

However, if the cavalry were to have their maximum shock value, that would be precisely the time when they should begin their forward move from behind the British front. The two arms might therefore impede each other. And, even more alarmingly, the cavalry might mask the guns at the very time they were getting into position to support the infantry advance on the third line. The result would be that either the infantry would be denied artillery protection or many of the horsed soldiers would fall victim to their own guns. There was a further problem. If the cavalry did get through, all the available roads would be needed to supply them with food and ammunition, leaving most infantry divisions disastrously short of those vital commodities. It must be recorded that after a desultory discussion no solutions were provided to these problems.

It may seem incredible that such vital matters were left unresolved. But there might be a clue in Rawlinson's opening remarks at the conference. He noted that the first major objectives mentioned by the Commander-in-Chief lay around Bapaume. But he went on to say that 'of course it will take us some time to arrive at that'. He then added:

> We have got to break the line here first in order to put that *proposed* operation into effect. If we are successful, as we *hope* we may be … it is *hoped* that there will be an opportunity of pushing the cavalry through.[30]

He concluded by saying: 'I have just given you … very broadly what the general trend of the operations will be in the event of our attaining a really decisive success. I will now turn to the operations of [the first day] itself.'

It seems reasonable to conclude that Rawlinson was not much alarmed at the difficulties that the cavalry operations would present to the infantry and artillery because he was not expecting them to eventuate. There are too many caveats in his opening statements ('proposed operation', 'it is hoped that', 'it will take us some time to arrive at that') to suggest any great faith in Haig's scheme. As had been the case for 1 July there is a strong suggestion that he was going through the motions of preparing for one kind of operation while actually preparing for another.

There were two artillery matters that remained to be considered. One was the perennial problem of cutting the wire and damaging the defences that could not be observed, the other was the weight of bombardment to be fired at the German defences.

The first problem particularly applied on the front of XIV Corps. There the Germans had constructed a defensive work called the Quadrilateral, which was supposed to have fallen into British hands by the time the offensive opened but had not. Neither this work nor the distant wire in the Combles Valley could be observed from any point behind the British front. The issue of bombarding unobservable defences was not new – it had arisen on many sections of the German front before 1 July. Rawlinson's solution was not new either. XIV Corps would have to rely on aerial observation to inform them if these defences were being destroyed. This had a chance of working in the case of the Quadrilateral – a large work not far distant from the British front line. Experience suggested that it had no chance of working in the case of a small objective such as wire. Time and again aerial photography had proved inconclusive as to whether belts of wire had been destroyed or merely rearranged by the bombardment. Yet in truth there was little more that could be done. The extension of the objective had left XIV Corps with a problem of observation which at this stage of the war was intractable.

The second artillery matter was conspicuous by its absence in any of the planning documents for 15 September. There was no discussion about the appropriate weight of bombardment needed to crush the enemy defences. Once more Rawlinson appears simply to have assembled as many guns and shells as possible and hoped that these would suffice.

This omission was not to prove as catastrophic as it had been on 1 July. It so happened that on 15 September the extension of the objectives by Haig to the German third line and beyond had little consequence for the artillery, because the third line was beyond the range of most British guns. Almost all of the 828,000 shells fired during the preliminary bombardment were therefore directed towards the first and second German trench systems.[31] This gave a weight of bombardment of twice that of 1 July (though half that of 14 July).[32] Nevertheless, the lack of attention to the bombardment was a matter of the greatest moment. On one section of the front (XIV Corps) the British did not have direct observation over the German trenches, a disadvantage not suffered on 14 July. Now, with a lesser ability to observe whether the shells were finding their target, they settled on a bombardment of half the intensity of that day. It must be presumed that by this period of the battle all commanders recognised the vital role of artillery in an attack. Yet they were prepared to send their men over the top without the sure knowledge that artillery calculations had been provided, and that their troops were adequately protected from both the distant enemy guns and machine gunners in the immediate defences which faced them.

A last-minute change was made to the 15 September plan by Haig. It involved an extension of the front of attack to include the capture of Martinpuich by the left of the Fourth Army and an attack on Courcelette by the 2 and 3 Canadian Divisions of the Reserve Army.[33] Haig's reasoning was in line with his increasing sense of euphoria and his conviction that a large cavalry sweep was in the offing. He wanted to eliminate these two fortified villages quickly, thereby opening the way for the Reserve Army promptly to advance northwards on the left flank of the Fourth. If this were accomplished, the German forces facing Allenby's Third Army would find their communications cut and might surrender without even being attacked. As a consequence, a similar situation would confront enemy forces ranged against the First Army and a similar result eventuate.[34] Rawlinson tried to resist this further commitment. He pleaded a shortage of troops. But Haig insisted and the Fourth Army Commander was forced to give way.[35]

In the days immediately preceding the battle Haig sent a series of exhortations to Rawlinson and to Gough not to neglect any opportunity to send the cavalry through.[36] It seems clear that Haig had begun to sense something of Rawlinson's scepticism about cavalry action. Following a report by Davidson on a visit to Fourth Army headquarters on the 10th, Haig again impressed on Rawlinson the need for 'bold action' to 'derive full value from the element of surprise, which, after all is fleeting! Moreover, the season for fighting is nearly over.'[37] He repeated essentially the same message to Rawlinson on the 11th and on the 14th – clear evidence of how seriously he entertained the grander aspects of his project. Rawlinson duly passed on these instructions to his corps commanders, but without great conviction – for he invariably added the caveat that the cavalry must not impede infantry or artillery operations and he emphasised how difficult cavalry deployment on a large scale would be.

What then was the final plan for Haig's war-winning operation? The infantry attack with accompanying tanks would be conducted by 11 divisions attacking on a 12,000-yard front distributed from left to right as follows:

| | *Corps* | *Division* | *Tanks* |
|---|---|---|---|
| Reserve Army | Canadian Corps (Byng) | 3 Canadian, 2 Canadian | 6 |
| Fourth Army | III Corps (Pulteney) | 15, 50, 47 | 12 |
| | XV Corps (Horne) | New Zealand, 41, 14 | 18 |
| | XIV Corps (Cavan) | Guards, 6, 56 | 18 |

Contingent on the success of these forces, the remaining British armies on the Western Front would come into play.

Four objectives were given to the infantry. The first was the German front line. The second (which concerned just III and XV Corps) comprised the immediate defences covering the village of Flers. The third involved all three corps from Fourth Army, and encompassed Flers and the ground to the east and west of it. The final infantry objective for the first phase was the capture of

Gueudecourt, Lesboeufs, and Morval by XV and XIV Corps in order to establish a defensive flank for the cavalry sweep. The total advance to be achieved by the attacking force was 5,000 yards on the right and 4,000 on the left. The troops were expected to advance in four jumps spread over 4.5 hours. As the battle would commence at 6.20 a.m., the cavalry advance would therefore commence shortly after 10.50 am, its objective the high ground around Rocquigny–Villers-au-Flos–Riencourt–Bapaume.

As for the tanks, they would generally operate in groups of three in line ahead. They would start at zero and aim to reach the first objective five minutes ahead of the infantry. Gaps 100 yards wide would be left in the creeping barrage along the route taken by the tanks. After consolidation of the first objectives the tanks followed by infantry would proceed to attack the second objective. Tank lanes would remain in the barrage up to this point, but then the barrage would extend along the whole front. The tanks were then to proceed to the third objective with the infantry still in the immediate rear. Here their participation would, for the moment, cease, and those still operational would be withdrawn to replenish fuel and ammunition. The fourth objective would be assaulted by the infantry alone, and only after the guns had been moved forward in order to bombard it.

# 21 Lumbering Tanks: The Battle of 15 September

## I

The preliminary bombardment for the new attack opened on 12 September. The weather, although fine in the morning, deteriorated later in the day. Showers persisted through most of the 13th, greatly hampering the aircraft which were attempting to spot for the artillery. On the 14th the weather cleared and a full day's shelling was possible but it is certain that as a result of the variable weather the bombardment was adversely affected, particularly on the front of XIV Corps.[1]

According to plan all corps left lanes unbombarded of at least 100 yards in width for their tanks. An airman far above the battle recorded the scene:

> When we climbed up to the lines, we found the whole front seemingly covered with a layer of dirty cotton-wool – the smoking shell-bursts. Across this were dark lanes, drawn as it might be by a child's stubby finger in the dirty snow. Here no shells were falling. Through these lanes lumbered the tanks.[2]

For this airman, the entry of the tank into battle represented a significant accretion of power. But for the troops on the ground the 'dark lanes' where 'no shells were falling' had in many instances an altogether different significance.

A good example of the negative impact is made evident by looking at the most rightward British division, the 56. This unit of XIV Corps had two tasks. First, it was to move forward on its right and establish a defensive flank facing Combles while French forces were carrying out a similar movement on the other side of the village. Converging attacks would then be arranged to capture it. Second, at the same time the 56 was to advance on its left to screen troops from the other two divisions of the corps as they advanced to capture the crucial villages of Morval, Lesboeufs, and Gueudecourt. The fall of these three villages would be the signal to unleash the cavalry, and was therefore vital if Haig's larger purpose was to come to pass.

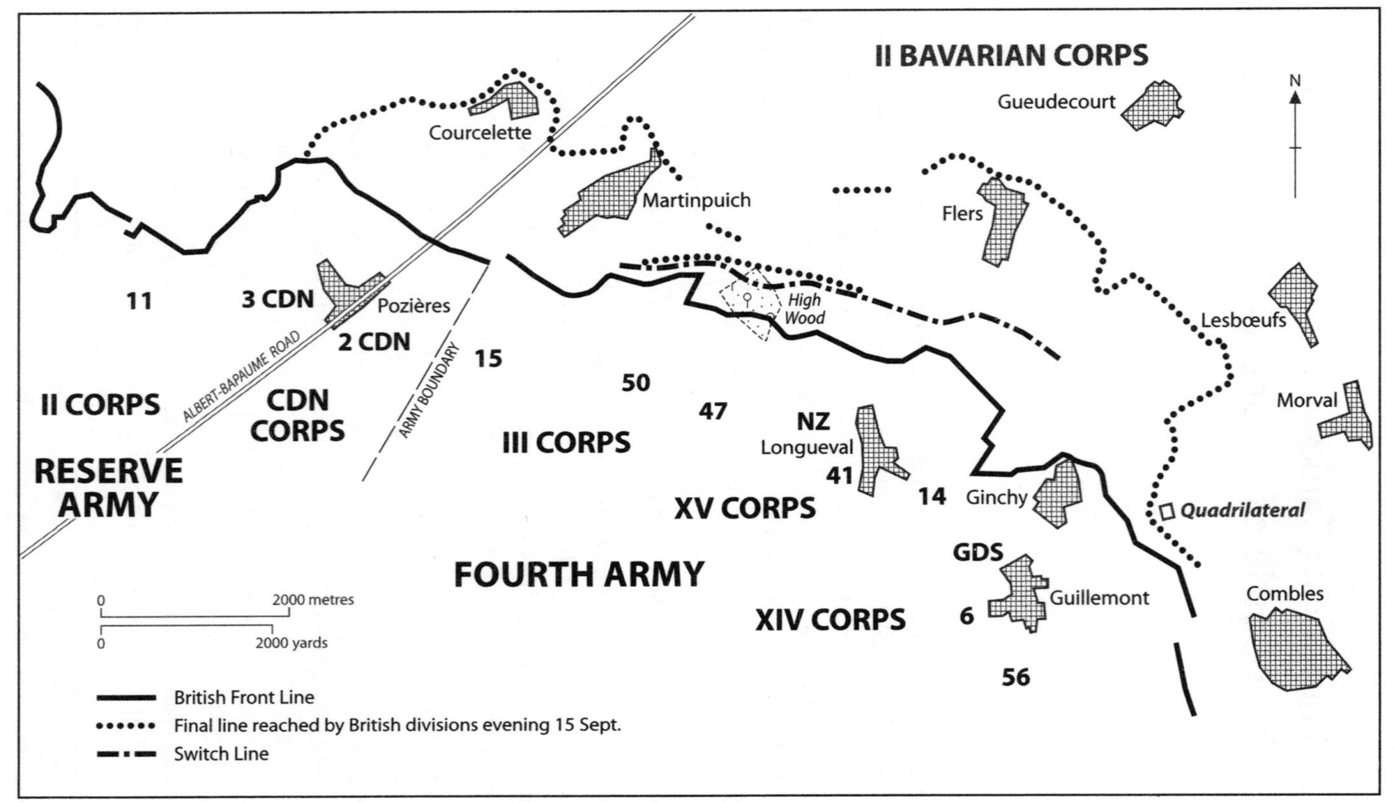


Tanks in Action, 15 September

The 56 Division comprehensively failed in its tasks. Of its three tanks, two broke down before reaching the British line. Thus there were no 'lumbering' tanks in this area, just German machine-gunners free from bombardment and with unimpeded opportunities to destroy the attacking infantry. The troops in the vicinity of these lanes were mown down, some assaulting battalions losing 90 per cent of their officers and 75 per cent of their other ranks.[3] The tank that did get through assisted a small advance around Leuze Wood.[4] That was all. As a result no solid defensive flank faced Combles and there were no troops to screen the advance on the distant villages. As it happened this was not of consequence, because no British troops made an appearance on this flank. Something had obviously gone wrong with the attack of the remaining divisions of XIV Corps.

Those divisions were the 6 and the Guards. In 1914 they had constituted part of the original BEF. Although much leavened by volunteers, this was perhaps the reason they had been chosen by Haig to secure the cavalry breakthrough. What soon became obvious was that a notable history was no substitute for a decent fire plan.

The problems of the 6 Division, although they were not to know it, had commenced long before zero hour. It will be recalled that this division faced a formidable German defensive work, the Quadrilateral. The task of destroying this work had been given to the heavy artillery, followed up by three tanks which would precede the infantry to subdue any defenders that had escaped the bombardment.[5] As it happened, during three days of shelling the heavy guns hardly touched the Quadrilateral. Partly this can be accounted for by the weather, which made observed shooting difficult. It seems that in addition, however, the gunners had located the Quadrilateral in the wrong area – on the reverse slope of the ridge instead of its summit and forward slope. An aerial photograph taken just before the attack reveals that the main defences were intact.[6]

What of the three tanks? Two broke down well behind the British line and took no part in the battle. The third reached the Quadrilateral and poured fire into the German defences. Next bullets striking the outside of the hull caused slivers of red hot metal to sheer off and ricochet around the interior, wounding some of the crew. Then bullets actually began to penetrate the hull. The Bavarians opposite 6 Division were using armour-piercing ammunition brought up to deal with the steel shields used by British snipers. That decided matters. The tank commander withdrew. Remarkably, he made it back to the British lines. But tanks would play no further role that day on the front of 6 Division.

It was now time for the men of the division to leave their trenches. Not only did they find the Quadrilateral intact and with no tanks present but the creeping barrage by arrangement was also nowhere to be seen. The command apparently had assumed that the preliminary bombardment would have done its job and that in any case the tanks would have 'flabbergasted' what German defenders remained. That is: assumptions about a bombardment which could not be observed and a weapon untried in war inspired the command to deny its infantry its sure method of protection. The creeping barrage, it may be noted, had been entirely dispensed with. It commenced beyond the Quadrilateral, some 750 yards in front of the infantry.[7] With enemy machine-gunners manning the parapet as the men deployed in no man's land, a bombardment this distant availed nothing and spelt disaster for the rightward attack.

In the leftward section of the divisional front, away from the Quadrilateral, it might be imagined that the attack stood a better chance. Here, the division was echeloned back some 500 yards from the Guards Division on the left. However, instead of trying to straighten the line to provide for a common start line for the infantry and artillery, the 6 Division's barrage was placed along an arbitrary line on the ground in order that it should conform with that fired for the Guards. So while the Guards' barrage coincided with an actual German trench, that in front of the left of 6 Division did not. In the indignant words of the divisional commander:

> The stationary barrage was put on this [arbitrary] line, where there was not a single German, instead of on the trench which was full of Germans, as one well knew for we had already been repelled from it [on the 12th].[8]

The result of all this was a disaster for the division. On the right the battalions were swept away by concentrated machine-gun fire from the Quadrilateral. Further left a similar fate befell the battalions facing the unbombarded German trench line. Within minutes the attack had collapsed with 3,000 casualties.[9] Throwing in a reserve brigade late in the day only added to the carnage.[10] By evening the 6 Division had lost 4,000 men for precisely no gains.

The 6 Division was one of the units which was supposed to open the way for the cavalry. Within ten minutes it had been shattered. All that remained was the Guards. Clearly they could not redeem the entire plan but it seemed feasible that they could still capture Lesboeufs, which might provide some basis for cavalry action on the 16th. The tanks proved of no help. Ten had been allotted to them but five broke down at once and three more wandered rather ineffectually into areas occupied by other divisions, where late in the day they did some useful subsidiary work in ending pockets of German resistance.[11]

So in the Guards' area of attack, what the tank lanes managed to accomplish was the creation of clear fields of fire for German machine gunners. Early on, this wreaked havoc on the Guards. Units soon became intermingled. Gaps appeared in some sections of the line and crowding in others; direction was lost; German trenches unknown to the British and therefore unbombarded added to the difficulty; flanking fire – especially from the right where the 6 Division had failed – caused further heavy casualties.[12]

Nevertheless, some attackers emerged unscathed through this hail of fire and managed to make some ground. How this happened is not at all clear. Some accounts suggest that the Bavarian troops in this area were in the process of being relieved and so were somewhat disorganised. Certainly, there could have been no 'tank panic' because none of the 'armoured creepers' were present at this time.[13] Perhaps also, the ferocity of the Guards' attack unnerved the Bavarians. Many of the British accounts speak of the unknown German trench as if it were some kind of dastardly ploy that warranted the 'slaughter' of its inhabitants which was carried out by the Guards.[14] Even after this trench had been captured more than one account notes that the men 'bayoneted all the Germans they found'.[15]

After some hours of fierce fighting, the defenders opposite the 2 Grenadiers broke and ran back towards their second line. Passing through, a follow-up formation (3 Grenadiers) considered at one point that the road to Lesboeufs was 'quite open'.[16] This was also the impression of the Irish Guards who reported that 'on reaching the top of the ridge the whole panorama of the landscape between Flers and Les Bouefs [was] disclosed in full view on the further slopes'.[17]

At this moment the Germans in the Lesboeufs area were certainly in disarray. But the position of the Guards was hardly secure. The leading units, looking towards the distant villages, were unsupported on either flank. Furthermore, a battery of German guns was coming into action against them. Shells soon started falling around the advanced troops.[18] And because of the carnage caused in the early moments of the attack some of the battalions were much reduced. In the case of 3 Grenadiers just 100 men remained.[19] Under these conditions it was thought prudent to consolidate the first objective and to dig in patrols slightly beyond to warn of German counter-attacks.[20]

The Guards had gained 2,000 yards on a 1,500-yard front, quite a feat in the circumstances. But this did not alter the fact that Haig's conception even now lay in ruins. The distant villages which were meant to be in British hands before the cavalry went forward were still 2,000 yards away. Along the whole of XIV Corps' front, only the Guards had captured even their first objective. Far from the tanks having 'flabbergasted' the Germans, many of the enemy in this sector would have been unaware of their existence. Overall, the optimistic predictions of collapsing German morale had proved unreliable as ever.

# II

The failure of the right wing of the British attack ensured that there would be no large cavalry sweep on the Somme. The task of the left flanking divisions was subsidiary: to guard the right flank as it moved forward in conjunction with the horsed soldiers. Ironically, they were completely successful.

Attacking were 2 Canadian Division from the Reserve Army and on its right 15 (Scottish) Division of Fourth Army.[21] Their task looked anything but simple. Standing in the path of the Canadians were the ruins of the large village of Courcelette. Similarly the ruins of Martinpuich confronted the 15th. As it happened, neither proved much of an obstacle. The Canadians had two advantages. First, they had detailed their seven tanks for mopping-up purposes only. So they would follow the infantry and no tank lanes were left in the barrage.[22] Second, the Germans conducted an ill-thought-out attack on some Canadian positions just before zero.[23] Not only was this operation quickly dealt with by Canadian front line units, but it left the forward German trenches packed with infantry, most of whom were caught by the preliminary bombardment. So when the Canadians followed what they described as 'our terrible Artillery barrage', they found the remaining Germans unusually willing to surrender.[24] Follow-up troops, pushing on to Courcelette, encountered troops described as of 'very poor quality',[25] who in any case were new arrivals on the Somme battlefield.[26] By 7.30 p.m. the village was in Canadian hands and patrols had even pushed beyond their designated final objectives.[27]

On the right of the Canadians the 15 Division also captured all of its objectives, including the ruins of Martinpuich. There was no assistance from the tanks, all of which arrived too late to take part in the battle.[28] In this area the enemy seemed to be taken by surprise, many of the defenders being caught in their dug-outs.[29] In addition, the morale of German troops around Martinpuich actually seemed in line with GHQ predictions. The defenders of the village, although having ample time to emerge from the cellars and strongpoints and employ their weapons, surrendered.[30] No fewer than 700 Germans including a battalion headquarters, were captured.[31] The left flank of the great advance, although already aborted by events on the right, was securely in British hands.

The 15 Division was part of III Corps which had two other divisions attacking that day, 50 to the left of High Wood and 47 from the wood itself. Their task was to capture the third German line to the left of Flers and later to form part of the northern advance of the infantry. Neither division got so far, although the 50 made reasonable progress. In this area the bombardment had proved particularly accurate and the attackers found few Germans remaining to defend the first line.[32] Further progress was then possible on the left because of the success of the neighbouring 15 Division. At the end of the day this sector of the divisional front lay just short of the German third position.[33]

On the right it was quite different. There, enfilading machine guns from High Wood halted the advance before it reached the first German line. Some further progress was made after the wood had fallen, but by this time casualties were high, troops had lost direction because of the dust kicked up by the barrage, and the two tanks which had accompanied them and performed some useful tasks in enfilading trenches were out of action. The men were eventually forced to dig in just short of the German second position, well short of their final objective.[34]

It may be imagined that the 47 Division had more immediate concerns than the grandiose objectives laid out for them in their operations orders. Their first objective was High Wood. This had been one of the objectives on 14 July, and of a series of subsequent operations. None had succeeded. On 15 September the Germans were still in occupation of the Switch Line which ran through the northern sector of the wood. Now the 47, a Territorial unit from south London which had fought at Aubers Ridge, Festubert, and Loos in 1915, had been given the task. It had one advantage. For the first time since 14 July, the wood was to be attacked as part of a broad-front operation, so that the Germans would not be able to concentrate all their artillery fire against it. There were, however, some significant negative factors. The first was General Pulteney, the commander of III Corps, who had decided to use the four tanks allotted to 47 Division inside the tangled wilderness of the wood instead of in outflanking movements around it. Furthermore, none of the tank officers had visited 47 Divisional staff to discuss the employment of artillery fire or where they proposed to enter the wood.[35] Then there was the fact that the British and German front line trenches in the wood were so close together that bombardment was difficult. For the period of the preliminary bombardment this was easily solved. The British troops were withdrawn and the wood subjected to heavy fire. But it was then decided that, just prior to zero, the men should reoccupy their original front line.[36] This meant that the problem of proximity which had been overcome for the preliminary bombardment now applied to the creeping barrage. And here the solution was quite lamentable. The command decided to commence the barrage (which anyway would have lanes left in it for the tanks) 150 yards *beyond* the German front line to avoid hitting their own troops.[37] This decision was neither sensible nor necessary. A new front line could have been dug in rear of the existing British line and the creeping barrage commenced in front of that. Finally, the map co-ordinates given to the artillery were wrong, so the creeping barrage actually commenced 200 to 250 yards behind the German front line.[38]

The result was predictable. Of the four tanks assigned to the division, two were ditched in old trenches behind the British front line in the wood. The third found the going so rough that it turned right out of the wood and shot up a trench full of troops, who happened to be British.[39] Nevertheless, the tank commander was awarded the Military Cross.[40] In the restrained words of this unit's War Diary, 'after a heated argument … the tank ceased fire and took no further part in the day's proceedings'.[41] A fourth tank by good luck and skilful driving actually arrived at the German front line and shot up a small group of enemy defenders, then proceeded through to the next rearward trench and shot that up as well. At this point its engine failed and the crew abandoned it. Making their way back to the British lines they accepted the surrender of a group of Germans on the way.[42] Despite this small success, Pulteney's decision to use the tanks inside the wood certainly prevented them from fulfilling even the limited potential they possessed in 1916.

As for the infantry, they were having to battle their way towards the distant creeping barrage which had 100-yard gaps in it. The men were met with such heavy fire from unbombarded German machine-gun positions that few survived to contribute to their respective war diaries. The best account of what happened comes from the unlikely source of a French interpreter assigned to the division.

> The 15th [Londons] were to rush a [German strongpoint] with the help of the Tanks. The 8th [Londons] were to debouch from the Wood and make for some redoubts on the downward slope beyond. The 6th [Londons] were to pass through the 15th and 8th, and make for a certain point in the German 3rd line …. The Artillery was put on the back positions principally and the Tanks and the 15th were left to deal with the first line. The Tanks are certainly wonderful things, and can go over all sorts of country except, perhaps, ground where tree trunks lie criss cross in all directions. Therefore when the 15th went over the top, they had a bad time with machine guns, though they took the [strongpoint] and lay down in front of the Old German Front Line. The 8th, coming up to pass through the 15th and carry on, instead of carrying on, had to support the 15th themselves …. Old Goodes and his merry men were then called in and did a record shoot with their Trench Mortars. The Huns stuck it until 750 bombs had been hurled at them and then held up a white flag. This ended the business in the Wood.[43]

It was a notable event. High Wood, which had resisted so many British attacks, had fallen. The combination of the broad-front attack, the heavy preliminary bombardment, and the final hurricane of trench mortar shells had overcome the ineptitude of the original plan. But it was only the first objective of the day. The German second and third lines were still to be assaulted. Not surprisingly, further substantial movement proved beyond the division. Most of its reserve battalions had been drawn into the fighting inside the wood. It was not until 6 p.m. that a motley composite force could be organised for a further advance. Some ground was gained but at heavy cost, one of the assaulting units being reduced to just 62 men of the 567 who attacked.[44] The survivors could do nothing more than dig in just short of the second German line.

## III

It fell to the divisions of XV Corps to make the most substantial advances of the day and it was in this sector that the tanks made an effective contribution. The corps had a series of formidable objectives. First they were to capture the Switch Line, then later the German second line and the fortified village of Flers, and then move on to the German third line around Gueudecourt.

Least successful was 14 Division on the right flank of the corps. This unit was heavily enfiladed by the machine-gunners who had wrought such devastation on the early attack of the Guards Division.[45] The unit also had trouble locating the Switch Line, which had in fact been obliterated by the artillery.[46] Nor could the division establish contact with the fast-moving 41 Division on its left. So as the reserve battalions attempted to move forward they found both their flanks unsupported. They dug in and held their positions, but they were short of the German second line and had no chance of advancing beyond.[47]

The two divisions of the corps which achieved the major advances of the day were the New Zealand and the 41, neither of which had seen action on the Somme. Along some sections of their area of attack the preliminary bombardment had been extremely effective. In the 41 Division area very few defenders in the front positions survived it and so despite the lanes left for the tanks the Switch Line was taken with few casualties. The attackers were also fortunate to have three tanks which were able to operate in advance of them and subdue or put to flight those who had survived the bombardment.[48]

In the New Zealand sector (where none of their four tanks appeared before zero) numerous German machine-gunners were still in their dug-outs when the infantry, moving fast behind the barrage, arrived.[49] So by 6.50 a.m., just 30 minutes after zero, the Switch Line had been captured. The only severe casualties had been suffered by the left of the New Zealand Division by flanking fire from High Wood.[50]

The second objective consisted of a line of trenches just south of Flers. It fell without incident. The troops ran into desultory German artillery fire, but when they reached the new line they found it almost deserted. By 7.20 a.m. detachments from the two divisions were in sight of Flers.[51]

Their third objective lay just beyond the ruins of Flers, in some trenches which made up part of the German second line. This was the moment when the tanks played their most significant part in the operations. On the front of 41 Division four tanks were still operational. These machines followed the creeping barrage (which it might be noted now had no gaps in it, demonstrating how unnecessary the tank lanes had been) into Flers village with the infantry close behind. Three machines fanned out to the right and left of the rubble and subdued any machine-guns that remained. The fourth lumbered up what remained of the main road and dealt with a machine-gun that was holding up the advance. All of this proved too much for the defenders. They fled back towards Gueudecourt and by 10 a.m. Flers and some of the German second line had been captured.[52]

Tanks were also assisting the New Zealanders. On the left of their advance,

> The 3rd bn. had been hung up by intact wire and heavy machine gun fire. At 10.30 a.m. 3 tanks arrived – one tank went to the extreme left of the sector … while another dealt with the wire and machine guns …. This enabled the 3rd bn. to take the Flers Line.[53]

On the right the panic caused by the tanks in Flers made the capture of the left of the village a relatively easy matter.

A portion of the German second line now lay in British hands, and that part of it running northwards towards Le Sars had been outflanked. Gueudecourt lay not far distant. It seemed that the centre of the Fourth Army was on the brink of a major victory. But this was not the case. The 41 Division's casualties were by this time considerable, and the units much intermixed. Such was the confusion that at one point an entire brigade actually fell back from Flers, leaving it open. The situation was restored by some reserve battalions before the enemy could take advantage of it, but these units could make no further advance. All tanks were now out of action and the German defence had recovered to the extent that they delivered several heavy counter-attacks from Gueudecourt. Just after 4.30 p.m., the order was sent out to consolidate what had been gained.[54] Nor could the New Zealanders progress. They attempted to advance north-west of Flers, but reports were coming in of German counter-attacks on High Wood and on Flers itself. It was thought prudent to dig in.[55] The great attack was over.

# 22 25 September

## I

On the evening of 15 September Rawlinson received reports from his corps commanders and issued his orders for the new day. He demanded that nothing less than a full-scale attack be undertaken immediately to enable the 'Cavalry Corps to push through to its objectives and complete the enemy defeat'.[1] The unreality of this order hardly needs emphasising. The Cavalry Corps had precisely the same chance of effecting a victory on the 16th as it had had the day before – that is, no chance at all. As for the infantry, the 6, Guards, and 47 Divisions were in no state to resume full-scale attacks and the remainder were in various degrees of disorder. What followed then from Rawlinson's instruction was not a concerted attack across the whole front but the series of small-scale, sporadic actions that had become a familiar pattern after a major attack on the Somme. On this occasion they produced exactly the same results as those following 14 July – no advances for quite heavy casualties.

By the morning of the 17th, the deteriorating weather and the exhaustion of British divisions holding the line made it obvious even to Rawlinson that there could be no large operations for some days. In any case, by this time Haig had a larger vision. After speaking to Foch and Gough he determined that a major offensive would be carried out from Thiepval to Maurepas. The Reserve Army and the French would be engaged as well as Rawlinson's forces.[2] In all, 10 divisions would be involved, with the aim of capturing Thiepval and the German third line around Le Transloy.

In the event, the same chronic inability to co-ordinate the action of the different armies foiled Haig's intent. The first destabilising factor was the weather. Rain persisted on the 18th, making it impossible to bring forward ammunition for the guns and supplies of all kinds for the troops. By the 20th the weather

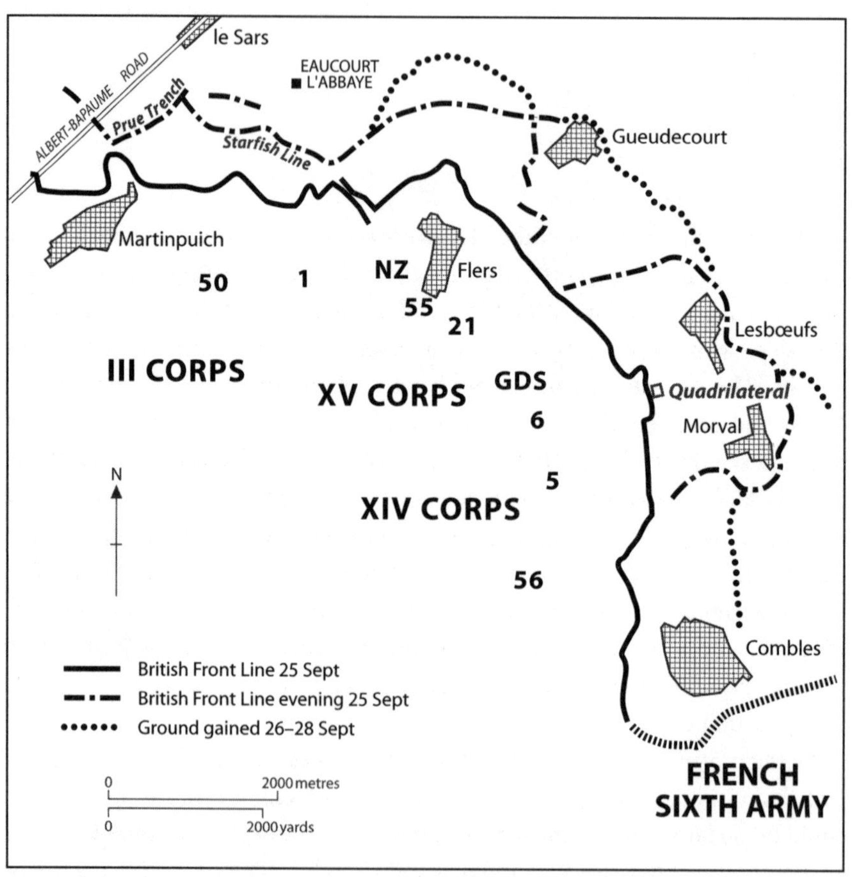
le Sars
EAUCOURT L'ABBAYE
ALBERT-BAPAUME ROAD
Prue Trench
Starfish Line
Gueudecourt
Martinpuich
50
1
NZ
Flers
55
21
Lesbœufs
III CORPS
XV CORPS
GDS
Quadrilateral
6
Morval
N
5
XIV CORPS
56
Combles
British Front Line 25 Sept
British Front Line evening 25 Sept
Ground gained 26–28 Sept
0
2000 metres
0
2000 yards
FRENCH SIXTH ARMY

25 September

had become so bad that operations were postponed until the 23rd.[3] Further bad weather imposed another delay until the 25th.[4]

Then there were the French. On the 18th Foch indicated that he would not be ready until the 21st because of ammunition shortages. He also insisted that any attack should take place in the afternoon so that artillery fire could be observed. (This was to have consequences for the operation as a whole which will be discussed later.) As the 21st approached Foch then made it clear that he could not meet that deadline. So heavy had been his expenditure in ammunition in beating off a German counter-attack on the 20th that he would need 48 hours to replace it.[5] This pushed the operation forward to the 23rd and then the bad weather delayed it again until the 25th. Nevertheless, the Fourth Army and the French were at least to go forward on the same day.

The same could not be said of the Reserve Army. Gough had decided to use a number of tanks to assist him in capturing Thiepval. This presented a problem. Because of French insistence that the attack by their forces and the Fourth Army take place in the afternoon, Haig reasoned that if Gough attacked at the same time his tanks would have to be brought forward in daylight, exposing them to the German artillery. He therefore decided that they must be used in the concealing 'mists of early morning'[6] and this meant that Gough's attack would go in on the 26th, the day after Rawlinson and the French. This made no sense. The advantages of a really broad front attack were being sacrificed for a weapon which had hardly proved itself of startling utility on the 15th. Nevertheless, Haig had made his decision. Then for reasons that are totally obscure, Gough made a different one. When the day of his attack arrived the tanks were not used in the early morning mists but in the early afternoon. Gough in fact attacked on the 26th at exactly the same time that the French and Rawlinson attacked on the 25th.

Rawlinson's plan therefore (Gough's will be discussed separately in the next chapter) was for 10 divisions to assault the German third line from Martinpuich on the left to Combles on the right. The French I and XXXII Corps would co-operate on the right. The decision to attack in the afternoon, forced on Rawlinson by the French, meant that no tanks could be used for the same reason expounded earlier by Haig regarding Gough's forces – tanks would be too vulnerable to artillery fire in broad daylight. So instead of leading the attack, several would follow the assault around dusk and deal with any German resistance lingering in the ruins of the villages in their third line.[7] What this meant was that the creeping barrage could be reintroduced as a method of infantry protection all along the front, for there would be no lanes required for the tanks. This decision, which was to have a crucial impact on the outcome of the battle, therefore came about not because of a reflective investigation of operations on the 15th but by accident. While the plan for the 25th (and, as it happened, the 26th) was being decided the start line for that operation had yet to be captured. This meant that the Quadrilateral and the unattained objectives between High Wood and Martinpuich, including Prue Trench and the Starfish Line, had first to be taken.

The 6 Division, which had failed before the Quadrilateral on the 15th, was assigned the task of assailing it again. At least the position of the German defensive work had now been established with some accuracy by the British artillery, and a bombardment of it began on the 17th.[8]

According to the 6 Division's War Diary, there is very little to say about this operation. The Quadrilateral fell after a brief fight, conducted like clockwork.[9] One is always wary of such descriptions of operations on the Western Front and indeed according to one participant in the attack nothing remotely approaching precision occurred on that day. Lt-Col. Dillon was an officer who had been left in reserve on the 15th. On the morning of the 18th he was ordered forward to report to his brigadier about the forthcoming operation. His diary then takes up the story:

> He [the Brigadier] then told me that the Colonel [of the attack battalion] had broken down, that the whole situation had altered, that I was in Command of the battn. and that we would attack at dawn, and that he would let me have orders as soon as possible. I had … a conference of C.O's, all of which was absolute Greek to me not knowing where the Bn. was or what we were going to attack etc. So I sat quiet and said yes and no and tried to look dignified. At about 5 p.m. we were all asked if we quite understood and as we all said yes the show finished. I then got hold of an intelligent young staff officer and in ten minutes, with my map, had chalked the whole thing and made him promise to send me orders at the first possible opportunity and then we went to my headquarters …. On arrival I found the adjutant in a state almost of collapse, the doctor wounded, and apparently no one knew where the companies were. Fortunately, the pressure was relieved with the arrival of orders …. [But] by this time … it was 8 p.m. and quite dark and the attack was to start at 5.50 am. Nobody seemed to know the way and everybody we met was dead or wounded …. It was getting very late now and the shelling was vy heavy, and I was really rather in trouble, as had I got straffed I had all the orders on me and nobody would have known what was happening . … At 5.30 I woke my Adjt. …. The barrage was just starting …. Our own guns had it all their own way for 15 minutes by which time the lads were over. …

> What happened was two of our Companies went over the top in front and got hit badly, a third (and this is where I disobeyed orders) came in from [a flank]. Rushed the Hun strong pts bombed and bayoneted down the trench. The two unfortunate Companies got up and went for the boche and it seems incredible but in *10* minutes they had the whole boche line. In the meantime my 4th Coy. had gone straight on and made a strong pt 600 yards beyond and they caught the remaining Germans across the open. We captured 500 yards of front, advanced 1,000 yds. One mortar, one machine gun, 100 German prisoners and countless bombs. German dead God knows.[10]

By such imprecise and un-clockwork methods did the dreaded Quadrilateral fall to the British.

Far to the left of 6 Division in the area of III Corps two new divisions (50 and 23) which had replaced 15 and 47 were also making ground. One of the battalions involved in this forward movement has described exactly how it was done:

> Orders were received from Bde for the Batt ... to dig at 7.30 pm a jumping off trench, midway between the front line ... and the Starfish Line, with a view to an attack on the latter, but the orders also stated that if, on completion of the jumping off trench, the covering party found that the Starfish line was lightly or not held at all, then the covering party was to enter it, and a garrison be put in.[11]

And this is exactly what happened. The Starfish Line was occupied and garrisoned without opposition. Later in the day Prue Trench was captured in a similar manner.[12] So by these means 50 Division had gained its start line for the big attack.

Meanwhile, similar operations were taking place on the front of 1 Division where other sections of the Starfish Line were captured,[13] and on the front of 23 Division where the remainder of Prue Trench was secured.[14] Though little heralded at the time, later in the war such operations, especially those carried out by the Australian Corps before the Battle of Amiens in August 1918, would become known as 'peaceful penetration' operations. The expression as it happened was coined by Rawlinson in his notes on these events.[15]

## II

The attack was to commence at 12.35 p.m. on 25 September. It was to be carried out by 10 divisions, five of which ( 23, 1, 55, 21, 5) had not been in action on 15 September. All corps would attack, but the main undertaking, the capture of Gueudecourt, Lesboeufs, and Morval – and consequently the German third line – was to be the task of XIV and XV Corps. III Corps would merely keep pace on the left to provide flank protection for XV Corps. There was on this occasion very little mention of the cavalry. One division of horsed soldiers was to be available to Fourth Army for unspecified purposes. There were to be no distant objectives. And because of this the artillery concentration against the defenders of the German front system was formidable, although Fourth Army headquarters seemed not to have calculated exactly what it would be.

In the two days before the battle, the British threw approximately 400,000 shells weighing about 7.5 million pounds into not more than 18,000 yards of enemy trench.[16] The bombardment therefore achieved a concentration of about 400 pounds of shell for every yard of trench attacked. This was 40 per cent higher than the bombardment of 15 September. As for the defences which received this weight of shell, they were more rudimentary than either the first or second German trench systems on 15 September. In addition the incessant British attacks since the 15th and the rainy weather between the 16th and the 22nd had prevented the Germans from strengthening their line. On the right, the XIV Corps was to capture Morval and Lesboeufs. The 56 Division was merely to provide flank protection, the main operation being carried out by (from right to left) the 5, 6, and Guards Divisions. The advance was to be made behind a creeping barrage fired across the whole front in three short jumps. Between each jump there was to be a pause of an hour for consolidation and reorganisation.[17] The total distance to be traversed was no more than 1,500 yards, giving the operation all the characteristics of a bite and hold attack.

The 56 Division accomplished its task with relative ease. Advancing under 'a most efficient enfilade artillery barrage' the battalions cleared Bouleux Wood and advanced some way beyond.[18] Combles was now outflanked to the right. Casualties, at 164, were modest by Somme standards.[19]

The main attack by XIV Corps was carried out by 5, 6, and the Guards Divisions. The 5 and 6 Divisions had a relatively easy time, gaining all their objectives including the ruins of Morval according to timetable. The pauses in the advance were found most useful for regrouping under the creeping barrage. There is no doubt that success on this part of the front was due to the combination of an accurate preliminary bombardment, accurate wire-cutting, and the relentless destructive capacity of the creeping barrage. The War Diary of a Norfolk battalion which led the 5 Division's assault makes this clear:

> Our artillery barrage was excellent, & we advanced with it, practically in it, & got to the objective at the very second it lifted …

> The Germans had got out of their trenches & were largely in shell-holes, a few in front (who were killed as we went up), the majority were in rear of the trench. Germans were killed in the shelters & in the trench, & at first, some as they attempted to come forward from the shell-holes – the remainder surrendered (about 150).[20]

Thus were the lessons of 'bite and hold' revealed once more to the lower levels of command. They would be lessons that the higher echelons of the British army would learn, discard, and learn again until the end of the war.

On the left of XIV Corps' attack, the experience of the much-tried Guards Division would demonstrate that many things could go wrong even in a successful attack and that the experience of battalions in the same attack could be quite different. On the right of their front the Guards faced a series of sunken roads and wire concealed in fields of crops.[21] In this sector the 2 Grenadiers found that the artillery had failed 'to cut a single strand of wire'.[22] They lost most of their officers in the process of cutting their way through it and then charging the German trenches.[23] Their War Diary has nothing but derision for the gunners:

> the co-operation of the Artillery was remarkable for its absence and a great deal of ammunition was uselessly expended on ground where no Germans were, and places where Germans could be seen were left untouched.[24]

On the other hand, the battalion immediately to the left of the Grenadiers found all the wire cut and resistance weak. They took their objective with just 14 casualties.[25] In the end the Guards Division secured all their objectives, including the ruins of Lesboeufs, but at a cost of 1,900 casualties – twice those of any other division of XIV Corps.[26]

On the left of XIV Corps were the three assault divisions of XV Corps, from right to left 21, 55, and the New Zealand Division. The 21 Division met with varying fortunes. Their 64 Brigade (on the left of the Guards) suffered severely from a German barrage which came down just two minutes after zero.[27] They then found their objective (Gird Trench) strongly manned with machine-guns and riflemen who took a heavy toll on the advancing troops.[28] Finally, when the survivors closed on Gird Trench they found that the artillery had left strong belts of wire in front of it untouched.[29] The few men now remaining had no option but to take shelter in shell holes and await the protection of the night.[30]

The 110 Brigade of 21 Division fared little better. The wire had not been cut on some sections of its front, the trenches were strongly held, and German fire soon reduced the brigade to such small numbers that they were forced to withdraw. A night attack was ordered but after a discussion between the divisional commander (Jeudwine) and the XV corps commander (Horne) more cautious counsels prevailed and it was cancelled.[31]

This failure left the British in a considerable quandary. To the north-east of XIV Corps the Gird Trench remained in enemy hands and it provided an excellent starting point for a counter attack southwards into the flank of Cavan's divisions. Should such an attack succeed, the whole British position around Lesboeufs and Morval would be threatened. Luckily for the British help was at hand. During the night a tank had been hidden in the ruins of Flers. It now moved off to a section of Gird Trench where the Guards were still hanging on. At 7.30 a.m. on the 26th, accompanied by bombing detachments from the 7 Leicesters, the tank

> started moving South Eastwards along the Gird Trench, first on one side of the trench and then on the other, firing its machine guns and being well supported by the bombers .... As the 'tank' moved down the trench the enemy surrendered freely .... By 8.30 a.m. the whole length of trench had been cleared .... In the capture of Gird trench, 8 officers and 362 other ranks of the enemy were made prisoners besides many killed. Our casualties were ridiculously small, about 5 in all. Over 1,000 yards of trench were captured in about 1 hour. What would have proved a difficult operation involving probably considerable losses was made easy entirely owing to the assistance rendered by the 'tank'.[32]

With the capture of Gird Trench, the road to Gueudecourt lay open. Patrols from the 6 Leicesters found the southern end of the village unoccupied. They then ran into some resistance from snipers and machine-guns but by dusk most opposition had ended and the village fell into their hands.[33] So the last of the three villages protecting the German third line (Gueudecourt, Lesboeufs, and Morval) was now secured.

The remainder of the battle need not detain us. The 55 and New Zealand Divisions, advancing behind an accurate and 'extremely steady' creeping barrage, captured the trench lines to the north-west of Gueudecourt with relative ease.[34]

As for III Corps, we have noted, most of its objectives were captured by 'peaceful penetration' methods before zero hour. On the 25th, the 1 and 50 Divisions gained ground to the north-west of Martinpuich. The 23 Division in the face of strong opposition on the Albert–Bapaume road broke off the attack.[35]

So ended the action of 25 September. In Somme terms it had been an outstanding success. The limited objective of the German third line had been captured from Martinpuich to Combles. As by default on 14 July and by design on this occasion, the efficacy of the bite and hold operation in conjunction with a formidable artillery accompaniment had been demonstrated. One tank had played a useful role around Gueudecourt, the cavalry no role at all. It was of course the guns that had effected the victory. The artillery had delivered sufficient of the infantry to their objectives to enable the small gains to be made. In terms of casualties as well, 5,000 in total for the 10 divisions, the cost was low by Western Front standards.

Did the fall of the third German line mean then that Rawlinson's forces now confronted open country where the cavalry might roam? It did not. The inexorable logic of Western Front fighting meant that while the British were making their modest gains in September, the Germans had not been idle. While Rawlinson's men crept towards Bapaume the German command ordered that a new defensive line be dug between Ligny-Thilloy and Le Transloy, a fifth line in front of Bapaume, and a sixth line further back.[36] Now these lines too would have to be breached before open country was reached. And by late September summer had departed, autumn had commenced and winter with its promise of rain and mud was very close. Whether Haig would respond to these matters was another question.

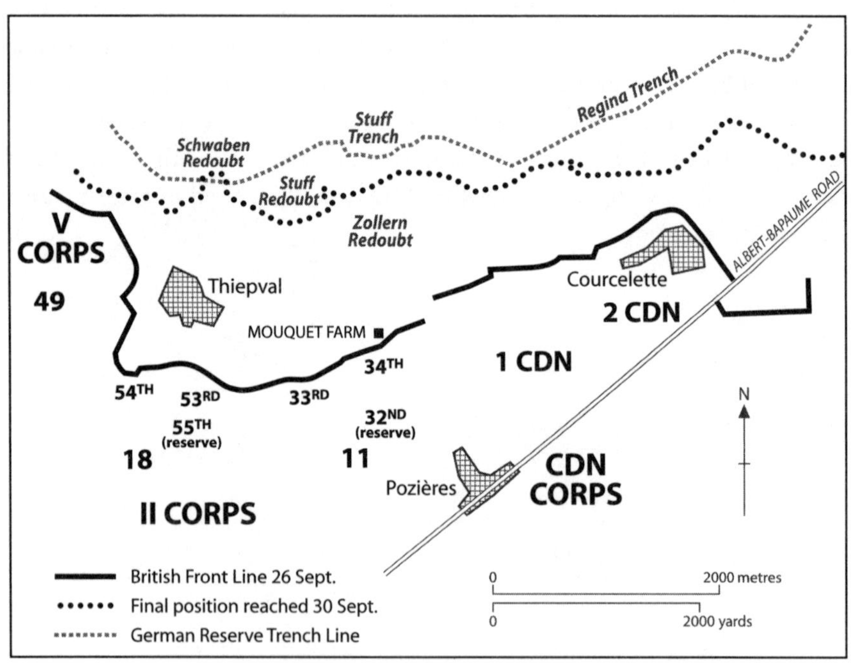


Thiepval Ridge, 26–30 September

# 23 'The Tragic Hill of Thiepval',[1] 26–30 September

## I

When we left the Reserve Army in early September the II Corps and the Australians were struggling towards Mouquet Farm. There were few further large operations on Gough's front until 26 September. One, however, is worthy of note, not for the results achieved, but for the reactions of the command to its complete failure. On 3 September, two divisions of II Corps (39 and 49) attacked to the north of Thiepval. The 49 Division was given the task, after a short bombardment, of assaulting the Schwaben Redoubt frontally. There was to be no attempt at surprise. Not unexpectedly, as this strongpoint had withstood the five-day artillery assault before 1 July, it failed. There were 1,800 casualties. No ground was gained. Gough, Jacob (the Commander of II Corps), and the divisional commander were in no doubt as to the cause of failure. It was not due to the total lack of originality or subtlety in the plan – it was due to the lack of 'martial qualities' in the troops.

The chorus of invective by the command against the assault battalions is remarkable. As well as the lack of martial spirit, Gough contributed want of 'discipline and motivation', 'ignorance on the part of the C.O.s', and 'poor spirit in the men'. Jacob added 'want of direction', 'stage-fright' (!!), and cowardice on the part of the brigadier. He pointed out that there were 'no casualties amongst C.O.'s' (a damning indictment indeed) and wanted entire battalions disbanded if they were unable to pull themselves together. The Divisional Commander was by comparison restrained, merely pointing to a lack of training and discipline (as though these matters were not part of his responsibility). These judgements, it may be noted, were passed on battalions that had lost between 30 and 50 per cent of their strength in failing to capture one of the strongest positions on the Western Front. Perhaps it was as well that most of the Reserve Army front was quiescent for the remainder of the month.[2]

# II

The origins and timing of the major attack by Gough's force on 26 September are shrouded in mystery. Earlier he had stated that the whole purpose of the crawl towards Mouquet Farm was to position his force to attack Thiepval from the rear. At some point in September this plan was scrapped (but operations to capture the farm were not) and a frontal assault on Thiepval substituted. We may surmise that the difficulty in capturing Mouquet Farm was the reason for the change, although none of the Reserve Army Papers, or Haig's diary, or any other source is specific about this. The date of the operation, as we have noted, was changed from the 25th (when it would have coincided with efforts by the Fourth Army) to the 26th in order to conceal the tanks in the early morning mists of the Thiepval Valley. But as was also noted, for reasons that are opaque and on which the sources are also silent, the start time was moved from morning to afternoon – 12.35 p.m., exactly the same time as Fourth Army operations, but a day later.

# III

For the attack on Thiepval and its ridge, Gough had assembled four assault divisions on a 6,000-yard front. On the right, the 2 and 1 Canadian Divisions would advance to the north and east of Courcelette and attempt to capture Regina Trench which lay just beyond the ridge line. Further left the 11 Division, in its first action since the Suvla Bay landing in August 1915, would capture Mouquet Farm and Zollern and Stuff Redoubts, and then advance beyond to Stuff Trench (as the continuation of Regina Trench was known in this area). The most difficult task would fall to the 18 Division, which had played so conspicuous a part in early operations of the Somme campaign. Since then it had been 'resting' in Flanders. Now it had been brought south and given the intimidating tasks of capturing Thiepval and the Schwaben Redoubt, strongpoints which had taken a fearful toll on the 36 and 32 Divisions on 1 July and which – apart from the ill-fated attempt of the 49 Division on 3 September – had not been attacked since.

The whole operation presented enormous difficulties to the Reserve Army. The final objective (Regina and Stuff Trenches) lay on a reverse slope, out of direct observation from the British line. But before that point was reached, in the II Corps sector, lay the five formidable objectives just mentioned: Mouquet

Farm, Zollern Redoubt, Stuff Redoubt, Thiepval, and Schwaben Redoubt. These fortified areas represented slightly different problems for the attack. On the surface, Mouquet Farm was now little more than rubble. However, underneath the debris lay three groups of cellars connected by a tunnel which ran in part behind the British front line. The entrances to the cellars were concealed in the ruins and not at all obvious to the attacking infantrymen. So even if an accurate creeping barrage could carry the assault battalions to the farm, it must lift while the soldiers sought out the entrances. This was the moment of danger. If the enemy machine-gunners and riflemen were to emerge before these entrances were located the attackers could find themselves assaulted from all sides.

The redoubts were perhaps even more difficult to subdue. Unlike Mouquet Farm they were some thousand yards beyond the British line. Thus the creeping barrage would have to be followed (and be fired accurately) for a much greater distance. And this generally meant that the progress of the troops would have to be as steady as the barrage (timed at 100 yards every three minutes in this case). Any delay and the troops would lose its protection and be exposed to fire from the redoubts. Moreover, the redoubts were extensive with deep dugouts impervious to the heaviest shells and with warrens of tunnels. So even if a part of the defences fell, a garrison reinforced via these tunnels might mount strong counter-attacks. Further, if the attacking troops got into a redoubt no artillery fire could assist them. The encounter would descend into close combat, a relatively rare phenomenon on the Western Front.

Thiepval had its own difficulties. Above ground hardly one stone stood on another. Below there were an estimated 144 cellars, any of which could house machine-gunners. A creeping barrage thus might carry an attacking force into the village but the occupants might emerge after the barrage had passed and fire on the assault troops from the rear as they moved on to other objectives.

What artillery arrangements were made to deal with these difficulties? As with so many battles at this time, the Reserve Army seems merely to have assembled as many guns as possible and hoped that they would prove sufficient, rather than calculating what might be necessary to subdue the German defence. In all they had 570 field guns and 270 howitzers for the operation on a 6,000-yard front. This gave them about the same artillery concentration as the Fourth Army on 15 September. That is, they would have twice the number of shells per yard of trench attacked as on 1 July but less than half that for the successful attack on 14 July.[3]

There were some positive aspects to the artillery plan. Those guns in the area of V Corps which were located west of the River Ancre would be able to fire on Thiepval in enfilade, thus enabling the fortress ruin to be attacked from three sides.

The second aspect was the weight of artillery with which Thiepval was to be deluged – approximately 100,000 shells, 40,000 of them from the heavy guns, an unprecedented weight of attack. Thiepval was also to be drenched with gas just before zero in order to incapacitate some of the dug-out dwellers.[4]

The preliminary bombardment commenced on 23 September. On the first day the weather was poor, making ground and aerial observation extremely difficult. After that it improved but autumn mists shrouded much of the low ground around Thiepval for some hours in the mornings and evenings, confining observation to a few hours a day. Nevertheless, from the 24th the spotting planes were able to report considerable destruction in many areas.

## IV

It is unnecessary to describe every aspect of this battle. Gough's operations from 26 to 30 September really revolved around the capture of Regina Trench in the Canadian sector and the five redoubts in II Corps sector so our narrative will concentrate on these intense struggles.

The Canadian experience can be briefly told. On the right, away from the strongpoints, the early objectives were taken with moderate losses.[5] On the left, units ran into strong enfilade fire from Mouquet Farm, Zollern, and Stuff Redoubts.[6] On subsequent days various attempts were made to advance on Regina Trench. All failed, the reverse slope again protecting an objective from British artillery fire. By the 30th, although some ground had been gained, Regina Trench was still securely in German hands.

Mouquet Farm, the first of the German strongpoints to be encountered, lay in the area of the rightward brigade of 11 Division (34 Brigade). Just before zero a special bombing party from the 9 Lancashire Fusiliers was to rush the farm and block its exits before the main attack went in. This was only partially successful. As the men were picking their way around the rubble heaps in an attempt to locate the exits, a machine-gun opened fire on them from a mound of rubble to the north.[7] It was undoubtedly this gun which took such a toll on the Canadian advance on the right and the other assault formations of 11 Division. By late afternoon the 11 Manchesters had been drawn into the fight but several enemy machine-guns were now in operation and causing heavy casualties.[8] Two tanks sent forward to help had ditched close by the farm. However, this was turned to advantage. Parties from the 11 Manchesters, the 5 Dorsets, and the 6 East Yorkshire Pioneers dismantled two of the machine-guns from the tanks and opened fire on the German defenders. Under this cover, bombing parties ran forward and threw explosive and smoke grenades down the entrances. At last (5.30 in the afternoon) the garrison, comprising one officer and 55 men, surrendered. No fewer than four battalions (the equivalent of a brigade of troops) had been involved in the five-hour struggle against this tiny force. But at last the farm which had been the target of Australian and Canadian operations for eight weeks fell to the veterans of Suvla Bay.[9]

Despite this considerable diversion of strength the main task of the 34 Brigade was the capture of Zollern and then Stuff Redoubt. Zollern was some 750 yards from the British front line and consisted of the usual cluster of all-round trench defences and dug-outs. Before zero the divisional commander had received reports that the strongpoint had been 'obliterated' by the heavy artillery.[10] The troops soon found that this was far from the case. Machine-guns from Zollern opened on them as soon as they left their trench.[11] What happened next remains obscure. Men from the 8 Northumberland certainly reached the redoubt. But by this time the barrage had been lost and those detailed to 'mop up' the dug-outs of the redoubt were dead,[12] and cohesion had been lost. Patrols sent forward to ascertain the position described the ground in front of the redoubt as 'an empty battlefield', perhaps the first time that expression had been used.[13] What they were observing was to become common in modern war – a battlefield so swept by hostile fire from concealed machine-guns that nothing could move on it. By nightfall in fact there was only one officer and 59 men from the Northumberland clinging to the southern face of Zollern. More battalions were prepared for the assault on the 27th but in the early morning officer patrols found the redoubt empty, evacuated during the night because of the successful advance of 33 Brigade on the left of 34.[14] Two redoubts had now fallen to 11 Division.

Stuff Redoubt was in the original German second line some 500 yards north-west of Zollern. It was, if anything, a more difficult prospect because it was obscured from observation from the British front. At the end of fighting on the 26th the closest troops to it were the remnants of the 34 Brigade close to Zollern. The fall of that strongpoint opened up the possibility of an advance on Stuff but the 34 Brigade was a spent force and the reserve brigade of the division (32) was moved forward.

The attack was to take place at 3 p.m. on the 27th by two battalions of the brigade. This was later postponed to 4 p.m. to give all units time to assemble but the orders to delay did not reach the 9 West Yorkshire. Perhaps because of the unusual spectacle of an attack by a lone battalion the Germans holding the south face were taken by surprise and the Yorkshires were able to establish a precarious grip on it.[15] Then one hour later the other battalion (6 Yorkshire)

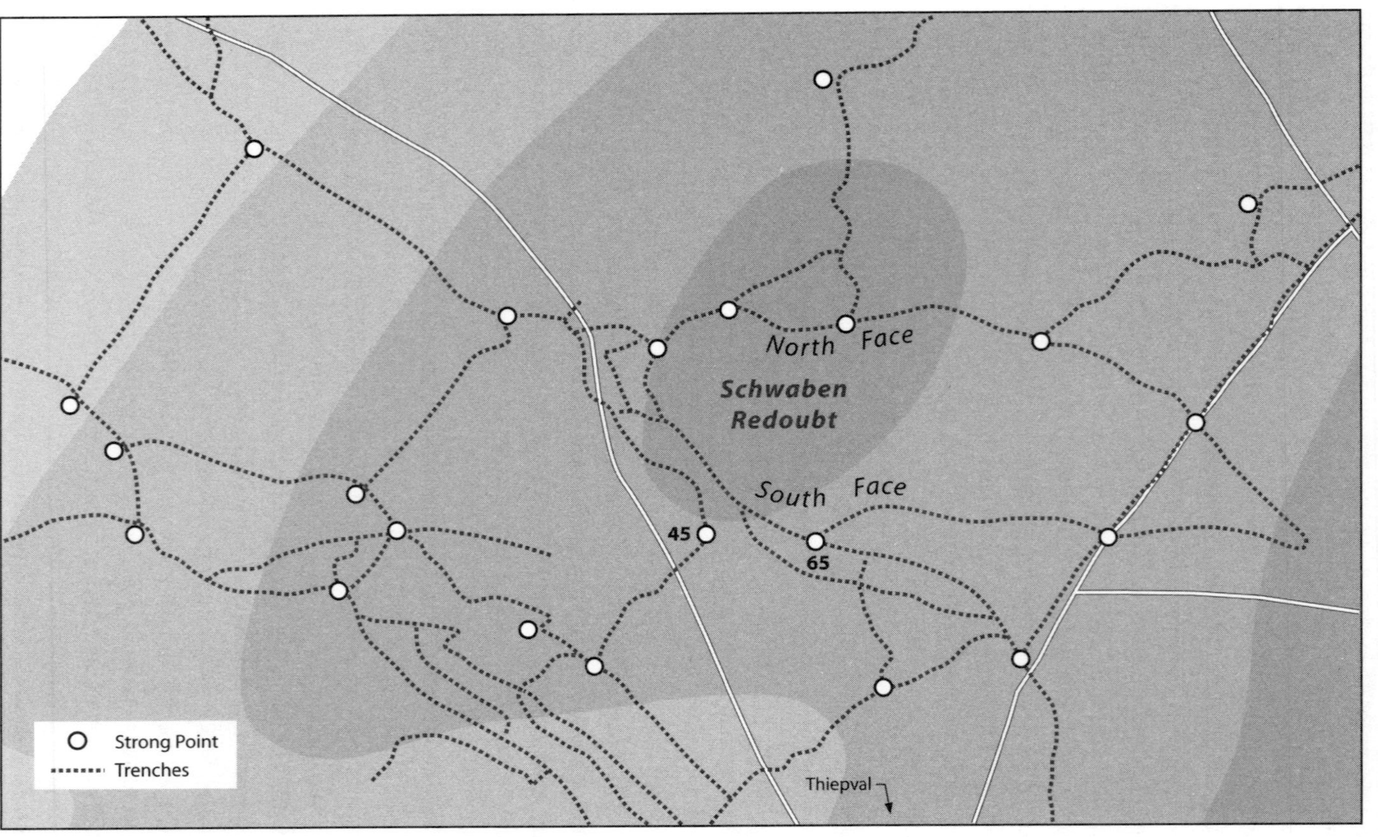


The Schwaben Redoubt, October

advanced, this time without any artillery support, as it had been fired at the original start time. This singular phenomenon also caught the Germans unawares and by just after 4 p.m. there were strong units of two battalions holding on to the southern section of Stuff Redoubt.[16] The fighting now degenerated into hand-to-hand combat in most confused conditions. Artillery support for an attack on the remainder of Stuff was almost impossible to arrange because the location of the troops was unknown and indeed some were in the underground tunnels of the redoubt. Several attempts to capture the north face of the redoubt were made over the next two days. All failed and by the end of the battle the northern section of Stuff Redoubt remained in German hands.[17]

Meanwhile the 18 Division had the daunting tasks of capturing Thiepval and the Schwaben Redoubt. Three reinforced battalions were to be used against Thiepval, 10 Essex from the 53 Brigade, and 12 Middlesex and 11 Fusiliers from 54 Brigade.[18] The Essex, which were only to capture the eastern tip of Thiepval, had the less difficult task. They advanced close behind the barrage at zero only to find that 'the enemy's machine guns and snipers had been completely dominated by our artillery'.[19] Casualties were 'negligible'.[20] Then the units found themselves under heavy enfilade fire from the north-west of the ruins and were forced to halt.[21]

Much thought had been given to the capture of Thiepval by the commander of the brigade, General Shoubridge. Each of the attack battalions was reinforced by a company of 'moppers-up' from other units who were to clear the large number of dug-outs known to honeycomb the ruins of the village. A third battalion was placed in close support either to assist the two lead battalions in getting forward or to supply additional parties to clear dug-outs. Two tanks were detailed to supplement the assault.[22]

The assault was grim from the start. The trenches and dug-outs in this area were too numerous for the bombardment to have dealt with them all effectively. Nor did the creeping barrage do much to assist except in the initial phase, because progress was far slower than its rate of creep. As the fighting progressed across the ruins the battle developed into an incoherent welter of hand-to-hand combat. Gradually, however, the British advanced. In the centre of Thiepval the artillery had been most effective and within an hour the Middlesex were approaching the ruins of Thiepval château until checked on the right by extremely deadly fire from that point. At this time the leading tank opportunely arrived and effectively dealt with the enemy's machine-guns around the château.[23] It seems that the intervention of this tank was crucial, the brigade narrative being doubtful if the attack could have proceeded beyond that point had not the château defences been eliminated.[24]

Even after the ruins of the château were occupied, progress was glacial. Snipers were encountered 'in every other shell hole', machine-gun fire was continuous, and every inch of ground had to be fought for. By 3.35 p.m. the north-eastern section of Thiepval was still holding out yet the leading battalion (12 Middlesex) 'had been practically expended' and the 11 Fusiliers 'were all split-up, in dug-out clearing parties and individual fights for points still holding out'.[25] Any hope of further advances now lay with the reserve battalion. That unit had in fact already been ordered forward. But it immediately ran into a very heavy barrage and many officers became cut off from their companies. With all recognisable landmarks now obliterated by the shelling, most remaining units lost direction. Just one company (without any officers) arrived at the front to reinforce the hard-pressed troops. As their numbers were insufficient to add any significant weight to the attack, it was decided to consolidate the line already held.[26]

Before an advance on the final objective, the Schwaben Redoubt, could be undertaken it was imperative that all of Thiepval be captured. So on the 27th, C Company of the 7 Bedfords, the only unit in position, was ordered to take it. The company narrative takes up the story:

> 2nd Lt. Adlam...went across the open under extremely heavy rifle & machine-gun fire from shell hole to shell hole [and] organised an assaulting party .... He collected a large quantity of German bombs and placing himself at the head of his party, commenced a whirlwind attack on the strong point. He personally out threw the enemy despite the fact they were using only egg bombs, and by the resolution and furiousness of his attack forced the enemy ... [back]. Realising this 2nd Lt. Adlam...led a final attack on the strongpoint despite the fact that he had been wounded in the leg. This work was extremely successful and 40 dead Germans were carried in the trenches later on – This heavy loss being due to 2nd Lt. Adlam's wonderful throwing.[27]

Thus did the remainder of Thiepval fall. Adlam was awarded the VC.

The attack on Schwaben could now proceed. As Maxse undoubtedly knew from accounts of 1 July, this was not something to be taken lightly. Of all the redoubts built into the German second line, it was without question the most formidable. Underneath the all-round trench defences lay a complex of tunnels, large enough for hospital facilities and a telephone exchange. Nevertheless, as Maxse also knew, the Ulstermen had briefly held sections of the redoubt for a short period. More methodical methods might produce a more permanent success.

Maxse erred on the side of prudence. As dawn broke on the 27th he contemplated the fact that most battalions of the 53 and 54 Brigades were shattered. The price for Thiepval had been high – 1,456 casualties,[28] something approaching 40 per cent of the attacking force. On the other hand Shoubridge of the 54 and the redoubtable Higginson of the 53 had done well and were familiar with the local situation. Maxse therefore halted all operations on the 27th and sent Shoubridge and Higginson battalions of the 55 Brigade as reinforcements, with orders to attack on the 28th.

The attempt by the 18 Division to capture the redoubt would last from 28 September to 6 October, by which time the Germans would still be in possession of the north-western corner. As many as eight battalions from the division (7 Queen's, 8 Suffolk, 8 East Surrey, 8 Norfolk, 7 Bedfords, 5 West Yorkshire, 6 Berkshire, 7 Buffs) took part in the fighting which occurred largely in the trenches, dug-outs, and tunnels of the redoubt. Once more, artillery support could protect the troops until they entered the maze of the redoubt but then was useless. The fighting was terribly confused and often degenerated into hand-to-hand combat which ebbed and flowed around the strongpoints (see map, 'The Schwaben Redoubt, October 1916', p. 254). The struggle for points 45 and 65 may serve as illustrations of the type of combat involved.

Both of these strongpoints were in the double trench system which formed the southern face of the redoubt. They were first attacked from the south-east on the morning of the 28th by the 7 Queen's and the 8 Suffolk. The going was very slippery due to overnight rain and the barrage was soon lost. The troops found themselves under heavy machine-gun fire from point 65. An hour later the fire was still so heavy that both battalions remained pinned down.[29] Then Captain Longbourne of the Queen's decided to take matters into his own hands:

> He took a bag of grenades and ran from shell hole to shell hole till he got within 25 yards of this strongpoint in which two machine guns were in action. From a shell hole he bombed the enemy and knocked out one machine gun. His bombs were then exhausted. It then became a duel between him and the Germans manning the second machine gun .... He beckoned to Private Waldron to bring him another bag of bombs. The fight was resumed, Captain Longbourne throwing the bombs and Private Waldron sniping any Germans who showed above the parapet. This went on for 45 minutes whilst the Germans were also throwing bombs but could not hit Captain Longbourne in his shell hole. Sergeant Parker then joined him and assisted by sniping. Finally Captain Longbourne had only two bombs left. He threw them into the enemy and simultaneously charged with Sergt. Parker and Private Waldon.

> Then these brave men found the crew of the gun had all been killed and they thus captured the strongpoint and subsequently received the surrender of 46 unwounded German prisoners who were hiding in dug-outs close by. Fifteen dead Germans were lying around the two machine-guns.[30]

By this means the British forced their way into the southern face of Schwaben Redoubt. And the fall of point 65 soon led to the capture of 45 as the Queen's bombed their way down the connecting trench.[31] This was not the end of the affair, however. At 6 a.m. on the 30th the Germans barraged point 45, now held by the 8 East Surrey. According to their account: 'Our men were attacked from two sides and outranged, especially by the small egg bomb and were driven back, with elements of 7th Queens, about 200 yards.'[32]

Later this position was retaken as part of a larger operation to capture the north face of the redoubt.[33] But the enemy guns had the range of this point and the British occupying troops were forced to evacuate it under heavy shell fire.[34] The point was reoccupied on 2 October and this time remained in British hands.[35] By the time the 18 Division was withdrawn it had taken all but the north-western face of Schwaben Redoubt. The cost of its capture was approximately 2,000 men.[36]

## V

So by the end of the Battle of Thiepval Ridge the British had advanced between 1,000 and 2,000 yards on a 6,000-yard front – gaining just over 5 square miles of territory. However, they were not yet securely on the ridge line. Regina Trench and sections of Stuff and Schwaben Redoubts were still in enemy hands. Casualties had also been heavy – 4,500 in 11 Division, 4,000 in 18 Division, and about 4,000 Canadians: a total of 12,500 men. German casualties are unknown but, given the fierce fighting around the redoubts, they cannot have been light.

The fighting for the Thiepval Ridge does reveal one of the myriad faces of war not so far conspicuous at the Battle of the Somme. More than once we have made the point that without adequate fire support (especially from the artillery) the endeavours of the infantry, however brave they might be, and however advanced their training and sophisticated their battle formations, usually came to naught. That factor is not absent here. Without the protection of the creeping barrage Canadian troops could hardly have got within 1,000 yards of Regina Trench or the British to the vicinity of Mouquet Farm, Zollern, Stuff, and the Schwaben Redoubt. If Thiepval had not been 'softened up' (that is, many of the defenders killed, wounded, or stunned) by the bombardment it would have resisted attack as it had on 1 July. But fighting for the redoubts themselves *was* largely a matter of individual or small group endeavour. A creeping barrage could not penetrate into a tunnel. Neither, except in the most fortunate (for the attackers) of circumstances, could the heavy shells of the preliminary bombardment. In these conditions, once the barrage had delivered the troops to the edge of the redoubts, they were on their own. What is worthy of note is that in this grim, intense, close-quarter fighting, the troops from the British New Army and the Dominions were quite capable of outfighting the German defenders. This scenario runs counter to a popular and tenacious view of the First World War – that man for man the Germans could outfight any other soldiers and that it was only the materiel superiority of the Allies that enabled them to prevail. But what we have just seen shows that given circumstances where training and individual courage could be brought to bear, men who in 1914 had been civilians around Grantham and Colchester outfought the German defenders who in some cases had occupied the defensive redoubts for months or even years.

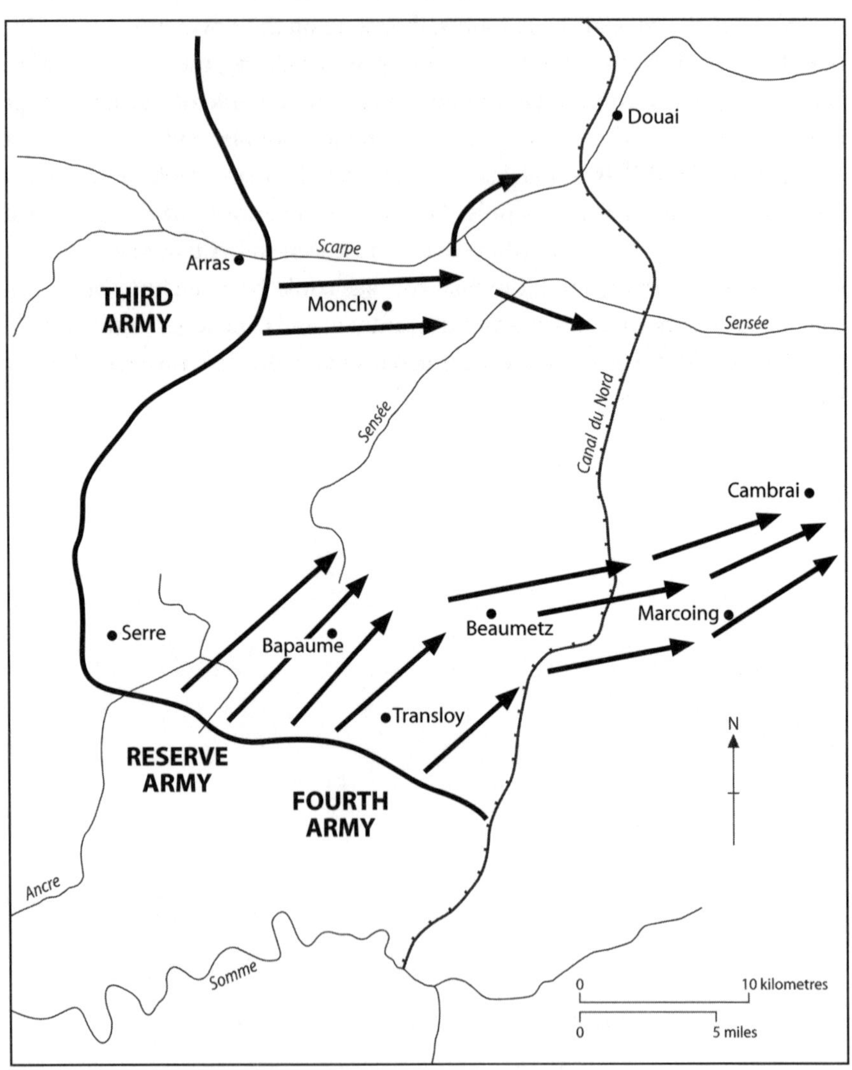


Haig's October Plan

# 24 'A Severe Trial of Body and Spirit': The Somme, October

## I

Despite their limitations, the operations from 15 September to 30 September were the most successful carried out by the British on the Somme. The two assaults by Fourth Army and one by the Reserve Army had captured as much ground as all operations between 1 July and 14 September. And there were other positive aspects on the British side that had emerged from the fighting. The creeping barrage as a method of infantry protection was now used as a matter of course by all divisions in the Fourth and Reserve Armies. Furthermore, although on 15 September the tanks had proved disappointing and even a negative factor, because of the disruption to the artillery plan, they had proved useful in certain circumstances. In Flers, Gueudecourt, and Thiepval they had enabled stubborn resistance in the ruined villages to be overcome quickly and at modest cost.

The experience of battle had alerted the tank experts to deficiencies in the Mark I tank. It was now recognised that a more powerful engine must be employed, that the armour protection must be increased to deal with German armour-piercing bullets, that a shorter version of the 6-pounder gun must be developed for greater ease of manoeuvre, and that the tracks must be tightened to avoid the tendency to spin off in rough going.[1] Finally, the British infantry in instances where the artillery could no longer be employed had outfought their German counterparts, even though the enemy were often occupying well-prepared defensive positions.

Set against these heartening aspects were some negative factors. The command seemed chronically unable to calculate exactly how much artillery was needed to capture particular objectives. The intervention of a Maxse might assist in the capture of a specific area such as Thiepval but the general *modus operandi* seemed to be to assemble as many guns as possible and hope for the best. A further problem was the inability of Haig to grasp the kind of operations that his army could conduct with at least some chance of success – that is, offensives limited in objectives to the range of the guns covering the infantry advance, and intended precisely to kill the maximum number of German soldiers with minimum loss to his own side. Always in this period when a major attack was announced the cavalry were assembled and distant objectives set. It was perhaps this hankering after the decisive battle that diverted the attention of the staff at GHQ from such matters as artillery concentration. What it ensured was that battles were never fought with the attritional factor at their centre, thus causing more casualties to the attacking British than were being inflicted on the defending Germans.

Another negative factor underlay this persistent overreaching. Optimism is a requirement that few commanders can do without. But optimism taken to ludicrous extremes is dangerous. Haig's conviction that, on the eve of all of his major offensives, German morale was on the brink of collapse underpinned his projected cavalry forays. Another example of unwarranted optimism is the assumption that major advances (in Somme terms) such as those of 15, 25, and 26 September were a sure sign of disintegrating enemy morale. The danger here lay in what might happen if Haig's armies, already worn down by hard fighting and somewhat disorganised as a result, were asked for additional efforts so as to push a supposedly tottering enemy over the edge. It will be recalled that the limited success of 14 July was followed by the disorganised, unco-ordinated, and ultimately futile attempts to gain ground. And if such a pattern reappeared in the aftermath of the September advances there were added dangers for Haig's armies which had not been present in mid-July.

The first was the fact that, except in small areas of the Reserve Army front still occupied by the Germans (Regina Trench and the areas of Stuff and Schwaben Redoubts), the British had reached the far edge of the Thiepval–Morval Ridge. Any advance from the ridge would see them lose this commanding position and descend into a valley. They would then face a gently slope to just beyond Bapaume. Thus any advance beyond their present position would restore the observation advantage to the Germans.

The second danger was that Haig had now reached a precarious point in the campaigning season. The latter half of September had been remarkably fine, with heavy rain falling on just two days – the 18th and 29th. Similar conditions were not to be expected in October. Mid-autumn often saw heavy rains in the Somme area, at a time when the British would be advancing from high ground to low. In these circumstances there was a considerable risk that the artillery would be blinded and that the men would be consigned to damp or boggy trenches for the winter.

A third danger concerned the Germans. Although most of their original defences (the first, second, and third lines) were now in British hands, in the weeks when the British army crawled towards the ridge the enemy had not been idle. A fourth line through Le Transloy now confronted the Fourth Army and aerial reconnaissance revealed that the Germans had commenced a fifth line in front of Bapaume and a sixth three miles further back.[2] None of these lines possessed the strength and complexity, in terms of dug-outs and breadth of wire, of the systems overrun so far. Yet reaching them required a five-mile advance – precisely the distance that Haig's armies had achieved in a three month campaign. Unless the enemy collapsed entirely, such a timetable would extend the campaign into the depths of winter. Would Haig be so reckless as to take the risk?

There was never a chance that he would do anything else. Even before operations on the Reserve Army front were concluded he had issued new orders to his army commanders. He instructed Rawlinson to capture the Transloy Line, Gough to advance on Loupart Wood from the south and Beaumont Hamel from the west, and Allenby (Third Army) to attack from around Gommecourt.[3] These were modest enough objectives with a maximum advance of about 2,500–3,000 yards. However, as always with Haig, there must be no pause while preparations for these operations were undertaken. He instructed the Fourth and Reserve Armies to secure 'as soon as possible' the outer defences of the Transloy Line and the remainder of Thiepval Ridge. In the case of the Thiepval Ridge this made sense in that it would place Gough's troops securely on the high ground. To the Fourth Army it made no sense at all, because it would allow no preparation time for the larger affair he intended and was bound to result in the hasty, ill-thought-out, narrow-front operations that invariably followed from such directives.

But then the larger affair to which these actions were intended as a prelude – the capture of the Transloy Line – itself made no sense. If successful it would see Rawlinson's troops descend from the high ground and press forward into a valley. This would lose them the advantage of observation and the valley would become a bog should the normal October rains set in.

It soon became clear why these factors did not weigh with Haig. The advance he had ordered was only the first step in an expanding design. Once more he was beginning to see distant vistas and far-away places as the true destination for his armies. The trend seems to have set in after a visit by Kavanagh (commanding the Cavalry Corps) on 30 September. The discussion commenced reasonably enough with Haig instructing Kavanagh to explore the area north of the River Ancre in case an attack from that direction might take the Germans by surprise.[4] Soon, however, the issue arose of a cavalry pursuit in the event of an enemy collapse. Haig told Kavanagh:

> I would aim at getting the enemy into a trap with the marshes to the east of Arras (around Hamel) on his N side and the Canal du Nord on the east of him. The latter is a brand new canal running in deep cuttings in places 150 feet deep.

This scenario would be brought about by a three army attack. Rawlinson would attack the Transloy Line and then advance north-east to Beaumetz. He would then swing due east, pass through Marcoing and encircle Cambrai from the south-east.[5]

Gough's movements were not spelt out with any precision. However he was to capture Achiet-le-Grand and then presumably operate on Rawlinson's left flank as the Fourth Army closed on Cambrai.

Allenby (who also visited Haig that day) would provide the northern pincer of the whole movement. He would attack south of Arras, capture the high ground around Beaurains–Monchy, cut off the enemy from the north and close the gap in the unfinished Canal du Nord with artillery fire. He would then undertake a further advance to trap the enemy in a pocket formed by Canal du Nord-Scheldt marshes around Hamel–Beaulencourt.

It is important to understand what this plan entailed. In Rawlinson's case, Beaumetz was eight miles from the recently captured Flers; Marcoing was a further eight miles distant, and to pass the Fourth Army to the south and east of Cambrai would have involved a further 8 miles advance. That is, Haig was postulating for the Fourth Army a 24-mile operation, six times the distance they had traversed in the campaign so far which had occupied a period of three months. For Gough the distances would have been approximately the same. As for Allenby, he had a mere 20 miles to cover but he had the additional task of rapidly moving his heavy artillery forward to deny to the Germans the gap in the Canal du Nord.

There was never a chance that any aspect of this plan would be put into effect. Successful cavalry operations would require the German army to have collapsed – down to the last machine-gun team and the last battery of guns. If even a few Germans were inclined to stand and fire these weapons the cavalry would be slaughtered. In addition a heavy toll would be taken on the infantry, now out of their trench defences, advancing at a walk across open country. Allenby's forces would bear a further burden. They would have to transport most of their heavy guns, and all the ammunition to support them, in rapid time over a distance of at least 15 miles across an area crisscrossed with trenches and barbed-wire entanglements. In short, this whole plan was preposterous in the conditions applying on the Western Front in late 1916.

It might of course be argued that this after all was just a contingency plan of the type developed by any well-run army. Certainly armies have contingency plans, but in this case Haig's had no chance of success if the enemy continued to fight (and would be unnecessary should they not). In other words this was not an example of prescient forward planning, it bore the characteristics of something concocted at the Mad Hatter's tea party.

It might also be argued that Haig's plan should not be taken seriously – that it was just an example of the Commander-in-Chief's imagination running away with him late at night while he was writing up his diary. A number of factors tell against this view. First, there is no reason to doubt that the conversations with Kavanagh, Rawlinson, Allenby, and Gough on which the diary entry is based actually took place. If Haig's imagination was running riot then he had no hesitation in sharing his fantasies with his army commanders – down to such points of detail as how particular locations were to be attacked.

There is an additional reason which indicates that Haig was serious about these operations. In the section of his diary where he goes into detail about the plan, he drew a thick line in the margin and indicated to Doris, his wife (who regularly typed out his manuscript diary), 'please do not copy this point'.[6] Two explanations suggest themselves. The first is that at the time Doris received the diary, the plan was still regarded as sufficiently secret for the number of copies of it to be kept to a minimum. But second, and in sharp contrast, by the time she received the diary the actual achievements of the British army had fallen so far short of the objectives stated in the plan as to make the entry embarrassing. What these scenarios have in common is that Haig was indeed serious about his grand October plan.

The importance of this episode lies not so much in the plan itself – not one section of which was ever implemented – as in what it revealed about the mind of the Commander-in-Chief. Even so late in the campaigning season as October, Haig was thinking in terms of Napoleonic decisive battles – discrete episodes which would either end the war or go a long way towards it. And decisive battles could only be brought about after a break-in, achieved by the infantry and artillery, was converted to a breakthrough by the cavalry. The awkward fact that the cavalry had no place on a modern battlefield pointed elsewhere: to the lamentable conclusion (from Haig's viewpoint) that limited objective operations with attrition should be the principal aim. This conclusion, it has to be stressed again, was one that Haig had spent most of the war avoiding. Breakthrough was his watchword, the cavalry his instrument, a vivid imagination his guide. And that would long continue to be the case

## II

Meanwhile, back at the front Rawlinson and Gough were wrestling with those sections of the Commander-in-Chief's design that it was possible to set in train. Even here Haig had placed a deadly ambiguity at the centre of his instructions. He had set the Transloy Ridge as the objective for the Fourth Army and Loupart Wood and Beaumont Hamel for Gough's forces. But he had also enjoined that there be no pause in operations and that objectives that lay within easy reach of these forces were to be captured at once.

Only in one area were useful gains made – when the units of XIV Corps eliminated a sharp salient in the British line around Eaucourt l'Abbaye. In other areas the Canadians failed to capture Regina Trench and fighting continued in Stuff and Schwaben Redoubts.[7]

Two features of the fighting are worthy of note. The first is that the German infantry resisted all attacks with its usual tenacity, only giving ground (as around Eaucourt) where it was tactically sensible to do so. The second matter is that from 1 to 6 October the 'enemy's artillery fire daily increased in violence and accuracy'.[8] Trenches were continually obliterated and attacks broken up.[9]

None of this indicated that the Germans were about to crack and fall back into the marshes designated for them by Haig. On the contrary it appeared that they were recovering from the setbacks of September. They were relieving tired divisions and strengthening their artillery. Between the end of September and 13 October the six divisions holding the line from Le Transloy to the Ancre were replaced by seven from other parts of the front, and from 15 September to 8 October 36½ additional heavy batteries were introduced and 36 worn-out batteries replaced.[10] It was the fruits of these efforts that the British infantry were noticing in early October. The high command unfortunately did not notice.

But then another factor intervened which the high command could not disregard. The weather, which had been remarkably fine since 15 September, broke. On 2 October heavy rain fell. The air observers were grounded and the artillery greatly hampered in their work. The 3rd was misty but on the 4th heavy rain returned and persisted on the 5th and 6th. All this disrupted Rawlinson and Gough's plan to capture the objectives immediately facing them – the outlying trenches of the Transloy Line and the remainder of the Thiepval Ridge. So heavy was the rain that the ground was reduced to a bog and the operation, set for the 5th, had to be postponed first until the 6th and then until the 7th.

It was at this point that the incessant attacks ordered by Haig took their toll on the troops and on the British plan. The Canadians, who had been trying to make ground towards Regina Trench since their failed attempt on 1 October, announced that they could not provide relief for their tired troops in time for an attack on the 7th. The French on the other hand would be ready by that date. It was decided that no simultaneous operations could take place – the Fourth Army and the French would attack on the 7th, the Reserve Army on the 8th.

Although the Fourth Army attack was only intended to be a preliminary to Haig's big push towards the swamps north of Cambrai, it was a large enough affair. One French division and six British divisions would attack with the intention of capturing the Transloy Line.

Taken as a whole, the attack was a failure. On most parts of the front the weather had not allowed sufficient aerial spotting for the guns to be directed with any accuracy on to the German trenches or batteries. Moreover, in some areas the Germans had positioned trenches behind small folds in the ground, which although close to the British front trenches, could not be directly observed.[11] In other areas the British ran into newly constructed German trenches of which neither the infantry nor the artillery was aware.[12] On yet other occasions resistance came not from defensive lines, but from machine-guns, placed either in shell holes on the flank of the attack or at a distance beyond the range of the creeping barrage.[13]

There was one small success on the left flank to show for this gloomy affair. There the 23 Division following close behind a creeping barrage jumped the defenders of Le Sars in their dug-outs before they could bring their weapons into play. By the end of the day the village was in British hands. This episode demonstrated yet again the efficacy of the creeping barrage when accurately fired against conventional defence.[14] Otherwise the weather, which should have cautioned against any attack, and the new German machine-gun tactics made the capture of intermediate positions protecting the Transloy Line impossible. There may have been another reason as well, noted by an acute observer in XV Corps. 'Perhaps,' the new commander of XV Corps General du Cane wrote, 'all concerned were too optimistic owing to the previous successes.'[15]

On the 8th it was the turn of the Reserve Army. Here the 3 and 1 Canadian Divisions attacked from the left of Le Sars with the objective of capturing their old nemesis, Regina Trench. They were no more successful than Rawlinson's troops. In many areas of the front the bombardment had failed to cut the wire and the Germans had adopted in some places the expedient of pushing rolls of barbed

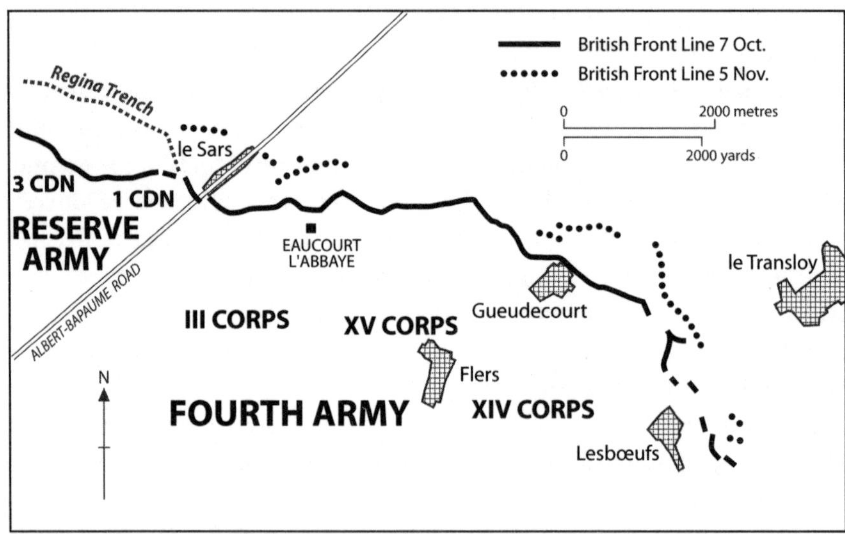


The October Battles

wire into no man's land at zero. The result was that most Canadians proceeded no further than the wire and were then shot down by German machine-gunners.[16] In small areas where the wire had been cut a few companies forced their way into Regina Trench but without support they were soon counter-attacked back. Only on the right where the success of 23 Division carried them through were they able to make any gains at all to the north-west of Le Sars.[17]

Gough did not see this matter as a command failure – he blamed the troops. After lunch on the 8th, Haig visited the Reserve Army Commander at Toutencourt and obtained the following reflections on the battle:

> He [Gough] was of opinion that the Canadian (3rd Division) had not done well. In some parts, they had not even left their trenches for the attack.[18]

The next attack on the outer defences of the Transloy Line was mounted on the 12th by five divisions of Fourth Army. The weather on the 10th and 11th was fine but dull with low cloud which prevented aerial observation. Nevertheless, the absence of rain was what decided the command to proceed. The results were much the same as those on the 7th – a few battalions gained 400–500 yards but none captured even their first objective.[19] The reports identified two factors which had led to failure. The first was the weather, which robbed the artillery of photographs and reconnaissance reports.[20] The second was well summed up by the commander of 30 Division:

> The principal cause of failure appears to me to have been due to a well organized enemy employment of machine gun fire. It remains to be discovered how we can deal with enemy machine guns, scattered all over this evenly but *not* placed in his trenches, which by indirect or long range fire can erect a 'barrage' on No Man's Land.[21]

One worrying aspect of the attack had been the high ratio of casualties among the Fourth Army battalions. The four battalions of 4 Division suffered 1,446 casualties, an average of 360 per battalion.[22] The 7 Seaforths from 9 Division suffered 467, the 2 York and Lancaster from 6 Division 200, the 7 Norfolks from 12 Division 222.[23] These are high figures but they are even more alarming when it is recognised that few battalions in the Fourth Army could muster more than 400 men for an attack.[24] The Royal Irish Fusiliers (4 Division) even had to summon the normal 10 per cent of officers and men left behind in any attack to build up sufficient strength to go over the top. One of its companies had just 76 men out of a normal complement of 250.[25] Incessant operations since mid-September had worn down the Fourth Army to the extent that even new divisions introduced to the front (and for the attack on the 12th, the 4, 6,

30, and 9 Divisions were designated as 'fresh') were running out of men. The weather, the new German tactics, and the loss of observation left the army with very poor prospects for future success.

The failure on the 12th caused much soul-searching at Fourth Army headquarters. A few home truths were beginning to clarify in Rawlinson's mind. He recorded in his diary:

> There are numerous [cases] of wire uncut, distant machine gun fire and strong counter attacks but the fact is that bosh [*sic*] put up a better fight of it this time and until we can reduce his [resistance?] further by shaking his moral[e] we shall not I fear drive him out of his present line though it is by no means a strong one. – In places it is difficult to oversee – Since we came forward off the high ground we have to a great extent lost the advantage we had over him of observation.[26]

Here at least was recognition that the new conditions, new tactics, and a new determination on the part of the enemy to resist were serious factors, which needed careful thought. Rawlinson followed up on these thoughts by calling his corps commanders with their artillery experts (and the Prince of Wales!) to a conference at his headquarters on the 13th.[27] After listening to his commanders for some hours, Rawlinson went on to produce a document summarising the reasons for failure. They were:

1. absence of surprise – all attacks occur between 12.00 noon and 3.00 pm;
2. difficulty of observation – because of poor weather [and, although he did not state it here, loss of the commanding position on the ridge];
3. recovering enemy resistance;
4. lack of clearly defined departure trenches to give the creeping barrage a regular starting line;
5. distant machine gun fire.[28]

His remedies were to state that any future attack required good aerial observation in order to deliver an accurate bombardment; to vary zero hour; to allow sufficient time to dig departure trenches so the artillery could be certain of their location, and to extend the creeping barrage so as to deal with the distant machine-guns.[29] (Cavan also suggested to Haig that the distant machine-guns be blinded by smoke shells.[30] Neither man seemed to realise that at this moment the Fourth Army had no smoke shells.[31])

But Rawlinson had wider concerns. Before even the first failed attempt against Le Transloy, Haig had visited headquarters with truly alarming news:

> He [Haig] is bent on continuing the battle until we are forced to stop by the weather, indeed he would like to go on all through the winter.[32]

Rawlinson pointed out that the three constraints were 'ammunition, weather and men'.[33] By this he meant that there was an insufficiency of the first and third commodities, and even had they been available the weather would prevent them being used optimally.

It was not that Haig was unaware that these problems existed. Indeed, on the following day he enumerated them in a letter to Robertson, the CIGS, as the three factors on which further operations would depend.[34] However, he did not act on this logic by announcing an immediate halt to operations. Instead he called for better rail communications to deliver more ammunition to the front and 'the utmost efforts of the Empire' (i.e. more men). As for the weather, Haig merely deemed that 'an ordinary winter' 'should not suffice to put a stop to my advance'.[35] In any case, he concluded, it was imperative to press on because although 'it was not possible to say how near to breaking point the enemy may be ... he has undoubtedly gone a long way towards it'.[36]

It would be satisfactory to report that the disastrous efforts of 7 and 12 October were sufficient to change Haig's view of the prospects of the campaign. But no such change took place. Another attack was ordered for the 18th.

In the event the attack was as complete a failure as those on the 7th and 12th. The bombardment had largely missed the German defences, the enemy artillery was still intact, and the attacking troops suffered from long-range machine-gun fire. Hardly any of the recommendations laid down by Rawlinson on the 13th seem to have been acted upon. A period of fine weather had not occurred – it rained or was cloudy for most days between 13 and 18 October – assembly trenches were not in many cases properly constructed because of the conditions, the barrage (perhaps because of lack of ammunition) had not been extended rearwards to take account of the German machine-gunners, and no smoke barrage was fired.[37] Only in one instance was a recommendation of the conference implemented. Zero hour had been changed from the afternoon to 3.40 a.m. As it happened, this made things worse. It meant that any attack would take place in the dark. Let the account of the 1 East Lancashire (4 Division) stand for many others on that day.

> At zero hour 3.40 am the weather conditions were appalling, pitch black, extremely cold, and pouring with rain. The waves advanced .... No organized line held by the enemy was met, but heavy machine gun and rifle fire was directed on to our waves from front and flanks.... [38]

The situation at the front was always obscure. No officers or Senior N.C.O.'s of [the leading companies] came back, and no messages were received back. I think that no rifles of the men who went forward could have been in working order 10 minutes after they left our lines. The ground was terribly torn up by shell fire, and as slippery as ice. The men kept on slipping and falling into the holes in the dark. The few who returned were one mass of mud from head to foot, and completely exhausted.[39]

Such were the fighting conditions in an 'ordinary winter'.

Even Haig was forced to modify his plans after this failure. Rain had continued to fall and so bad were the conditions that the Official History, a work not noted for its vivid prose, was moved to eloquence:

By the middle of October conditions behind the battlefront were so bad as to make mere existence a severe trial of body and spirit. Little could be seen from the air through the rain and mist, so counter-battery work suffered and it was often impossible to locate with accuracy the new German trenches and shell-hole positions. Objectives could not always be identified from ground level, so that it is no matter of surprise or censure that the British artillery sometimes fired short or placed its barrages too far ahead. Bursts of high-explosive were smothered in the ooze; many guns had been continuously in action for over two months and were too worn for accurate fire; in some particularly flooded battery positions sinking platforms had to be restored with any battle debris which came to hand. The ground was so deep in mud that to move one 18-pounder ten or twelve horses were often needed, and to supplement the supplies brought by light-railway and packhorse, ammunition had to be dragged up on sledges improvised of sheets of corrugated iron. The infantry, sometimes wet to the skin and almost exhausted before zero hour, were often condemned to struggle painfully forward through the mud under heavy fire against objectives vaguely defined and difficult of recognition.[40]

An artilleryman reflecting on conditions after the war confirmed these observations:

The 11th. Brigade R.F.A., in which I was commanding A Batty., was in action close to MOUQUET FARM, within a few yards of what appeared on the maps as a road, and which, judging by the orders which we received, when we were withdrawn in November, was believed by the Staff to be a road. Actually for hundreds of yards round the Battery positions there was not a square inch of the original surface of the ground visible; the whole area was a mass of shell craters of every calibre of shell, all running into each other,

> and superimposed on each other. The road was merely a line of craters, and it was so completely under water the whole time that it was never possible to see where they were. One battery tried to use it once, and in the first few yards lost a mule in a large hole.
>
> Ammunition was brought up on a light railway, to within a quarter of a mile of the battery positions, and horses came up every morning from the wagon lines to transfer it in pack to the batteries. This railway was shelled and broken every night, and the ammunition often did not arrive until midday. Meanwhile the unfortunate horses and their drivers had to hang about, often in pouring rain, always in unspeakable mud, for hours; the only water available was the foul water in the shell holes and when they returned to the wagon lines at dusk or after dark both men and horses were done in; while the shoeing smiths were up half the night replacing shoes which had been sucked off in the mud. It was not unknown for a horse to lose three shoes during the day. My [quartermaster] established himself in an abandoned dug-out on the edge of this morass, not too far from the battery, to which stores and rations for the battery were taken by wagon, and were brought on in pack at convenient times. My request that, to save the horses, I might supply myself with ammuntion in the same way, was curtly refused; the railway had been made to supply us, and we were to use it, happen what might. No Artillery Staff Officer ever came near us, except once, when the Corps Commander, Sir C. Jacob, came to see us, and they had to accompany him.
>
> At my battery position two cases occurred of the ground collapsing into, presumably, holes made underground by heavy delay action H.E. shell. In one case two men of a gun detachment were completely overcome by the poisonous fumes thus released; they were still unconscious when they left the battery, but whether they died or not I do not know. In the other case the collapse was under the feet of an officer sleeping in a shelter and he was not hurt.
>
> When it came to evacuating the positions one battery dismounted its guns in order to get them out. In my own case orders received at 11 a.m. gave me three hours to pass a certain cross-roads; but although we started getting the guns out as soon as the teams arrived my last vehicle only managed to clear the point in question at 6 p.m. the following day.
>
> The very fact that such orders could be issued proves that the Staff had not the remotest idea of what conditions were like in the line.[41]

Operations on this part of the front, it seemed evident, would have to be suspended. But Haig refused to draw this conclusion. Certainly in a note to Rawlinson and Gough written on the 18th, he considerably scaled back his expectations of earlier in the month. The Third Army would now not take part in operations and the Reserve and Fourth Armies' objectives were limited to those that were facing them (the Miraumont Spur and the Transloy Line respectively).[42] But this was to miss the point. Distant objectives such as Cambrai and the marshes east of Arras had all along been unrealistic propositions. But in the weather conditions in which Haig was now operating, so was the Transloy Line. This did not mean that the odd yard of coagulated mud might not be wrested from the enemy. But given the lack of accurate fire support these trivial gains would be bought at prohibitive cost.

It might be thought that Rawlinson, on receiving this missive from Haig, would register the strongest protest at continuing on after a trio of failures. The contrary proved to be the case. At a conference of his corps commanders called on the afternoon of the 18th and when it was clear that his latest effort had failed, he said:

> the attack [scheduled for the 23rd] was to be made with a large number of troops organized in depth, and every effort was to be made to make it a success, as it was most undesirable to remain for the Winter in the position on the low ground which we now occupy.[43]

This too was to miss an important point. Did not the failures of 7, 12, and 18 October suggest that the Fourth Army lacked the power to improve on its position on the low ground? Certainly it was undesirable to remain in a slough of mud, but the time to make this point had been back in September when the ridge had been captured. Now all the Fourth Army commander was doing was committing his hapless troops to another series of attacks in the most unpropitious of circumstances.

The results of Rawlinson's fourth effort were the same as the first three. A few sections of trench were captured but they were of no consequence. The 4 Division suffered 1,200 casualties, the 8 Division somewhat more.[44]

We last encountered 8 Division when it had failed so disastrously on 1 July. On that occasion the commander of 25 Brigade of the division, responding to his superiors, had included the percentage casualties suffered by his assault battalions, thereby making clear the calamity which had befallen his unit. After 23 October the commander of the same brigade, although a different officer, went through the same exercise. Of the four attacking battalions the casualties suffered amounted to 59 per cent, 39 per cent, 51 per cent and 38 per cent of their strength.[45] These percentages were certainly less than the figures for 1 July, which ranged from 53 per cent to 92 per cent. However, they were high enough, and with miscellaneous casualties to units such as the machine-gun companies amounted to 50 per cent of the strength of this unit. And it may be added that these casualties were suffered, not in pursuit (however misguided) of the larger purpose of 1 July, but in order to capture two insignificant lines of mud called Zenith and Misty Trenches.

The prospects for future operations were now extremely bleak. Incessant rain had turned the battlefield into a quagmire. Only with the greatest difficulty could ammunition for the guns and food and water for the troops reach the front. The mud confined all traffic supplying the Fourth Army to a single narrow road from Longueval to Flers. The German artillery soon became aware of this. Every two minutes the road in the vicinity of Flers was the recipient of a salvo of 5.9-inch shells.[46]

The consequent conditions for the troops in the front line were laid bare by a GHQ staff officer, Lord Gort. (By 1940 he was the commander of the British army.) After a visit to the front Gort passed on to Haig a number of comments. These describe men 'living on cold food and standing up to their knees in mud and water', afflicted by trench foot and in too poor a physical condition to conduct an attack successfully. Those moving up to the front were reduced to 'a state of physical exhaustion in a very short time' by the condition of the road. And so all-encompassing was the mud that troops making an attack had to 'help each other out of the fire trenches as they cannot get out unaided'.[47] Another source described attacking infantry as not only unable to keep up with their own creeping barrage but as being reduced to almost stationary targets in no man's land for the enemy machine-gunners.[48]

At this time another factor, which had already affected operations, began to reveal itself, as an officer subsequently commented:

> By the time the troops got to the area [of the front] the actual trench system, owing to shelling and new digging by both sides and errors in map compilation bore little recognisable resemblance to the actual trench system.[49]

What this meant was that commanders and staff officers and artillerymen were using maps that now bore no relation to reality. This could lead to farcical situations where men occupying a trench fired in the wrong direction on troops moving forward to relieve them. Moreover, it made it impossible for the artillery to give close support to an attack.[50]

Notwithstanding these conditions, Haig was determined to maintain the offensive. For 5 November he ordered what would be the seventh British attack on the Transloy Line, even giving Rawlinson objectives beyond that point: 'I told him that when Le Transloy is captured, arrangements must be made to push on at once to Beaulencourt in co-operation with the French. The XIV Corps had only planned to take Le Transloy.'[51]

The revelation that even the capture of Le Transloy would not end the ordeal of the troops provoked a minor revolt – not, it should be noted, from Rawlinson but from the corps commander responsible for carrying out the attack. Lord Cavan, the commander of XIV Corps, wrote to Rawlinson in terms not often employed to their superiors by high-ranking officers on the Western Front:

> With a full and complete sense of my responsibility I feel it my bounden duty to put in writing my considered opinion as to the attack ordered to take place on Nov 5th....
>
> An advance [on Le Transloy] from my present position with the troops at my disposal has practically no chance of success on account of the heavy enfilade fire of machine guns and artillery from the north, and the enormous distance we have to advance against a strongly prepared position, owing to the failure to advance our line in the recent operations....
>
> I perfectly acknowledge the necessity of not leaving the French left in the air [and]...I assert my readiness to sacrifice the British right rather than jeopardise the French...but I feel that I am bound to ask if this is the intention, for a sacrifice it must be. It does not appear that a failure would much assist the French, and there is a danger of this attack shaking the confidence of the men and officers in their commanders.
>
> No one who has not visited the front trenches can really know the state of exhaustion to which the men are reduced.[52]

Even this missive, with its suggestion that the higher command were neglecting to acquaint themselves with the situation at the front, did not alter the determination of Haig and Rawlinson. In reply to Cavan, Rawlinson emphasised 'the importance of meeting our obligations with the French'. And he insisted that a minor attack scheduled for later that day (3 November) should be allowed to proceed as it 'would form a useful test of what might be expected to be accomplished on the 5th'.[53]

The attack on the afternoon of the 3rd did indeed prove a 'useful test': it accomplished nothing at all. Rawlinson was not deterred. He concluded that the cause of failure was a want of vigour on the part of XIV Corps headquarters, and he decreed that the attack on the 5th would proceed as planned. Cavan, however, was not about to submit. He insisted that he would not attack until Rawlinson himself had seen conditions at the front.[54] Cavan won his point. As he later recalled, after viewing the front line 'R was equally convinced...that an attack was impossible.'[55] And Rawlinson was able to persuade Haig that operations to assist the French should be scaled down to trench raids and artillery support.[56]

Yet Cavan's commendable display of plain speaking availed his forces nothing. After an interview with Foch, Haig reversed his decision. The operation on the 5th was to go ahead after all.[57] The Fourth Army was thus committed to the attack despite the advice of the army commander and the corps commander whose task it was to carry it out. To make matters worse, the plan promulgated by Haig made no tactical sense. The XIV Corps was ordered to mount two attacks by widely separated formations. This allowed the Germans in the intervening ground to bring to bear devastating enfilade machine-gun fire on the hapless troops. That is, Haig was ordering a repetition of precisely that type of attack which had caused him, two months previously, to warn Rawlinson that 'something was wanting in the methods employed'. The operation failed at a cost of 2,000 casualties.[58]

This was not quite the end of the battle on the Fourth Army front. Attacks – generally small scale and usually futile even when a trench was occasionally wrested from the enemy – continued throughout November. Nor were these operations cheap. The 50 and the 33 Divisions suffered 2,200 casualties each in November, the 17 Division 1,300, the 8,750 and the Australian Corps (which re-entered the battle on 5 November) several thousand. So in operations that improved the tactical position of the Fourth Army not a whit, almost a division of infantry was cast away. But by then attention had turned away from the Fourth Army. In this last phase of the battle it was the Reserve (now renamed the Fifth Army) that held centre stage.

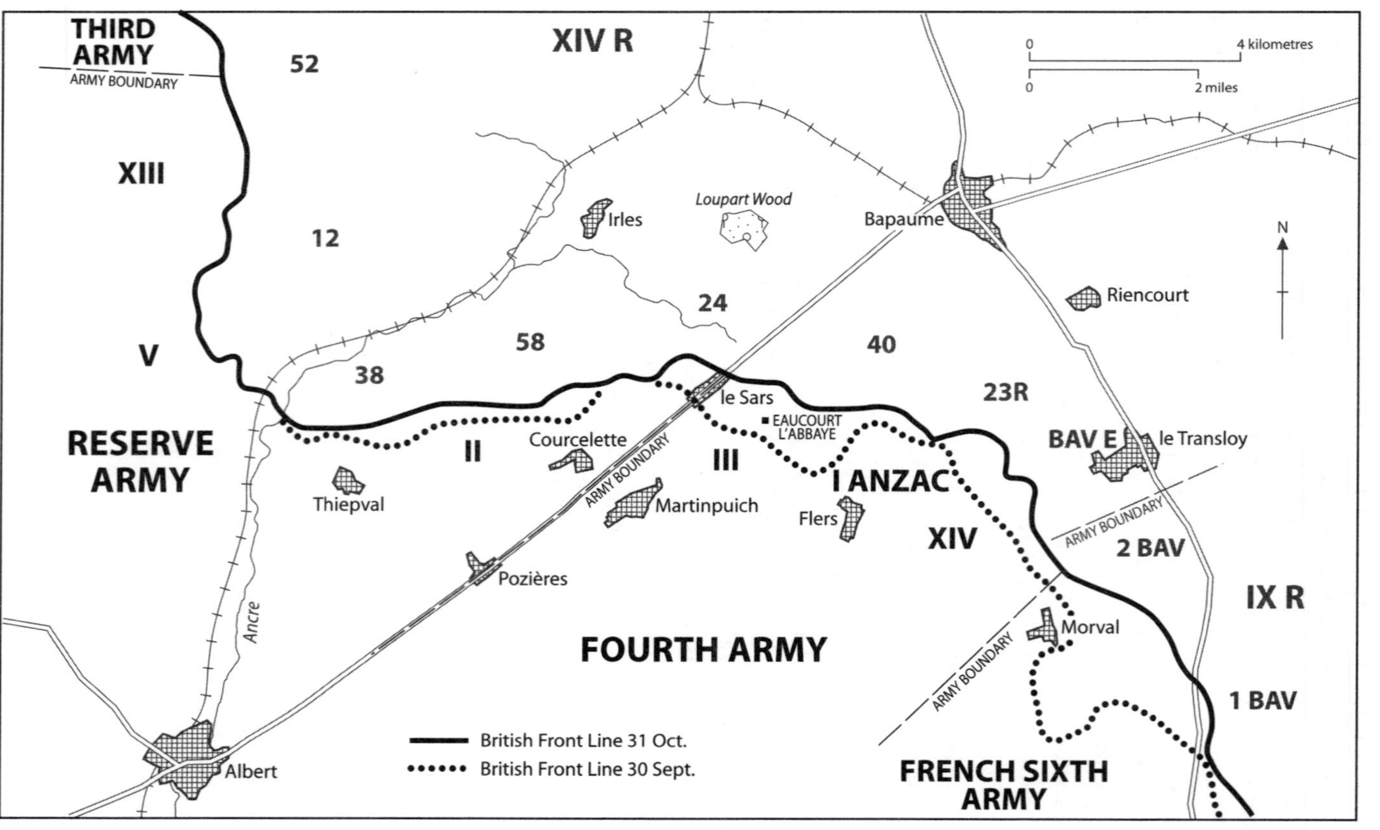


Gains Made, October

# 25 'We Must Keep Going!': The Politicians and the Somme Campaign, September–October

## I

As autumn set in and the Somme operations sustained mounting casualties for little progress, there seemed no gleam of promise for the Entente powers.

Since back in July it had become clear that the British offensive was not going to achieve a swift advance into German-held territory, and that the Germans were abandoning their campaign at Verdun. The proclaimed reason for maintaining the Somme offensive had therefore changed. For the British, success was simply defined as pinning the Germans to the west. So the Russians were enabled to continue their advance, and the Romanians were attracted into joining the fray.

In September and October, these justifications dramatically unravelled. Correspondingly, the validity of continuing the Somme operation came ever more steadily into question.

## II

Early in September, Asquith spent three days on the Somme, including a visit to Fricourt. Reporting to the War Committee on his return, he endeavoured to provide a hopeful picture.[1] Haig and Joffre, he reported, were 'on very good terms'. At Fricourt he had found the general, officers, and men 'all in the highest spirits'. The 7 Division, preparing to attack Ginchy, were 'full of confidence', and even though their assault did not prove 'entirely successful', an action two days later by the Irish had rendered it a 'successful operation'.

Yet the overall account presented by Asquith was largely negative. 'The advance,' he admitted, 'was a question of push, push, push and must necessarily be slow work.' While Robertson was assuring the War Committee that the

Germans, although fighting as well as ever up to a certain point, gave up more easily than formerly, Asquith provided no evidence that the enemy was approaching disintegration. He had, he said, seen a large number of German prisoners, 'and they were fine men and looked well fed'. He related that he had asked Allenby, former commander of the cavalry and now in charge of the Third Army, about the chances of employing Britain's sole weapon of exploitation. Allenby was not hopeful. He held that 'It was no use sending Cavalry through a small opening...it would be a great mistake to send Cavalry forward unless they can take a whole length of front.'

When Curzon asked of the Prime Minister whether it was expected to push through the enemy line by Christmas, Asquith 'did not think so'. This caused Grey, the Foreign Minister, to observe that 'the situation was not much affected [that is, improved] if the Germans were not pushed back'. Asquith countered with the familiar, but increasingly threadbare, claim 'that we kept the Germans occupied, that many were being killed, and there were numerous prisoners'.

Grey's response to this indicated the mounting uncertainty which the Somme campaign was generating: 'we must keep going, but he wanted to know what it leads to.' He went on to offer the speculation that 'surely the rest of the German line must be affected by this pushing back'. Robertson's response was less than reassuring:

> There was nothing else to be done.

Curzon, inquiring about the nation's ability to fill the gaps caused by the ongoing burden of casualties, received no greater comfort. Robertson told him that recruitment was the reverse of reassuring. The British army, he said, would by next March be short by 400,000 men, and he wanted to know how they were to be obtained. (His eyes, plainly, were directed towards the 2.5 million men employed in essential industries or otherwise exempted.) Robertson also made it clear that they could not look to the French to make up the deficiencies of manpower. He quoted Joffre as saying that the French army 'could not help feeling the strain of reduction', and might soon be asking the British to take over part of the French section of the Western Front.

As far as the Somme campaign was concerned, only one glimmer of hope presented itself at this 12 September meeting. The British were preparing to throw an entirely new weapon into the fray: what hitherto had been called 'the caterpillar machine-gun destroyer', but now was becoming known as 'the tank'. Yet on the eve of its first employment (on 15 September) the new weapon was as much a source of bewilderment as of hope. Asquith acknowledged that the tanks were only an experiment, and anticipated that they would prove decidedly vulnerable: 'They could be knocked out with ease by an artillery barrage.' There was also a problem with numbers. When, the previous December, Haig had taken over as British commander on the Western Front, he had – sight unseen – been highly enthusiastic about the new weapon, and had promptly ordered 1,000. But, according to Asquith, by the second week in September just 62 of these machines were available.

The view was general in the War Committee that the successful employment of tanks depended on surprise. This meant that they must make a great impact on first employment. A problem resulted. Should tanks be thrown into battle straight away, when only a few score were available, or should they be put on hold until the day – plainly well distant – when they could be employed in large numbers? The Prime Minister implied that this was still an open question, telling his colleagues that Haig had not yet decided how and when to use them. Given that Haig was going to launch them just three days later, this is hard to credit.

In the event the War Committee – despite its concern that the tank might cease to be of value once its existence had been exposed – dodged the issue. Grey held that the timing of their first use must be left to the man on the spot. Asquith judged that 'the question could be safely left to Sir Douglas Haig'. No one, apparently, dissented.

As it happened, only a small number of tanks were to hand when they made their début on 15 September. Robertson told the War Committee at its next meeting that 48 tanks had been deployed, of which 30 had got beyond the start line, 24 had done good work, and four had received direct hits. Their appearance, it was remarked, had attracted great attention in the press and among the public. Robertson, asked by Grey whether the tanks had achieved as much 'as the newspapers said', insisted that they had been 'a big success'.[2] The fact that they had been used only in small quantity, and were no longer a secret, passed without comment. But it is noteworthy how rarely, thereafter, the War Committee returned to the subject of the tank's part in the Somme battle. Indeed by the beginning of October the committee was wondering whether it was worthwhile to continue producing tanks, since the enemy had probably already devised means of dealing with them.

So, the tank's 'big success' on 15 September was plainly relative, and had not transformed the conflict on the Western Front. The great offensive must continue to be a matter of 'push, push, push'.

# III

Over the same meeting that pondered the situation on the Somme and worried over the possible uses of the tank, other matters cast their shadow. These lay far from the fields of France, but related to the Somme campaign by calling in question its much-touted justification: that, however meagre its accomplishments, it was serving a large purpose by robbing the German command of strategic initiative.

Robertson on 12 September referred to mounting evidence that, over time, the Germans had withdrawn 11 divisions from the Somme front, some of which had been traced to the east. This, he said, bore out the view that he had recently expressed, that Hindenburg's preference lay in actions on the Eastern rather than the Western Front. What he did not go on to remark, and what nobody chose to draw to his attention, was that this statement demolished his many assurances that, on account of the Somme, the Germans no longer possessed the capacity to act on their preferences.[3]

Robertson read from a recent memo of his, with which Joffre concurred, 'that the German High Command may be tempted to undertake offensive action against certain points on the Eastern Front'. The reaction of the British and French high commands was predictable. They proposed to thwart Hindenburg's plans 'by a continued offensive' in the west, with the French and British intensifying their effort while they retained the advantage of fine weather. (Robertson's next observation was to quote Joffre's earlier comment that the French army was a declining asset. So it was clear which of the Western Allies would have to do the intensifying.)

Britain's civilian leaders did not dissent from this judgement. The War committee resolved that it agreed 'with the Chief of the Imperial General Staff that the proper course to be followed in the present situation is to continue the offensive on the Western Front with all energy and with the full powers at the disposal of the French and ourselves'. In other words, where hitherto the rationale of the Somme offensive had been that it prevented the Germans from attacking on the Eastern Front, now it was justified because the Germans were about to do just that.

In another respect the overall situation, notwithstanding the unrelenting Allied offensive in the West, was changing. As noted previously, the early success of Russian forces against Austria-Hungary had at last persuaded Romania to come in on the side of the Entente powers. This event had brought enormous cheer to the Allies and dismay to the rulers of Germany. Both reactions, it rapidly became evident, were premature.

In no time at all, Romania's entry into the war began transforming itself into an Allied calamity. On 12 September Robertson spoke bluntly to the War Committee about the ineptitude of the Romanian command. It had spread its forces along the frontier in the worst possible way. 'The dispositions exhibited an extraordinary amateurishness.' At the same time, Robertson said, the Romanian government was proving resentful. Their Prime Minister was 'rather upset, and implied the Allies had not kept faith'. In Romania's view, the Allies had done nothing to aid them, and had allowed the Germans to transfer nine divisions from the Somme to the Balkans.

Robertson challenged these complaints. He asserted that the nine divisions had gone to the Russian front, not the Romanian. And he insisted that the French and British had made serious endeavours to activate their forces at Salonika, so tying the Bulgarians to their southern front and restricting their power to concentrate against Romania.

Yet it could not be concealed that neither the Anglo-French exertions on the Somme nor their activation of the Salonika front was proving of much help to the Romanians. Curzon referred to the numerical dominance of the Allies at Salonika and inquired whether more could not be done. Robertson had to explain that some elements in the Salonika forces were performing ill, and that Sarrail's leadership of the Allied campaign there, having for some time been under a cloud, was proving decidedly faulty. The most that Robertson could hope for from action in Salonika was that it might keep the Bulgarians in place. 'He had always said[,] and said again, that our troops could not get through.' For the Romanians, this was hardly enough.

## IV

The implicit, if hitherto rarely expressed, conflict within the British political command concerning the orientation of strategy, West or East, came to a head in early October. But it had been establishing itself for at least a month.

Up to the end of August, Robertson believed (as he assured Haig) that in matters of strategy the Somme operation retained general support in the War Committee. But on 7 September his tone changed as he discerned that elements in the committee were beginning to contemplate the diversion of military resources to another area. Robertson told Haig:

> I find Lloyd George has got the Servian fit again [i.e. was dismayed at the way Britain was failing to aid its allies in the Balkans, just as – in Lloyd George's view – Britain had done regarding Serbia in 1915] and maintains we have

> been wrong all along & the French have been right, as shown by Rumania's coming in. He thinks Hindenburg will now go for Rumania with <u>more</u> troops.[4]

For a few weeks more, the War Committee went along with Robertson's view that the best way to assist Romania was for Haig to hammer away on the Somme. But by early October, with the peril to Romania now acute (Robertson admitted to the War Committee that the enemy were within 80 miles of Bucharest), and with Haig's endeavours apparently having no effect on German activity in the Balkans, another view was making itself heard. Lloyd George's 'Servian fit' was taking hold.

The matter expressed itself at a War Committee meeting on 9 October. Robertson, in an attempt to head off dangerous tendencies, had elicited from Haig an astonishing statement (which enjoyed Robertson's 'entire agreement'):

> The C-in-C urged most strongly that he should be empowered to continue the offensive on the Western Front without intermission. Sir Douglas Haig had stated that he could not too strongly urge that the utmost efforts of the Empire be devoted to enabling him to continue the offensive. There were fair grounds for hope that very far-reaching success, affording full compensation for all that had been done to attain it, might be gained in the near future by a vigorous maintenance of our offensive in that theatre.[5]

Any relaxation of his army's efforts on the Somme would enable the enemy both to recover himself and to strengthen his defences, with the result that much of the great advantage already gained would be lost.

Robertson immediately turned the discussion in the direction of the Balkans and the imperilled state of Romania. But he did so only in the context of three premises. First, Romania had brought its problems upon itself by the ineptitude of its military command. Second, the only Allied power in a position to help Romania – and, if so inclined, well placed to help it – was Russia. Third, Britain must take no action in the Balkans (such as sending additional British divisions to Salonika) which would diminish the primacy, and the great promise, of the Somme campaign.[6]

This last point did not, as it had done hitherto, refer to the Somme's supposed capacity to take pressure off Romania – a proposition now beyond belief. It referred to the promised potential of the Somme campaign to accomplish, even now, great things in its own right. As Robertson proclaimed, he agreed with Haig that if they pursued vigorously the offensive on the Western Front, 'we might achieve something really substantial'. That is, as the Somme campaign ceased to have the potential to achieve anything at all of substance – or, at the very least, anything more of substance – its principal advocates' promises became ever more grandiose, and ever less credible.[7]

Lloyd George spoke next. He did not even comment on the supposed attractions offered by persistence on the Somme. Instead, he directed himself to the looming Allied disaster in the Balkans. Hindenburg, he argued, was rejecting the policy of seeking victory on the Western Front, where the Germans could well retreat some five to fifteen miles without relinquishing anything of importance. The German commander wanted a great victory in the Balkans. Britain in this struggle had never supported any of the small nations in Eastern Europe, and its prestige would disappear if Romania was wiped out. So: 'a Conference should be assembled at once' representing the general staffs of the French, Italian, and British armies, 'to go thoroughly into the Romanian situation and to devise some measures which would enable our honour to be saved.'[8]

The War Committee resolved to place on hold Lloyd George's proposed conference, but only while it secured from the British commander at Salonika the answer to three questions: would a vigorous advance from Salonika be of real aid to Romania; how soon could such an advance be accomplished; and – should the Western Allies send to Salonika an extra eight divisions – what would this achieve?

The clear divergence concerning the principal orientation of British strategy evident at this meeting generated – as Asquith related to Hankey in 'a full and most amusing account' – 'a frightful row between Ll. George and Robertson'. The 'row' took the form of an 'acrimonious correspondence'.[9]

Robertson set the ball rolling.[10] He was basing his protest on the fact that, when first appointed CIGS under Kitchener, the latter's reputation had been at a severe discount. So Robertson had been able to secure recognition as the War Committee's sole spokesman on military matters. When Kitchener was drowned and Lloyd George took his place, this arrangement (despite Lloyd George's unblemished reputation) had not officially been abrogated. This gave Robertson his opportunity.

On 11 October, in the letter opening the 'acrimonious correspondence', Robertson reminded Lloyd George that a month earlier, responding to the pending German assault on Romania, he had told the War Committee that 'our best assistance would be the prosecution of the offensive on the Western Front combined with vigorous action by the [existing] Salonika forces.' The War Committee had agreed. On 9 October he had repeated this advice, stressing that the dispatch of additional forces to Salonika 'would be unsound and probably useless'. But this time the matter had not gone well. The cause was Lloyd George:

> You felt it your duty to disagree with this advice and recommended certain action being taken by the Committee with the object of inducing France and Italy to combine with us in sending to Salonika a reinforcement of some 8 additional divisions.

Worse, the War Committee had directed Robertson to ask Joffre for his opinion 'on certain points regarding which I had already given my opinion'. That is (in Robertson's view):

> (a) A plan of campaign was contemplated entirely contrary to the conclusions of the War Committee a month ago.
> (b) My advice was set aside and the advice of a foreign general sought.

This 'want of confidence in my advice', Robertson protested, was causing him 'grave concern'. He expected, in his position as CIGS, to be 'able to count upon the support of the Secretary of State for War in regard to the military plans which he puts forward for the consideration of the War Committee'. If the War Committee decided to embark on a military operation which he had made it clear he considered unsound, then:

> I could not be responsible for conducting this very difficult war under these conditions.

This was a strong rebuke. But if Robertson thought that a powerful protest and implied threat of resignation would bring Lloyd George to heel, he was quickly disillusioned.

Lloyd George replied the same day. He noted that in conversations between them since the 9 October meeting, 'you made no protest against my taking a line of my own on Romania'. He went on:

> Tonight's letter would therefore have caused me some surprise had not a leading newspaper proprietor [obviously Northcliffe] given me the pith of its contents [some] hours before it was dispatched to me .... This great journalist even threatened publication unless I withdrew immediately from the position I had taken up.

With his tongue firmly in his cheek, Lloyd George added:

> Of course you could not have authorised such a breach of confidence & discipline. But unfortunately this kind of thing is of frequent occurrence in the service & must be stopped in the best interests of the Army .... this state of things is an outrage on all the best traditions of the service.

There were, Lloyd George went on, two points that must be settled immediately. 'One is the point of discipline I have raised. The present position is intolerable.' The other was the matter Robertson had raised. He did not doubt Robertson's 'supreme responsibility in all matters affecting strategy & the direction of military operations – subject of course to the War Council [i.e. War Committee]'. But he questioned whether this meant that, as War Secretary, he himself had only the right to 'choose between the position of a dummy or a pure advocate of all opinions expressed by my military advisers' – not the right to express an independent view on the war.

> I am perhaps overanxious that our prestige and honour should be saved in the East....I know what will be said here if after bringing Roumania to aid us we look on whilst she is being butchered before our eyes without taking the most serious risks to rescue her.

Lloyd George closed with the conventional expression of admiration for Robertson's 'great gifts' and of his desire to co-operate with him, but then produced the sting in the tail:

> You must not ask me to play the part of a mere dummy. I am not in the least suited for the part.

This sharp exchange would not greatly affect the course of events. As October proceeded, Lloyd George became ever more dismayed at the impending conquest of Romania: 'the biggest blow of the war' and an event which, by handing to Germany the Romanian harvest and oilfields, would 'probably prolong the war for another two years'. But he was aware that nothing could be done. By the time any reinforcements could get there, he conceded, the Romanians would already have made peace. Had extra British and French divisions been dispatched two months ago (i.e. at the time he had been seized by his 'Servian fit'), Lloyd George claimed on 24 October, they would have had a real influence, but not now.[11]

What makes these matters of note, especially in terms of outcome on the battlefield, was not the issue that generated so powerful a dispute. It was the issue which the War Committee – including Lloyd George – chose to disregard so that it could get on with agonising about the Balkans.

The 9 October meeting, it will be recalled, began with Robertson presenting, and supporting, a document by Haig pleading for the continuance of the campaign on the Somme. Haig was not, be it noted, commenting on possible action at Salonika (which, anyway, was strictly not his business). Nor was he discussing the relative merits of action on the Somme as against action in the Balkans. He was expounding the considerable (if notably unspecified) array of beneficial results which, even this late in the year, would spring from a continued British offensive in France: 'very far reaching success … in the near future' 'affording full compensation for all that had been done to attain it'.[12]

So improbable, it may be speculated, did the War Committee find these flights of fancy that it simply disregarded them. The conclusions recorded for its meeting of 9 October make interesting reading, but principally for what is not there. An extensive account is given of the decisions taken concerning the crisis in the Balkans. But regarding proposed events on the Western Front, all that is offered is evasion: namely a statement that Haig had sent a document urging the continuation of the Somme offensive 'without intermission'. This was in no sense a 'conclusion': merely a repetition of something already contained in the body of the minutes.

The silence of the War Committee on this matter amounted, however bizarrely, to large action on its part – much larger, in terms of consequences, than anything which resulted from the protracted wranglings about Salonika and Romania. The British military command, with winter fast approaching, and with no justification for its foreshadowed action apart from unargued forecasting of improbable achievements, was proposing to embark upon several further weeks of life-consuming endeavours on the Somme. It might be assumed that such operations could only proceed after the War Committee, with due consideration, accepted the promises and gave its authorisation. If it did not accept the promises, it would presumably withhold authorisation.

Nothing of the sort proved to be the case.

Haig made his bid for authorisation. The War Committee thought so little of his promises that it did not care even to discuss them. So no authorisation was given. Yet the operations went ahead anyway, and the War Committee made no objection. Clearly, this was what it had expected to happen. Long ago, when the sun was shining and hopes were high, it had endorsed the proposal to launch a great attack on the Somme. Now, with hopes vanished and the sun well and truly set, its endorsement remained and it chose not to comment.

This exercise in passing by on the other side could not fail to have consequences. The War Committee, by saying nothing in response to Haig's message, had done a momentous thing. It had opened the way to the dismal last weeks of the Somme campaign.

# 26 The Political Battle: Beaumont Hamel, 13–19 November

## I

When we last left the Reserve Army, Stuff and Schwaben Redoubts were still partially in German hands and a third attempt to capture Regina Trench by the Canadians had failed. While this was happening Haig and Gough had decided on a major operation north of the Ancre to capture Beaumont Hamel. In the meantime, however, to assist that operation by obtaining observation over the Ancre on the right of the attack, it was decided that II Corps should attack south of the river. The purpose was to seize the high ground, the path to which was blocked by the German hold on Schwaben, Stuff, and Regina.

Stuff Redoubt was easily captured. On 9 October a battalion from 25 Division following close behind a creeping barrage drove the Germans from its north face.[1] But in one aspect the result was disappointing. The redoubt gave no observation in the direction of Beaumont Hamel. To obtain that an area just to the north of the redoubt, known as the Mounds, would have to be captured.[2] Another operation was prepared.

The Schwaben Redoubt proved more formidable and the Reserve Army planning methods left much to be desired. At the same time that the attack on Stuff Redoubt was being mounted, the 39 Division attacked Schwaben. But it did so with just three companies, with no preliminary bombardment and at night so there was no creeping barrage. The results were predictable. The alert defenders cut down most of the companies in no man's land and the few who managed to penetrate the north face of the redoubt were soon driven out by counter-attack. The brigade commander was moved to point out the inadequacies of the plan – no bombardment of the redoubt in order to destroy the dug-outs, no creeping barrage, no weight in the attack.[3]

On this occasion his strictures received attention. On the 14th, after a two-day bombardment, three battalions of 118 Brigade attacked Schwaben behind a

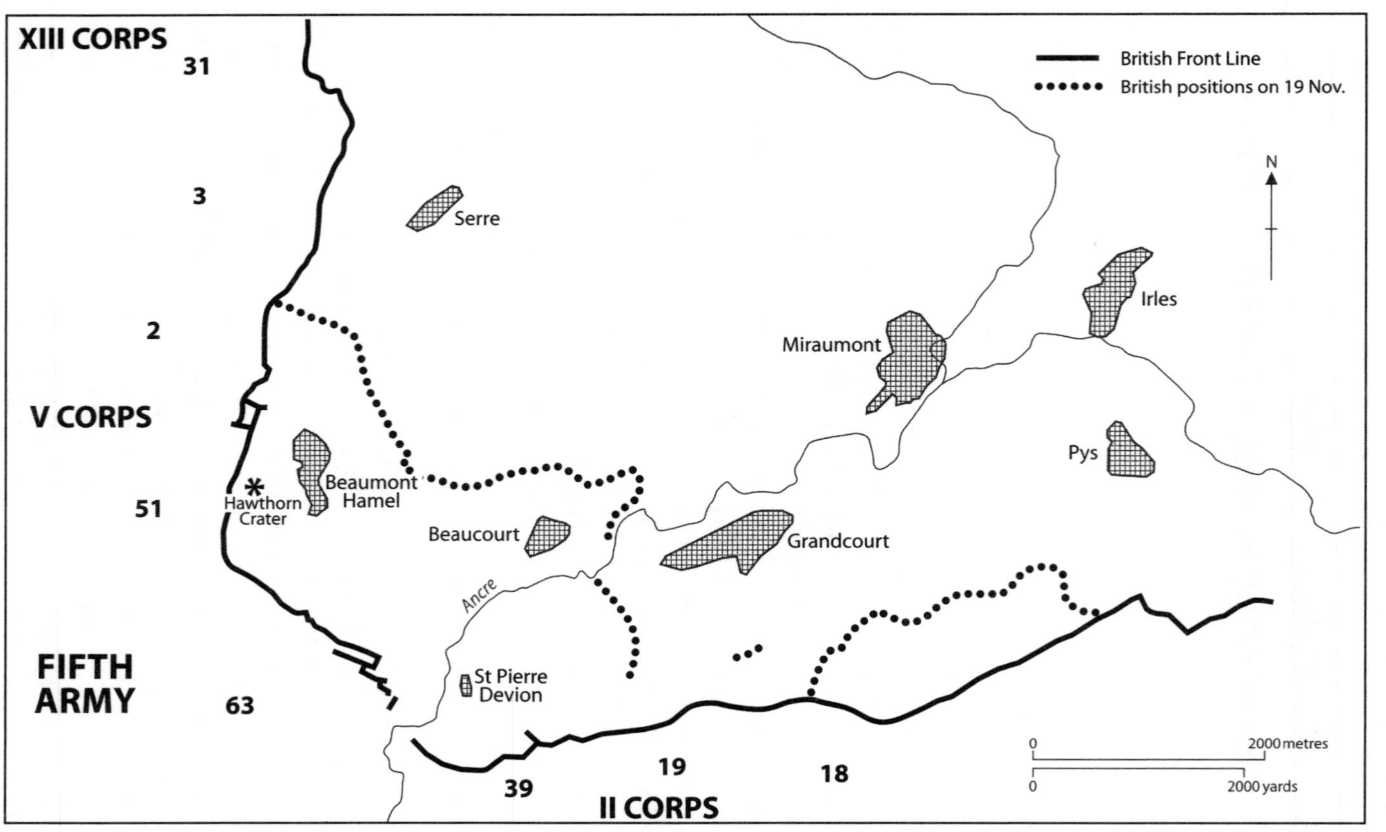


Beaumont Hamel, 13–19 November

creeping barrage. Even then the results hung in the balance. The wire had not been cut in all places, enemy shelling was heavy, and some troops lost direction.[4] However, along most of the front the troops stuck close to the creeping barrage and moved into the German line before the enemy had fully realised that an assault was imminent.[5] So at last the Schwaben Redoubt fell to the British. And while this was happening the 25 Division captured the Mounds.[6] Observation to the immediate right of the great attack had been secured.

Regina Trench remained. This obstacle, awkwardly sited on the reverse slope of the heights above the Ancre, had resisted almost constant attack since 26 September. In this operation too the Reserve Army planners had absorbed some valuable lessons. In particular there would be no narrow-front, small-scale attack. Regina Trench (and its extension to the west, Stuff Trench) would be assailed by four divisions (39, 25, 18, 4 Canadian). The attack went in at 12.06 a.m. At 12.35 a.m. it was over, all objectives having been captured. The 25 Division report admirably summarises the reasons for success along the entire front:

> (a) very careful previous preparation;
> (b) the fact that the battalions engaged were kept comparatively fresh in spite of bad weather and much work;
> (c) the excellent artillery preparation which had evidently demoralised the enemy greatly;
> (d) the complete surprise effected. In this connection...[it] completely covered the assembly of our troops;
> (e) the confidence with which our men advanced close up to the artillery barrage, and the excellence of the barrage;
> (f) the feeble German counter artillery work.[7]

So now, with the Ancre heights in his hands, Gough could finally contemplate the northern operation first suggested by Haig some two months before.

## II

It will be recalled that as a part of the great battle of 15 September, Haig intended the Reserve Army to sweep north to cover the inward flank of the Fourth Army as it advanced on Cambrai–Arras. Since then much had changed. The advance had not occurred and operations in October had become bogged down. Yet the idea of an advance by Gough's army had not been abandoned, merely scaled down.

The first of these less ambitious plans reached Gough on 29 September. The Reserve Army, in combination with the Fourth Army on its right, was to launch a two-pronged attack. From Thiepval it would advance northward to a line Loupart Wood–Irles–Miraumont. At the same time it would advance eastward, capture Beaumont Hamel and also advance on Miraumont, attempting to cut off the German forces retreating in front of the British forces advancing from Thiepval. Simultaneously, the Third Army would capture Gommecourt.

If this was less ambitious than Haig's plan before 15 September, it was still ambitious enough. It was proposing a five mile advance by the Reserve Army which if successful would capture in one operation more ground than it had accomplished in three months of campaigning. In the event, of course, this plan had to be abandoned because of the repeated failure of Gough's men to secure the desired start line of the Ancre heights.

The almost continual rainfall in the first two weeks of October soon forced a second reappraisal. Gough cancelled existing orders and limited his converging attack to the line Pys–Irles.[8] Optimistically, 45 tanks were assigned to the operation.[9]

But despite three more days of continuous rain and after watching the total failure of Rawlinson's effort on 18 October, Haig began to slip back into his old ways. 'Success,' he told Gough, 'will be exploited at once in an easterly and north-easterly direction, under the orders of G.O.C. Reserve Army to such extent as in his judgement the forces at his disposal renders possible.'[10]

Continuing bad weather and Gough's need to capture the Ancre Heights put the northern operation on hold. But then the relatively easy victory of 21 October quickly revived optimism at Reserve Army headquarters. Gough now announced that after he had captured the line Pys–Irles, he would push on to Miraumont and then unleash the cavalry to secure the high ground between Loupart Wood and Achiet-le-Petit. A follow-up formation of infantry would then secure the final objective some two miles to the north-east of this position.[11]

In the rainy days that followed, confidence among the command perversely increased. On the 24th Haig informed Gough that if there was an initial success he would place a second cavalry division at his disposal and a third if more successes followed that.[12]

All this was completely divorced from reality. Conditions at the front were so bad that even minor infantry operations were having to be cancelled because of the bog. The idea of three divisions of cavalry (about 18,000 horses) operating in such mud beggars imagination. Yet that is exactly what Haig and Gough were contemplating.

Nevertheless, the rain which had been continuous from 24 October to 3 November did impose some more cautious appraisals on the British command.[13] The Fifth Army (as the Reserve Army had become on 1 November) was now authorised to postpone any operation until the weather improved.[14] In any case the attack was now only to be 'limited', the final objectives being St-Pierre Divion, Beaucourt, and Serre.[15]

There the matter rested until 8 November.

Then Gough received a surprise visit from Kiggell, Haig's Chief of Staff. So startling was the information conveyed to the Fifth Army Commander, and so potentially dangerous to his command were its consequences, that Gough took the precaution of having a full record of this and subsequent visits made for his protection. In part Kiggell said the following:

> He explained that there was to be a conference of the Allied Commanders on the 15th, and that the British position would be somewhat strengthened if it should be possible for the Fifth Army to win some success before that date. There was no desire to pressure Gough into an action where the prospect of success was not sufficiently good to justify the risk, but on the other hand a tactical success would very probably have far reaching results.[16]

This was placing Gough in an uncomfortable situation. If an operation would strengthen Haig's position at an inter-Allied conference, and even a tactical success would have 'far-reaching' results, the claim that the command did not wish to pressure Gough into action was spurious. He had received an offer that no army commander could refuse.

Gough clearly understood that unless the weather was atrocious he would have to attack. So he called a conference of his three corps commanders to discuss possibilities. A strong wave of realism swept over this meeting. It was decided that the maximum that should be attempted was the capture of the first objective of the scaled-down operation, entailing an advance of just 1,000 yards. Fanshawe and Congreve, who would be making the northern attack, opined that if this was captured, then the next objectives – Serre and Beaucourt – could also be taken. Jacob, commanding the southern advance, and presented with a final objective of only 1,000 yards, promised to conform to either option.[17]

During the next two days opinion at Fifth Army headquarters fluctuated. Although only a small amount of rain fell the weather remained overcast and misty. Nevertheless, the ground was drying fast. Gough therefore decided to attack on the 13th.

Messages emanating from GHQ were decidedly mixed. On the morning of the 12th Kiggell assured Gough that the last thing Haig would need was a battle 'in unfavourable tactical conditions'.[18] Then the Commander-in-Chief himself arrived. Haig reiterated the difficulties of ground and weather and unhelpfully added that 'nothing was so costly as a failure'.[19]

But at the same time he told Gough that 'a success at this time was much wanted'. This was for three reasons – to give heart to the hard-pressed Romanians, to convince Russia that its allies were active, and

> lastly, on the account of the Chantilly Conference which meets on Wednesday. The British position will doubtless be much stronger (as resources are short) if I could appear there on top of the capture of Beaumont Hamel, for instance, and 3000 German prisoners.[20]

There was much sophistry in all this. It is difficult to imagine that the fall of Beaumont Hamel would energise the Romanians or prove to the Russians that Haig had the Germans by the throat. His third reason was more to the point. But even this requires comment. 'The British position' at an inter-Allied conference would hardly be much strengthened by the capture of the heap of rubble that was Beaumont Hamel. Nor was Haig's position likely to be much improved by the capture of a village 116 days after it had been scheduled to fall.

Yet Haig was desperate for anything he could describe as a success. He knew that the atrocious weather was placing out of court his aspirations to go on attacking all through the winter. Consequently Gough's November operation constituted his last throw. Had Gough not even told him that if the operation did not go ahead there would be nothing for it but to shut down the battle? So anything that could be described as a success, even if it was an advance of just 1,000 or 2,000 yards, would serve as a positive end to the campaign. No one was going to remind Haig that Beaumont Hamel had been an objective for the first day. Members of the War Committee attending Chantilly were bound to have collective amnesia on this point – after all, they had presided over the 116 days of the battle. And success was important to Haig – the Battle of the Somme must be seen as having some sort of triumphant conclusion.

So the question hanging over this last phase of the campaign was: could even the capture of Beaumont Hamel be accomplished in such unfavourable conditions?

## III

The preliminary bombardment began on the early morning of 6 November. Most of the guns were concentrated on the area which had given so much trouble on

1 July – that around Beaumont Hamel and St-Pierre Divion. High-explosive shells deluged both localities. In addition, steps were taken to subdue the machine-gunners on the crest behind Beaumont Hamel who had taken such a toll on the first day. As the enemy machine-gunners were not in concrete emplacements but concealed in shell holes and other natural features, it was decided in this operation to blanket the whole ridge with machine-gun fire. No fewer than 40 guns were used for this work and as a result not one enemy machine-gun on this ridge came into action during the entire attack.[21]

It also appears that the Fifth Army had realised the crucial nature of the creeping barrage. A typical operation order for the battle stated:

> THE ESSENTIAL PRINCIPLE is that the leading infantry should follow so closely on the heels of the barrage that the enemy has no time to recover or man his machine guns before they are on him.
>
> In all the most successful attacks of recent months the assaulting infantry had crept TO WITHIN 50 YARDS of their own barrage, ready to rush in the moment it lifts off the objective.
>
> This principle will be assiduously impressed on all ranks both by lectures and in practice attacks, so that every man thoroughly understands that his safety lies in getting close up to the barrage and that he must wait for no orders to advance the moment the barrage lifts.[22]

The attack commenced at 5.45 a.m. – that is, in the dark. Even after the sun rose, visibility did not substantially improve for some time because of the thick fog.

On the extreme left of the attack it was soon discovered that not even the most accurate creeping barrage could protect the infantry if conditions were such that they could not follow it. On the very flank of the attack the same division (31), but certainly not the same men, advanced against the same objective (Serre) as on 1 July. The results were also pretty much the same. The ground was so bad that the 'men sank up to their waists' in mud and so lost the protection of the barrage. One unit declared the ground 'impassable to Infantry with their war equipment' and said that 'it would have been difficult for a man in running costume, under peace conditions' to traverse it. They were met by heavy machine-gun fire and although some penetrated as far as the third German line they were soon isolated and driven back by counter-attack.[23]

The next division on the left fared no better. At the end of the day they had gained precisely no ground at a cost of over 1,000 casualties. One of the battalions involved listed the reasons for failure, which may serve as a useful summary for the failure of them all:

1. loss of direction in the dark and fog
2. loss of most officers in the early phase of the attack because of unsubdued machine-guns
3. the broken and muddy ground
4. uncut wire
5. the invisibility of the barrage in the mist
6. the strength of the German Second line which had been missed by the barrage
7. Rifles becoming clogged and therefore useless because of the mud.[24]

The left of the next division (2) also failed for much the same reasons: uncut wire, boggy ground, and loss of the barrage, all of which meant that Gough's great blow had entirely failed on the northern third of its front.[25]

Fortunately for the British, the southern two-thirds of the attack fared somewhat better. The right of 2 Division found the going firmer and the mist lighter. So they could see the barrage and follow close behind it. As a result they were able to jump the German dug-out dwellers as they emerged, and capture the German line. Follow-up battalions pressing close behind them passed through and on to the German third line, which by 6.15 a.m. was in British hands.[26]

The key to the battle, however, lay to the south, where Beaumont Hamel and St-Pierre Divion were to be attacked. The first of these objectives lay in the area of 51 Division, which was to assault Beaumont Hamel and advance to the strong German trench beyond. In this sector a mine was blown near the same area as that of the Hawthorn Redoubt on 1 July and for the same purpose – to prevent German machine-gunners in the salient formed by the redoubt from enfilading troops advancing to its right and left. On this occasion the expedient was successful. The 30,000 pounds of ammonal was blown at zero and the troops (who had moved into no man's land beforehand) occupied the mine crater.[27]

Beaumont Hamel still proved difficult. Even though the machine-gunners on the ridge behind it had been killed or neutralised and 'there was scarcely a square yard in the village which was not torn up by shellfire, the deep dugouts ... escaped'.[28] Machine-gunners emerging from these dug-outs stopped the attack on the western outskirts of the village. On this occasion, however, because of the success of the mine explosion to the north, reinforcements could be sent to take the defenders of the village in flank. By 10.45 a.m. Beaumont Hamel, which had defied Haig's armies since July, had fallen.[29]

That was in fact the sum total of 51 Division's success on that day. An attempt was made around noon to advance on the second objective – the trench due east of the village. It failed. By this time the protection of the creeping barrage had been lost. And there were just too few troops remaining to constitute a weighty and coherent attack. The capture of Beaumont Hamel had exacted a fearful toll on the assault battalions. The Seaforth Highlanders had suffered over 50 per cent casualties, the Argyll and Sutherland Highlanders 40 per cent, and many others were of the same order.[30] Corps headquarters wisely cancelled the projected follow-up, calculating that with their main objective captured further advances could await the new day.[31]

While 51 Division was capturing Beaumont Hamel, the 63 Division to its south was making the largest gains of the day. This division had bizarre origins. It commenced life as the Royal Naval Division, when in 1914 the navy discovered that it had men surplus to requirements for its ships. These were then supplemented by some army units to bring the division up to strength. It saw service in such Churchillian adventures as the Antwerp expedition of 1914 and Gallipoli in 1915. In 1916 it was transferred to France and renamed the 63 Division, though it retained its naval connection by having battalions named after admirals, such as Hood, Drake, and Anson.[32] This was its first battle on the Western Front.

Essentially the 63 succeeded in its initial advance for the same reasons as the 51. The fog aided surprise and blinded the enemy artillery. The wire was well cut and the creeping barrage carried the troops to the outskirts of the German third line. One detachment, under the leadership of Lt.-Col. Freyburg, even pushed on to the outskirts of Beaucourt. Then German resistance stiffened. The artillery had missed sections of the third line and the defences of Beaucourt were still intact. After several hastily arranged and botched attempts at further advances, the corps ordered a halt until the 14th.[33]

South of the Ancre only the 39 Division was to make a substantial advance. Here the main obstacle was St-Pierre Divion with its 'highly developed system of dug-outs and tunnels'.[34] Owing to some excellent artillery arrangements that assigned a 4.5-inch howitzer to every known dug-out and tunnel entrance, the village was captured. The German garrison fled but ran straight into the path of the other assault battalions. The result was that for once the number of prisoners taken (1,380) exceeded the casualties (587).[35]

On the 14th, with Haig on his way to the Chantilly conference, operations to press on and capture the original objectives were undertaken by all divisions. All failed. The artillery were now uncertain as to the exact location of the forward troops, units were disorganised, and attacks could not be coordinated. No ground was gained.[36]

Nevertheless, despite these barren results, Gough issued orders that operations were to continue on the 15th. But Haig was now at Chantilly, where a vigorous debate was proceeding about whether more troops should be sent to

Salonika. (The Russians, Romanians, and Serbs were in favour, the British and French military were against, their governments sat on the fence.) That night Haig dined with Asquith who he reported, was 'very pleased with our successes'.[37] After this meeting, Haig sent Gough, with whom he was in touch by courier, the following order:

> [you] are not to undertake any attack on a large scale until after the return of the Commander-in-Chief.[38]

Clearly the battle had served Haig's purpose and he was worried that Gough might jeopardise his position by launching further attacks about which Mr Asquith might not be so pleased.

But Gough was not giving up easily. He sent another message to Haig on the evening of the 16th saying that both corps commanders thought 'the proposed operation had very good prospects of success'.[39] By this time the conference was over. Its main decisions had proved very satisfactory to Haig. The Allies had decided that the Western theatre was decisive, that the British and French would 'press' the enemy through the winter as far as climatic conditions permitted, and that they would resume the offensive in the New Year.[40]

Haig now felt less constrained. He gave Gough approval for strictly limited operations 'if the weather remained satisfactory'.[41] In the event it did, at least to the extent that no further rain fell. On the 18th operations resumed. On the left the newly introduced 32 and 37 Divisions gained some ground to the south of Serre and Freyburg's force captured Beaucourt.[42] To the south of the Ancre the 19, 18, and 4 Canadian Division also made some rather inconsequential gains.[43] But the cost of these efforts was exceedingly high. The 32 and 37 Divisions suffered about 5,000 casualties between them, the divisions of II Corps around the same.[44]

The bitterness caused by the conditions under which these attacks were made reverberated for years. In 1936 an officer who took part in the II Corps attack wrote to the Official Historian:

> This was the only occasion in which I saw men dead from exhaustion from their efforts to get out of the mud. At Passchendaele I saw men mud bound but they could be dragged out, but at the Ancre at this time, we were pitchforked into the quagmire in the dark and there was no possibility of a man helping the one next to him ....It was the very worst instance I came across of what appeared to be a cruel useless sacrifice of life and the climatic conditions alone made it clear ... to the very stupidest brain that no success could possibly result. [45]

The loss of 10,000 men for no important gain had a sobering effect on Haig. At Chantilly, he had agreed to resume the offensive on the Somme in the following year. And he was already in receipt of a letter from Rawlinson warning him that unless operations halted there might be insufficient men to conduct operations of any magnitude in the spring.[46] The commander-in-chief therefore finally decided to wind down the battle. This did not mean that all activity on the Somme ceased. As the Australians, who had just entered the front line in the Fourth Army sector, were to discover, trench raids and minor operations of a more or less purposeless nature would continue all winter. But as for major attacks, this was the end. To all intents and purposes, the Battle of the Somme concluded on 18 November.

The operations around Beaumont Hamel in November 1916 reveal a number of interesting facets about the high command and the nature of the battle. First, they demonstrated that if the end result was important enough – in this case Haig's standing with the government and the Allies – objectives could be limited to the practicable, and the wherewithal in terms of artillery support could be found to ensure a high chance of success. Haig was quite capable of turning his attention to a limited 'bite and hold' operation if the circumstances required it. Second, it revealed just how many resources were required, especially in adverse weather, to make any kind of advance on the Somme. As much ammunition was expended in this attack as had been on the much longer front on 1 July. Yet for all the success proclaimed for the Beaumont Hamel operation, the results were in fact very meagre. The maximum advance was just over 2,000 yards and the amount of territory gained inconsiderable. And for this effort, no fewer than 11 divisions had been used, at a cost to V Corps of around 15,000 men and to II Corps of at least half that number. In other words over 22,000 men, or the infantry of two divisions, had been consumed for no great purpose.

Furthermore, the battle showed that if Haig was so minded he could follow its progress in close detail and call it off immediately the advances were not deemed commensurate with the cost. This may be contrasted with his behaviour during August. Then, after being slow to appreciate that the battle was drifting, he seemed incapable of or unwilling to impose his will upon it. This effectively disposes of the notion that, during the Somme campaign, Haig acted as he did (or failed to act) because events had gone beyond his control.

# 27 Reflections on the British at the Somme

## I

In the long history of the British army, the Battle of the Somme was its bloodiest encounter. Between 1 July and mid-November 1916, 432,000 of its soldiers became casualties, or about 3,600 for every day of battle. Set out in a table of the divisions which fought at the Somme the casualty list is in some ways more sobering even than these stark totals reveal.

| *Division* | *Casualties* | *Division* | *Casualties* |
|---|---|---|---|
| 30 | 17 374 | 14 | 7 643 |
| 18 | 13 323 | 55 | 7 624 |
| 21 | 13 044 | 47 | 7 560 |
| 5 | 12 667 | 4 Aust. | 7 248 |
| 17 | 12 613 | 39 | 7 215 |
| 56 | 12 333 | Guards | 7 204 |
| 34 | 12 036 | 6 | 6 966 |
| 25 | 11 239 | 2 Can. | 6 876 |
| 12 | 11 089 | 20 | 6 854 |
| 33 | 10 787 | 1 Can. | 6 555 |
| 9 | 10 538 | 23 | 6 282 |
| 4 | 10 496 | 51 | 6 202 |
| 1 | 10 451 | 24 | 6 119 |
| 3 | 10 377 | 48 | 6 115 |
| 7 | 10 237 | 41 | 5 928 |
| 19 | 9 830 | 31 | 5 902 |
| NZ | 9 408 | 36 | 5 482 |
| 8 | 8 969 | 32 | 5 272 |
| 11 | 8 954 | 15 | 4 877 |
| 49 | 8 461 | 35 | 4 663 |
| 2 Aust. | 8 113 | 16 | 4 330 |
| 50 | 7 902 | 4 Can. | 4 311 |

| | | | |
|---|---|---|---|
| 1 Aust. | 7 883 | 63 | 4 075 |
| 2 | 7 856 | 38 | 3 876 |
| 29 | 7 703 | 46 | 2648 |
| 1 Can. | 7 469 | 37 | 2 000 |

In addition the cavalry suffered 71 casualties.

It is worth repeating that the nominal infantry strength of a division at the Somme was about 12,000 men but that the average strength was closer to 10,000. What the table reveals then is that 15 divisions of the 52 engaged in the battle lost their entire infantry strength or in some cases more. In addition the table reveals that the average casualty bill for a division was 8,500 or between 70 and 85 per cent of the divisional infantry strength.

Of the 432,000 casualties probably 150,000 died and another 100,000 were too seriously wounded to serve again as infantry (or in most cases in any other capacity). That is, the Somme destroyed for ever the fighting capability of 250,000 men, or the infantry strength of 25 divisions. One out of every two British soldiers who fought on the Somme never fought again.

What of the German casualties? There is no need to enter into the controversies surrounding the German casualty figures as discussed in the British Official History. M. J. Williams and others have effectively demolished the arguments put forward by Edmonds in his desperate attempt to establish some equivalence between the British and the German figures. The most thorough analysis of the German figures for the Somme campaign appears in Winston Churchill's *The World Crisis*. Churchill developed an early interest in this matter probably as a result of the War Committee's cursory rejection of his memorandum on the subject in August 1916. His figures for German casualties were supplied to him by the Reichsarchiv in Germany in the 1920s and there is no reason to doubt their accuracy. For the period July to October 1916 he states that approximately 200,000 casualties were inflicted on the Germans by the British at the Somme.[1] To this figure should be added those German casualties suffered during the preliminary bombardment and those suffered in November. Neither figure is known with any accuracy but another source gives the total German casualty figures for the battle for June to December as 237,000 and this figure is not at all at odds with Churchill's total for the shorter period.[2] Deducting a figure of some 7,000 for the rather sporadic fighting in December would give a total of 230,000 suffered by the Germans against the British.

This is a truly startling figure, compared with the 432,000 British. What it reveals is that every casualty inflicted on the Germans by the British cost them almost two casualties of their own. If these statistics are taken as a measure there is no doubt which side emerged as the winner. Haig was wearing out his own armies at a much higher rate than he was wearing down his opponents'.

Given that it was the British who mounted all the major attacks at the Somme, the disparity in casualties is not perhaps surprising. But since it was the British who had superiority in the air and in artillery, the most lethal weapon on the Western Front, perhaps it is.

Air superiority conferred significant advantages. Aircraft could be left largely unmolested to direct artillery fire and to take photographs of German defensive positions. However, at the Somme these advantages were negated by a number of factors. The first and most serious was the weather. There was so much cloud and rain even at the height of summer in July and August that for many days, as noted by General Horne, aircraft could not be deployed. In addition, artillery accuracy had not reached such a high state of development at the Somme that aerial observation could always be used to good effect. Adjustment to the range of a gun was a slow matter which substantially reduced the number of shells that could be fired during a day. And the interpretation of aerial photographs had not reached in 1916 the level of precision obtained later in the war. Overall then, aerial superiority was not the asset it would become in 1918.

What of artillery superiority? Haig's gunners fired around 19 million shells at the Germans between the opening of the preliminary bombardment and the end of the battle. This amounted to deluging the enemy with just less than 150,000 shells each day. We have no way of knowing what the Germans fired in retaliation, but the repeated statements made about the constancy and ferocity of British shelling which appear in their regimental accounts leave no doubt that it was less than they were receiving.

Several factors lessened the effect of this artillery predominance. The first was that because the British were always on the attack their gunners were required to eliminate small or distant targets – trench lines, machine-gun posts, batteries – that were difficult to hit. On the defensive, the enemy had the relatively simpler task of firing their shells into the general area where the British were forming up or moving into no man's land. In these circumstances a lesser number of shells fired by the defenders might find more targets than a greater number fired by the attackers.

Then there was the fact that the British were continually fighting themselves into positions where the Germans could take maximum toll with their lesser resources. The northern flank on 1 July, the right angle around Delville Wood in July and August, and the Pozières–Mouquet Farm salient in the same period are three of the more extreme examples where the British exposed their troops to intense enemy artillery retaliation.

Added to this was the policy of small, narrow-front attacks which enabled the Germans to concentrate what guns they had against the relatively small number of British troops which might be advancing on any given occasion. Given all these factors and the primitive state of artillery accuracy, the British cast away much of the advantage artillery superiority might have given them.

## II

What can be said about the performance of the British army? Let us start our investigation by considering the infantry.

Overall, the soldiers of Haig's armies have not emerged well from accounts of the battle. The troops, especially of the New Armies, have been categorised as green, under-trained, and lacking in initiative. This view appears to have three distinct origins. The first is the British command (especially Haig, Rawlinson, and Gough) who often commented on the poor material with which they had to work. The second is the conventional view of the first day of battle when it is said that the troops could carry out no more complicated manoeuvres than advancing shoulder to shoulder at a slow walk. The third origin consists of the various German accounts which categorise the Somme as a *Materialschlacht*, a battle of resources in which the more lavishly munitioned but poorly trained British soldiers pushed back a more skilful enemy.

All these criticisms can be largely discounted. The comments of Haig and his army commanders were usually self-serving, a mere cover for inadequate planning or for the impossible objectives set for the infantry. As for the image of the unthinking Tommy, plodding to his doom on 1 July, we have demonstrated that it is entirely fallacious. The battalion commanders certainly thought the troops under their command capable of quite sophisticated manoeuvres and planned accordingly. These plans came to naught not because of any inadequacy of the men but because of the inadequacy of the fire support given them and without which they were in no position to practise their skills. The German criticisms are curious and revealing. The post-war writers of these accounts failed to grasp that the consequence of the failure of the Schlieffen Plan meant that the war was bound to develop into a battle of resources. That they still thought otherwise in the 1920s and 1930s – that inferiority in resources could be compensated by skilled infantry – was to play its role in the road to war in 1939.

In fact, the British infantry when they were adequately supported by firepower – the factor that was the determinant of victory on the Western Front – could perform as well as their enemy. This is demonstrated by the actions of

XIII Corps on 1 July, by the Fourth Army in the opening stages of the 14 July operation, by the successful attack on 25 September, and by the fighting around the redoubts by the Reserve Army in September and October. Whatever failings the Somme demonstrated in the British army, it is hard to argue that the performance of the combat infantry was one of them.

What of the intermediate levels of command? In most cases we know very little about the brigadiers and divisional generals on the British side. Higginson of 53 Brigade stands out as a commander who would never hesitate to point out the impossible nature of what his men were often asked to do and the inadequate planning which usually accompanied such orders. Maxse is the best known of the divisional commanders and some of his operations (1 July in the south, the capture of Thiepval in September) bear the hallmarks of well-thought-out affairs. Yet when his division was thrown into the chaotic situation around Delville Wood in mid-July it could perform no better than any other division. A similar point could be made about Tudor (9 Division), who developed some innovatory fire support tactics which aided the advance of his division on 14 July, but who found himself powerless in the shambles that resulted. Similarly Walker (1 Australian Division) who led his men with skill in the capture of Pozières laboured without success against the disastrous Mouquet Farm operations which were subsequently forced on him.

The point to be made about all of these examples is that it was often not the quality of the brigade or divisional command that led to success but the position in which their troops were placed by decisions made elsewhere. Thus if fire support was adequate a well-trained division could exercise its skill and capture its objectives. If such support was absent a Maxse, Tudor, or Walker could make no difference whatever.

The corps commanders could have slightly more influence on a battle. This could be in a negative sense, as with Pulteney in his unimaginative plan for III Corps before 1 July or in his insistence that tanks could traverse High Wood on 15 September. Similarly, Hunter-Weston had a malign effect on VIII Corps in his artillery arrangements on 1 July and in his insistence on detonating the Hawthorn mine 10 minutes before zero hour. Horne is more of an enigma. He was not without insight, as his remarks in his letters to his wife reveal. However, he rarely seemed able to translate these insights into action. Moreover at times his obtuseness could be breathtaking – as in September when he revealed that he could not understand the purpose of a creeping barrage. Of the others, Congreve did well when the artillery provided him with the preconditions for success but floundered when it did not. Cavan was the only corps commander to resist (momentarily) a futile attack ordered from above, but under pressure he soon capitulated. In the end no corps commander was blessed with enough insight or courage to place those insights before the higher command and hence to influence decisively the course of the battle.

Of the army commanders, Gough need not detain us. His grasp of the tactical situation facing his army seemed always limited, his dithering over the best way to capture Thiepval was disastrous for his troops and his 'victory' at Beaumont Hamel much overrated. His performance at the Somme should have seen him sink into a well-deserved obscurity. Perversely, in 1917, the opposite was to happen.

Rawlinson is a more complicated figure. In 1915 he was one of the originators of the 'bite and hold' concept of battle and on several occasions at the Somme he tried to revert to this style of warfare. His original plans for 1 July and 15 September were certainly more realistic than those he was required by Haig to implement. But when challenged by the Commander-in-Chief, his grip on the concept seemed so uncertain, or his obedience to authority so ingrained, that he soon found himself attempting to carry out the more grandiose plans foisted on him by GHQ. Whatever the reason, it was Haig's conceptions which were implemented, usually with disastrous results. Certainly Rawlinson seems to have lacked fixity of purpose. Having declared one course of action sensible (well-thought-out, large-scale attacks) he often proceeded in a quite different course (hastily prepared, small-scale operations) to the great detriment of his army. The troops surely deserved better than this from one in such high authority.

What of Haig? Any analysis of the military aspects of the Somme campaign has to conclude with an assessment of his performance. It was Haig who set the parameters for battle before 1 July and on any subsequent occasion when a major attack was in the offing. It was Haig who decided on what resources would be directed towards a particular operation, what objectives would be set and whether an attack would continue or be closed down.

At his own estimation he achieved three great things at the Battle of the Somme. He relieved the pressure on the French at Verdun and thus saved their army to fight another day. He pinned the German army to the Western Front, thus relieving pressure on the Russians. And he commenced a well-thought-out process whereby the German army was to be worn out in 'one continuous battle' over the next two years.

None of these claims stands up to close scrutiny. The Somme was planned by Haig without any relation to Verdun. His first plan for the battle indeed had as an integral component assisting the French armies to his immediate south by attacking down the Thiepval Ridge towards them; but this had nothing to do with Verdun. Moreover, when the French contribution to the Somme diminished as a result of Verdun, Haig reoriented his plan so that his armies would advance north-east (away from the French) and win the campaign on their own account. The Somme eventually directed German attention away from Verdun, but that was never Haig's intention.

As for pinning the Germans to the Western Front, this was simply not true. Fifteen German divisions left for the east during the course of the battle and this number proved quite capable of overrunning Romania when that country rashly entered the war on the Allied side.

The 'one continuous battle' argument is the merest sophistry. The Somme was never fought by Haig as the first step of a wearing-out campaign. On 1 July, 14 July, 15 September, and in early October he developed plans that were meant to win the campaign (if not the war) at a single stroke. Not until the very end of the battle was any mention made of the necessity for a campaign in 1917, let alone 1918. As we will see, it was the decisive battle, not attrition, that lay at the heart of Haig's conception of war.

On routine matters of command he performed badly. He proved incapable of co-ordinating the actions of his two armies, which as a consequence hardly ever carried out a joint attack. Nor in other ways did Haig seek to impose his authority on the battlefield. In the shambles into which the campaign sank in the latter half of July and August Haig only belatedly sought to intervene and then failed to follow through to ensure that his instructions were being obeyed by his lower-order commanders. The battle thus drifted along, seemingly out of control of anyone on the British side.

On the more important matters of the higher tactical and strategic conduct of the battle his performance was, except in one respect, even worse.

In the matter of modern technology Haig was not the troglodyte of legend. He adopted weapons such as heavy artillery, the tank, and aircraft. However, he was unable to use these modern weapons to develop an appropriate strategy. He persisted in relying not on his more modern weaponry but on the cavalry. Throughout the campaign he regarded the cavalry as a battle-winning or even war-winning weapon of exploitation. This was to have particularly disastrous consequences for the first day of the Somme. To clear the field for a cavalry sweep Haig spread his already inadequate artillery fire across the entire German defensive system. As a result, most enemy machine-guns and batteries survived to wreak havoc on the British attack.

On many subsequent occasions (14 July, 15 September, early October) the cavalry were massed and distant objectives, ranging from 50 to 100 miles, were set. Each of these strokes was designed to be a campaign or war-winning affair. The fact that 18 months of warfare had demonstrated that cavalry could not live on a modern battlefield was stubbornly resisted by Haig. His problem seems to have been that without a weapon of exploitation his whole conception of warfare, which was rooted somewhere in the nineteenthth century, would lie in ruins. In this he was the very opposite of an attritional general. He considered that wars were won by decisive battles and that battles could only be decisive if large amounts of ground were gained and that this could only be accomplished by the cavalry. None of his major battles was planned with attrition in mind. Indeed, only at one point in the campaign (early August) does he admit that he is in a 'wearing-out' phase, but says that it is just a temporary condition until he can mass his forces for another decisive effort. In acting thus, Haig was in denial about the reality of warfare on the Western Front. No conceivable method of fighting in that maze of trench defences, barbed wire, and massed artillery and machine-guns could have been cheap. As the French General Mangin said, 'whatever you do, you lose a lot of men'. But by 1916, as every battle in 1915 had demonstrated, the only sure way of proceeding was to accumulate such weaponry and shells as could blast the enemy from one defensive line to another, along the way ensuring that the casualties of the attacking side were minimised and those on the defending side maximised. The aim of an 'attritional' general was not therefore to gain ground but to kill the enemy in such numbers that his powers of resistance would be gradually worn down. Haig did not have the deadliness, the fixity of purpose, or the type of mind that could make such precise calculations of the munitions and guns required to achieve such results. He was in fact, and contrary to legend, much more of a romantic than was required on the Western Front. So far from having too little imagination, he had too much. He could envisage cavalry sweeps and decisive battles more in keeping with Napoleonic conceptions than with industrial war.

## III

The final arbiter of the British fortunes at the Somme was the civilian War Committee. It is melancholy to report that this group of generally intelligent men carried out their tasks with no more understanding of the imperatives which faced them than did Haig.

They started well enough. Their constitutional authority to determine British strategy was asserted at an early stage in the discussions about the nature of the 1916 campaign. If a group of civilians insisted that in the last analysis it would be they who decided the relatively trivial matter of how many horses the British army would have on the Western Front, what else might they not determine?

As a group, the War Committee also insisted that any new offensive in the west in 1916 should not be launched prematurely, that it should be adequately munitioned and sensibly conducted. Indeed, they insisted on canvassing all other options to the Western Front before they agreed to an offensive in that area at all. Thus Balfour wanted the Eastern theatre to be thoroughly examined for possible offensive action, while others suggested Turkey, Russia, Romania, and Italy. In the end the impracticalities of major operations in all these theatres and the awkward fact that the greater part of the German army lay in France and Belgium led them to sanction an offensive in the west.

Nevertheless, having agreed to the operation, the War Committee sought assurances from Kitchener and Lloyd George that the battle would be fought with due regard for manpower resources and would not be fought until a superiority of guns and munitions could be guaranteed. These assurances were duly given.

But the assurances of Kitchener and Lloyd George were meaningless. Kitchener did not seek out details from Haig as to how he intended to conduct the battle – this despite the fact that Rawlinson had warned the War Minister in March that Haig might attempt a foolhardy operation designed to break the German line at a blow. Nor was Lloyd George aware of how Haig intended to use the munitions and guns supplied him or whether they would be sufficient for the front and depth of defences to be assailed. In short, having sanctioned the operation, the War Committee was never certain about the nature and purpose of what they had sanctioned.

When battle was joined, the committee's performance rapidly deteriorated. It was clear from discussions held with Hankey as early as 3 July that its members were uneasy about the high casualties and the lack of progress on the Somme. Yet in committee these same members always accepted without question the casualty figures supplied to them by Robertson. The figures on the German side were often inconsistent and sometimes downright unbelievable. Into this latter category fell the figures given by Robertson to refute the Churchill memorandum of early August. Here was a chance for the War Committee to assert its authority and question whether 1,250,000 Germans could have been laid low on the Somme when only 160,000 British had become casualties. The committee not only ducked this question, they formally sent their congratulations to Haig on the development of the battle.

Why was the civilian leadership of Britain acting in this extraordinary way? They almost certainly failed to voice their concerns because of the lack of a clear alternative. Closing down the operation on the Somme was hardly an option, with the French still hard-pressed. Moreover, the Russians seemed to require a continuance of the British offensive if their successes against the Austro-Hungarians were to continue.

In the months that followed, the War Committee, despite mounting concern, did nothing. In this period the definition of what the Somme was meant to achieve kept being altered. By early September the pretence that significant amounts of ground were being gained had ceased to be credible. With the crushing of Romania at the end of the period it could hardly be said that German troops were being kept away from the Eastern Front. From then on, the only justification for the continuance of the battle became the killing of enemy troops. And this at a time when it was only too obvious that the chief military adviser to the committee was supplying it with sets of enemy casualty figures that were becoming less and less believable.

Then in early October Haig (of all people) supplied the committee with an excuse to close the battle down. In a memorandum he asked for permission to continue the offensive. Most members of the committee were by this time thoroughly alarmed by the drain on British manpower and its likely effect on the ability of the country to continue the war. Yet they not only passed up the opportunity Haig had given them, they failed even to discuss his request. This was the moment when the civilian leadership indicated in the most dramatic way that it had lost the nerve to assert its authority over Haig and Robertson. A threat to resign on the part of the CIGS over renewed civilian interest in Salonika resulted in much huffing and puffing, but no action The battle ran its muddy, bloody, and inconclusive course. The civilian leadership therefore failed the men for whom they claimed to be trustees. The soldiers who became casualties in their hundreds of thousands fought well in a good cause. But they deserved a plan and competent leadership as well as a cause.

# Epilogue: The End of It All, November 1916

## I

On 3 November 1916, the War Committee of the British cabinet held an unscheduled and unusual meeting. No agenda paper was issued. And a major section of the conclusions was handwritten, not (as was customary) typed. These sections carried the directive 'Not to be printed or circulated'.[1]

The initiator of this gathering was Lloyd George, with Hankey proposing to him that it should consist only of cabinet ministers unaccompanied by advisers. ('This had been my suggestion to Lloyd George,' Hankey confided to his diary, 'so that he might air his views freely unhampered by the presence of that old dragon Robertson.') Lloyd George's action reflected his dismay at the way in which the war was proceeding. And it gave expression to his determination that matters must be conducted by different methods to different ends. With the benefit of hindsight, this meeting may be seen as the opening episode of a process by which, within a month, Asquith would be forced out of office and Lloyd George would become Prime Minister.

## II

Lloyd George began the gathering by reading a telegram which he had received from a leading Romanian statesman, M. Take-Jonescu. It took the form of an appeal directly to Lloyd George.

Romania, the writer stated, had been at war for two months, and had suffered heavy casualties. The cause of Romania's difficulties, 'which every day become more forcible', was 'lack of heavy artillery'. 'Our front is enormous; we cannot indefinitely replace heavy guns by infantry attacks.' Only one country could make good Romania's lack of artillery, given that Russia had insufficient for its own needs. 'We have asked help of England; they do not give it us.'

Lloyd George had drafted a reply, which was approved by the War Committee. It recognised the 'serious need' for the Allies to give every support to the 'gallant Roumanian Army in their terrible struggle for the defence of their country'. The Western Allies had recently sent 90,000 additional troops, with appropriate weaponry, to Salonika, raising the force there to 450,000. It had also sent to Romania 400 machine-guns. But it was difficult to send more heavy guns, 'owing to [the] urgent necessity for keeping up heavy pressure on Germans on the Western Front in order to prevent their detaching fresh divisions from the West to join the forces attacking Roumania'. But they were sending several batteries to Russia to use on the Romanian front, and with French aid would send as many further guns 'as restricted transport facilities will allow'. Thereby the condition of Allied forces on the Eastern Front, as concerned heavy guns and ammunition, 'must continue [*sic*] steadily to improve from now onward'.

This set of communications was intended by Lloyd George to introduce a wide-ranging survey of the 'General Military Policy of the Allies'. Again, Lloyd George produced a document addressed to him. Its author was the Chief of the Imperial General Staff. Lloyd George had asked Robertson, for the benefit of the War Committee, to provide his judgement on 'the probable duration of the war'.

Robertson found this request 'very difficult'. The duration of any war, he suggested, was hard to estimate. And this conflict, with its wide-ranging objectives and its vast involvement of non-military matters (such as 'large questions of international finance and commerce'), was particularly difficult.

Further, many matters were not subject to accurate estimation. The Allies might have greater manpower than their adversaries. But what did this signify when Germany had the advantages of interior position and could totally dominate the actions of the Central Powers, whereas its opponents were alarmingly diverse?

> Russia is corrupt, badly armed and administered, and will not improve her communications; Italy refuses to move men from her own country; Rumania runs away.

As far as the Western Front was concerned, 'we and the French have been steadily gaining a moral[e] and material ascendancy over the enemy'. And as far as Britain was concerned, 'it is still within our power to put more men and more guns into the field'. With these, and as long as Britain did not 'fritter away our efforts in non-vital theatres' and Russia could be supplied with heavy artillery, it was possible to hope that 'the pressure upon the enemy on both fronts will not be less severe' than heretofore. But

> we cannot hope for a conclusion in our favour unless and until we make full and appropriate use of all our resources. We have not yet taken the steps to this and we ought to take them at once.

## III

Lloyd George characterised this missive as 'one of the most serious documents on the war that he had read'.

He proceeded to put his own gloss on it. He stated bluntly that Britain was not getting on with the war. The enemy had recovered the initiative, was in occupation of expanding territory, and had four million men in reserve. 'At no point had the Allies achieved a definite, clear success.' The Somme campaign had possessed three objectives: to relieve Verdun; to break the German line or capture some strategic objective; to pin German troops to the Western Front and so enable the Russians both to succeed themselves and to safeguard Romania. Only in the first respect had it fulfilled its purpose. On the second and third, it had clearly failed.

So how was the war to be brought to an end? What was the plan? As concerned the policy of attrition, 'the losses of the Allies were greater than those of the enemy'. Germany was more careful of its men and was prepared to abandon territory. The Allies, fighting for their own land, could not do this.

Lloyd George then referred to a variety of difficulties facing the Allies. There was the current shipping problem and the 'growing danger from submarines'. There was the food situation and the financial situation. There were threats to the solidarity of the Entente. And there were problems on the home front: the public expected victories, and would experience severe disappointment when it realised that no victory was likely to result from the Somme battle.

Lloyd George insisted that, as far as the public was concerned, responsibility for the conduct of the war rested with the politicians, and above all with the War Committee. He proposed therefore that a meeting should be called between the responsible political leaders of Britain, France, and Italy 'to take stock of the situation'. It would then confer with its Eastern ally to settle strategic differences between them (for example there was the view of General Alexieff that 'only a victory over [the] Germans in the Balkans can have a decisive influence in the war'). Lloyd George proposed a small conference of ministers from Britain, France, and Italy, followed by a military conference in Russia.

These remarks opened the way to a discussion of considerable note. Above all, the War Committee expressed 'general agreement' with the 'general tenor' of Lloyd George's remarks, although some members considered them 'unduly pessimistic'. In particular:

> It was generally agreed that the offensive on the Somme, if continued next year, was not likely to lead to decisive results, and that the losses might make too heavy a drain on our resources having regard to the results to be anticipated.

In a powerful comment on the disappointing outcome of the long and bloody endeavour on the Somme battlefield, the War Committee agreed 'that we should examine whether a decision might not be reached in another theatre'. And the projected conference of representatives from Britain, France, and Italy was to consist just of political leaders, without military representatives.

## IV

Lloyd George, as Hankey noted in his diary, was delighted with the outcome of the meeting, and not least with its judgement upon the Somme campaign. His response is noteworthy, particularly as the verdict here passed on the Somme campaign by the political masters who had authorised and watched over it was devastating.

In the opinion of the Secretary of State for War, 'We were not getting on with the war', 'the enemy had recovered the initiative', 'at no point had the Allies achieved a definite, clear success', and the 'policy of attrition' had inflicted greater losses on the Allies than on their enemies.

It may be deemed a grimly realistic assessment. In all probability, it was the crucial factor (admittedly in company with many other alarming events) that had reduced the Asquith government to such ill-repute that a change of regime was imminent. It appeared to lead irresistibly to the conclusion that the massive Western Front offensive of 1916 would also be the last. For it seemed irresistibly to follow that the War Minister – shortly to become Prime Minister – would not, after casting so negative a judgement on the Somme endeavour, authorise another such undertaking.

Lloyd George had been coming steadily to this conclusion. Back in September, while visiting the Western Front, he had made dismissive remarks concerning Haig's conduct of the battle. And one month after taking over the Prime Ministership, he would tell his private secretary:

> Haig does not care how many men he loses. He just squanders the lives of these boys. I mean to save some of them in the future....I am their trustee.[2]

That meant, apparently, that there would not be another Battle of the Somme.

But it is necessary to notice a countervailing matter. We have observed that, in August, the back-bencher Winston Churchill had led the way in producing statements convincingly condemnatory of the Somme strategy. The marked deficiency of Churchill's paper had lain in its failure to suggest any alternative, and preferable, way of proceeding. The same was glaringly the case with Lloyd George's strictures in November. After all, there was no reason to believe that his proposed assemblage of political leaders from Britain, France, and Italy would come up with a radically different way of conducting the war. The Balkans had provided no consolation in 1916. The Italians had needed rescue from many misfortunes. The Russians were a spent force. And Romania was an already-past calamity. So where, if not on the Western Front, would the British launch an attack?

Yet there was no question that Lloyd George, in supreme command, might place Britain on the defensive and allow its allies to bear unaided the burden of undertaking offensive operations. Back in June, Lloyd George had been driven to advocate an attack on the Somme by the near-collapse of France, Britain's only dependable ally. If France was to be kept fighting, Britain must remain a conspicuous participant in an offensive strategy somewhere.

Further, the huge groundswell of opinion in Britain favourable to Lloyd George's assuming leadership in the war had not been generated by a desire to run down Britain's involvement in the fighting. It sprang from the conviction that he alone could end 'wait and see' and devise the combative means to carry the war to victory. That is, he was expected to engage in a yet more ruthless mobilisation and employment of Britain's resources. This expectation appeared soundly based. As he had made clear in mid-1916, when President Wilson had appeared ready to propose a negotiated peace, Lloyd George would have no truck with half-measures or limited commitments. This, he insisted, would be 'a fight to a finish, to a knock out'. The war under his direction would result in triumph, but apparently without the loss of British lives entailed in the methods of Sir Douglas Haig.

This failure to propose any concrete alternative to the Somme strategy would in the following year produce grim consequences. In 1917, Britain (along with France) would – notwithstanding the accession of a British Prime Minister opposed both to a Western Front strategy and to the military commander who conducted it – prosecute yet further large and unproductive offensives on the Western Front. So despite the negative judgement on Britain's 1916 strategy delivered, on Lloyd George's incentive, by the War Committee during the last days of the Somme campaign, that tragic endeavour would not prove the nadir of British strategy in the First World War.

# Notes

## 1 The Context

1. David Lloyd George, *War Memoirs VI* (London, Ivor Nicholson & Watson, 1933), p. 373.

## 2 'Absolutely Astonishing'

1. In June 1915 the War Council had become the Dardanelles Committee. In December of that year it became the War Committee.
2. All quotations in this chapter are taken from the minutes of the War Committee of the British cabinet for 18 May 1916. They are to be found in the series CAB 42 in the Public Record Office.

## 3 Decision-making, January–February

1. War Committee Minutes 28/12/15, CAB 42/6/14, Microfilm copy in the Australian Defence Force Academy Library.
2. War Committee Minutes 23/11/15, CAB 42/5/20.
3. Dardanelles Committee Minutes 30/10/15, CAB 42/4/20 and War Committee Minutes 15/11/15, CAB 42/5/12.
4. See the minutes and conclusions in CAB 42/6/14.
5. See 'Note By Mr Balfour on the Minutes of the War Committee, December 28, 1915', dated 29/12/15 in CAB 42/7/5 and another memorandum by Balfour dated 27/12/15 also in CAB 42/7/5.
6. Ibid.
7. See 'Note by the Secretary of State for War' 8/1/16 in CAB 42/7/5.
8. For the comments by Asquith, Austen Chamberlain, McKenna, and Lloyd George detailed below see War Committee Minutes 13/1/16, CAB 42/7/5.
9. For the discussion that follows see the War Committee Minutes for 22/2/16 in CAB 42/9/3.

## 4 Decision-making, March–June

1. War Committee Minutes 10/3/16, CAB 42/10/9.
2. War Committee Minutes 21/3/16, CAB 42/11/6.
3. Ibid.
4. Ibid.
5. Ibid.
6. War Committee Minutes 23/3/16, CAB 42/11/9.
7. Ibid.
8. Ibid.
9. Ibid.
10. Ibid.
11. See Chapter 5.
12. War Committee Minutes 7/4/16, CAB 42/12/5.
13. Ibid.
14. Ibid.
15. Ibid.
16. See the discussion of this matter in the War Committee Minutes 28/4/16, CAB 42/12/12.

17. War Committee Minutes 10/5/16, CAB 42/13/6.
18. War Committee Minutes 17/5/16, CAB 42/14/1.
19. War Committee Minutes 18/5/16, CAB 42/14/2.
20. Ibid.
21. War Committee Minutes 26/5/16,CAB 42/14/11.
22. Ibid.
23. Ibid.
24. War Committee Minutes 6/6/16, CAB 42/15/4.
25. Ibid.
26. Ibid.
27. Ibid.
28. Ibid.
29. War Committee Minutes 7/6/16, CAB 42/15/6.
30. War Committee Minutes 21/6/16, CAB 42/15/10.
31. Ibid.
32. Ibid.
33. Ibid.
34. War Committee Minutes 22/6/16, CAB 42/15/11.
35. War Committee Minutes 30/6/16 CAB 42/15/15.
36. Ibid.
37. War Committee Minutes 22/6/16 CAB 42/15/11.
38. Ibid.

## 5 'Grasping at the Shadow'

1. Haig to Joffre 1/2/16, WO 158/14.
2. See Rawlinson's Diary for 12 and 21 February 1916, Rawlinson Papers, Churchill College, Cambridge.
3. Ibid., 21/6/16.
4. Ibid., 25/2/16.
5. Fourth Army Intelligence report 17/1/16, Montgomery-Massingberd Papers, Liddell Hart Centre, King's College, London.
6. The detail of the German defensive system is drawn from G. C. Wynne, *If Germany Attacks: The Battle in Depth in the West* (London, Faber and Faber, 1940), pp. 100–1.
7. W. S. Churchill, *The World Crisis 1916–1918, Part 1* (London, Thornton Butterworth, 1927), p. 172.
8. Rawlinson to Kitchener 9/3/16, Rawlinson Letters, National Army Museum, London, 5201/33/18 [hereafter NAM].
9. Rawlinson Diary 2/3/16.
10. Rawlinson Short Note Diary 17/3/16, NAM. Rawlinson wrote two diaries. The more extensive one with long daily entries is in Churchill College, Cambridge. The diary in the National Army Museum consists mainly of short notes about meetings attended, people met, etc.
11. George Cassar, *Kitchener: Architect of Victory* (London: Kimber, 1977), pp. 466–7.
12. Rawlinson Diary 30/3/16.
13. Ibid.
14. Fourth Army Conference 30/3/16, Fourth Army Papers V1, Imperial War Museum [hereafter IWM].
15. Rawlinson Diary 31/3/16.
16. 'Plan for Offensive by Fourth Army 3/4/16', in IV Army Summary of Operations, WO 158/233.
17. Ibid. All further references to the 3 April plan come from this document.
18. Haig to Rawlinson 13/4/16 (OAD 710/1) in 'Battle of the Somme: Preparations by the Fourth Army', Fourth Army Papers V1, IWM [hereafter, Fourth Army Somme Preparations].
19. Haig Diary 5/4/16, Haig Papers, National Library of Scotland. See this entry for his detailed comments on the plan and the entry of 8/4/16 for his talk with Rawlinson. Haig's marginalia on Rawlinson's plan can be found in the copy in the Public Record Office, WO 158/233. All other mentions of the plan are taken from the copy in the IWM.
20. This and subsequent quotations from Haig to Rawlinson are taken from 13/4/16 in Fourth Army Somme Preparations.
21. Haig to Joffre 10/4/16, ibid.

22. Ibid.
23. Haig's marginalia on Rawlinson's plan of 3/4/16 in WO 158/233.
24. Haig to Rawlinson 13/4/16.
25. Ibid.
26. Haig's marginalia on Rawlinson's plan of 3/4/16.
27. Rawlinson to GHQ 19/4/16, WO 158/233.
28. Ibid.
29. Ibid.
30. Ibid.
31. Haig's marginalia on Rawlinson's memorandum of 19/4/16.
32. Rawlinson to GHQ 19/4/16.
33. Haig's marginalia on the above document.
34. Haig to Rawlinson 16/5/16 in Sir James Edmonds, *Military Operations: France and Belgium, 1916, Appendix Volume 1* (London, Macmillan, 1932) Appendix 11, p. 33 [hereafter *Somme Appendix V1*].
35. Sir James Edmonds, *Military Operations: France and Belgium 1916 V1* (London, Macmillan, 1932), p. 257 [hereafter Edmonds, *1916 V1*].
36. Rawlinson to Haig 10/5/16 in Fourth Army Papers V5, IWM and GHQ to Rawlinson 17/5/16, ibid.
37. See Table 3.1 in Elizabeth Greenhalgh, 'A Study in Alliance Warfare: The Battle of the Somme, 1916' (MA thesis, University of New South Wales, 1996).
38. Edmonds, *1916 V1*, p. 47.
39. Ibid., p. 193.
40. Gough to Kiggell 1/5/16, WO 158/245.
41. Haig's marginalia on this document.
42. Ibid.
43. Fourth Army Operation Order 5/6/16, Fourth Army Papers V7, IWM.
44. Fourth Army Operation Order No. 2 14/6/16, ibid.
45. Ibid.
46. Fourth Army to Second Indian Cavalry Division 14/6/16, ibid.
47. Haig to Rawlinson 16/6/16 (OAD 12) in *Somme Appendix V1*, Appendix 13, pp. 86–7.
48. Haig to Rawlinson and Gough 21/6/16, WO 158/245.
49. Haig to Robertson 1/6/16, WO 158/21. The authors are grateful to Elizabeth Greenhalgh for drawing this letter to their attention and to Gunther Rothenburg for explaining to them the dynamics of Jena.
50. 'Report of the Army Commanders' Remarks at the Conference held at Fourth Army Headquarters, 22nd June 1916', in Fourth Army Papers, V6, IWM.
51. 'Remarks Based on Recent IV Corps Artillery Operations With An Appendix & Estimate of Ammunition Required', 6/10/15, Rawlinson Papers, 5201/33/67, NAM.
52. Conference at Army HQ 17/5/16, Fourth Army Somme Preparations.
53. Ibid.
54. Rawlinson to GHQ 10/5/16. Fourth Army Papers V5, IWM.
55. Plan for Offensive by Fourth Army 3/4/16.
56. Kiggell to Rawlinson 20/6/16 (OAD 15), Fourth Army Papers V5.
57. Ibid.
58. Rawlinson to GHQ 21/6/16, ibid.
59. Ibid.
60. Ibid.
61. Plan for Offensive by Fourth Army 3/4/16.
62. *Der Weltkrieg V10* [the German official history] (Berlin, Mittler, 1936), p.345.
63. VIII Corps Heavy Artillery Programme, in 29 Division War Diary June 1916, WO 95/2230.
64. Rawlinson to GHQ 10/5/16.
65. Brigadier E. C. Anstey, 'The History of the Royal Artillery 1914–1918' (unpublished draft history), in the Royal Artillery Institution Library, Woolwich, pp. 117–18.
66. X Corps, undated, untitled document in X Corps Heavy Artillery War Diary June 1916, WO 95/863.

## 6 'Favourable Results Are Not Anticipated'

1. This point and much else in this section relies on the excellent account of training the New Armies by Peter Simkins, *Kitchener's Army: The Raising of the New Armies, 1914–16* (Manchester: Manchester University Press, 1988), Chapter 12.
2. Ibid., p. 297.
3. Reginald Cockburn (KRRC) quoted ibid., p. 303.
4. Simkins, *Kitchener's Army*, p. 293
5. It is reproduced in full in *Somme Appendix V1*, Appendix 17, pp. 125–30.
6. Ibid., p. 128.
7. See 'Fourth Army Tactical Notes', *Somme Appendix V1*, Appendix 18 and especially pp. 141–4.
8. Rawlinson, Address to Commanding Officers, n.d., Rawlinson Papers 1/6, Churchill College, Cambridge.
9. See the valuable discussion of information dissemination and training in Paddy Griffith, *Battle Tactics on the Western Front: The British Army's Art of Attack 1916–18* (New Haven/London, Yale University Press, 1994), Chapter 10.
10. Edmonds, *1916 V1*, p. 272.
11. 32 Division: 'Report on Operations 21st June to 4th July, and from 8th to 15th July', 32 Division War Diary July 1916, WO 95/2368.
12. Maxse to Montgomery 31/7/16, Maxse Papers 69/53/8, IWM.
13. XIII Corps: 'Narrative of Events: Operations of the XIII Corps during the period 1st July to 15 August, 1916', XIII Corps War Diary July 1916, WO 95/895.
14. General Maxse, 'The Battle of the Somme', Maxse Papers, 69/56/6.
15. Ibid.
16. 'Notes of a Conference held at Army Headquarters on the 16 April 1916', Fourth Army Papers V1, IWM.
17. 'Fourth Army Tactical Notes', p. 144.
18. Ibid., p. 134.
19. Ibid., pp.134–6.
20. Rawlinson Diary 24–26 June, in Rawlinson Papers, Churchill College, Cambridge.
21. Ibid., 27/6/16.
22. Ibid., 28/6/16.
23. X Corps Heavy Artillery Progress Report 25th–26th June, X Corps Heavy Artillery War Diary June 1916, WO 95/866.
24. Ibid., 26–27 June.
25. See reports ibid. for 27–28, 28–29, 29–30 June.
26. 32 Division: 'Report on Preparations and Action of 32nd Divisional Artillery during Operations of July 1916', 32 Division War Diary June 1916, WO 95/2368.
27. See for example Lt-Col. E. Thesiger (XV Corps) to Edmonds 3/5/30 and Major-Gen T. A. Tancred (VIII Corps) to Edmonds 28/10/29 complaining about these matters, in Somme Correspondence CAB 45/191.
28. Thesiger to Edmonds 3/5/30.
29. See Edmonds, *1916 V1*, pp. 122–3. Also Anstey, 'History of the Royal Artillery', p. 112.
30. Note by Brigadier-General Whitfield in his unclassified papers in the IWM.
31. Cassel Papers, unclassified, IWM.
32. See X Corps Heavy Artillery Progress Reports for the period of the preliminary bombardment in X Corps Heavy Artillery War Diary June 1916, WO 95/866.
33. Ibid. See also 21 Division, Daily Summary of Information for the period of the preliminary bombardment in 21 Division War Diary June 1916, WO 95/2130.
34. 21 Division Daily Summary of Information 24–30 June in 21 Division War Diary June 1916, WO 95/2130.
35. Report on a visit to III Corps by Brigadier-General R. P. Benson, Commanding Heavy Artillery V Corps, AWM 26/6/45/2.

36. Ibid.
37. These reports come from a wide variety of sources. The Fourth Army noted the effect of wire-cutting in its Daily Summary of Operations, Fourth Army Papers, V1, IWM. For VIII Corps see 'Special Wire-Cutting Reports' in VIII Corps War Diary June 1916, WO 95/820; 'Extracts from War Diary 1st Heavy Artillery Group VIII Corps', AWM 26/6/49/52; 29 Division, 'Reports on Raids', 29 Division War Diary June 1916, WO 95/2280; 29 Division 'Daily Summary' 24–30 June ibid.; 4 Division Raid Reports in 4 Division War Diary June 1916, WO 95/1444. For X Corps see X Corps Artillery Progress Reports 23–30 June, X Corps Heavy Artillery War Diary June 1916, WO 95/866; 32 Division 'Report on Operations 21st June to 4th July and from 8th to 15th July' in 32 Division War Diary July 1916, WO 95/2368; 32 Division Daily Intelligence Summaries 24–30 June 1916, in 32 Division War Diary June 1916, WO 95/2367. For III Corps see 'III Corps Weekly Reports on Operations', III Corps War Diary June 1916, WO 95/672; 34 Division 'Summary of Information 24–30 June', 34 Division War Diary June 1916, WO 95/2432; 34 Division Report on Raids ibid.; 34 Division 'Special Wire Reports', ibid.; 34 Division Patrol Reports, ibid. For XV Corps see 21 Division 'Daily Summary of Information 23–29 June', 21 Division War Diary June 1916, WO 95/2130. For XIII Corps see 30 Division 'Weekly Intelligence Summaries', 30 Division War Diary June 1916, WO 95/2310; 30 Division Patrol Reports 26–30 June, ibid.; 30 Division War Diary 24–30 June, ibid.; 18 Division War Diary 24–30 June, WO 95/2015.
38. Haig Diary 28/6/16, National Library of Scotland.
39. Rawlinson Diary 30/6/16.
40. The weight and number of shells used in the preliminary bombardment can be calculated from a document, 'Artillery Shells fired on 1 July 1916', Rawlinson Papers 1/6.
41. For patrol reports in general see the sources quoted in note 37.
42. 'Report by O C 1st Royal Dublin Fusiliers 29/6/16', 29 Division War Diary June 1916, WO 95/2280.
43. 'Report by O C 1st Essex 29/6/16', ibid.
44. For XV and XIII Corps reports see the sources quoted for these corps in note 37.
45. For the interrogation reports see the Fourth Army Intelligence Reports 24–30 June 1916 in WO 157/171 and also the Fourth Army War Diary for the same date in Fourth Army Papers V1.
46. 'Notes from Examination of Prisoners of 111 Infantry Regiment' in Fourth Army Daily Intelligence Reports, WO 157/171.
47. Ibid.
48. Interrogation of a prisoner who surrendered to XV Corps 29/6/16, ibid.
49. Interrogation of prisoners captured north of Thiepval 26-27/6/16, ibid.
50. Interrogation of Prisoner Hornung 27/6/16, ibid.
51. Fourth Army Daily Intelligence Summary 30/7/16, ibid.
52. For a discussion of factors affecting artillery accuracy see Robin Prior and Trevor Wilson, *Command on the Western Front: The Military career of Sir Henry Rawlinson 1914–1918* (Oxford/Cambridge, Mass.: Blackwell, 1992), Chapter 4.
53. Anstey, 'History of the Royal Artillery', p. 118.
54. Ibid.
55. H. A. Jones, *The War in the Air*, vol. 2 (Oxford: Clarendon Press, 1969) pp. 175–6; Peter Mead, *The Eye in the Air: History of Air Observation and Reconnaissance for the Army 1785–1945* (London, HMSO, 1983) p. 78.

56. See Rawlinson's Diary 24–30 June 1916.
57. For these reports see note 37.
58. Ibid.

## 7 'A Short Life'

1. Edmonds, *1916 V1*, p. 460.
2. Ibid., p. 474.
3. Captain Wilfrid Miles, *Military Operations: France and Belgium 1916 V2* (London: Macmillan, 1938), p. 425 [hereafter, Miles, *1916 V2*].
4. Jack Horsfall and Nigel Cave, *Serre* (London: Leo Cooper, 1996) pp. 39–40.
5. Miles, *1916 V2*, p. 425.
6. Ibid., p. 429.
7. Major-General R. N. Harvey [Inspector of Mines GHQ] to Edmonds 28/10/29, CAB 45/189.
8. Ibid.
9. Ibid.
10. Major-General Lord Ruthven [Staff Officer VIII Corps] to Edmonds 30/10/29, CAB 45/189.
11. 'Action of the VIII Corps Artillery on July 1st 1916', in VIII Corps Heavy Artillery War Diary July 1916, WO 95/825.
12. 'Narrative of the Operations of the VIII Corps on 1st July 1916', in VIII Corps War Diary July 1916, WO 95/820.
13. 'Operations of 94th Infantry Brigade, on July 1st, 1916', in 31 Division War Diary July 1916, WO 95/2341.
14. See 1 East Lancashire War Diary for 1/7/16 in WO 95/1498.
15. See War Diary of 1 King's Own Regiment for 1/7/16 in WO 95/1506.
16. 'Report of the Operations of the 29th Division from the 30th June to the Night of the 1/2 July', in 29 Division War Diary July 1916, WO 95/2280.
17. For example, see L. Milner, *A History of the 15th (Service) Battalion (1st Leeds) The Prince of Wales Own (West Yorkshire) Regiment 1914–1918* (London: Leo Cooper, 1991).
18. Special Order of the Day by Brigadier-General H. C. Rees in 31 Division War Diary July 1916, WO 95/2341.
19. See VIII Corps Narrative and 94 Brigade Narrative.
20. John Bickersteth (ed.), *The Bickersteth Diaries 1914–1918* (London, Leo Cooper, 1996), p. 100.
21. Horsfall and Cave, *Serre*, pp. 67–8. The numbers killed come from Ernest W. Bell, *Soldiers Killed on the First Day of the Somme* (Bolton, Lancs: Bell, 1977).
22. Special Order of the Day by Brigadier-General H. C. Rees in 31 Division War Diary July 1916.
23. See VIII Corps Narrative, 94 Brigade Narrative.
24. R. A. Sparling, *History of the 12th (Service) Battalion York and Lancaster Regiment* (Sheffield: The Regiment, 1920), p. 63.
25. 16 West Yorkshire War Diary 1/7/16, WO 95/2341.
26. See VIII Corps Narrative and 94 Brigade Narrative.
27. J. C. D. Inglis to Edmonds 13/11/29, CAB 45/135.
28. Casualties calculated from divisional narratives, Miles, *1916 V2* and Horsfall and Cave, *Serre*.
29. See VIII Corps Narrative and Report on Operations of the 29 Division.
30. 'Account of Action, 1st July 1916, Attack of 1st Lancashire Fusiliers on Beaumont Hamel', 1 Lancashire Fusiliers War Diary July 1916, WO 95/2300.
31. J. Ashurst, *My Bit: A Lancashire Fusilier at War 1914–1918*, ed. Richard Holmes (Marlborough, Crowood, 1987), p. 99.
32. Report on Operations of the 29 Division.
33. Ibid.
34. 1 Battalion Newfoundland Regiment War Diary 1/7/16, WO 95/2308.
35. Ibid.; Nigel Cave, *Beaumont Hamel* (London: Leo Cooper, 1994), pp. 57–64; Dr D. W. Parsons, 'The New-

foundland Regiment: An Analysis of Those Wounded on 1 July 1916', *Stand-To*, no. 22, Spring 1988, pp. 16–17.

36. J. W. Burrows, *The Essex Regiment* (Southend-on-Sea: Burrows & Son, 1931), p. 211.
37. Report on Operations of the 29 Division.
38. See VIII Corps Narrative.
39. '8th Battalion: The Royal Warwickshire Regiment' by Col. N. R. Ludlow. This is a pamphlet dated 1/7/18 in the 1/8 Warwicks' War Diary July 1916, WO 95/2756.
40. 'Operations on 1st July, 1916', in 4 Division War Diary July 1916, WO 95/1445.
41. See account in 1 East Lancashire War Diary July 1916, WO 95/1498.
42. 4 Division, 'Operations'.
43. This section has been reconstructed from the 4 Division's 'Messages Received on the Telephone 1st July 1916', in 4 Division War Diary.

## 8 'The Enemy's Fire Was So Intense'

1. For much of this detail we have drawn on the excellent book by Michael Stedman, *Thiepval* (London: Leo Cooper, 1995), Chapter 2.
2. For X Corps Artillery see the daily progress reports in their Heavy Artillery War Diary for June 1916, WO 95/844.
3. War Diary of 14 Royal Irish Rifles 1/7/16, WO 95/2511.
4. The Boyne anniversary can only be made to coincide with 1 July if the Julian calendar is used. Since 1751 Britain had used the Gregorian calendar, which subtracted 11 days from the year. Since that time the Boyne was deemed to have fallen on 12 July. Cyril Falls, in his history of the division claims that celebrations of the Boyne within the division took place on both dates. By the latter date it is a wonder that celebrations of any kind could have occurred. The story that some of the officers wore the orange sashes of their order as they went over the top is a myth. The authors are grateful to Professor Keith Jeffrey for this last point.
5. 'Short Account of the Attack by the 12th (S) Bn Royal Irish Rifles on 1st July 1916', 12 Royal Irish Rifles War Diary 1/7/16, WO 95/2506. For other battalions involved in the attack to the north of the Ancre see 9 Royal Irish Fusiliers War Diary 1/7/16 in WO 95/2505 (they suffered 535 casualties out of 600) and 13 Royal Irish Rifles War Diary 1/7/16 in WO 95/2506.
6. Account of 36 Division Operations 1/7/16, 36 Division War Diary July 1916, WO 95/2491.
7. Ibid.
8. *Schlachten des Weltkrieg: Somme-Nord V1* (Oldenburg: Stallung, 1927), pp. 36–7. This is an official monograph issued by the Reichsarchiv [hereafter *Somme-Nord*].
9. Ibid.
10. Account of the 36 Division.
11. See War Diary of 8 Royal Irish Rifles and 10 Royal Irish Rifles for 1/7/16 in WO 95/2503.
12. War Diary of 8 Royal Irish Rifles.
13. Stedman, *Thiepval*, pp. 79–80.
14. Account of the 36 Division.
15. Ibid.
16. Stedman, *Thiepval*, p. 81.
17. Edmonds, *1916 V1*, p. 402.
18. War Diary of the 16 Northumberland Fusiliers 1/7/16, WO 95/2398.
19. Michael Stedman, *Salford Pals* (London: Leo Cooper, 1993), pp. 88–9. The 15 Lancashire Fusiliers were popularly known as the Salford Pals.
20. 'Report on Operations 21 June to 4th July, and from 8th to 15th July', 32 Division War Diary July 1916, WO 95/2368.
21. The expression is Stedman's. See *Salford Pals*, p. 99.
22. War Diary of 16 Lancashire Fusiliers 1/7/16, WO 95/2397.
23. 32 Division 'Report on Operations'.
24. Ibid.

25. 1 Dorset War Diary 1/7/16, WO 95/2392; 19 Lancashire Fusiliers War Diary 1/7/16, WO 95/2394.
26. 1 Dorset War Diary 1/7/16.
27. 2 Manchesters War Diary 1/7/16, WO 95/2392.

## 9 'Wave after Wave Were Mown Down'

1 For an excellent description of the area see Michael Stedman, *La Boisselle* (London: Leo Cooper, 1997), Chapters 1 and 2.
2 See note 50, Chapter 6.
3 Diary of Captain Reginald Leetham, uncatalogued collection, IWM.
4 8 Division Preliminary Operation Order No. 107, 12/6/16, 8 Division War Diary June 1916, WO 95/1675.
5 34 Division Operation Order No. 16, 15/6/16, 34 Division War Diary June 1916, WO 95/2432.
6 Edmonds, *1916 V1*, pp. 374–5.
7 Major H. M. Hanc[?] OC 179 Tunnelling Company to Edmonds, June 1930, CAB 45/134.
8 III Corps: Summary of Operations 1 to 7 July, 1916, III Corps War Diary June 1916, WO 95/673; 34 Division, 'Use of Smoke', in 34 Division Operation Order 15/6/16 quoted above.
9 III Corps Summary of Operations.
10 'Brief Narrative of course of the action compiled from reports and various other reliable sources', 70 Brigade War Diary July 1916, WO 95/2185.
11 8 Kings Own Yorkshire Light Infantry War Diary 1/7/16, WO 95/2187; 'Statement of Operations by the 8th York and Lancaster Regiment on 1st July, 1916' in their War Diary for 1/7/16, WO 95/2188.
12 70 Brigade, 'Brief Narrative'.
13 Ibid.
14 'Account of the part taken by 11th (Service) Battalion The Sherwood Foresters in the operation of 1st July 1916', in 11 Sherwood Foresters War Diary 1/7/16, WO 95/2187.
15 Ibid.
16 70 Brigade, 'Brief Narrative'.
17. Ibid.
18 The figures for the survivors can only be regarded as approximate. They have been compiled from battalion accounts and from Edmonds, *1916 V1*, pp. 389, n.1.
19 'Report on Action of July 1st 1916 [by 2 Lincolnshire Battalion]', in 25 Brigade War Diary July 1916, WO 95/1726.
20 25 Brigade, 'Report on Operations about Ovillers July 1st 1916', ibid.
21 See for example, 'Report of Operations of July 1st' [of 1 Royal Irish Rifles, a support battalion in 25 Brigade], ibid.
22 The table has been compiled from the 25 Brigade account already quoted and 'Report of the part taken by the 2nd Battalion Devonshire Regiment During the Attack on Pozieres [*sic*] on 1st July 1916', in 2 Devonshire War Diary July 1916, WO 95/1712; 2 Middlesex War Diary 1/7/16, WO 95/1713; 2 West Yorkshire War Diary 1/7/16, WO 95/1714.
23 25 Brigade, 'Report of Operations about Ovillers'.
24 Ibid. Hooroosh or hurroosh was a word much used by commanders in the First World War. It was a favourite expression of Rawlinson's, who on many occasions used it in the same sense as Tuson, that is to describe an all-out attack in which distant objectives would be reached rapidly. According to the *Oxford English Dictionary* the word originated in medieval times as 'hurish', a cry used to drive cattle. Melville employed it in *Moby Dick* (1851) and Kipling in his *Plain Tales from the Hills* (1888) – 'There was a wild huroosh at the Club', presumably meaning an outcry. Its last use was by the *News Chronicle* in 1959 when they reported 'Sex hormones went off with a great hooroosh'.

25 34 Division Operation Order No. 16, 15/6/16.

26 Ibid.; 15 Royal Scots War Diary 1/7/16, WO 95/2457. The Royal Scots were one of the units affected by the delay.

27 Graham Stewart and John Sheen, *Tyneside Scottish* (Barnsley: Leo Cooper, 1999), p. 96.

28 Ibid., p. 98.

29 20 Northumberland Fusiliers War Diary 1/7/16, WO 95/2462; 23 Northumberland Fusiliers War Diary 1/7/16, WO 95/2463.

30 21 Northumberland Fusiliers War Diary 1/7/16, WO 95/2462.

31 11 Suffolk War Diary 1/7/16, WO 95/2458.

32 ? to Edmonds 21/3/30, CAB 45/133.

33 15 & 16 Royal Scots War Diaries 1/7/16, WO 95/2547 and WO 95/2548 respectively.

34 Report on Operations – 103 Brigade War Diary 1/7/16, WO 95/2432.

35 25 Northumberland Fusiliers War Diary 1/7/16, WO 95/2467.

36 See eyewitness accounts in John Sheen, *Tyneside Irish* (Barnsley: Leo Cooper, 1998), pp. 95, 96, and 98. The last of these calls the action 'splendid'.

37 27 Northumberland Fusiliers War Diary 1/7/16, WO 95/2467.

38 Report on Operations – 103 Brigade.

39 Sheen, *Tyneside Irish*, p. 111.

## 10 'Cowering Men in Field Grey'

1 XV Corps Scheme of Attack April 1916, XV Corps War Diary April–June 1916, WO 95/921; 7 Division: Artillery Instruction for Forthcoming Operations and Explanatory Notes in Edmonds *1916 V1*, Appendix Volume, Appendix 25; Operation attack orders (9 KOYLI) in their War Diary June 1916, WO 95/2162.

2 See *Les Armes françaises dans la grande guerre* (Hereafter *French Official History*) Tome IV, vol. 2 annexes, VI Armée order 29/6/16, p. 707 and Map 15 which shows the positioning of VI Army heavy artillery batteries on the eve of the battle.

3 See note in Edmonds, *1916 VI*, p. 344. *Der Weltkrieg, V10* also admits to the loss of many guns in this area (p. 350).

4 XV Corps Operation Order No. 3, 16/6/16, XV Corps War Diary April–July 1916, WO 95/921.

5 64 Brigade account 1/7/16, 64 Brigade War Diary July 1916, WO 95/2159; 9 KOYLI War Diary 1/7/16.

6 64 Brigade Account 1/7/16, emphasis added.

7 Edmonds, *1916 VI*, p. 358

8 10 York and Lancaster Battalion: 'Operations July 1st 1916–July 4th 1916', WO 95/2158; 8 Lincolns: 'Operations 1/7/16', WO 95/2158.

9 This brigade was from XV Corps reserve. It had been attached to 21 Division for the main attack.

10 The account in 50 Brigade War Diary, WO 95/1998 is very sketchy.

11 For the epic story of an officer and 20 men who survived, consult the index (under Philip Howe) of Martin Middlebrook's *The First Day on the Somme* (London: Allen Lane, 1971).

12 17 Division War Diary 1/7/16, WO 95/1981.

13 'Notes on Attacks Carried Out By 7th Division in July, 1916', 7 Division War Diary July–Dec. 1916, WO 95/1631.

14 'Report on part taken by the 2nd Border Regiment in the engagement by Mametz on the 1st July 1916', 2 Borders War Diary July 1916, WO 95/1655.

15 Account by the Adjutant 9 Devons in their War Diary, 1/7/16, WO 95/1656.

16 2 Gordon Highlanders War Diary 1/7/16, WO 95/1656.

17 7 Division, 'Narrative of Operations from 1st to 5th July, 1916', in 7 Division War Diary, WO 95/1655.

18 XV Corps War Diary 1/7/16, WO 95/921.

19 50 Brigade War Diary 1/7/16. The Battalion was the 7 Green Howards.

20 Edmonds, *1916 VI*, p. 364.

21 Ibid., p. 363.
22 Gerald Gliddon, *The Battle of the Somme: A Topographical History* (Stroud: Sutton, 1996), p. 324.
23 Graham Maddocks, *Montauban*, (Barnsley: Leo Cooper, 1999), p. 47.
24 'Report on Operations, 30th Division, July 1st 'till 10 am July 5th', 30 Division War Diary July 1916, WO 95/2310.
25 Edmonds, *1916 V1*, p. 344.
26 Ibid.
27 Ibid.; 'Report on Operations, 30th Division'.
28 XIII Corps Plan of Operations quoted in Edmonds, *1916 V1, Somme Appendices*, Appendix 21, pp. 157–8.
29 Anstey, 'History of the Royal Artillery', p. 117.
30 Weekly Mine Report, 183rd Tunnelling Co. Regiment in 18 Division War Diary July 1916, WO 95/2015.
31 Maxse, 'The Battle of the Somme', Maxse Papers 69/53/6, IWM.
32 Account of S.T. Fuller, Fuller Papers 86/32/1, IWM.
33 53 Brigade 'Abbreviated Report on Operations from 23rd June and 20th July, 1916', AWM 26/6/48/23.
34 The 7 Queens from this brigade suffered almost 500 casualties. See Edmonds, *1916, V1*, p. 340, n.1. See also 'Short Report on the Action of July 1st 1916' by 7 Queen's in their War Diary, WO 95/2051 and 8 East Surrey War Diary 1/7/16, WO 95/2050.
35 'The Account of the Operations of the 54th Infantry Brigade during the Battle of the Somme between the 23rd June and 20th July 1916', Maxse Papers 63/53/7; 53 Brigade: 'Abbreviated Report on Operations'.
36 Captain Bull to 7 Bedfords War Diarist, in 7 Bedfords War Diary 1/7/16, WO 95/2043.
37 Untitled account of action on 1 July, in 7 Bedfords War Diary.
38 See untitled Bedfords account; 'Report on Attack, July 1st, 1916', by 11 Royal Fusiliers, WO 95/2045. The brigade account is in the Maxse Papers 63/53/7.
39 'Report by Captain A.G. Kirchington "B" Company [7/Buffs] on Operations of 1st July 1916', WO 95/2049. It was the task of this company to attack the crater area.
40 See 7 Queen's 'Short Report'.
41 Maxse, 'The Battle of the Somme'.
42 'Report on Operations, 30th Division.'
43 Ibid.
44 See their entry in Ernest W. Bell, *Soldiers Killed on the First Day of the Somme.*
45 Maddocks, *Montauban*, p. 93.
46 Ibid.
47 'Report on Operations, 30 Division.'
48 'Account of the Battle of 1st July 1916 for Glatz Redoubt and Montauban by Lieut. Colonel E.H. Trotter D.S.O. Commanding 18th Ser[vice] Battalion "The Kings' Liverpool Regiment"', 18 King's War Diary July 1916, WO 95/2330.
49 Maddocks, *Montauban*, p. 83.
50 Trotter, 'Account of the Battle of 1st July'.
51 'Report on Operations, 30 Division.'
52 Ibid; War Diary of 2 Royal Scots Fusiliers 1/7/16, WO 95/2340.
53 Maddocks, *Montauban*, p. 104.
54 Gliddon, *Battle of the Somme*, p. 274.
55 Unnamed, uncatalogued account, IWM.
56 Ibid.; 'Report on Operations of 17 Manchester Regiment on 1st and 2nd July 1916', WO 95/2339.
57 'Report on Operations, 30 Division.'

## 11 Reflections on 1 July

1. John Buchan, *The Battle of the Somme* (London: Nelson, 1917), p. 31.
2. B.H. Liddell Hart, *A History of the World War 1914–1918* (London: Faber, 1930), p. 315.
3. Ibid. p. 314.
4. Edmonds, *1916 V1*, p. 487.
5. C.M.F. Cruttwell, *A History of the*

*Great War 1914–1918* (Oxford: Oxford University Press, 1934), p. 266.
6. John Terraine, *Douglas Haig: The Educated Soldier* (London: Hutchinson, 1963), p. 204.
7. Martin Middlebrook, *The First Day on the Somme* (London: Allen Lane, 1971), p. 276; Corelli Barnett, *The Great War* (London: Hutchinson, 1979), p. 76; Paul Kennedy 'Britain', in A.H. Millett and Williamson Murray (eds), *Military Effectiveness V1: The First World War* (London: Allen & Unwin, 1988), p. 84; BBC TV *The Great War*, 1999.
8. A.H. Farrar-Hockley, *The Somme*, (London: Pan, 1970), pp. 113–32.
9. A. H Farrar-Hockley, 'The Somme and Passchendaele; Ordeal by Fire 1916–17', in P. Young and J. P. Lawford, *History of the British Army* (London: Barker, 1970), pp. 223–4.
10. Omar Bartov, 'Man and the Mass: Reality and the Heroic Image in War', in *Murder in our Midst: The Holocaust, Industrial Killing and Representation* (New York: Oxford University Press, 1996), p. 15.

## 12 'Ill-Considered Attacks on a Small Front'

1. Haig Diary 1/7/16, National Library of Scotland.
2. Ibid. 2/7/16.
3. Rawlinson Diary 1/7/16, Churchill College, Cambridge.
4. Ibid. 2/7/16.
5. Ibid. 1/7/16.
6. Fourth Army operation order No. 3, 1/7/16, Fourth Army Papers V7, IWM; 'Note of an interview at Fourth Army Headquarters, Querrieu at mid-day, 2 July, 1916', AWM 252/A116.
7. Haig Diary 3/7/16; Lieutenant-General Sir Sidney Clive Diary 3/7/16, CAB 45/201/2. General Clive was a British liaison officer with the French X Army.
8. Clive Diary 4/7/16.
9. Fourth Army Operations Orders 3/7/16, Fourth Army Papers V1, IWM.
10. Ibid.
11. III Corps Summary of Operations 1st to 7th July, 1916, III Corps War Diary July 1916, WO 95/673.
12. X Corps Report on Operations for Week Ending 6 p. m. July 7th, X Corps War Diary July 1916, WO 95/851.
13. 19 Division War Diary July 1916, WO 95/2053.
14. 8 North Stafford War Diary 3/7/16, WO 95/2085.
15. 9 Royal Welsh Fusiliers War Diary 3/7/16, WO 95/2092.
16. One of the six battalions involved, the 8 North Staffords, suffered 284 casualties. The whole episode provides a good example of the hazards of using a single war diary as a source. The diary of 19 Division, while giving the correct position for its men at the end of the battle, conveys the clear impression that the whole operation was a success. See their account in the entry for 3/7/16 in WO 95/2053.
17. X Corps Report on Operations for Week Ending 6 p. m. July 7th.
18. 'Account of Operations July 1st to July 9th in which the 12th Division took part', 12 Division War Diary July 1916, WO 95/1823.
19. See the War Diary of the leading unit, the 6 Royal West Kent in WO 95/1861 and the supporting battalion, 6/Buffs in WO 95/1860.
20. 12 Division 'Account of Operations'.
21. Ibid.
22. Major-General Sir Arthur B. Scott and P. Middleton Brumwell, *History of the 12th (Eastern) Division in the Great War, 1914–1918* (London: Nisbit & Co., 1923), p. 54.
23. Fourth Army Operations Orders 3/7/16.
24. Haig to Rawlinson and Gough 4/7/16 (OAD 42) in IV Army Summary of Operations, WO 158/234.
25. Haig to Rawlinson and Gough 6/7/16 (OAD 49) Fourth Army Papers V1.

26. 'Narrative of the operations 23rd Division July 1–10 Capture of Horse Shoe Trench, Bailiff Wood and Contalmaison,' 23 Division War Diary June 1916, WO 95/2167.
27. 17 Division War Diary June 1916, WO 95/1891.
28. The two sources cited above yield these facts.
29. 23 Division Narrative of Operations; Miles, *1916 V2*, p. 58 gives the 17 Division casualties between 1 and 11 July as 4,771 but it is likely that at least 1,000 of these were suffered on the first day.
30. 19 Division War Diary July 1916, WO 95/2053; 34 Division War Diary July 1916, WO 95/2432.
31. G. Grogan to Edmonds 10/4/30, CAB 45/134.
32. Ibid.
33. James Dundas to Edmonds 1/7/30, CAB 45/133.
34. Colin Hughes, *Mametz: Lloyd George's 'Welsh Army' at the Battle of the Somme*, 2nd edn (Gerrards Cross: Orion Press, 1982), p. 67. The account that follows relies heavily on this excellent narrative of events in Mametz Wood from 5 to 14 July.
35. 38 Division War Diary July 1916, WO 95/2539.
36. 'Notes on Attack Carried Out by 7th Division in July 1916', 7 Division War Diary July 1916, WO 95/1631.
37. See the War Diaries of the 17 and 38 Divisions for this matter and note that the times of the main attacks always differed even on the rare occasions when an attempt at co-ordination was made.
38. See Hughes, *Mametz*, which spells out these lamentable happenings in great detail; also 38 Division War Diary.
39. Miles, *1916 V2*, p. 54.
40. For casualty figures see ibid., pp. 47–58.
41. Figures have been arrived at from an analysis of the attacks detailed in Chris McCarthy, *The Somme: The Day by Day Account* (London: Arms & Armour, 1993) and from Miles, *1916 V2*.
42. Hughes, *Mametz*, p. 70.
43. *Der Weltkrieg V10*, p. 355.

## 13 'Cavalry Sharpening Their Swords', 14 July

1. Haig to Rawlinson 2/7/16, Fourth Army Papers V1, IWM.
2. Ibid.
3. Fourth Army Operation Order No. 4, 8/7/16, Fourth Army War Diary July 1916, WO 95/431.
4. Haig Diary 5/7/16, National Library of Scotland.
5. Rawlinson Diary 10/7/16, Churchill College, Cambridge.
6. Ibid.
7. Haig Diary 10/7/16.
8. 'Note of discussion as to attack of Longueval Plateau and the Commander-in-Chief's decision thereon'(OAD 60) 11/7/16, Fourth Army Papers, V1.
9. Congreve Diary 11/7/16, Congreve Papers, private hands.
10. Horne Diary 11/7/16, Horne Papers, 62/54/9, IWM.
11. For these discussions see 'Note of discussion as to attack of Longueval Plateau'.
12. Rawlinson Diary 11/7/16.
13. Haig Diary 12/7/16.
14. Congreve Diary 11/7/16; Haig Diary 12/7/16.
15. Artillery statistics have been taken from, 'Battle of the Somme: Artillery Notes and Statistics'. There are no detailed figures for the 14 July bombardment. The number of howitzer shells fired and their weight have been obtained by assuming that the proportion of heavy howitzer shells to shells fired by the field artillery was the same as that for 1 July. As the proportion of howitzers to total number of guns in the Fourth Army was slightly higher on 14 July than it had been on 1 July (31% as against 29%), this seems a safe assumption.

16. Fourth Army Operation Order No. 4, 8/7/16.
17. Fourth Army – Cavalry Commanders Conference 11/7/16, Fourth Army Papers V1.
18. Fourth Army Intelligence Report 9/7/16, Fourth Army Papers V12, IWM.
19. Fourth Army – Cavalry Commanders Conference 11/7/16.
20. Fourth Army – GHQ Conference 12/7/16, Fourth Army Papers V1.
21. Kiggell to Montgomery 11/7/16, ibid.
22. Ibid.
23. 'Instructions for the Action of Cavalry on Z Day', quoted in Miles, *1916 V2*, Appendix Volume, Appendix 4.
24. Haig Diary 13/7/16.
25. 'General idea of future plans in the event of the attack of the enemys 2nd line between Longueval and Bazentin-le-Petit being successful', 13/7/16, Fourth Army Papers V7, IWM.
26. Haig to Robertson 8/7/16, AWM 252/A99.
27. Rawlinson Diary 11/7/16.
28. 3 Division, 'Attack on the Longueval–Bazentin Position', 3 Division War Diary July 1916, WO 95/1377.
29. 9 Division, 'Narrative of Events 11–20 July', 9 Division War Diary July 1916, WO 95/1735.
30. 3 Division, 'Attack on the Longueval–Bazentin Position'.
31. See 'Operations of 21st Division', Fourth Army Papers V1 and 6 Leicesters, 'Narrative of Action' in their War Diary for 14/7/16, WO 95/2164. This unit lost over 500 casualties on 14 July.
32. 7 Division,'Narrative of Operations from 11th to 20th July, 1916', in 7 Division War Diary July 1916, WO 95/1655.
33. 3 Division, 'Attack on the Longueval–Bazentin Position'.
34. 9 Division War Diary 14/7/16, WO 95/1735.
35. For this phase of the fighting see 'Operations of the 21st Division'; 7 Division, 'Narrative'.
36. 6 Leicesters (21 Division), 'Narrative of Action'; 2 Royal Irish Rifles ( 7 Division) War Diary 14/7/16, WO 95/1662.
37. 9 Division War Diary 14/7/16, WO 95/1735; John Ewing, *The History of the 9th (Scottish) Division 1914–1919* (London: John Murray, 1921), pp. 116–17; Nigel Cave, *Delville Wood* (Barnsley: Leo Cooper, 1999), p.44.
38. The casualty figures are to be found in the war diaries mentioned above.
39. Fourth Army Telegrams to GHQ, 7.35 p. m., 14 July, GHQ War Diary July 1916, WO 95/5.
40. Secunderabad Cavalry Brigade, 'Narrative of Events – 14 July 1916', in their War Diary July 1916, WO 95/921.
41. Ibid.
42. Brigadier-General H. C. Potter to Edmonds 20/3/30, CAB 45/190. Another eyewitness needs to be noted here. Major-General Munshill-Ford was the commander of an infantry brigade trying to occupy High Wood. He was in no doubt that the Germans were occupying a trench within the wood in strength before his troops arrived. See Munshill-Ford to Edmonds n.d., CAB 45/136. Any testimony from aerial observers that the wood was unoccupied had little value, as the wood still had sufficient canopy to conceal trench lines and their garrisons.
43. *Somme-Nord V1*, p. 29.
44. See 91 Brigade War Diary 14/7/16 ,WO 95/1666. See 7 Division War Diary for the same date in WO 95/1631 for the difficulties in co-ordinating an attack on the wood.
45. Rawlinson to Lady Rawlinson, Cowans, Archibald Murray, Bagot, and Derby 18/7/16, Rawlinson Papers 5201/33/18, NAM.

## 14 'We Are a Bit Stuck', 15–31 July

1. Rawlinson Diary 15/7/16, Churchill College, Cambridge.
2. Ibid.

3. Fourth Army Conference 16/7/16, Fourth Army Papers V2, IWM.
4. Ibid.
5. Chris McCarthy, *The Somme: The Day by Day Account* (London: Arms & Armour, 1993), pp. 51–3.
6. Fourth Army Operation Order 16/7/16, AWM 26/6/41/33.
7. Fourth Army War Diary 17/7/16, Fourth Army Papers V2.
8. Rawlinson–Fayolle Conference 19/7/16, AWM 26/6/41/33.
9. Fourth Army War Diary 22/7/16.
10. 1 South African Brigade Narrative 15/7/16, WO 95/1777. See also the German battery positions marked on the map in WO 153/1623.
11. 9 Division, 'Narrative of Events', 9 Division War Diary July 1916, WO 95/1735.
12. See Haig's Diary for 17 and 19 July for these gnomic utterances.
13. 'Remarks by Brig-General Higginson' 1/8/16, in Maxse Papers 69/53/6, IWM.
14. Higginson to Edmonds 1/1/34, CAB 45/134.
15. Miles, *1916 V2*, p. 105.
16. Haig Diary 21/7/16; Rawlinson Diary 22/7/16.
17. See Miles, *1916 V2*, pp. 113, 136; Rawlinson Diary 22/7/16.
18. H.A. Jones, *The War in the Air*, vol. 2 (London: Hamish Hamilton, 1969), p. 239.
19. 19 Division War Diary 21/7/16, WO 95/2503.
20. 1 Royal West Kent War Diary July 1916, WO 95/1554.
21. To further complicate matters, XV Corps, of which 5 Division was a part, thought that the left of the division attacked at 1. 30 a.m. in line with 51 Division on its left. There is no mention in XV Corps War Diary of the 10 p. m. start. See XV Corps War Diary July 1916, WO 95/921.
22. 1 Royal West Kent War Diary July 1916; 13 Royal Warwickshire War Diary July 1916, WO 95/1556. The quotation comes from the Warwicks' diary.
23. 1 Brigade, 'Narrative of operations 23rd July 1916', 1 Brigade War Diary, July 1916, WO 95/1261; 2 Brigade, 'Report on Operations Night 22/23rd July, 1916', 2 Brigade War Diary July 1916, WO 95/1267.
24. Miles, *1916 V2*, p. 138.
25. 51 Division War Diary July 1916, WO 95/2845.
26. 5 Division War Diary July 1916, WO 95/1513. See also a letter from an officer of 9 Brigade (3 Division) to Edmonds 12/1/34 in CAB 45/138.
27. *Somme-Nord*, *V1*, p. 188.
28. G.C. Wynne, *If Germany Attacks* (London: Faber, 1940), p. 123. See also *Somme-Nord*, *V1*, p. 188.
29. 21 Brigade (30 Division) War Diary July 1916, WO 95/2327.
30. Haig Diary 23/7/16; Rawlinson Diary 23/7/16.
31. Rawlinson Diary 24–26/7/16.
32. XIII Corps Artillery Operation Order No. 6, 26/7/16; 2 Division War Diary July 1916, WO 95/1291; Miles, *1916 V2*, p. 157.
33. Rawlinson Diary 27/7/16.
34. 'Battle of the Somme Artillery Notes and Statistics', Rawlinson Papers 5201/33/71, NAM.
35. 2 Division Report in their War Diary July 1916.
36. Horne letters to his wife, 62/54/9, IWM.
37. Haig Diary 23/7/16.
38. Ibid., 24/7/16.
39. 90 Infantry Brigade, 'Report on Operations, 30th July 1916', in 30 Division War Diary July 1916, WO 95/2310; 2 Royal Scots Fusiliers War Diary 30/7/16, WO 95/2340.
40. 7 King's Own War Diary 30/7/16, WO 95/2078.
41. GHQ, Instruction (OA 256) 16/7/16, Fourth Army War Diary July 1916, Fourth Army Papers,V2.

42. '35th Divisional Artillery: Operations 21st to 30th July inclusive 1916', in 30 Division War Diary July 1916.
43. Ibid.

## 15 'Something Wanting in the Methods Employed', 1 August–12 September

1. Haig to Rawlinson and Gough 2/8/16 (OAD 91) in Miles, *1916 V2*, Appendices, Appendix 13, p. 34.
2. Ibid.
3. All quotations are ibid.
4. See 'Battle of the Somme: Artillery Notes and Statistics'.
5. 13 Durham Light Infantry War Diary 4/5 Aug. 1916, WO 95/2182.
6. Rawlinson–Fayolle Conference 5/8/16, Fourth Army Papers V2, IWM.
7. 55 Division, 'Operations 25/7 to 15/8', 55 Division War Diary Aug. 1916, WO 95/2900; '2 Division Report on Operations 8–9 Aug.', 2 Division War Diary August 1916, WO 95/1292; 2 Division 'Notes on Experience Gained During The Recent Operations', ibid.
8. 55 Division 'Operations'; 'Report by Corporal Shaw C Company 1/4 Royal Lancashire Fusiliers 8/8/16', in 'Battle Operations Carried Out By 1/4 Btn Royal Lancashire Fusiliers From 8th Aug. 1916', in their War Diary August 1916, WO 95/2922
9. Haig Diary 8/8/16, National Library of Scotland.
10. 1/5 Loyal North Lancashire (55 Division) War Diary 8–9/8/16, WO 95/2929.
11. Ibid.
12. Unknown correspondent to Edmonds n.d., CAB 45/132.
13. Rawlinson Diary 8/8/16, Churchill College, Cambridge.
14. Ibid., 9/8/16.
15. 'Notes of an Interview at Querrieu, at 11.00 a.m., 9th August, 1916, between [Rawlinson, Kiggell, Montgomery, and Davidson]', Fourth Army Papers V2.
16. Ibid.
17. Haig Diary 10/8/16.
18. After Cavan's sickness was reported to him Haig commented that the corps headquarters 'was surrounded by French troops, who are most unsanitary in their habits and the houses are full of fleas'. Haig Diary 17/8/16.
19. 6 Battalion Cameron Highlanders, 'Notes on Operations on Night 12/13 Aug.', in their War Diary August 1916, WO 95/1945.
20. 9 East Surrey War Diary 16/8/16, WO 95/2215.
21. Miles, *1916 V2*, p. 190. Fayolle incurred the wrath of Foch for the action but the intervention of the French commander came too late to affect the decision. See Foch to Fayolle 17/8/16, French Official History, V4/2, Annex 2947, p. 729.
22. Rawlinson, 'Notes for Conference 18/8/16, Rawlinson Papers 1/6, Churchill College, Cambridge.
23. 'Operations on the Somme: 1st July to 18th November 1916: Casualties By Division', AWM 252/A106; 'Report on Operations of 3rd Division 10th–21 August, 1916 in Vicinity of Guillemont', 3 Division War Diary August 1916, WO 95/1378.
24. 3 Division, 'Report on Operations'.
25. 1 Division War Diary 18/8/16, WO 95/1231.
26. 33 Division, untitled account of the action on the 18th in their War Diary Aug. 1916, WO 95/2405.
27. Ibid.
28. 14 (Light) Division, 'Summary of operations – August 18th, 1916', 14 Division War Diary Aug. 1916, WO 95/1867.
29. See 8 Buffs War Diary 18/8/16, WO 95/2207 and 3 Rifle Brigade War Diary 18/8/16, WO 95/2206.
30. 3 Division 'Report on Operations'; 8 East Yorkshire War Diary and untitled account of the action on 18/8/16, WO 95/1424; 1 Gordon Highlanders, 'Report on Operations in Maltz Horn

Ravine 16th to 20th August 1916', 1 Gordon Highlanders War Diary Aug. 1916, WO 95/1435.

31. Haig Diary 20/8/16.
32. Haig to Rawlinson (OAD 116), 19/8/16, AWM 26/6/4/41.
33. Haig to Rawlinson (OAD 123), 24/8/16, Fourth Army Papers V5, IWM.
34. Ibid.
35. Ibid.
36. Ibid.
37. Haig Diary 24/8/16.
38. For the weather conditions see Fourth Army War Diary in the Fourth Army Papers, IWM for the relevant days.
39. Haig Diary 29/8/16.
40. *Der Weltkrieg V10*, p. 56
41. Ibid.
42. See Somme Artillery Notes and Statistics for the comparative figures.
43. Account of Lt A.M. Little quoted in the 2/KOSB War Diary 3/9/16, WO 95/1552.
44. 'Report on Operations Carried Out By 5th Division from 3rd to 5th September 1916', 5 Division War Diary Sept. 1916, WO 95/1517.
45. Miles, *1916 V2*, p. 253, n.3.
46. See 1 Duke of Cornwall Light Infantry War Diary 3/9/16 in WO 95/1557.
47. 'Report on Operations by the 59th Infantry Brigade on 2nd 3rd and 4th … in the capture of Guillemont', 59 Brigade War Diary Sept. 1916, WO 95/2112; Captain J. A. C. Pennyquick to Edmonds 30/10/35, CAB 45/136.
48. Ibid.
49. 'Operations Carried out by the 20th (Light) Division on 3rd, 4th and 5th September', 20 Division War Diary Sept. 1916, WO 95/2095.
50. Miles, *1916 V2*, p. 257 n.3; 'Report on Operations carried out by 5th Division'; 'Operations Carried out by 20th (Light) Division'.
51. 7 Division Operation Order 31/8/16, 7 Division War Diary Sept. 1916, WO 95/1631.
52. 'Report of the Operations Carried Out by the 7th Division Between 26th August and 8 September Including the Attack on Ginchy', ibid.
53. '1st Infantry Brigade Narrative of Operations – 3rd September 1916', 1st Brigade War Diary Sept. 1916, WO 95/1261.
54. See 16 Division War Diary for Sept. 1916, WO 95/1969; 9 Royal Dublin Fusiliers War Diary 9/9/16, WO 95/1974.

## 16 'A Hell of a Time'

1. Haig to Rawlinson and Gough 18/7/16 (OAD 76), Fourth Army Papers V2, IWM.
2. 'Report on the Operations of First Australian Division at Pozieres', AWM 26/6/51/27; 'Summary of Operations for week ending 6 p.m. Friday July 28th', AWM 26/6/50/15.
3. 'Report on Operations of First Australian Division'. Gough disputed this. In a post-war letter to Edmonds he claimed that he 'gave Walker no choice' in the direction of attack but decided it himself. Gough to Edmonds 16/6/39, CAB 45/134.
4. See the important article by Gary Sheffield, 'The Australians at Pozières: Command and Control on the Somme, 1916', in David French and Brian Holden Reid (eds), *The British General Staff: Reform and Innovation c. 1890–1939* (London, Cass, 2002), pp. 112–26.
5. 'Report on Operations of First Australian Division'.
6. C. E. W. Bean, *The Official History of Australia in the War of 1914–1918, vol. 4: The Australian Imperial Forces in France in 1916* (Sydney: Angus & Robertson, 1938) pp. 484–5. [Hereafter, *Bean*, Australian Official History.[
7. First Australian Division Operation Order No. 31, 20/7/16, AWM 26/6/51/28.

8. 11 Australian Battalion account in 3rd Australian Infantry Brigade War Diary, Part 1, 23–26 July 1916, AWM 26/6/54/12.
9. *Bean*, Australian Official History, p. 509.
10. Graham Keech, *Pozières* (Barnsley: Leo Cooper, 1998), p. 55.
11. 10 Australian Battalion account in the 3rd Infantry Brigade War Diary.
12. 144 Brigade, 'Report on attack 12.30 a.m. 23rd July', in 1/6 Gloucesters War Diary July 1916, WO 95/2758.
13. Ibid.
14. Miles, *1916 V2*, pp. 144–5.
15. Keech,*Pozières*, p. 57.
16. Ibid.
17. Ibid., pp. 58–9.
18. *Bean*, Australian Official History, p. 549.
19. 'Report on Operations of First Australian Division'.
20. Account of Sergeant E. J. Rule, quoted in C. E. W. Bean, *Anzac to Amiens* (Canberra: Australian War Memorial, 1961), p. 249.
21. The success achieved by this division and most other Australian divisions on the Somme was ascribed by the Official Historian to the leadership qualities of brigade and battalion commanders. The fact is that such undoubted qualities as these men exhibited were useless without proper fire support.
22. 'Report on Action of 28th/29th July', 2 Australian Division, AWM 26/6/56/4.
23. Patrol Reports from 5 Australian Brigade 28/7/16, AWM 26/6/63A/1A.
24. Report on Action 28/29 July by 2 Australian Division.
25. Ibid.
26. These points are taken from Section 6, 'Deductions' in the above document.
27. 2 Australian Division, 'Report on Action of 4th/5th August', AWM 26/6/56/4.
28. Neil Malcolm to Birdwood 3/8/16, AWM 26/6/30/15.
29. Birdwood to Reserve Army HQ 4/8/16, ibid.
30. *Bean*, Australian Official History, p. 724.
31. Reserve Army Operation Order SG 21/8/16, AWM 26/6/42/3.
32. Reserve Army Operation Order 20/8/16, ibid.
33. See Chapter 20 for details of Haig's plan.
34. *Bean*, Australian Official History, p. 763.
35. Ibid., p. 731.
36. 1 Anzac Corps Royal Artillery War Diary 21/8/16, AWM 26/6/2/52.
37. Ibid.
38. Ibid.
39. 'Operations carried out by the 7th East Surrey Regt on the night of the 12/13th August 1916 near Ovillers', in their War Diary Aug. 1916, WO 95/1862.
40. 1/8 Royal Warwickshire War Diary 27/8/16, WO 95/2756.
41. Lt Rhodes to Major Herbert 7.30 p.m. 14/6/16. Private collection of 50 battalion records kindly made available by Ashley Ekins.
42. Quoted in *Bean*, Australian Official History, p. 763.
43. 13 Battalion message in AWM 26/6/60/6.
44. *Bean*, Australian Official History, p. 763.
45. See the messages in AWM 26/6/60/6.
46. *Bean*, Australian Official History, p. 769.
47. Ibid.
48. Ibid., p. 770.
49. Ibid.

## 17 Summary, 15 July–12 September

1. The casualty statistics for the Somme are summarised in a useful untitled doument in the Australian War Memorial which divides the actions of each division into periods and gives the casualties for each of them. However, the casualties for some divisions are not given exactly for the period under discussion here and on occasions we have had to make estimates.

The figures for the three Australian divisions which fought on the Somme, strangely, are not included but they can easily be obtained from the Australian Official History.

2. The number of attacks made by a division has been calculated from McCarthy, *The Somme Day by Day* and *Bean*, supplemented where necessary by the war diaries.
3. These figures come from a table, 'Statement Showing Number of Days Each Division Has Been in Front Line in Somme Battle from 1st July to 23rd November, 1916', in AWM 252/A106.
4. These figures have been derived from McCarthy, *The Somme*, the Official History, and the war diaries.
5. We know that it is the case from a series of maps showing the locations of the German guns in WO 153/1218.
6. M. H. Dendry to Edmonds 16/6/34, CAB 45/133.
7. See *Field Service Regulations* (London: HMSO, 1909) for the paucity of advice offered by official doctrine.
8. These statistics and comments come from a book compiled by the American Expeditionary Force Intelligence Section entitled, *Histories of Two Hundred and Fifty-One Divisions of the German Army which Participated in the War (1914–1918)* (London: Stamp Exchange, 1989). (Reprint of the 1920 edition.)
9. Figures derived from 'Fourth Army Ammunition Expenditure', in 'Battle of The Somme: Artillery Notes and Statistics'. To these figures (6.25 million) have been added one quarter of this total to include shells fired by the Reserve Army which are not otherwise available.
10. *Der Weltkrieg V10*, p. 374.
11. The number of German counter-attacks has been calculated from those mentioned in the Fourth Army 'Somme telegrams' and a proportional estimate for those carried out against the Reserve Army. The number should undoubtedly be taken as a minimum as many small counter-attacks would have gone unrecorded. The number for the British has been calculated from McCarthy and the Official History.

## 18 The Politicians and the Somme Campaign, July–August

1. Hankey Diary 3/7/16, Churchill College, Cambridge.
2. Robertson to Kiggell 5/7/16, Kiggell Papers IV, Liddell Hart Centre, King's College, London.
3. War Committee Minutes 11/7/16, CAB 42/16/6.
4. Ibid.
5. Ibid.
6. War Committee Minutes 6/7/16, CAB 42/16/1.
7. This and the previous quotations are taken from the War Committee Minutes 18/7/16, CAB 42/16/8.
8. War Committee Minutes 20/7/16, CAB 42/16/10.
9. Ibid.
10. Ibid.
11. Ibid.
12. War Committee Minutes 28/7/16, CAB 42/16/11.
13. Quoted in John Grigg, *Lloyd George: From Peace to War 1912–1916* (London: Methuen, 1985), p. 378. Readers seeking a more detailed examination of Lloyd George's role in this period should read this fine biography.
14. All quotations from this document are taken from the copy in W. S. Churchill, *The World Crisis* (London: Thornton Butterworth, 1927), Part 3, pp. 187–92.
15. Robertson to Haig 7/8/16, quoted in *The Military Correspondence of Field Marshal Sir William Robertson, Chief of the Imperial General Staff, December 1915–February 1918*, ed. David R. Woodward (London: Bodley Head, for the Army Records Society, 1989),

p. 79 In the same letter, Robertson referred to 'Winston … and various degommed [i.e. sacked] people' as 'the swines'.

16. Robertson Paper for the War Committee 1/8/16, CAB 42/17/1. In a letter to Haig written at the same time, Robertson said that he had presented German casualties to the War Committee at 750,000. But he repeats the figure of 'dead loss' (the crucial figure) as being 600,000. See Woodward, *Correspondence of Sir William Robertson*, p. 76.
17. War Committee Minutes 5/8/16, CAB 42/17/3.
18. Ibid.
19. Ibid.
20. Ibid.
21. Robertson to Haig 8/8/16, ibid., pp. 79–80.
22. For Lloyd George's comments see the War Committee Minutes 10/8/16, CAB 42/17/5.
23. Ibid.
24. War Committee Minutes 18/8/16, CAB 42/17/11.
25. This and previous quotations are ibid.
26. Ibid.
27. War Committee Minutes 30/8/16, CAB 42/18/16.

## 19 One Division's Somme

1. Statement showing number of days each division has been in the front line in the Somme Battle from 1 July to 31 October 1916, WO 153/1265.
2. 'Casualties by divisions', an untitled document in the Australian War Memorial, listing casualties suffered by all divisions during the Somme, AWM 252/206.
3. This figure has been arrived at by adding most of those listed as missing to the 'killed' category.
4. These figures have been calculated from the war diaries of the division and its constituent parts. These are: 1 Division, WO 95/1231; 1 Brigade, WO 95/1266; 2 Brigade WO 95/1273; 3 Brigade, WO 95/1276; 10 Gloucester, 8 Royal Berkshire, WO 95/1265; 1 Cameron, WO 95/1264; 1 Black Watch, WO 95/1263; 2 Royal Sussex, WO 95/1269; 1 Loyal North Lancashire, WO 95/1270; 1 KRRC, WO 95/1270; 1 Northamptonshire, WO 95/1271; 1 South Wales Borderers, WO 95/1280; 2 Welch, WO 95/1281; 2 Royal Munster Fusiliers, WO 95/1279; 1 Gloucester, WO 95/1278.
5. 2 South Wales Borderers War Diary, WO 95/1280.
6. Ibid., 25/7/16.
7. Ibid., 28/7/16.
8. Ibid., 1–4/8/16.
9. Ibid., 13/8/16.
10. Ibid.
11. Ibid., 5/8/16.
12. Ibid., 6/8/16.
13. Ibid., 9/8/16.
14. Ibid., 10/8/16.
15. Ibid., 8/8/16.
16. Ibid., 12/8/16.
17. Ibid., 1/8/16.
18. 1 Black Watch War Diary July 1916, WO 95/1263.
19. Brigadier-General A. W. Pagan, *Infantry: An Account of the 1st Gloucester Regiment during the War 1914–1918* (Aldershot: Gale & Polden, 1951), p. 95.
20. Ibid.
21. 2 Welch War Diary 12/7/16.
22. 1 Gloucester War Diary 19, 20, 21/7/16.
23. 1 Northamptonshire War Diary 12/7/16.
24. Ibid.
25. 1 South Wales Borderers War Diary 14/7/16.
26. Ibid.
27. Ibid., 15/7/16.
28. Ibid., 17/7/16.
29. Ibid., 18/7/16.
30. 10 Gloucesters War Diary 10–14/7/16.
31. 2 Royal Sussex War Diary 14–17/8/16.
32. Ibid., 19–21/8/16.
33. All the above details can be found in the 2 Welch War Diary.

34. See their respective war diaries for these details.
35. 2 Royal Munster Fusiliers Report on operations 24/8/16 in their War Diary.
36. 8 Royal Berkshire War Diary 18/8/16.
37. See their respective war diaries for these details.
38. 1 Gloucester War Diary 16-17/7/16.
39. 3 Brigade War Diary July 1916.

## 20 'An Operation Planned on Bolder Lines'

1. Haig Diary 16/8/16, National Library of Scotland.
2. Haig to Rawlinson 16/8/16 (OAD 111), AWM 26/6/41/41.
3. Ibid.
4. Haig to Rawlinson 19/8/16 (OAD 116), AWM 26/6/41/41.
5. Haig Diary 26/8/16.
6. Rawlinson Diary 26/8/16, Churchill College, Cambridge.
7. Ibid., 28/8/16.
8. Ibid.
9. Rawlinson to GHQ 28/8/16, Fourth Army Papers V5, IWM.
10. Ibid.
11. Haig Diary 29/8/16.
12. Haig to Rawlinson 31/8/16 (OAD 132), Fourth Army Papers V3, IWM.
13. Ibid.
14. All quotations are from Haig to Rawlinson and Gough 1/9/16 (but written 31/8/16) (OAD 131), in AWM 26/6/41/43.
15. See *Das K.B. 14 Infanterie Regiment Hartmann* (Munich, 1931), pp. 174–8; Major Hetzer, *Das K.B. 9 Infanterie Regiment Wrede* (Munich: Schlick, 1928), p. 92; Major A. Ritter, *Das K.B. 18 Infanterie Regiment Prinz Ludwig-Ferdinand* (Munich: Bayerisches Kriegsarchiv, 1926), pp. 154–9.
16. *K.B. 18*, p. 151.
17. See for example the account in *Das K.B. 10 Infanterie Regiment König* (Munich: Bayerisches Kriegsarchiv, 1925), pp. 245–52.
18. GHQ–, 'Notes on Tank Organisation and Equipment' in Miles *1916 V2* Appendices, Appendix 15, pp. 39–45; Trevor Pidgeon, *The Tanks at Flers V1*, 2 vols (Cobham, Surrey: Fairmile, 1995), pp. 34–5.
19. David J. Childs, *A Peripheral Weapon? The Production and Employment of British Tanks in the First World War* (Westport, Conn.: Greenwood, 1999), p. 127.
20. These and other quotations are all taken from the minutes of a conference at Fourth Army Headquarters, 31/8/16, Rawlinson Papers, Churchill College, Cambridge, 1/6.
21. All quotations taken from Rawlinson to Haig 31/8/16, Fourth Army Papers V2, IWM.
22. Rawlinson Diary 2/9/16.
23. Ibid., 6/9/16.
24. Haig to Rawlinson 7/9/16, Fourth Army Papers V5.
25. Haig to Rawlinson 4/9/16, AWM 252/A102.
26. Haig to Bacon 10/9/16, ibid.
27. Haig to Gough 13/9/16, ibid.
28. Ibid.
29. 'Note of a Conference held at Fourth Army Headquarters, 5th September, 1916', Fourth Army Papers V6, IWM. Subsequent quotations about the plan come from this document.
30. Ibid., emphasis added.
31. 'Battle of the Somme: Artillery Notes and Statistics'.
32. The length of trench to be attacked has been calculated by the same methods employed for the other battles.
33. Haig to Rawlinson and Gough 13/9/16 (OAD 146), WO 158/246.
34. Ibid.
35. Rawlinson Diary 14/9/16.
36. See OAD 146 quoted earlier and GHQ/Fourth Army Conference 14/9/16 (OAD 148), WO 158/246.
37. Haig Diary 10/9/16.

## 21 Lumbering Tanks

1. For weather conditions see Haig's Diary 12, 13, 14 Sept. 1916, National Library of Scotland.
2. Cecil Lewis, *Sagittarius Rising* (London: Corgi, 1969), pp. 102–3. (reprint of 1936 edn).
3. 'Operations of 169th Brigade on Somme Front', AWM 26/6/44/43; 1/1 Londons War Diary 15/9/16, WO 95/2949.
4. 'Operations of 169th Brigade'; See also an untitled account in 56 Division War Diary 15/9/16, WO 95/2932.
5. 'Centre Divisional Artillery, XIV Corps, Operation Order No.3', in 6 Divison War Diary 12/9/15, WO 95/1582.
6. A convincing argument for this interpretation is made by Trevor Pidgeon in *The Tanks at Flers*, pp. 77–8. This chapter owes much to the meticulous research in Pidgeon's book.
7. Note by GOC 6 Division to XIV Corps, 6 Division War Diary Sept. 1916.
8. Ibid.
9. 16 Brigade War Diary 15/9/16, WO95/1605; 'Operations of the 6th Division Between the 12th–18th September, 1916, at the Quadrilateral', 6 Division War Diary.
10. Ibid.
11. Pidgeon, *The Tanks at Flers*, pp. 96–8.
12. See the 1 Coldstream and 3 Grenadiers War Diaries, both in WO 95/1217, for a sense of the confusion which accompanied the attack.
13. This is the rather quaint name given to the tanks by the war diarist of 1 Scots Guards. See their War Diary for 15/9/16 in WO 95/1219. The name helps remind us of the novelty of the weapon.
14. Untitled account by GOC Guards Division in 2 Grenadiers War Diary 15/9/16, WO 95/1215.
15. 2 Grenadiers War Diary 15/9/16.
16. 3 Grenadiers War Diary 15/9/16, WO 95/1217.
17. 1 Irish Guards War Diary 15/9/16, WO 95/1216.
18. Ibid.
19. 3 Grenadiers War Diary 15/9/16.
20. See GOC 6 Division account quoted on p. 232.
21. 3 Canadian Division was attacking with the 2nd but its task was merely to keep pace with any progress made by that division.
22. Pidgeon, *The Tanks at Flers*, p. 127.
23. Untitled report of operations by 4 Canadian Brigade in their War Diary, WO 95/3811.
24. Ibid.
25. Account by Lt-Col. Coutlie (42 Canadian Battalion) quoted in Paul Reed, *Courcelette* (London: Leo Cooper, 1998) p. 56.
26. *Histories of Two Hundred and Fifty-one Divisions of the German Army which participated in the War, 1914-1918* (Washington, 1920), p. 465.
27. 5 Canadian Brigade War Diary 15/9/16, WO 95/3820.
28. 46 Brigade, 'Narrative of Events from 12th September, 1916 to 17th September, 1916', 46 Brigade War Diary 15/9/16, WO 95/1913.
29. See 10/11 Highland Light Infantry, 'Report on Operations 13th to 17th September, 1916', WO 95/1952; 10 Cameronians (Scottish Rifles) War Diary 15/9/16, WO 95/1954.
30. Ibid.
31. Lt-Col. J. Stewart and John Buchan, *The Fifteenth (Scottish) Division 1914–1919* (Edinburgh: Blackwood, 1926), p. 93.
32. '50th Division, September 1916', 50 Division War Diary, WO 95/2809.
33. Ibid.
34. Edward Wyrall, *The History of the 50th Division 1914–1919* (London: Lund Humphries, 1939), pp. 149–50.
35. W. Muirhead-Murray to Edmonds 16/5/35, CAB 45/136.

36. 47th (London) Division Operation Order No.99, 47 Division War Diary Sept. 1916, WO 95/2701.
37. Ibid.
38. Pidgeon, *The Tanks at Flers*, p. 108.
39. 47 Division, 'Report on Operations 15th–19th September 1916', 47 Division War Diary, Sept. 1916.
40. Pidgeon, *The Tanks at Flers*, p. 105.
41. 1/6 London War Diary 15/9/16, WO 95/2729.
42. Pidgeon, *The Tanks at Flers*, p. 106.
43. G. de Caux to Colonel Gore-Browne 30/9/19, Gore-Browne Papers, IWM, 88/52/1.
44. Alan H. Maude, *The 47th (London) Division 1914–1919* (London: Amalgamated Press, 1922), p. 65.
45. See, for example, the War Diary of 8 Somerset Light Infantry 15/9/16, WO 95/1902, which was operating on this flank.
46. 8 King's Royal Rifle Corps War Diary 15/9/16, WO 95/1895.
47. 7 Rifle Brigade War Diary 15/9/16, WO 95/1896.
48. 'Report of Action at Flers By 122 Infantry Brigade' (41 Division), 122 Brigade War Diary, WO 95/2632.
49. Account by 2 New Zealand Brigade in their War Diary, WO 95/3693.
50. 'Operations of the New Zealand Division 15/9/16', Fourth Army Papers, V3, IWM.
51. Ibid.; Report by 122 Brigade.
52. 'Operations of the 41st Division', Fourth Army Papers, V3.
53. 'Operations of the New Zealand Division'.
54. 'Operations of the 41st Division'.
55. 'Operations of the New Zealand Division'.

## 22 25 September

1. Fourth Army Operation Order 15/9/16, Fourth Army Papers, V8, IWM.
2. Haig Diary 17/9/16, National Library of Scotland.
3. Rawlinson Diary 20/9/16, Churchill College, Cambridge.
4. Haig Diary 21/9/16.
5. Ibid.
6. Ibid.
7. 'Notes on Operations between 14th September and 8th October 1916', Rawlinson Papers, RAGVQ 2522/2/79, NAM.
8. 'Operations of the 6th Division between the 12th–18th September, 1916, at the Quadrilateral', 6 Division War Diary Sept. 1916, WO 95/1582.
9. Ibid.
10. Account of Lt-Col. H.M. Dillon, uncatalogued, IWM.
11. 14 Northumberland Fusiliers War Diary 21/9/16, WO 95/2828.
12. Ibid.
13. 1 Cameron Highlanders War Diary 21/9/16, WO 95/1264.
14. 'Report on Operations of 23rd Division from 19th September to 8th October, 1916', 23 Division War Diary Sept. 1916, WO 95/2168.
15. See his 'Notes on Operations between 14th September and 8th October', quoted above.
16. 'Battle of the Somme: Artillery Notes and Statistics', Table C. This table gives the number of shells used. The weight of shell devoted to trench destruction is based on the figure for 15 September and adjusted for the lesser number of shells. The length of trench attacked has been calculated by the usual method.
17. XIV Corps Operation Order No. 59, 20/9/16, XIV Corps War Diary Sept. 1916, WO 95/911.
18. 'Account of Operations carried out by 56th Division During Sept. and October 1916', 56 Division War Diary September 1916, WO 95/2932.
19. 'Narrative of operations carried out by XIV Corps against LesBoeuf, Morval and Combles on September 25th, 26th, 27th, and 28th', XIV Corps War Diary Sept. 1916.

20. 1 Norfolk War Diary 25/9/16, WO 95/1573.
21. General Fielding (GOC Guards Division) to Cavan 26/9/16, Guards Division War Diary Sept. 1916, WO 95/1191.
22. 2 Grenadiers, 'Narrative of events for 24th–25th Sept 1916', WO 95/1215.
23. Ibid.
24. Ibid.
25. 'Narrative of operations carried out by XIV Corps … on September 25th'.
26. Ibid.
27. 9 Leicesters War Diary 25/9/16, WO 95/2165.
28. 'Operations of the 21st Division, 15th September–1st October 1916', 21 Division War Diary Sept. 1916, WO 95/2131.
29. 1 East Yorkshire War Diary 25/9/16, WO 95/2161.
30. Ibid.
31. 'Operations of the 21st Division'.
32. 'An account of operation on morning of Sept. 26th in which a "Tank" was employed', 21 Division War Diary September 1916.
33. 6 Leicesters War Diary 25/9/16, WO 95/2164.
34. The quotation comes from Colonel H. Stewart, *The New Zealand Division 1916–1919: A Popular History Based on Official Records* (Auckland: Whitcombe & Tombs, 1921), p. 99.
35. Miles, *1916 V2*, p. 381.
36. Ibid., pp. 382–4; Jones, *War in the Air V2*, pp. 285–7.

## 23 'The Tragic Hill of Thiepval', 26–30 September

1. F. Scott Fitzgerald, *Tender is the Night* (Harmondsworth: Penguin, 1986), p. 124.
2. All quotations are taken from a file regarding this fiasco in the 49 Division War Diary for Sept. 1916, WO95/2766.
3. Miles, *1916 V2*, p. 393.
4. General Maxse, 'The 18th Division in the Battle of Ancre', 18 Division War Diary Sept. 1916, WO 95/2015.
5. 6 Canadian Brigade Operations 26–30 Sept., WO 95/3807.
6. Miles, *1916 V2*, pp. 396–7.
7. 9 Lancashire Fusiliers 'Report on Attack – September 26th–28th, 1916', in their War Diary 26/9/16, WO 95/1820.
8. 11 Manchester War Diary 26/9/16, WO 95/1821.
9. 34 Brigade War Diary 26/9/16, WO 95/1818.
10. 'G.O.C's Comments on the Late Operations 26/9/16–1/10/16', 11 Division War Diary Sept. 1916, WO 95/1806.
11. 9 Lancashire Fusiliers 'Report on Attack'; 8 Northumberland Fusiliers 'Report on Operations for week ending 30th September 1916' in their War Diary 26/9/16, WO 95/1821.
12. 8 Northumberland Fusiliers 'Report on Operations'.
13. Miles, *1916 V2*, p. 401.
14. Ibid.
15. 9 West Yorkshire War Diary 27/9/16, WO 95/1809.
16. 'Report on the Operations of the 32nd Infantry Brigade during the attack on Stuff Redoubt and Hessian Trench from the 26th September 1916 to 30th September 1916', 32 Brigade War Diary Sept. 1916, WO 95/1806.
17. 32 Brigade, 'Report on Operations'.
18. Maxse, '18th Division in the Battle of Ancre'.
19. 'Report on the Operations carried out by the 53rd Infantry Brigade in the Thiepval area from 24th–29th Sept. 1916', Maxse Papers 69/53/9, IWM.
20. Ibid.
21. Ibid.
22. 'Report on Operations of the 54th Infantry Brigade during the capture of Thiepval and the subsequent attack on the Schwaben Redoubt' 26–28 Sept. 1916, Maxse Papers, 69/53/9.
23. Ibid.
24. Ibid.
25. Ibid.
26. 'Narrative of the part played by the 6th Battalion Northamptonshire

Regiment in the capture of Thiepval on the 26th September 1916', 6 Northampton War Diary Sept. 1916, WO 95/2044.
27. 7 Bedfords War Diary 27/9/16, 'Account of Captain L.H. Keys', WO 95/2043.
28. Maxse, 'The 18th Division in the Battle of Ancre'.
29. 7 Queen's 'Short Description of the Action of Sept. 28th 1916', 7 Queen's War Diary Sept. 1916, WO 95/2051.
30. Maxse, 'The 18th Division in the Battle of Ancre'.
31. Ibid.
32. 8 East Surrey, 'Report on the attack on the north face of the Schwaben Redoubt – September 30th', 8 East Surrey War Diary Sept. 1916, WO 95/2050.
33. Ibid.
34. 18 Division 'Report on operations for week ending 6 p.m. October 6th, 1916', 18 Division War Diary Sept. 1916.
35. Ibid.
36. Maxse 'The 18th Division in the Battle of Ancre'.

## 24 'A Severe Trial of Body and Spirit'

1. Ellis to the Ministry of Munitions 30/9/16, WO 158/836.
2. Miles, *1916 V2*, pp. 382–4; Jones, *War in the Air V2*, pp. 285–7.
3. Haig to Third, Fourth, Reserve Armies 29/9/16 (OAD 159), WO 158/246.
4. All quotations in this section are taken from Haig's diary entry of 30/9/16. Haig Diary, National Library of Scotland.
5. Some of this detail is elaborated by Haig in his diary entry of 1/10/16.
6. Haig manuscript diary.
7. See Miles, *1916 V2*, pp. 449–51 for Canadian operations and pp. 432–4 for III Corps' operations.
8. 'Report on operations of 23rd Division from 19th September, 1916 to 8th October, 1916', 23 Division War Diary Sept. 1916, WO 95/2168.
9. Ibid.
10. Miles, *1916 V2*, p. 455, n. ii.
11. '20th (Light) Division Operations 6th, 7th and 8th October, 1916', 20 Division War Diary Oct. 1916, WO 95/2095.
12. 1/7 London (47 Division) War Diary 7/10/16, WO 95/2730; 12 Division War Diary 7/10/16, WO 95/1824.
13. 'Operations of 189 Brigade (56 Division) on the Somme Front', AWM 26/6/49/43; 124 Brigade (41 Division) Report of Operations 7/10/16, 124 Brigade War Diary Oct. 1916, WO 95/2640.
14. 23 Division, 'Report on Operations – October 1916', 23 Division War Diary Oct. 1916.
15. Comments by du Cane on 41 Division Reasons for Failure on 7/10/16, in XV Corps War Diary Oct. 1916, WO 95/922.
16. 3 Canadian Division, 'Narrative of Operations from 3rd October to 11th October, 1916', 3 Canadian Division War Diary Oct. 1916, WO 95/3837.
17. Ibid.
18. Haig Diary 8/10/16.
19. Fourth Army Summary of Operations, 7 Oct., 1916, Fourth Army War Diary, Fourth Army Papers V4, IWM.
20. 30 Division, 'Report on Operations 30 Division: October 1916', 30 Division War Diary Oct. 1916, WO 95/2311.
21. Ibid.
22. 4 Division, 'Narrative 12/10/16', 4 Division War Diary Oct. 1916, WO 95/1445.
23. See their respective war diaries for 12/10/16 in WO 95/1445, WO 95/1610, and WO 95/1858.
24. Royal Irish Fusiliers War Diary 12/10/16, WO 95/1482.
25. Ibid.
26. Rawlinson Diary 12/10/16, Churchill College, Cambridge.
27. Report of a conference at Heilly 13/10/16, AWM 26/6/41/46.
28. Fourth Army Document 299/48(G), 12/10/16, in AWM 26/6/41/46.
29. Rawlinson Diary 13/10/16; Conference

at Heilly 13/10/16.

30. Haig Diary 14/10/16.
31. Miles, *1916 V2*, p. 443, n.1.
32. Rawlinson Diary 6/10/16.
33. Ibid.
34. Haig to Robertson 7/10/16, WO 158/21 (Commander-in-Chief, CIGS, Secretary of State for War Correspondence).
35. Ibid.
36. Ibid.
37. See 4 Division 'Narrative 18/10/16' in 4 Division War Diary 18/10/16; Rawlinson in his diary for 13/10/16 is commenting that the state of the ground did not allow an extension of his light rail system to bring shells to the front.
38. 1 East Lancashire War Diary 18/10/16, WO 95/1498.
39. Ibid.
40. Miles, *1916 V2*, pp. 457–8.
41. G.P. MacClellan to Edmonds, 15/10/1936, CAB 45/134.
42. Haig to Gough and Rawlinson 18/10/16 (OAD 182), AWM 26/6/105/35.
43. Fourth Army Conference 18/10/16 in Fourth Army Papers V6, IWM.
44. 4 Division 'Narrative 23/10/16', 4th Division War Diary Oct. 1916; 8th Division 'Report on Operations Octr. 19th–30th 1916', in 8 Division War Diary Oct. 1916, WO 95/1675.
45. 25 Brigade 'Report on Operations Octr. 19th–30th 1916', 25 Brigade War Diary Oct. 1916, WO 95/1675.
46. Captain R.O. Russell, *The History of the 11th (Lewisham) Battalion, The Queen's Own, Royal West Kent Regiment* (London: Lewisham Newspaper Co., 1934), p. 78.
47. 'Report by Major Gort 3/11/16', AWM 45, Bundle 31.
48. Lt.-Col. J. H. Boraston and Captain Cyril E.O. Bax, *The Eighth Division in War, 1914–1918* (London: Medici Society, 1926), pp. 87–8.
49. C. E. Hudson to Edmonds 28/2/36, CAB 45/134.
50. Ibid.
51. Haig Diary 22/10/16.
52. Cavan to Rawlinson 3/11/16, AWM 45, Bundle 31.
53. Haig to Rawlinson (OAD 205). This is an untitled, undated document summarising letters relating to the attack on 5 November in Fourth Army Papers V5, IWM.
54. Rawlinson Diary 3/11/16.
55. Cavan to Edmonds 9/4/36, CAB 45/132.
56. Haig to Rawlinson (OAD 205).
57. Ibid.
58. *Bean*, Australian Official History, p. 915.

## 25 'We Must Keep Going!'

1. Asquith's report and the subsequent discussion are taken from the War Committee Minutes 12/9/16, CAB 42/19/6.
2. War Committee Minutes 18/9/16, CAB 42/20/3.
3. Robertson's remarks and the subsequent discussion are taken from the War Committee Minutes of 12/9/16, CAB 42/19/6.
4. Robertson to Haig 7/9/16 quoted in David R. Woodward (ed.), *Military Correspondence of Field Marshal Sir William Robertson: Chief of the Imperial General Staff, December 1915–1918*, p. 85.
5. War Committee Minutes 9/10/16, CAB 42/21/3.
6. Ibid.
7. Ibid.
8. Ibid.
9. Hankey Diary 12/10/16, Churchill College, Cambridge.
10. The correspondence between Robertson and Lloyd George is to be found in Woodward (ed.), *Correspondence of Sir William Robertson*, pp. 90–6.
11. War Committee Minutes 24/10/16, CAB 42/2/5.
12. See the War Committee Minutes 9/10/16, CAB 42/21/3.

## 26 The Political Battle

1. 25 Division, 'Somme Battle', AWM 26/6/48/43.
2. Ibid.
3. 16 Sherwood Foresters War Diary 9/10/16, WO 95/2587.
4. 4/5 Black Watch, 'An account of the action at the Schwaben Redoubt' 14/10/16, 4/5 Black Watch War Diary Oct. 1916, WO 95/2591.
5. 'Operations of the 1/1st, The Cambridgeshire Regiment 14th–16th October 1916' 1/1 Cambridgeshire War Diary Oct. 1916, WO 95/2590.
6. 25 Division, 'Somme Battle'.
7. Ibid.
8. Reserve Army Operation Order No. 32, 15/10/16, AWM 252/A112.
9. Ibid.
10. Haig to Rawlinson and Gough (OAD 182), 18/10/16, AWM 26/6/105/35.
11. Reserve Army Operation Order No. 33, 21/10/16, WO 158/256.
12. Haig to Gough 24/10/16 (OAD 187), WO 158/256.
13. For the weather conditions at the front see Haig's diary, National Library of Scotland, or the very useful chronology in Gliddon, *The Battle of the Somme*, pp. 415–24.
14. Haig to Gough 3/11/16 (OAD 199), WO 158/246.
15. Haig to Gough 5/11/16 (OAD 207), WO 158/246.
16. 'Memorandum on Operations' by Neil Malcolm 13/11/16, WO 158/256.
17. Ibid.
18. Ibid.
19. Haig Diary 12/11/16.
20. Ibid.
21. 'Report on Machine Gun Work during recent operations at Beaumont Hamel', 51 Division War Diary, WO 95/2845.
22. 51 Division Operation Orders 22/10/16, ibid.
23. 'Report of Operations of XIII Corps for Week ending 6 p. m. 17.11.16', XIII Corps War Diary Nov. 1916, WO 95/896; George Lindsay (3 Division) to Edmonds 25/1/37, CAB 45/134.
24. 2 Royal Sussex, 'Report on Operations November 13th', 2 Royal Sussex War Diary Nov. 1916, WO 95/1437.
25. See 1 King's and 17 Middlesex War Diaries for 13 Nov., 1916 in WO 95/1359 and WO 95/1361 respectively.
26. Miles, *1916 V2*, p. 492.
27. Ibid.
28. 51 Division, 'Report on Operations of November 13th–15th Including the Capture of Beaumont Hamel', 51 Division War Diary Nov. 1916.
29. Ibid.
30. Ibid.
31. V Corps 'Summary of Operations, November 11th–17th, 1916', V Corps War Diary, Nov. 1916, WO 95/747.
32. Martin Middlebrook, *Your Country Needs You* (Barnsley: Leo Cooper, 2000), pp. 37–8.
33. 63 Division, untitled narrative, 63 Division War Diary Nov. 1916, WO 95/3093.
34. 4/5 Black Watch War Diary 13/11/16, WO 95/2591.
35. 39 Division, 'Report on the Battle of the Ancre: 13th November 1916', 39 Division War Diary Nov. 1916, WO 95/2565.
36. Miles, *1916 V2*, pp. 504–8.
37. Haig Diary 15/11/16.
38. Note by CGS (Kiggell) OAD 279, 17/11/16, WO 158/246.
39. Ibid.
40. Haig Diary 16/11/16.
41. Note by CGS 17/11/16.
42. V Corps 'Summary of Operations 18th–25th November, 1916', V Corps War Diary, Nov. 1916.
43. II Corps Operations 19/10–1/12 1916, II Corps War Diary, Nov. 1916, WO 95/638.
44. Miles, *1916 V2*, pp. 414–22.
45. L. W. Kentish to Edmonds 19/11/36, CAB 45/135.
46. Rawlinson to GHQ 7/11/16, Fourth Army Papers V5, IWM.

## 27 Reflections on the British at the Somme

1. Winston S. Churchill, *The World Crisis 1916–1918*, Part 1 (London: Thornton Butterworth, 1927), Table B, facing p. 52.
2. Great Britain, War Office Statistics of the Military Effort of the British Empire, 1914–1920, (London: War Office, 1922).

## 28 Epilogue

1. All quotations in this chapter are drawn from the War Committee Minutes of 3/11/16, CAB 42/22/13.
2. Frances Stevenson's Diary, 12/1/7, quoted in *Lloyd George: A Diary by Frances Stevenson* (London: Hutchinson, 1971), p. 139.

# Bibliography


## 1. Official Manuscript Collections

### *Cabinet Papers, Public Record Office, Kew*

CAB 42 War Committee Minutes and Conclusions (Microfilm)
CAB 45 Postwar Official History Correspondence

### *War Office Papers, Public Record Office, Kew*

WO 95 Operational War Diaries
WO 106 Directorate of Military Operations Files
WO 153 Operational Artillery Maps
WO 157 Directorate of Military Intelligence Files
WO 158 Miscellaneous Operations Files

### *Australian War Memorial Records, Canberra*

AWM 26 Operations Files, 1914–18 War
AWM 45 Copies of British war diaries and other records
AWM 51 AWM security classified records (a series of operational documents and high-level correspondence between GHQ and army commanders)
AWM 252 Miscellaneous high-level British records

## 2. Private Papers

### *Imperial War Museum, London*

Major A.J. Anderson
Lieutenant R.J. Blackadder
Major A.E. Bundy
A.P. Burke
F.L. Cassel
Captain G.N. Clark
Major R.S. Cockburn
Lieutenant-Colonel E.H.E. Collen
Private F. Collins
R. Cude
Lieutenant-Colonel H.M. Dillon
Viscount Dillon
B.F. Eccles
Fourth Army Papers (46 vols)
S.T. Fuller

Captain L. Gameson
Captain L. Garrison
Colonel Gore-Browne
Captain J.T. Harrod
General H. Horne
Captain R. Leetham
Lieutenant Kenneth Macardle
Captain C.K. McKerrow
Sergeant F. de Margrey
General Sir I. Maxse
Captain C.C. May
Miscellaneous – 3/34 Artillery Tank Lane Map
Captain H.B. Owens
Captain D.H. Pegler
Major P.H. Pilditch
Lieutenant G.C. Pratt
Colonel F.J. Rice
Lieutenant W.B. St Leger
Sergeant F. Spencer
B.W. Whayman
Brigadier–General Whitfield
Lieutenant F. Wollcombe

### *Liddell Hart Centre for Military Archives, King's College, London*

Reverend John Bloxam
Lieutenant-General Sir Sidney Clive
Brigadier-General Sir James E. Edmonds
Lieutenant-General Sir L. Kiggell
Field Marshal Sir A.A. Montgomery-Massingberd
Field Marshal Sir William Robertson

### *Royal Artillery Institution, Woolwich*

Colonel E.G. Angus
Brigadier E.C. Anstey
Captain A.F. Becke
Lieutenant-Colonel A.H. Burne
Major T.H. Davidson
Lieutenant J. Hussey
Captain W.B. Mackie
Brigadier E.E. Mockler-Ferryman
Major S.W.H. Rawlins
Major-General Sir H.H. Tudor

### *Others*

Field Marshal Earl Cavan, Public Record Office, Kew
Field Marshal Sir Douglas Haig, National Library of Scotland, Edinburgh
Lord Hankey, Churchill College, Cambridge
General Sir Henry Rawlinson, Churchill College, Cambridge; National Army Museum, London
Major Clive Wigram, Royal Archives, Windsor

## 3 Books and Articles

American Expeditionary Force Intelligence Section, *Histories of Two Hundred and Fifty-One Divisions of the German Army which participated in the War (1914–1918)* (London: Stamp Exchange, 1989). Reprint of 1920 edn

Brigadier E.C. Anstey, 'History of the Royal Artillery' (unpublished)

*Les Armées françaises dans la grande guere*, 103 vols (Paris: Imprimerie Nationale 1922–38).

J. Ashurst, *My Bit: A Lancashire Fusilier at War 1914–1918*, ed. Richard Holmes (Marlborough: Crowood, 1987)

C.T. Atkinson, *The History of the South Wales Borderers, 1914–18* (London: Medici Society, 1931)

—— *The Queen's Own Royal West Kent Regiment, 1914–1919* (London: Simpkin Marshall, 1924)

—— *The Seventh Division, 1914–1918* (London: John Murray, 1927)

A.H. Atteridge, *History of the 17th Northern Division* (Glasgow: Maclehose, 1929)

Lt-Col. W.S. Austin, *The Official History of the New Zealand Rifle Brigade* (Wellington: Watkins, 1924)

T.M. Banks and R.A. Chell, *With the 10th Essex in France* (London: Gay & Hancock, 1924)

Corelli Barnett, *The Great War* (London: Hutchinson, 1979)

Omer Bartov, *Murder in Our Midst: The Holocaust, Industrial Killing and Representation* (New York: Oxford University Press, 1996)

C.E.W. Bean, *Official History of Australia in the War of 1914–18*, vol. 4: *The Australian Imperial Forces in France: 1916* (Sydney: Angus & Robertson, 1938)

——, *Anzac to Amiens* (Canberra: Australian War Memorial, 1961)

Major A.F. Becke, 'The Coming of the Creeping Barrage', *Journal of the Royal Artillery*, vol. 58, 1931–2, pp. 19–42

W.C. Belford, *Legs-Eleven: Being the Story of the 11th Battalion AIF in the Great War of 1914–1918* (Perth: Imperial Printing Co., 1940)

Ernest W. Bell, *Soldiers Killed on the First Day of the Somme* (Bolton: Bell, 1977)

S.G. Bennett, *The 4th Canadian Mounted Rifles 1914–1919* (Toronto: Murray Printing, 1926)

R. Berkeley, *The History of the Rifle Brigade in the War of 1914–1918* (London: Rifle Brigade Club, 1927)

Brevet-Col. B.A. Bethell, *Modern Guns and Gunnery* (Woolwich: Cattermole, 1910)

F.W. Bewsher, *History of the 51st (Highland) Division, 1914–1918* (Edinburgh: Blackwood, 1921)

John Bickersteth (ed.), *The Bickersteth Diaries 1914–1918* (London: Leo Cooper, 1996)

Shelford Bidwell, 'An Approach to Military History', *Army Quarterly*, Jan. 1949, pp. 243–6

—— *Gunners at War* (London: Arrow Books, 1972)

—— and Dominick Graham, *Coalitions, Politicians & Generals: Some Aspects of Command in Two World Wars* (London/New York: Brassey's, 1993)

—— and Dominick Graham, *Fire-Power: British Army Weapons and Theories of War, 1904–45* (London: Allen & Unwin, 1982)

Lt-Gen. Sir Noel Birch, 'Artillery Development in the Great War', *Army Quarterly*, vol. 1, 1920–21, pp. 79–89

Robert Blake (ed.), *The Private Papers of Douglas Haig*, 1914–1919 (London: Eyre & Spottiswoode, 1952)

Capt. O.G. Body, 'Lessons of the Great War: The Barrage versus Concentration on Selected Targets', *Journal of the Royal Artillery*, vol. 53, 1926, pp. 59–67

Lt-Col. J.H. Boraston, *Sir Douglas Haig's Despatches* (London: Dent, 1919)

Lt-Col. S.H. Boraston, and Cptn Cyril E.O. Bax, *The Eighth Division in War, 1914–1918* (London: Medici Society, 1926)

Lawrence Bragg and Others, *Artillery Survey in the First World War* (London: Field Survey Association, 1971)

V. Brahms, *The Spirit of the 42nd: Narrative of the 42nd Battalion, 11th Infantry Brigade, 3rd Division, Australian Imperial Forces, during the Great War* (Brisbane: 42nd Battalion AIF Association, 1938)

Lt-Col. C.N.F. Broad, 'Army Intelligence and Counter-battery Work', *Journal of the Royal Artillery*, vol. 49, 1922–3, pp. 187–98, 221–42

—— 'The Development of Artillery Tactics 1914–1918', *Journal of the Royal Artillery*, vol. 49, 1922–3, pp. 62–81, 127–48

Lt-Col. A.F. Brooke, 'The Evolution of Artillery in the Great War', *Journal of the Royal Artillery*, vol. 51, 1924–5, pp. 359–72; vol. 52, 1925–6, pp. 37–51, 369–87; vol. 53, pp. 233–49

Ian Malcolm Brown, *British Logistics on the Western Front 1914–1919* (Westport, Conn.: Praeger, 1998)

John Buchan, *The Battle of the Somme* (London: Nelson, 1917)

——*The History of the South African Forces in France* (London: Nelson, 1920)

J.W. Burrows, *The Essex Regiment* (Southend-on-Sea: Burrows & Son, 1931)

Lt J.R. Byrne, *New Zealand Artillery in the Field 1914–1918* (Auckland: Whitcombe & Tombs, 1922)

W.A. Carne, *In Good Company – An Account of the 5th Machine Gun Company AIF in Search of Peace 1915–19* (Melbourne: 5th Machine Gun Company, 1937)

George Cassar, *Kitchener: Architect of Victory* (London: Kimber, 1977)

N. Cave, *Beaumont Hamel* (London: Leo Cooper, 1994)

——, *Delville Wood* (Barnsley: Leo Cooper, 1999)

Brigadier-General John Charteris, *At G.H.Q.* (London: Cassell, 1931)

—— *Field Marshal Earl Haig* (London: Cassell, 1929)

T.P. Chataway, *History of the 15th Battalion, Australian Imperial Force: War of 1914–1918* (Brisbane: William Brooks, 1948)

David S. Childs, *A Peripheral Weapon? The Production and Employment of British Tanks in the First World War* (Westport, Conn.: Greenwood, 1999)

W.S. Churchill, *The World Crisis 1916–1918*, (London: Thornton Butterworth, 1927)

Captain E.J. Colliver and Lieutenant B.H. Richardson, *The Forty-Third: The Story and Official History of the 43rd Battalion, A.I.F.* (Adelaide: Rigby, 1920)

J.O. Coop, *The Story of the 55th Division* (Liverpool: Daily Post, 1919)

Duff Cooper, *Haig* (2 vols) (London: Faber & Faber, 1935)

D.J. Corrigall, *The History of the Twentieth Canadian Battalion (Central Ontario Regiment) Canadian Expeditionary Force in the Great War* (Toronto: Stony & Cox, 1935)

Lt-Col. W.D. Croft, 'The Influence of Tanks upon Tactics', *Journal of the Royal United Services Institute*, Feb. 1922, pp. 39–53

—— *Three Years with the 9th (Scottish) Division* (London: Murray, 1919)

A. Crookenden, *The History of the Cheshire Regiment in the Great War* (Chester: Crookenden, 1939)

C.M.F. Cruttwell, *A History of the Great War 1914–1918* (Oxford: Oxford University Press, 1934)

Major-General Sir John Davidson, *Haig: Master of the Field* (London: Peter Nevill, 1953)

A. Dean and E.W. Gutteridge, *The Seventh Battalion AIF: A Résumé of the Activities of the Seventh Battalion in the Great War, 1914–1918* (Melbourne: Dean & Gutteridge, 1933)

George A.B. Dewar and Lt-Col. J.H. Boraston, *Sir Douglas Haig's Command: December 19, 1915 to November 11, 1918* (2 vols) (London: Constable, 1922)

Sir James E. Edmonds, *Military Operations: France and Belgium 1916, Volume 1* (London: Macmillan, 1932)

J. Ewing, *History of the 9th (Scottish) Division, 1914–1919* (London: John Murray, 1921)

—— *The Royal Scots 1914–1919* (Edinburgh: Oliver & Boyd, 1925)

E. Fairey, *The 38th Battalion A.I.F.* (Bendigo: Bendigo Advertiser, 1920)

Cyril Falls, *History of the Thirty-Sixth (Ulster) Division* (London: McCaw Stevenson & Orr, 1922)

—— *Life of a Regiment*, vol. 4: *The Gordon Highlanders in the First World War, 1914–1919* (Aberdeen: Aberdeen University Press, 1958)

General Sir Martin Farndale, *History of the Royal Regiment of Artillery: Western Front* (Woolwich: Royal Artillery Institution, 1986)
A.H. Farrar-Hockley, *Goughie: The Life of General Sir Hubert Gough* (London: Hart-Davis/MacGibbon, 1975)
—— *The Somme* (London: Pan, 1970)
*Field Service Regulations* (London: HMSO, 1909)
R.R. Freeman, *Hurcombe's Hungry Half Hundred: A Memorial History of the 50th Battalion A.I.F., 1916–1919* (Adelaide: Peacock Publications, 1991)
David French and Brian Holden Reid (eds), *The British General Staff: Reform and Innovation c. 1890–1939* (London: Cass, 2002)
J.F.C. Fuller, *Tanks in the Great War* (London: John Murray, 1920)
S. Gillon, *Story of the 29th Division* (London: Nelson, 1925)
Gerald Gliddon, *The Battle of the Somme: A Topographical History* (Stroud: Sutton, 1996)
E.G. Godfrey, *The Cast-Iron Sixth: A History of the Sixth Battalion London Regiment* (London: Old Comrades Association, 1938)
E. Gorman, *'With the Twenty-Second': A History of the Twenty-Second Battalion, A.I.F. 1914–1919* (Melbourne: H.H. Champion, 1919)
Lt-Col. A.A. Goschen, 'Artillery Tactics', *Journal of the Royal Artillery*, vol. 52, 1924, pp. 254–60
General Sir Hubert Gough, *The Fifth Army* (London: Hodder & Stoughton, 1931)
Andrew S. Green, 'Sir James Edmonds and the Official Military Histories of the Great War 1915–1948' (Ph.D. thesis, University of Leeds, 1999)
Elizabeth Greenhalgh, 'A Study in Alliance Warfare: The Battle of the Somme 1916' (MA (Hons.) thesis, University of New South Wales, 1996)
W.E. Grey, *The 2nd City of London Regiment (Royal Fusiliers) in the Great War* (London: Regimental HQ, 1922)
Paddy Griffith, *Battle Tactics on the Western Front: The British Army's Art of Attack 1916–18* (New Haven/London: Yale University Press, 1994)
—— *Forward into Battle: Infantry Tactics from Waterloo to Vietnam* (London: Antony Bird, 1982)
John Grigg, *Lloyd George: From Peace to War 1912–1916* (London: Methuen, 1985)
F.C. Grimwade, *The War History of the 4th Battalion, the London Regiment (Royal Fusiliers), 1914–1919* (London: Regimental HQ, 1922)
Lt-Col. R.G.A. Hamilton (Master of Belhaven), *The War Diary of the Master of Belhaven 1914–1918* (London: John Murray, 1924)
Lord Hankey, *The Supreme Command, 1914–1918*, 2 vols (London: Allen & Unwin, 1961)
S. Hare, *The Annals of the King's Royal Rifle Corps* (London: John Murray, 1932)
Major H.C. Harrison, 'Calibration and Ranging', *Journal of the Royal Artillery*, vol. 47, 1920, pp. 265–8
B.H. Liddell Hart, *A History of the World War 1914–1918* (London: Faber, 1930)
—— *The Tanks*, vol. 1: *1914–1939* (London: Cassell, 1959)
Fred R. van Hartesveldt, *The Battles of the Somme: Historiography and Annoted Bibliography* (Westport, Conn.: Greenwood, 1996)
J. Hayes, *The Eighty Fifth in France and Flanders* (Halifax: Royal Print, 1920)
C. Headlam, *History of the Guards Division in the Great War* (London: John Murray, 1924)
J.Q. Henriques, *War History of the 1st Battalion, Queen's Westminster Rifles, 1914–1918* (London: Medici Society, 1923)
Major Hetzer, *Das K.B. 9, Infanterie Regiment Wrede* (Munich: Schlick 1928)
*Historical Records of the Queen's Own Cameron Highlanders* (London: Blackwood, 1909–31)
Ian V. Hogg, *The Guns 1914–18* (London: Pan, 1973)
—— and L.F. Thurston, *British Artillery Weapons and Ammunition 1914–1918* (London: Ian Allen, 1973)
Jack Horsfall and Nigel Cave, *Serre* (London: Leo Cooper, 1996)
Major N. Hudson, 'Trench-Mortars in the Great War', *Journal of the Royal Artillery*, vol. 42, 1920, pp. 17–31

Jackson Hughes, 'The Monstrous Anger of the Guns: British Artillery Tactics on the Western Front in the First World War' (Ph.D. thesis, University of Adelaide, 1994)
Colin Hughs, *Mametz: Lloyd George's 'Welsh Army' at the Battle of the Somme* (Gerrard's Cross: Orion Press, 1982)
A.H. Hussey and D.S. Inman, *The Fifth Division in the Great War* (London: Nisbet, 1921)
G.S. Hutchison, *The Thirty-Third Division in France and Flanders, 1915–1919* (London: Waterloo, 1921)
Capt. V.E. Inglefield, *History of the Twentieth (Light) Division* (London: Nisbet, 1921)
John A. Innes, *Flash Spotters and South Rangers: How they Lived, Worked and Fought in the Great War* (London: Allen & Unwin, 1935)
H.S. Jervis, *The 2nd Munsters in France* (Aldershot: Gale & Polden, 1922)
H.A. Jones, *The War in the Air*, vol. 2 (London: Hamish Hamilton, 1969) (reprint of 1928 edn)
—— *The War in the Air*, vol. 6 and one vol. of appendices (Oxford: Clarendon Press, 1937)
H.K. Kahan, *The 28th Battalion, Australian Imperial Force: A Record of War Service* (n.p.: H.K. Kahan, 1968)
*Das K.B. 10 Infanterie Regiment König* (Munich: Bayerisches Kriegsarchiv, 1925)
*Das K.B. 14 Infanterie Regiment Hartmann* (Munich, 1931)
Graham Keech, *Pozières* (Barnsley: Leo Cooper, 1998)
E.J. Kennedy, *With the Immortal Seventh Division* (London: Hodder & Stoughton, 1916)
H.B. Kennedy, *War Record of the 21st London Regiment, First Surrey Rifles 1914–1919* (London: Skinner, 1928)
A.W. Keown, *Forward with the 5th: The Story of Five Years' War Service Fifth Infantry Battalion A.I.F.* (Melbourne: Specialty, 1921)
C.L. Kingsford, *The Story of the Royal Warwickshire Regiment* (London: Newnes, 1921)
Col. R.M. St G. Kirke, 'Some Aspects of Artillery Development during the First World War on the Western Front', *Journal of the Royal Artillery*, vol. 101, Sept. 1974, pp. 130–40
J.C. Latter, *The History of the Lancashire Fusiliers, 1914–1918*, 2 vols (Aldershot: Gale & Polden, 1949)
Cecil Lewis, *Sagittarius Rising* (London: Corgi, 1969)
Peter H. Liddle, *The Battle of the Somme: A Reappraisal* (London: Leo Cooper, 1992)
David Lloyd George, *War Memoirs, IV* (London: Ivor Nicholson, 1933)
C.B.L. Lock, *The Fighting 10th – A South Australian Centenary Souvenir of the 10th Battalion, A.I.F. 1914–19* (Adelaide: Webb & Son, 1936)
C. Longmore, *The Old Sixteenth: Being a Record of the 16th Battalion A.I.F., during the Great War, 1914–1918* (Perth: History Committee 16th Battalion, 1929)
C.E.B. Lowe, *Siege Battery 94 during the World War* (London: Werner Laurie, 1919)
General E. Ludendorff, *My War Memories 1914–1918* (London: Hutchinson, 1919)
Captain Timothy L. Lupfer, *The Dynamics of Doctrine: The Changes in German Tactical Doctrine during the First World War* (Leavenworth Papers no. 4) (Leavenworth, Kansas: Combat Studies Institute, 1981)
Chris McCarthy, *The Somme: The Day by Day Account* (London: Arms & Armour, 1993)
J. McCartney-Filgate, *History of the 33rd Division Artillery in the War, 1914–1918* (London: Vacher, 1921)
K.W. Mackenzie, *The Story of the Seventeenth Battalion A.I.F. in the Great War 1914–1918* (Sydney: Shipping Newspapers, 1946)
Major-General M.N. Macleod, 'A Sapper Secret Weapon of World War 1', *Royal Engineers Journal*, vol. 68, 1954, pp. 275–81
Graham Maddocks, *Montauban* (Barnsley: Leo Cooper, 1999)
Great Britain: War Office, Statistics of the Military Effort of the British Empire, 1914–20 (London: War Office, 1922).
Laurie Magnus, *The West Riding Territorials in the Great War* (London: Kegan Paul, 1920)
General Sir James Marshall-Cornwall, *Haig as Military Commander* (London: Batsford, 1973)
A.H. Maude, *The 47th (London) Division, 1914–1919* (London: Amalgamated Press, 1922)

Paul Maze, *A Frenchman in Khaki* (London: Heinemann, 1934)
Peter Mead, *The Eye in the Air: History of Air Observation and Reconnaissance for the Army 1785–1945* (London: HMSO, 1983)
Charles Messenger, *Trench Fighting 1914–18* (London: Pan/Ballantine, 1973)
Martin Middlebrook, *The First Day on the Somme* (London: Allen Lane, 1971)
—— *Your Country Needs You* (Barnsley: Leo Cooper, 2000)
Captain Wilfred Miles, *Military Operations: France and Belgium 1916*, vol. 2 (London: Macmillan, 1938)
A.H. Millett and Williamson Murray (eds), *Military Effectiveness V1: The First World War* (London: Allen & Unwin, 1988)
L. Milner, *A History of the 15th (Service) Battalion (1st Leeds) The Prince of Wales Own (West Yorkshire) Regiment 1914–1918* (London: Leo Cooper, 1991)
J.E. Munby, *A History of the 38th Division* (London: Rees, 1920)
C.C.R. Murphy, *The History of the Suffolk Regiment, 1914–1927* (London: Hutchinson, 1928)
W.W. Murray, *The History of the 2nd Canadian Battalion (East Ontario Regiment) Canadian Expeditionary Force in the Great War, 1914–1919* (Ottawa: Mortimer/Historical Committee, 2nd Battalion, CEF, 1947)
Captain G.H.F. Nichols, *The 18th Division in the Great War* (Edinburgh: Blackwood, 1922)
Col. G.W.L. Nicholson, *Canadian Expeditionary Force 1914–1919* (Ottawa: Queen's Printer, 1962)
—— *The Gunners of Canada: The History of the Royal Regiment of Canadian Artillery* (Beaceville, Quebec: Imprimerie L'Eclaireur, 1976)
H.C. O'Neill, *The Royal Fusiliers in the Great War* (London: Heinemann, 1922)
Douglas Orgill, *The Tank: Studies in the Development and Use of a Weapon* (London: Heinemann, 1970)
Brigadier-General A.W. Pagan, *Infantry: An Account of the 1st Gloucester Regiment during the War 1914–1918* (Aldershot: Gale & Polden, 1951)
Christopher Page, *Command in the Royal Naval Division* (Staplehurst, Kent: Spellmont, 1999)
Dr D.W. Parsons, 'The Newfoundland Regiment: An Analysis of those Wounded on 1 July 1916, *Stand-To*,' no. 22, Spring 1988, pp. 16–17
Brigadier A.L. Pemberton, *The Development of Artillery Tactics and Equipment* (London: War Office, 1950)
Major John Penrose, 'Survey for Batteries', *Journal of the Royal Artillery*, vol. 49, 1922–3, pp. 253–70
Trevor Pidgeon, *The Tanks at Flers* (2 vols) (Cobham, Surrey: Fairmile, 1995)
Robin Prior, *Churchill's 'World Crisis' as History* (London: Croom Helm, 1983)
—— and Trevor Wilson, *Command on the Western Front: The Military Career of Sir Henry Rawlinson, 1914–18* (Oxford/Cambridge, Mass.: Blackwell, 1992)
Paul Reed, *Courcelette* (Barnsley: Leo Cooper, 1998)
Michael Renshaw, *Mametz Wood* (Barnsley: Leo Cooper, 1999)
Major Ritter, *Das K.B. Infanterie Regiment Prinz Ludwig-Ferdinand* (Munich: Bayerisches Kriegsarchiv, 1926)
Stephen Roskill, *Hankey: Man of Secrets*, vol. 1 (London: Collins, 1970)
Captain R.B. Ross, *The Fifty-First in France* (London: Hodder & Stoughton, 1918)
Lt-Col. Sir John Ross-of-Bladensburg, *The Coldstream Guards 1914–1918*, vol. 2 (London: Oxford University Press, 1928)
Lt-Col. H. Rowan-Robinson, 'The Limited Objective', *Army Quarterly*, vol. 2, 1921, pp. 119–27
A. Russell, *The Machine Gunner* (Kineton, Warwickshire: Roundwood, 1977)
Captain R.O. Russell, *The History of the 11th (Lewisham) Battalion, The Queen's Own, Royal West Kent Regiment* (London: Lewisham Newspaper Co., 1934)
Lt-Col. H.R. Sandilands, *The 23rd Division, 1914–1919* (Edinburgh: Blackwood, 1925)
J.W. Sandilands and N. Macleod, *The History of the 7th Battalion Queen's Own Cameron Highlanders* (Stirling: Mackay, 1922)

Major-General Sir Arthur B. Scott and P. Middleton Brumwell, *History of the 12th (Eastern) Division in the Great War, 1914–1918* (London: Nisbit & Co., 1923)

*Shlacten der Weltkrieg: Somme-Nord*, 2 vols (Oldenburg: Stallung, 1927)

Mark Severn, *The Gambardier: Giving some Account of the Heavy and Siege Artillery in France, 1914–18* (London: Benn, 1930)

W. Seymour, *The History of the Rifle Brigade in the War of 1914–1918*, 2 vols (London: Rifle Brigade Club, 1936)

J. Shakespear, *The Thirty-Fourth Division 1915–1919* (London: Wetherby, 1921)

John Sheen, *Tyneside Irish* (Barnsley: Leo Cooper, 1998)

Gary Sheffield, *Forgotten Victory: The First World War Myths and Realities* (London: Headline, 2001)

—— *The Somme* (London: Cassell, 2003)

Peter Simkins, *Kitchener's Army: The Raising of the New Armies, 1914–1916* (Manchester: Manchester University Press, 1988)

C.R. Simpson, *History of the Lincolnshire Regiment, 1914–1918* (London: Medici Society, 1931)

E.K.G. Sixsmith, *Douglas Haig* (London: Weidenfeld & Nicolson, 1976)

R.A. Sparling, *History of the 12th (Service) Battalion (York and Lancaster) Regiment* (Sheffield: The Regiment, 1920)

F.W. Speed, *Esprit de Corps: The History of the Victorian Scottish Regiment and the Fifth Infantry Battalion* (Sydney: Allen & Unwin, 1988)

Michael Stedman, *Fricourt-Mametz* (London: Leo Cooper, 1997)

—— *Guillemont* (Barnsley: Leo Cooper, 1998)

—— *La Boisselle* (London: Leo Cooper, 1997)

—— *Salford Pals* (London: Leo Cooper, 1993)

—— *Thiepval* (London: Leo Cooper, 1995)

F.H. Stevens, *The Story of the 5th Pioneer Battalion A.I.F.* (Adelaide: Callotype, 1937)

Graham Stewart and John Sheen, *Tyneside Scottish* (Barnsley: Leo Cooper, 1999)

Col. H. Stewart, *The New Zealand Division 1916–1919: A Popular History based on Official Records* (Auckland: Whitcombe & Tombs, 1921)

J. Stewart and J. Buchan, *The Fifteenth (Scottish) Division, 1914–1919* (Edinburgh: Blackwood, 1926)

A.J.P. Taylor (ed.), *Lloyd George: A Diary by Frances Stevenson* (London: Hutchinson, 1971)

F.W. Taylor and T.A. Cusack, *Nulli Secundis: A History of the Second Battalion A.I.F. 1914–1919* (Sydney: New Century Press, 1942)

John Terraine, *Douglas Haig: The Educated Soldier* (London: Hutchinson, 1963)

—— 'Mortality and Morale', *R.U.S.I. Journal*, vol. 112, Nov. 1967, pp. 364–9

—— *The Smoke and the Fire: Myths and Anti-Myths of War 1861–1945* (London: Sidgwick & Jackson, 1980)

—— *The Western Front 1914–18* (London: Arrow, 1970)

—— *White Heat: The New Warfare 1914–18* (London: Sidgwick & Jackson, 1982)

Tim Travers, *The Killing Ground: The British Army, the Western Front and the Emergence of Modern Warfare 1900–1918* (London: Allen & Unwin, 1987)

A. Wade, *The War of the Guns* (London: Batsford, 1936)

N. Wanliss, *The History of the Fourteenth Battalion A.I.F. Being the Story of the Vicissitudes of an Australian Unit during the Great War* (Melbourne: Arrow Printery, 1929)

C.H.D. Ward, *The 56th Division – 1st London Territorial Division* (London: John Murray, 1921)

—— *Regimental Records of the Royal Welch Fusiliers vol. III: 1914–1918 France and Flanders* (London: Forster Groom, 1928)

Major-General A.G. Wauchope, *A History of the Black Watch (Royal Highlanders) in the Great War, 1914–1918* 3 vols (London: Medici Society, 1926)

*Der Weltkrieg V10* (Berlin: Mittler, 1936)

Ray Westlake, *British Battalions on the Somme* (London: Leo Cooper, 1994)

T.A. White, *The History of the Thirteenth Battalion A.I.F.* (Sydney: Tyrrells, 1924)

Lt-Col. F.E. Whitton, *History of the 40th Division* (Aldershot: Gale & Polden, n.d.)
Trevor Wilson, *The Myriad Faces of War* (Cambridge: Polity, 1986)
—— (ed.), *The Political Diaries of C.P. Scott 1911–1928* (London: Collins, 1970)
Denis Winter, *Death's Men: Soldiers of the Great War* (London: Allen Lane, 1978)
—— *Haig's Command: A Reassessment* (Harmondsworth: Viking, 1991)
Lt-Col. H. St J.L. Winterbotham, 'Geographical and Survey Work in France, especially in connection with Artillery', *Journal of the Royal Artillery*, vol. 46, 1919, pp. 154–72
David R. Woodward, *Lloyd George and the Generals* (East Brunswick, NJ: Associated University Presses, 1983)
— (ed.), *The Military Correspondence of Field-Marshal Sir William Robertson, Chief of the Imperial General Staff, December 1915–February 1918* (London: Bodley Head, for the Army Records Society, 1989)
E. Wren, *Randwick to Hargicourt: History of the 3rd Battalion A.I.F.* (Sydney: Ronald G. McDonald, 1935)
C.M. Wrench, *Campaigning with the Fighting 9th* (n.p.: Boolarong Publications, 1985)
H.C. Wylly, *The Border Regiment in the Great War* (Aldershot: Gale & Polden, 1924)
—— *The First and Second Battalions, The Sherwood Foresters (Nottingham and Derbyshire Regiment) in the Great War* (Aldershot: Gale & Polden, 1926)
—— *The Green Howards in the Great War* (privately printed, 1926)
—— *History of the 1st and 2nd Battalions, the Leicestershire Regiment in the Great War* (Aldershot: Gale & Polden, 1928)
G.C. Wynne, *If Germany Attacks: The Battle in Depth in the West* (London: Faber, 1940)
E. Wyrall, *The Gloucestershire Regiment in the War, 1914–1918: The Records of the 1st (28th), 2nd (61st), 3rd (Special Reserve) and 4th, 5th and 6th (First Line T.A.) Battalions* (London: Methuen, 1931)
—— *The History of the King's Regiment (Liverpool)* (London: Arnold, 1928–30)
—— *The History of the 19th Division, 1914–1918* (London: Arnold, 1932)
—— *The History of the 50th Division, 1914–1919* (London: Lund Humphries, 1939)
P. Young and J.P. Lawford, *History of the British Army* (London: Barker, 1970)

# Index